Atlantic Africa and the Spanish Caribbean,
1570–1640

This book was the winner of the
JAMESTOWN PRIZE
for 2015.

Atlantic Africa

AND THE

Spanish Caribbean, 1570–1640

DAVID WHEAT

Published for the Omohundro Institute of
Early American History and Culture, Williamsburg, Virginia,
by the University of North Carolina Press, Chapel Hill

The Omohundro Institute of Early American History and Culture is sponsored by the College of William and Mary. On November 15, 1996, the Institute adopted the present name in honor of a bequest from Malvern H. Omohundro, Jr.

Manufactured in the United States of America
Library of Congress Cataloging-in-Publication Data

Cover illustration: Puerto de Bayaha. Detail. [Circa 1575–1605]. España. Ministerio de Educación, Cultura y Deporte. Archivo General de Indias. Mapas y Planos, Santo Domingo, 3.

Library of Congress Cataloging-in-Publication Data
Names: Wheat, David, 1977– author.
Title: Atlantic Africa and the Spanish Caribbean, 1570-1640 / David Wheat.
Description: Chapel Hill : Published for the Omohundro Institute of Early
    American History and Culture, Williamsburg, Virginia, by the University of
    North Carolina Press, [2016] | Includes bibliographical references and index.
Identifiers: LCCN 2015041271 | ISBN 9781469623412 (cloth : alk. paper) |
    ISBN 9781469623801 (ebook)   SUBJECTS: LCSH: Spain—Colonies—Caribbean
    Area—History—17th century. | Spain—Colonies—Caribbean Area—
    History—16th century. | Atlantic Coast (Africa)—History—17th century. |
    Atlantic Coast (Africa)—History—16th century. | Slave trade—Africa, West—
    History—17th century. | Slave trade—Africa, West—History—16th century. |
    Slavery—Caribbean Area—17th century. | Slavery—Caribbean Area—16th
    century. | Blacks—Caribbean Area—17th century. |
    Blacks—Caribbean Area—16th century.
Classification: LCC F1621 .W47 2016 | DDC 966/.02—dc23 LC record available at
    http://lccn.loc.gov/2015041271

Parts of Chapter 4 draw on the previously published article, *"Nharas* and *Morenas Horras:* A Luso-African Model for the Social History of the Spanish Caribbean, c. 1570–1640," *Journal of Early Modern History,* XIV (2010), 119–150.

The paper in this book meets the guidelines for permanence and durability of the Committee on Production Guidelines for Book Longevity of the Council on Library Resources.

The University of North Carolina Press has been a member of the Green Press Initiative since 2003.

cloth   20   19   18   17   16   1   2   3   4   5

For SEILA *and* MICAELA

Acknowledgments

This book would not have been possible without a great deal of help from many individuals and institutions over the past twelve to fifteen years. I am immensely grateful to my mentor Jane Landers for more kindnesses, and more adventures, than I could possibly enumerate. Even as I filled out graduate school application forms, having recently read *Black Society in Spanish Florida*, I never anticipated that I would soon be following Jane to far-flung research sites scattered across the globe: from Saint Augustine to Toronto, from Azrou to Veracruz, from the Aflao border post to Old Havana, where someone would give half of my lunch to a stray dog named Rita. In addition to supervising my graduate training at Vanderbilt University, where this project first took shape as a Ph.D. dissertation, Jane was (and remains) a vital source of guidance and encouragement.

Other faculty members in Vanderbilt's History Department were tremendously supportive; in particular, I would like to acknowledge Dan Usner, Marshall Eakin, and Katie Crawford. I am also grateful to Anthère Nzabatsinda. Interlibrary Loan staff at the Jean and Alexander Heard Library, Vanderbilt University, Nashville, Tennessee, provided invaluable aid. Paula Covington trained me in research methods, and, at my request, acquired all twenty-two volumes of António Brásio's *Monumenta Missionária Africana* for the library. I began my archival research in Spain under the auspices of a College of Arts and Sciences Summer Research Award in 2005; further research was made possible by a Fulbright Institute of International Education Fellowship and the Conference on Latin American History's Lydia Cabrera Award. A Graduate School Dissertation Enhancement grant permitted me to travel to Bogotá and Cartagena, Colombia, for additional research in 2008, and a fellowship at the Robert Penn Warren Center for the Humanities, directed by Mona Frederick, allowed me to visit archives in Lisbon and to devote the 2008–2009 academic year to writing. Throughout my time in Nashville, I benefited from the hospitality, companionship, and good graces of friends and family. I would especially like to thank Rick Moore, Philippe Adell, Pablo Gómez, Kathrin Seidl, and my brother Jeremy Wheat.

Thanks are also due in no small measure to the many archivists and scholars who facilitated my research. I am greatly indebted to staff at the Archivo General de Indias (AGI) in Seville, where I conducted research for twenty months in 2005–2006 and where Mark Lentz, J. Michael Francis, Esther González, Jeremy Baskes, and the late Fernando Serrano Mangas, among many other friends and scholars, provided camaraderie and guidance. In Cuba, I am grateful to staff members in Havana's cathedral, where in 2004 and 2006, as a graduate assistant on the preservation project *Ecclesiastical and Secular Sources for Slave Societies,* I helped Jane Landers and Oscar Grandío Moráguez digitize parish records that figure prominently in this study. In the Archivo Nacional de Cuba, I learned that Havana's early notarial records were in poor condition and thus unavailable for consultation; Coralia Alonso Valdés mitigated my disappointment by graciously directing me to a useful database of notarial record abstracts. Renée Soulodre-La France was indispensable in helping me make the most of an all-too-brief visit to the wonderful Archivo General de la Nación in Bogotá, Colombia, and I remain grateful to Pablo Gómez, Sara Gómez Zuluaga, and Margarita Zuluaga Tobon for their hospitality in Bogotá and Medellín. In Lisbon, Jessica Dionne, Walter Hawthorne, and Daniel Domingues da Silva acquainted me with the Arquivo Histórico Ultramarino and the Arquivo Nacional da Torre do Tombo in summer 2008, and John Thornton generously shared notes from his own extensive work in both of these archives.

The Department of History at Michigan State University (MSU) has been my academic home since 2009, and I feel extremely fortunate to have been able to continue working on this project in such a collegial and supportive environment. Special thanks to Walter Hawthorne, Pero Dagbovie, Ben Smith, Glenn Chambers, Ed Murphy, and my fellow Alabamian Peter Beattie. I am also grateful to David Bailey, Liam Brockey, Emily Conroy-Krutz, Denise Demitriou, Kirsten Fermaglich, LaShawn Harris, Charles Keith, Matt Pauly, Roger Rosentreter, Mindy Smith, Helen Veit, and John Waller. Thanks also to Jorge Felipe González. For assistance and timely advice on matters ranging from fiscal and administrative issues to winter survival skills, I thank Deb Greer, Elyse Hansen, Jeanna Norris, and Chris Root. The MSU library has been a fantastic resource, and Mary Jo Zeter kindly helped me locate several elusive published collections. A one-semester release from teaching duties in 2011 permitted me to write a new chapter, and I completed a draft of the entire manuscript under the auspices of a National Endowment for the Humanities Faculty Fellowship in 2012–2013. A HARP-Production Award from MSU's Office of the Vice President for Research and Graduate Studies provided funding for map production fees and a subvention to help offset manufacturing costs. For each of these sources of support, I am deeply grateful.

During the years I researched and wrote this book, I was very fortunate to exchange ideas with many other scholars at archives and conferences and via e-mail. Alex Borucki, António de Almeida Mendes, Antonio García de León, Armin Schwegler, Ben Smith, Consoli Fernández, David Eltis, Derrick Spires, Fabrício Prado, Frank Knight, George Brooks, Gerhard Seibert, Ida Altman, Ivor Miller, Jim Amelang, Joe Miller, John Thornton, José da Silva Horta, Juanjo Ponce-Vázquez, Kristen Block, Leo Garafolo, Linda Newson, María Cristina Navarrete, Maria Manuel Torrão, Maria João Soares, Mike Larosa, Nicolas Ngou-Mve, Paul Lovejoy, Peter Mark, Phil Morgan, Rina Cáceres, and Toby Green shared their knowledge of primary and secondary sources, copies of their own work before publication, or encouraging words that meant far more to me than they probably realized. Jane Landers, Walter Hawthorne, Manolo Fernández Chaves, Rafa Pérez García, Pablo Gómez, Kara Schultz, Gabriel Rocha, and Marc Eagle supported my research in all of the above-mentioned ways and provided much-appreciated feedback as I revised my book manuscript.

Any errors that may remain are mine alone, but a great deal of credit is due to the editorial staff of the Omohundro Institute of Early American History and Culture. In addition to the extraordinarily helpful suggestions provided by Ida Altman and one anonymous reader, Fredrika Teute's insightful comments and queries vastly improved the manuscript, to say the least. I would also like to thank Nadine Zimmerli, and Kaylan Stevenson for her skillful—nay, heroic—copyediting.

Finally, it is a pleasure to acknowledge my gratitude to my parents, John R. Wheat and Patricia H. Wheat, to my siblings and siblings-in-law, Jeremy, Ellen, Emily, and John, and to the entire González Estrecha family, especially my in-laws Julio González Zahinos and Micaela Estrecha Flores, for their long-standing support. To Rick and Suzanne Moore and to Andre and Erika and the Brown-Binion family I also offer my heartfelt thanks. For their love, and for their patience, my deepest gratitude is to Seila González Estrecha and to our daughter Micaela; this book is dedicated to them.

Contents

List of Illustrations

Abbreviations

AEA	*Anuario de Estudios Americanos*
AHR	*American Historical Review*
Americas	*The Americas: A Quarterly Review of Latin American History*
ARB	*Africana Research Bulletin*
CEA	*Cahiers d'études africaines*
CLAR	*Colonial Latin American Review*
HA	*History in Africa: A Journal of Method*
HAHR	*Hispanic American Historical Review*
IJAHS	*International Journal of African Historical Studies*
JAH	*Journal of African History*
JEMH	*Journal of Early Modern History*
JGSWGL	*Jahrbuch für Geschichte von Staat, Wirtschaft und Gesellschaft Lateinamerikas*
JNH	*Journal of Negro History*
JWH	*Journal of World History*
MMA(1)	António Brásio, comp., *Monumenta Missionária Africana: África Ocidental,* 15 vols. (Lisbon, 1952–1988)
MMA(2)	António Brásio, comp., *Monumenta Missionária Africana: África Ocidental,* 2a Sér., 7 vols. (Lisbon, 1958–1998)
NWIG	*Nieuwe West-Indische Gids / New West Indian Guide*
RCHA	*Revista Complutense de História de América*
RHES	*Revista de História Económica e Social*
RIEA	*Revista Internacional de Estudos Africanos*
RIHGB	*Revista do Instituto Histórico e Geográfico Brasileiro*
SA	*Slavery and Abolition*
Voyages	*Voyages: The Transatlantic Slave Trade Database* (2010), www.slavevoyages.org
WMQ	*William and Mary Quarterly*

Editorial Note

For the sake of convenience, historians of colonial Latin America and the Caribbean have long employed the easily recognizable term "Spain" as shorthand for the Crown of Castile. I have largely done the same. However, readers should bear in mind that early modern Spain was not culturally, linguistically, or politically uniform. Under the Hapsburgs or Austrias, the Spanish empire consisted of multiple kingdoms, principalities, and duchies, along with their respective provinces and overseas colonies. Although these various polities maintained many of their own laws and traditions, the highest echelons of government within each—including the kingdoms of Portugal and the Algarve and the entire Portuguese empire, from 1580 to 1640—were ostensibly reduced to governorships or viceroyalties subject to the authority of the Hapsburg monarchs and their councillors based in Valladolid or Madrid. With very few exceptions, Spain's colonies in the Americas were treated as overseas territories of the Crown of Castile, governed by Castilian law and traditions and heavily influenced by colonists arriving from Andalusia and Extremadura. Yet, these Old World migrants were accompanied and followed by others from all regions of the Iberian Peninsula and elsewhere. Global economic networks, clandestine migration, and slave trafficking made Spanish (Castilian) colonization of the Americas an extremely international affair. Links to Portugal and the Luso-Atlantic world were of particular importance for the settlement of the Spanish Caribbean.

The archival materials consulted for this study were written before the widespread adoption of standardized spelling and rarely employ capitalization, diacritical marks, or punctuation along the lines of modern Spanish or Portuguese. For clarity, all names have been capitalized, and abbreviated given names (mª, francª, juº, xptobal) have been spelled out in full (María, Francisca, Juan, Cristóbal). Modern diacritics have been added to Spanish given names and, less frequently (since most of the sources examined were written in Spanish), to Portuguese given names when spelled as such. Abbreviated surnames (rrº, frz) have also been spelled out in full (Rodrigues, Fernandez), although, for surnames in particular, I have attempted to respect the spelling provided in original sources, adding diacritical marks for only a few individuals in conformity with their appearance in other published secondary works. For given names and surnames beginning with "rr" or "y" (rrodrigo, ysabel), those letters have been changed to "R" (Rodrigo) and "I" (Isabel), respectively. The letters "V" and "B" at the beginning of names have been switched to conform to modern spellings as well (Benito instead of Venito, Ventura instead of Bentura). Otherwise, in many instances, I have retained common spellings such as the use of the letter "ç" (Gostança, Ceçilia)—common in modern Portuguese but no longer used in Spanish—or the letter "y" falling within words (Antonyo, Luysa). The names of individuals who appear in multiple sources are typically spelled differently in each; in such cases I have generally chosen one spelling to avoid confusion.

In colonial Spanish American sources, Sub-Saharan Africans are frequently ascribed "nations" or "lands" in lieu of a surname or in addition to a surname. I have capitalized these ethnonyms and toponyms throughout. Early modern Iberians spelled these terms in various ways (Yalonga, for example, might also appear as Gelonga). As with Iberian names, I chose one preferred spelling for each ethnonym, unless quoting directly from an archival source. When referring to individuals who were ascribed ethnonyms as surnames, however, I treat their surname the same way as Iberian surnames, leaving historical spellings more or less intact. Some of these ethnonyms can be matched with known historical or modern ethnolinguistic groups, which also may be spelled or pronounced differently in French, English, Portuguese, or in those groups' own languages. Here, too, I employ only one spelling for each modern group (for example, Yalunka instead of Jalonke or Djallonké). Throughout the book, when historical ethnonyms can be matched with more recent enthnolinguistic identities, to distinguish between the two I express the historical terms in quotation marks and modern group names in parentheses, as follows: "Yalonga" (Yalunka).

In addition to Iberian names and African ethnonyms, sub-Saharan Africans and people of African descent are frequently described in early Spanish Caribbean sources as either *negro* or *negra* ("black"), *moreno* or *morena* ("brown"), and *mulato* or *mulata* ("mulatto," which in the Caribbean usually meant a lighter-skinned person of mixed African and Iberian ancestry). These racial categories were somewhat flexible. In the Iberian world, race was not yet the primary factor determining who could or could not be enslaved and often appears to have been less important as a marker of personal identity than religious and political loyalties or association with a specific household or extended family. The categories "negro" and "moreno" were clearly mutable—the same person could be called "negra" or "morena" depending on the circumstances—and both terms were often used as a reference to general social categories rather than a straightforward description of an individual's skin tone. Indeed, the color "moreno" was not particularly associated with people of African heritage; Spanish sailors were also regularly described as having skin, especially their faces, *de color moreno* (brown in color).

By the 1570s, the smallest and most basic unit of currency, against which all other monies of account could be measured, was the *maravedí*. The *real,* worth 34 maravedís, was probably the most common silver coin in circulation. The *peso* of unassayed or common silver *(plata corriente)* was worth eight reales, or 272 maravedís (the phrase "piece of eight" is derived from *peso de a ocho reales*). Pesos of assayed silver *(plata ensayada)* were worth the considerably higher sum of 450 maravedís. These values could change over time and from one location to another; by this time, pesos of gold *(oro)* were used less commonly in the Caribbean but held values of approximately 400 maravedís and upwards. *Ducados,* or ducats, were the equivalent of 375 maravedís, or eleven reales. The silver mark *(marca de plata)* was worth 2,210 maravedís, or sixty-five reales.

Prologue

From his concealed position on the river's opposite bank, Pedro Yalonga observed the Englishmen who had come to Panama in search of Spanish American silver. Setting sail in 1595 with twenty-seven ships and twenty-five hundred men, the infamous pirate and privateer Sir Francis Drake had already assaulted Puerto Rico, Riohacha, and Santa Marta before turning to Panama. When his fleet landed at Nombre de Dios in January 1596, the city was deserted; its inhabitants had received ample warning and retreated into the interior. Only a few volunteers remained nearby in Santiago del Príncipe, a village of resettled maroons. The previous day, several English soldiers had been prevented from drawing water at the mouth of the Factor River when an enslaved African man known as Pedro Yalonga (also Pedro Zape Yalonga) "shot and killed one." The others, "believing there were many of our people lying in ambush[,] fled in terror[,] leaving their water jugs behind." Now an entire "squadron of English musketeers and pikemen" had come "to secure the river[,] to be able to take water unharmed." Accompanied by several other volunteers, including four members of "the free black infantry of Santiago del Príncipe," Pedro Yalonga saw that they were led by "an Englishman dressed in green velvet with gold fringe," who carried "a scepter in his hand." Turning to his companions, Pedro Yalonga told them, *"Señores[,]* I want to fell the one in green[,] who seems an important man." With these words, he moved within range, aimed his harquebus, and fired; the officer clad in velvet immediately "fell to the ground dead." After crying out and firing a volley in some disorder, the English carried their sergeant major back to their encampment in Nombre de Dios, where he was buried with lowered flags and muted drums. Discreetly following them, Pedro Yalonga and his colleagues witnessed Drake himself receive the deceased officer, showing "much sadness and great sentiment."[1]

1. All translations are the author's unless otherwise noted. "Pedro Yalonga esclavo sobre q se le de livertad por lo q ha servido," May 24–June 12, 1596, AGI-Panamá 44, n.56 (2), fols. 1r–13r. This file was not microfilmed with the rest of the *legajo* (bundle of documents); I am grateful to AGI staff for

Standing before a notary several months later, Pedro Yalonga retold these events, noting that "I[,] Pedro Zape Yalonga[,] black slave . . . showed up with my arms to serve his majesty and to kill[,] as I killed[,] the sergeant major of the English armada[,] and other Englishmen[,] in the encounters that presented themselves." Like enslaved people elsewhere in colonial Spanish America, Pedro Yalonga was able to use his record of military service as grounds for pursuing freedom within Spanish Caribbean society. His bid for manumission had the support of local authorities, who permitted him to dictate a formal petition to a scribe whom they provided. Yalonga's letter included an *interrogatorio,* or set of questions, to be answered by witnesses of his choosing. The testimonies subsequently given by former maroons Sebastian de Madrid, Don Pedro Zape, and Matheo Congo—infantry captain, field marshal, and *alcalde ordinario* (municipal mayor) of Santiago del Príncipe, respectively—provide a striking glimpse of African participation in Spanish Caribbean defenses during the late sixteenth century. As military effectives defending Panama's Caribbean coastline, Pedro Yalonga and his ex-maroon companions fit well within colonial Latin American historiography, foreshadowing the geopolitical importance of the region's free colored militias two centuries later. The spokesman he authorized to deliver his petition to the Spanish crown and Council of the Indies was none other than Don Diego Suares de Amaya, *alcalde mayor* (chief local magistrate) and captain general of Nombre de Dios. In an introductory note, the captain general drew attention to Africans' importance in holding the Spanish territory, arguing that Pedro Yalonga's manumission would "inspire the rest of the blacks in the province to serve Your Highness with the same fervor and loyalty." On August 6, 1597, less than three weeks after Yalonga's petition was presented before the royal court in Madrid, the crown issued a decree instructing Nombre de Dios's city council to free him in recognition of his services and to pay his manumission price, if necessary, with funds from the royal treasury.[2]

---

allowing me to consult the original. According to English sources, which did not yet use the Gregorian calendar, Drake's fleet landed in Nombre de Dios in December 1595; see Kenneth R. Andrews, ed., *The Last Voyage of Drake and Hawkins* (Cambridge, 1972), 5–6, 12–15, 35–44, 87–88, 94–95. On Bayano maroons' relocation to the pueblos of Santa Cruz la Real and Santiago del Príncipe in the 1580s, see María del Carmen Mena García, *La sociedad de Panamá en el siglo XVI* (Seville, 1984), 422–425; Jean-Pierre Tardieu, *Cimarrones de Panamá: La forja de una identidad afroamericana en el siglo XVI* (Madrid, 2009), 183–243. For a description of Santiago del Príncipe in 1596, see Carol F. Jopling, comp., *Indios y negros en Panamá en los siglos XVI y XVII: Selecciones de los documentos del Archivo General de Indias* (Antigua, Guatemala, 1994), 411.

2. "Pedro Yalonga," May 24–June 12, 1596, AGI-Panamá 44, n.56 (2), fols. 1r–12r. Though recorded by notaries, Pedro Yalonga's petition and interrogatorio are dictated in first person on fols. 3r–5v. For

UNLIKE DRAKE'S ALLIANCE with maroons on the Isthmus of Panama during the early 1570s, the prominent roles played by Africans and people of color in frustrating Drake's final voyage to the Caribbean two decades later are rarely recognized. English accounts of Drake's unsuccessful invasion of Panama in 1595–1596 mention the loss of Sergeant Major General Arnold Baskerville, "a gallant gentleman," but fail to elaborate on the circumstances of his death. Free and enslaved black volunteers' efforts to deny Drake's forces access to water, to hinder their attack on Santiago del Príncipe, or to prevent them from advancing toward Panama City—fighting alongside Spanish soldiers, in the latter case—are scarcely mentioned in English sources. Although maroons serving as Drake's scouts or guides in the 1570s regularly appear in popular histories, historians have only begun to pay equal attention to the "free black infantry of Santiago del Príncipe" who rendered services to the Spanish crown in the 1590s—and almost certainly included some of the same men who had sided with Drake two decades earlier.[3]

Much to the chagrin of northern European interlopers, and sometimes surprising even Spanish officials, Africans and people of African descent often contributed to early Spanish Caribbean defenses in similar circumstances. Yet, occasional military service was in fact one of the less significant ways that they shored up Spanish territorial claims in the Caribbean basin during the sixteenth and seventeenth centuries. Following the catastrophic decline of the region's Amerindian populations, and with relatively weak immigration from Iberia, African forced migrants increasingly performed the basic functions of colonization. By the mid-sixteenth century, as the postconquest placer mining, pearl fishing, and sugar industries faded, free

the crown's response, see Mena García, *La sociedad,* 373; Jopling, comp., *Indios y negros,* 475. See also Jane Landers, "Transforming Bondsmen into Vassals: Arming Slaves in Colonial Spanish America," in Christopher Leslie Brown and Philip D. Morgan, eds., *Arming Slaves: From Classical Times to the Modern Age* (New Haven, Conn., 2006), 120–145; Andrews, ed., *Last Voyage,* 96–98, 211–212; Kenneth R. Andrews, *The Spanish Caribbean: Trade and Plunder, 1530–1630* (New Haven, Conn., 1978), 36; Paul E. Hoffman, *The Spanish Crown and the Defense of the Caribbean, 1535–1585: Precedent, Patrimonialism, and Royal Parsimony* (Baton Rouge, Ill., 1980), 41–42.

3. For the death of Baskerville, see Andrews, ed., *Last Voyage,* 96. For useful discussion of Drake's alliance with maroons in the 1570s, see Carlos F. Guillot, *Negros rebeldes y negros cimarrones; Perfil afro-americano en la historia del Nuevo Mundo durante el siglo XVI* (Buenos Aires, 1961), 170–175; Andrews, *Spanish Caribbean,* 135–141; Hoffman, *Spanish Crown,* 1–2; Kris E. Lane, *Pillaging the Empire: Piracy in the Americas, 1500–1750* (Armonk, N.Y., 1998), 40–43; Tardieu, *Cimarrones de Panamá,* 126–144. For rare mention of free people of color contesting Drake's raid in the same region two decades later, see Kenneth R. Andrews, *Drake's Voyages: A Re-Assessment of Their Place in Elizabethan Maritime Expansion* (New York, 1967), 175. Michael Guasco provides excellent analysis of this episode in Guasco, *Slaves and Englishmen: Human Bondage in the Early Modern Atlantic World* (Philadelphia, 2014), 80–91.

and enslaved Africans formed the backbone of the Spanish Caribbean's labor force, performing a wide variety of occupations in urban seaports, on farms and ranches, and in transportation sectors. Well before 1600, Africans and people of African descent constituted demographic majorities in several major areas of Spanish settlement, both in the islands and along the Caribbean's southern littoral. Port cities and hinterlands remained under Spanish rule but were sustained by the transatlantic slave trade; events in western Africa and precedents in the Luso-Atlantic world shaped colonial societies as much as influences from early modern Spain. Viewed in this context, the actions of sub-Saharan Africans like Pedro Yalonga are not particularly surprising. After all, they defended towns that were, in many ways, their own.[4]

4. As Kristen Block observes, English troops attacking Española in 1655 were surprised to find that "substantial numbers of blacks were among those defending 'Spanish' territory from English invasion." See Block, *Ordinary Lives in the Early Caribbean: Religion, Colonial Competition, and the Politics of Profit* (Athens, Ga., 2012), 137.

Introduction

In 1534, city council members in San Juan, Puerto Rico, described the island's heavy reliance on enslaved sub-Saharan African workers as a necessary evil: "Like one who has the wolf by its ears, so that it is neither good to let it go nor to keep holding on, in the end we cannot live without black people; it is they who are the laborers, and no Spanish person will work here." Spanish colonial administrators throughout the circum-Caribbean made similar assertions during much of the following century, long after the decline of early mining and sugar industries and even in areas where these activities had always been of limited economic importance. In 1588, Cartagena's governor noted: "In this land, . . . Spaniards provide no service whatsoever, especially the lower occupations which no household can do without. Those who are employed here are all blacks." Likewise in his description of Panama in 1575, a high court magistrate of the Audiencia of Tierra Firme explained: "The workers and servants are all blacks, because no white people will offer themselves for service, for this reason the number of blacks in this kingdom is large." In the 1620s, Havana's city council members recorded that "all the haciendas are operated with slaves, and there is no one else to make use of, particularly on this island, since native-born Indians are lacking." If sub-Saharan Africans were initially brought to the Caribbean islands in the early 1500s to undertake specialized tasks in mines and on sugar plantations, by the late sixteenth century, they and their descendants performed most of the labors necessary to support Spanish colonization.[1]

1. Vicente Murga, comp., *Historia documental de Puerto Rico*, I, *El concejo o cabildo de la ciudad de San Juan de Puerto Rico (1527–1550)* (Río Piedras, Puerto Rico, 1956), 146–149; Carta de Don Pedro de Lodeña, Feb. 13, 1588, AGI-SF 37, r.6, n.76, fol. 5v; Alonso Criado de Castilla, "Description of the Kingdom of Tierra Firme," (Panama, 1575), in Manuel M. de Peralta, comp., *Costa-Rica, Nicaragua y Panamá en el siglo XVI: Su historia y sus límites según los documentos del Archivo de Indias de Sevilla, del de Simancas, etc.* (Madrid, 1883), 535; Alejandro de la Fuente, "Introducción al estudio de la trata en Cuba, siglos XVI y XVII," *Santiago*, LXI (March 1986), 165. Drawn from general reports addressed to the

Despite occasionally voicing discomfort that black slaves outnumbered Iberian residents, colonial Spanish Caribbean authorities' general reports to the crown and the Council of the Indies frequently mentioned the need for additional slaves, repeatedly identifying them as the only available labor force. In addition to extending Iberian slaving practices, the transportation of Africans to Spanish Caribbean colonies replicated early modern Spanish towns' reliance on migration from outside to sustain or increase population levels. But in-migration to Caribbean settlements represented a modification of Iberian precedents. Unlike in Castilian cities, where workers were siphoned away from smaller villages and rural areas within the Iberian peninsula, in the Spanish Caribbean most new arrivals would be involuntary migrants from West and West Central Africa. Though forced African migrants have rarely been viewed as full-fledged settlers, their ubiquity in the sixteenth- and early-seventeenth-century Caribbean adds considerable weight to the speculation that, by 1650, more than half the new settlers in the western hemisphere were Africans. Indeed, by the early 1580s Spanish officials in Panama would comment that there were "at least three times as many slaves as Spaniards" in the region.[2]

Africans' presence in the Spanish Caribbean was especially pronounced after the devastation of the region's Amerindian populations, given that Castilian *chapetones* (ruddy-cheeked, new arrivals) preferred destinations in New Spain and Peru. A brief comparison of the two migration streams during the final decades of the sixteenth century confirms the demographic predominance of Africans and people of African origin in Spain's circum-

Spanish crown and other metropolitan authorities, statements explaining local reliance on African laborers served to justify requests for authorization to import additional captives or for legislation regulating slave prices. An exception to this rule is *oidor* (magistrate) Criado de Castilla's remarkable "Description of the Kingdom of Tierra Firme," a rather straightforward account of the physical and demographic characteristics of Spanish settlements in Panama.

2. David E. Vassberg, *The Village and the Outside World in Golden Age Castile: Mobility and Migration in Everyday Rural Life* (Cambridge, 1996), 74; John Thornton, *Africa and Africans in the Making of the Atlantic World, 1400–1800,* 2d ed. (Cambridge, 1998), 14; Carta de Juan de Vivero, contador de Tierra Firme, May 23, 1581, AGI-Panamá 33, n.121, fol. 2r. Even while drawing attention to the dangers posed by Panama's demographic composition in light of conflict with the maroon state of Bayano, Vivero explicitly recognized that Panama relied heavily on enslaved workers for "todo el servicio . . . por la ffalta de yndios" (all types of labor . . . for lack of Indians). On Africans' increasing presence in the Greater Antilles after the mid-1520s with the arrival of slave ships directly from Africa, see Genaro Rodríguez Morel, "The Sugar Economy of Española in the Sixteenth Century," in Stuart B. Schwartz, ed., *Tropical Babylons: Sugar and the Making of the Atlantic World, 1450–1680* (Chapel Hill, N.C., 2004), 85–114; António de Almeida Mendes, "The Foundations of the System: A Reassessment of the Slave Trade to the Spanish Americas in the Sixteenth and Seventeenth Centuries," in David Eltis and David Richardson, eds., *Extending the Frontiers: Essays on the New Transatlantic Slave Trade Database* (New Haven, Conn., 2008), 63–94.

Caribbean colonies. Between 1579 and 1600, nearly ten thousand individuals received authorization to travel from Seville to the Spanish Americas; among those who specified their intended destinations, a little more than two-thirds were bound for either New Spain or Peru. Even if this figure were doubled to account for clandestine emigration, the total number of all migrants from Iberia to any destination in the Spanish Americas still falls well short of the minimum number of African captives—29,386—presently known to have disembarked in the single port of Cartagena de Indias between 1585 and 1600.[3]

The Spanish empire's reliance on Africans to populate and sustain its Caribbean colonies stands in stark contrast to other European powers' use of voluntary or indentured European migrants for these purposes. Although western European expansion in the Americas might be imagined as a series of interactions between native Americans, white settlers, and black slaves, these ostensibly primordial categories cannot adequately explain the development of Spanish Caribbean sites in which racial descriptors often failed to correspond to fixed legal, social, or economic status. Nearly forty thousand African and African-descended workers inhabited Spanish Caribbean seaports and rural areas by the first decade of the seventeenth century, revealing that in the early modern Iberian world, settlers—or more accurately, *pobladores,* those who peopled Iberian colonies overseas—were often anything but white or European.[4]

3. Calculated from David Wheat, "The Afro-Portuguese Maritime World and the Foundations of Spanish Caribbean Society, 1570–1640" (Ph.D. diss., Vanderbilt University, 2009), 252–256. On Iberian migration, see Peter Boyd-Bowman, "Patterns of Spanish Emigration to the Indies until 1600," *HAHR,* LVI (1976), 580–604; Ida Altman, *Emigrants and Society: Extremadura and America in the Sixteenth Century* (Berkeley, Calif., 1989), 168–173; Linda A. Newson, "The Demographic Impact of Colonization," in Victor Bulmer-Thomas, John H. Coatsworth, and Roberto Cortés Conde, eds., *Cambridge Economic History of Latin America,* I, *The Colonial Era and the Short Nineteenth Century* (New York, 2006), I, 152–163; Auke Pieter Jacobs, "Legal and Illegal Emigration from Seville, 1550–1650," in Ida Altman and James Horn, eds., *"To Make America": European Emigration in the Early Modern Period* (Berkeley, Calif., 1991), 59–84. On Amerindian population decline, see Sherburne F. Cook and Woodrow Borah, "The Aboriginal Population of Hispaniola," in *Essays in Population History: Mexico and the Caribbean* (Berkeley, Calif., 1971), I, 376–410; Noble David Cook, "Disease and the Depopulation of Hispaniola, 1492–1518," *CLAR,* II (1993), 213–245; Massimo Livi-Bacci, "Return to Hispaniola: Reassessing a Demographic Catastrophe," *HAHR,* LXXXIII (2003), 3–51.

4. For population estimates, see Appendix 1. In addition to its association with whiteness, the English-language term "settler" implies cultural practices that were not prevalent in Iberian colonies. On English notions of "settlement," usually associated with houses, gardens, and boundary markers such as fences, see Patricia Seed, *Ceremonies of Possession in Europe's Conquest of the New World, 1492–1640* (Cambridge, 1995), 16–40, 177. In Spanish, the words closest in meaning to the English verb "to settle" are *fortificar* (to fortify) and *poblar* (to people); see P. E. H. Hair, trans. and ed., *To Defend Your Empire and the Faith: Advice on a Global Strategy Offered c.1590 to Philip, King of Spain and Portugal, by Manoel de Andrada Castel Blanco* (Liverpool, England, 1990), 262–263.

A closer look at early Spanish Caribbean populations undercuts the primacy of white settlers as presented in many historical narratives and complicates the very notion of European colonization of the Americas. Sub-Saharan Africans' importance in Spain's settlement of the circum-Caribbean also adds a new dimension to the idea that Spanish rulers' efforts in co-opting other peoples through collaboration and negotiation contributed to the growth and longevity of the Spanish empire. Africans actively participated in the Spanish exploration and invasion of the Greater Antilles, Mexico, and Florida, and within the French empire, by the late eighteenth century, free *mulâtres* (a term used to denote people of mixed African and European ancestry) constituted a powerful planter class in parts of French Saint-Domingue. The terms "conquistador" and "planter" are now understood to have included black conquistadors and mulâtre planters. During the sixteenth and early seventeenth centuries, Africans' participation in Iberian overseas expansion was even more pronounced in processes of colonization or settlement.[5]

Africans' roles as de facto colonists in the early Spanish Caribbean challenge two long-standing assumptions: first, that a large-scale, export-oriented sugar industry was the intrinsic destiny of all Caribbean colonies and, second, that slavery was primarily important for colonies oriented toward extraction or exploitation, rather than settlement. Although slavery and sugar production often define Caribbean history, early Spanish Caribbean colonization did not immediately establish and maintain a large-scale, export-oriented sugar industry. For historians anticipating the rise of the sugar complex, the islands remained essentially uncultivated until the second half of the seventeenth century, when they were captured or ceded to other European powers who promptly established plantations, or until the very late eighteenth and nineteenth centuries, when Cuba and Puerto Rico became major sugar producers in their own right. Areas that never developed extensive sugar industries—including the Caribbean's entire southern littoral from Venezuela to Panama—-do not fit this version of Caribbean history. Not unlike Anglocentric accounts in which maroons offer aid to English protagonists and then seemingly vanish, sugar-centered

5. Henry Kamen, *Empire: How Spain Became a World Power, 1492–1763* (New York, 2003), 488; Regina Grafe and Alejandra Irigoin, "A Stakeholder Empire: The Political Economy of Spanish Imperial Rule in America," *Economic History Review*, LXV (2012), 609–651; Ricardo E. Alegría, *Juan Garrido: El conquistador negro en las Antillas, Florida, México y California, c. 1502–1540* (San Juan, Puerto Rico, 1990); Matthew Restall, "Black Conquistadors: Armed Africans in Early Spanish America," *Americas*, LVII (2000), 171–205; C. L. R. James, *The Black Jacobins: Toussaint L'Ouverture and the San Domingo Revolution* (New York, 1963), 36–44, 163–173.

frameworks leave the impression that, in the Caribbean, slavery only became historically significant—and Africans only become visible—with the
arrival of northern Europeans and the establishment of sugar plantations.[6]

Latin American historiography's traditional emphasis on Spanish colonization and silver extraction in highland areas, largely at the expense of major
Amerindian populations, is a third factor contributing to the invisibility
of African roles in the settlement of the Spanish Caribbean. Unlike other
Spanish American colonies that featured a "black middle," with people of
African origin vastly outnumbered by an Amerindian demographic base,
after the mid-1500s Spain's Caribbean colonies possessed neither an abundance of silver nor large Amerindian societies. Instead, as Spanish colonization of the region realigned around major sea roads, labor forces in port
cities began to include greater numbers of sub-Saharan Africans and their
descendants, who consequently began to form larger percentages of the
colonial population. The Spanish Caribbean after the 1520s has long been
dismissed as ancillary, at best, to events elsewhere that have become central
narratives in colonial Latin American history. But these ports' function
within a broader imperial system fueled social and economic developments
that intensified Spanish colonization despite the absence of silver mines.[7]

In his classic study of northern European incursions into the early
Spanish Caribbean, Kenneth R. Andrews describes four types of Spanish

6. On "settlement" as opposed to "exploitation" colonies, see Franklin W. Knight, *The Caribbean: The Genesis of a Fragmented Nationalism,* 3d ed. (New York, 2012), 47–60. For description of the early Spanish Caribbean as a "backwater" that remained underdeveloped until the establishment of export-oriented plantation agriculture under English or French rule, see, for example, Sidney W. Mintz, *Three Ancient Colonies: Caribbean Themes and Variations* (Cambridge, Mass., 2010), 10, 27, 88, 137–141, 171, 209. For critiques of the tendency to equate sugar production with growth, development, or successful colonization, see Alejandro de la Fuente, "Sugar and Slavery in Early Colonial Cuba," in Schwartz, ed., *Tropical Babylons,* 115–157; Alberto Abello Vives and Ernesto Bassi Arévalo, "Un Caribe por fuera de la ruta de la plantación," in Vives, comp., *Un Caribe sin plantación* (San Andrés, Colombia, 2006), 11–44; Juan José Ponce Vázquez, "Social and Political Survival at the Edge of Empire: Spanish Local Elites in Hispaniola, 1580–1697" (Ph.D. diss., University of Pennsylvania, 2011), 7–9. On the relative value of silver and sugar exports, see Alex Borucki, David Eltis, and David Wheat, "Atlantic History and the Slave Trade to Spanish America," *AHR,* CXX (2015), 435–436.

7. On Africans' demographic presence in New Spain, see Colin A. Palmer, *Slaves of the White God: Blacks in Mexico, 1570–1650* (Cambridge, Mass., 1976), 39; Matthew Restall, *The Black Middle: Africans, Mayas, and Spaniards in Colonial Yucatan* (Stanford, Calif., 2009), 13. Echoing colonial-era European perspectives, historians have often portrayed circum-Caribbean lowlands unfavorably in comparison to cooler, drier climates that would have been unfamiliar for many African migrants. For references to Cartagena de Indias as a place of "sweltering heat" and "stench" and to Nombre de Dios and Portobelo as "tropical pest-holes," "groups of squalid huts," and "hot, sickly shanty towns," see Fredrick P. Bowser, *The African Slave in Colonial Peru, 1524–1650* (Stanford, Calif., 1974), 53, 62; Murdo J. MacLeod, "Spain and America: The Atlantic Trade, 1492–1720," in Leslie Bethell, ed., *The Cambridge History of Latin America* (Cambridge, 1984), I, 352–353.

settlements in the region: sugar colonies, mining colonies, pearl fisheries, and commercial entrepôts. Although this typology still holds for the early sixteenth century, it is not particularly useful for visualizing the region after approximately 1570. By this time, the sugar industry in Española and Puerto Rico had faded drastically; it had never really even gotten off the ground in Cuba. Gold and copper mining continued in areas such as Concepción (Panama), El Cobre (Cuba), and Cocorote (Venezuela), but none of these sites was remotely as important as the mining operations extracting precious metals from Peru, New Spain, or the New Kingdom of Granada. The Caribbean pearling industry had likewise declined considerably by the mid-sixteenth century: Cubagua's pearl fisheries were exhausted by the 1530s, and the island was depopulated after an earthquake in 1541. Pearls were still being collected around La Margarita in the early seventeenth century, but the island clearly was no longer a "little Peru."[8]

During the final third of the sixteenth century, the Spanish Caribbean evolved as Spain reorganized and consolidated its imperial structures. The transatlantic circuit known as the *Carrera de Indias* was established in the early 1560s and would remain the standard itinerary for annual convoys of merchant ships for most of the next two centuries. The Spanish American empire that emerged afterward concentrated on silver-producing areas on the mainland, with strategically located port cities protecting north Atlantic shipping lanes and the fleet system that linked Spain to its main overseas sources of wealth. By the 1570s, the same fortified seaports that hosted the Indies fleets simultaneously served as shipyards, slaving hubs, and centers for regional trade. With as many as seven thousand temporary residents passing through Havana alone each year, the fleets—and various imperial resources allocated to protect them—spurred the port's remarkable growth during the late sixteenth century. Cartagena de Indias was

---

8. Kenneth R. Andrews, *The Spanish Caribbean: Trade and Plunder, 1530–1630* (New Haven, Conn., 1978), 31–33; John J. TePaske, *A New World of Gold and Silver,* ed. Kendall W. Brown (Leiden, 2010), 21, 54–57; Morel, "Sugar Economy," in Schwartz, ed., *Tropical Babylons,* 107–109; Robyn Patricia Woodward, "Medieval Legacies: The Industrial Archaeology of an Early Sixteenth-Century Sugar Mill at Sevilla la Nueva, Jamaica" (Ph.D. diss., Simon Fraser University, 2006), 71–73; Michael Perri, "'Ruined and Lost': Spanish Destruction of the Pearl Coast in the Early Sixteenth Century," *Environment and History,* XV (2009), 129–161. On La Margarita as "el Piru chiquito," see Oficiales reales de la Margarita a S. M., Sept. 19, 1621, AGI-SD 183, r.2, n.64. Pearl fishing declined somewhat later (around 1640) off Panama's Pacific coast; see Alfredo Castillero Calvo, *Sociedad, economía y cultura material: Historia urbana de Panamá la Vieja* (Panama, 2006), 613. Caribbean pearl fisheries remained an important point of reference even after their production had diminished; see Molly A. Warsh, "Adorning Empire: A History of the Early Modern Pearl Trade, 1492–1688" (Ph.D. diss., Johns Hopkins University, 2009), 185–216.

officially accorded the title "city" in 1575, and, two decades later, royal officials stationed there compared it to Lima and Mexico City as "one of the three [cities] of the Indies." By the 1590s, Cartagena was considered "the most principal and most visited port in all of the Indies," and, according to Admiral Cristóbal de Erauso, Cartagena and Havana were "the two best ports in all Christendom." Panama City, together with the smaller ports of Nombre de Dios and Portobelo, was equally vital as a linchpin connecting Spanish Atlantic shipping to the Pacific Ocean and Peru. Though considerably less prosperous than Cartagena or Havana, Santo Domingo retained importance as one of the region's larger port cities and as seat of a superior appellate court with jurisdiction over much of the Caribbean. Although other settlements that had once produced gold, sugar, and pearls were now abandoned or marginalized, these ports thrived as administrative centers, defensive bulwarks, transit points, and hubs for transoceanic commerce.[9]

Meanwhile in rural and semirural hinterlands all around the Spanish Caribbean's commercial entrepôts, as the port cities grew—and as mining, sugar, and pearl fishing industries dwindled—farming, ranching, and food processing became increasingly significant economic activities, geared not only toward local consumption but also toward intra-American trade and transoceanic export. In addition to specie from mining sites in central Mexico and the Andes, Indies fleets departed for Spain with Caribbean commodities including hides, ginger, and timber as well as tobacco, sugar, and pearls. Though Cartagena, Havana, Santo Domingo, Panama City, and other urban centers consumed much of the livestock and agricultural goods produced locally, extant shipping records for the late sixteenth and early seventeenth centuries also reveal a vibrant regional economy, featuring the exchange of foodstuffs such as maize, pork, cacao, flour, manatee lard, and cassava bread within, and even beyond, the circum-Caribbean. These and other "fruits of the land" were themselves the products of intracolonial trade networks, linking hinterlands and ports within colonies and Spanish

9. Knight, *Caribbean*, 31; Alejandro de la Fuente, with César García del Pino and Bernardo Iglesias Delgado, *Havana and the Atlantic in the Sixteenth Century* (Chapel Hill, N.C., 2008), 55; Donaldo Bossa Herazo, *Nomenclátor Cartagenero* (Bogotá, 2007), 22–23, 28–29; Alonso de Tapia y Joan de Yturrieta Alcevia a S. M., June 25, 1594, AGI-SF 72, n.91, fol. 2r ("siendo ella [esta ciudad] tan principal y una de las tres de las yndias"); Fernández de Medina a S. M., July 1, 1599, AGI-SF 94, n.26 ("el puerto mas prinçipal y cursado de las Indias"); Leví Marrero, *Cuba: Economía y sociedad: Siglo XVI: La economía* (Madrid, 1974), II, 147–148 ("los dos mejores puertos de la Cristiandad"); Christopher Ward, *Imperial Panama: Commerce and Conflict in Isthmian America, 1550–1800* (Albuquerque, N.Mex., 1993), 55–137; Marc Eagle, "The Audiencia of Santo Domingo in the Seventeenth Century" (Ph.D. diss., Tulane University, 2005).

American colonies to one another: cacao produced in Venezuela was in high demand in Mexico; Panama exported hides not only to Spain but also to Peru.[10]

After the mid-sixteenth century, the greater part of the labors mentioned above were increasingly performed by Africans and people of African descent. Despite a severe drop-off in mining and sugar production, the transatlantic slave trade not only continued but also escalated during the late sixteenth century. Estimates suggest that, between 1580 and 1640, nearly 450,000 African captives disembarked in Spanish American ports—all of which, except for Buenos Aires, were located in the Caribbean. An unknown percentage of these captives were then reexported to Peru, Mexico, and other destinations, but many remained within the circum-Caribbean.[11]

In settlements throughout the Caribbean, less than a century after Spain began to colonize the region, labors once undertaken by enslaved and coerced Indians were performed by Africans. But, no less significantly, Africans were employed in occupations more common to townsmen and rural workers in Iberia and in other Iberian colonies across the Atlantic. They labored on farms, raising food crops such as maize, yuca, and plantains and export crops such as tobacco and ginger. They worked as ranch hands, drovers, canoemen, sailors, dockworkers, cooks, domestics, carpenters, caulkers, seamstresses, cobblers, blacksmiths, laundresses, masons, musicians, and warehouse guards. In other words, Spanish Caribbean colonies increasingly relied on enslaved African workers to sustain economies that were rapidly moving away from the very activities historians most commonly associate with slave labor. Rather than supporting export-oriented plantation

10. Isabelo Macías Domínguez, *Cuba en la primera mitad del siglo XVII* (Seville, 1978), 147–170, 517–629; Nicolás del Castillo Mathieu, *La llave de las Indias* (Bogotá, 1981), 133–150; Robert J. Ferry, "Encomienda, African Slavery, and Agriculture in Seventeenth-Century Caracas," *HAHR*, LXI (1981), 609–635; María del Carmen Borrego Plá, *Cartagena de Indias en el siglo XVI* (Seville, 1983), 62–69, 373–400, 410; Juana Gil-Bermejo García, *La Española: Anotaciones históricas (1600–1650)* (Seville, 1983), 111–131, 140–157, 192–198; Eduardo Arcila Farias, dir., *Hacienda y comercio de Venezuela en el siglo XVI* (Caracas, 1983), 137–154; María del Carmen Mena García, *La sociedad de Panamá en el siglo XVI* (Seville, 1984), 157–161; Arcila Farias, dir., *Hacienda y comercio de Venezuela en el siglo XVII: 1601–1650* (Caracas, 1986), 61–141, 221–301; Elsa Gelpí Baíz, *Siglo en blanco: Estudio de la economía azucarera en el Puerto Rico del siglo XVI (1540–1612)* (San Juan, Puerto Rico, 2000), 97–99; Antonino Vidal Ortega, *Cartagena de Indias y la región histórica del Caribe, 1580–1640* (Seville, 2002), 167–208; de la Fuente, *Havana*, 21, 43–50, 127–134; Castillero Calvo, *Sociedad, economía y cultura material*, 496, 537–547.

11. Borucki, Eltis, and Wheat, "Atlantic History and the Slave Trade," *AHR*, CXX (2015), 440–442. See also Enriqueta Vila Vilar, *Hispanoamérica y el comercio de esclavos: Los asientos portugueses* (Seville, 1977), 209; Castillero Calvo, *Sociedad, economía y cultura material*, 579–585; Mendes, "Foundations," in Eltis and Richardson, eds., *Extending the Frontiers*, 77–83. On Buenos Aires, see Kara D. Schultz, "'The Kingdom of Angola Is Not Very Far from Here': The South Atlantic Slave Port of Buenos Aires, 1585–1640," *SA*, XXXVI (2015), 424–444.

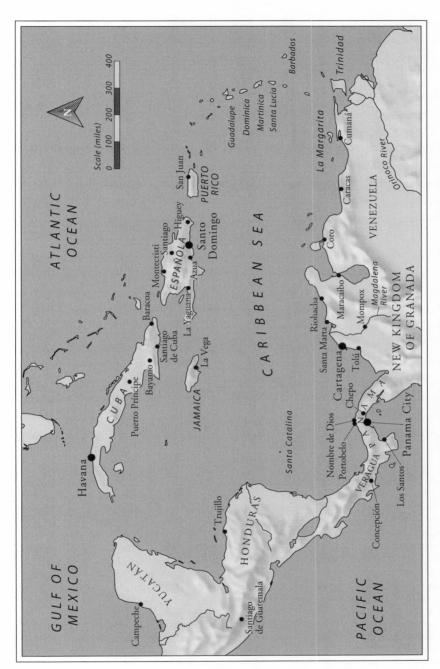

Map 1 Selected Spanish Caribbean Settlements, circa 1600. Drawn by James DeGrand

economies, by the late sixteenth century the slave trade reinforced Spanish overseas expansion by providing surrogate colonists: a versatile labor force that had become absolutely essential for the basic functioning of Spanish colonial society.[12]

Despite Africans' demographic presence and economic importance in Spanish Caribbean settlements during the late sixteenth and early seventeenth centuries, their political power was limited. Even the most heavily Africanized ports remained Spanish, governed by civil, military, and religious officials appointed by metropolitan authorities. Some Africans and people of African origin did enjoy a degree of political power in very localized contexts, but their subordinates were virtually always other Africans and Afrocreoles. Thus, Matheo Congo and Don Pedro Zape served as *alcalde ordinario* (municipal mayor) and *maestre de campo* (field marshal), respectively, in the ex-maroon village of Santiago del Príncipe; and men like Julián de la Torre, Agustín Martin, and Melchor de Salazar were *alguaciles de los negros* ("sheriffs of the blacks"), captains of free black militias, and leaders of work crews composed of free people of color in Havana, Cartagena, and Panama. But local town and city councils invariably included few, if any, sub-Saharan Africans or people of African descent.[13]

Yet, rather than being confined to cane fields or remote mining sites, Africans became Spain's colonists, or settlers, in the Caribbean. By 1600, African migrants and their descendants constituted "black majorities" in Española and Panama, in the province of Cartagena, in western Cuba, and probably in Puerto Rico (see Appendix 1). Whereas in early modern Iberia people of African origin lived and worked side by side with larger numbers

12. Vila Vilar, *Hispanoamérica*, 215. See also David Eltis, "Free and Coerced Transatlantic Migrations: Some Comparisons," *AHR*, LXXXVIII (1983), 251–280; Thornton, *Africa and Africans*, 42; Felipe Fernández-Armesto, *Millennium: A History of the Last Thousand Years* (New York, 1995), 269–275; Ira Berlin, "From Creole to African: Atlantic Creoles and the Origins of African-American Society in Mainland North America," *WMQ*, 3d Ser., LIII (1996), 282; Enriqueta Vila Vilar, with Wim Klooster, "Forced African Settlement: The Basis of Forced Settlement: Africa and Its Trading Conditions," in Pieter C. Emmer and German Carrera Damas, eds., *General History of the Caribbean*, II, *New Societies: The Caribbean in the Long Sixteenth Century* (London, 1999), II, 159–179; María Cristina Navarrete, *Génesis y desarrollo de la esclavitud en Colombia, siglos XVI y XVII* (Cali, Colombia, 2005), 162; Restall, *Black Middle*, 9–15.

13. "Pedro Yalonga esclavo sobre q se le de livertad por lo q ha servido," May 24–June 12, 1596, AGI-Panamá 44, n.56 (2), fols. 7v–8v, 11r–12r; Emilio Roig de Leuchsenring, dir., *Actas capitulares del Ayuntamiento de La Habana* (Havana, 1937–), tomo II, 166–167; Carol F. Jopling, comp., *Indios y negros en Panamá en los siglos XVI y XVII: Selecciones de los documentos del Archivo General de Indias* (Antigua, Guatemala, 1994), 448; Irene A. Wright, ed. and trans., *Further English Voyages to Spanish America, 1583–1594: Documents from the Archives of the Indies at Seville Illustrating English Voyages to the Caribbean, the Spanish Main, Florida, and Virginia* (London, 1951), 127–129; Caja de la Habana, 1636–1639, AGI-Ctdra 1118, n.1, pliegos 15–16.

of Iberians of low socioeconomic status, in these Spanish Caribbean settlements they almost completely replaced their Iberian counterparts, filling nearly all of the nonelite social and economic roles that Iberian migrants strove to avoid. At the same time, in Santiago de Cuba and Jamaica, where people described as "black" or "*mulato*" or "slaves" constituted at least substantial minorities (that is, from one-third to one-half of the population)—and even in places like Florida, Yucatán, Guatemala, Honduras, and much of Venezuela, where Amerindian communities maintained their demographic predominance—African migrants performed tasks typically done by Iberian townsmen and agricultural laborers in Spain and Portugal. Like other residents of the Spanish Americas, free and enslaved people of African origin sometimes colluded with foreign interlopers, but they also fought against foreign invasion. They participated extensively in the Catholic Church and other colonial institutions. As permanent residents of Spanish Caribbean population centers, they outnumbered even the most powerful of maroon communities: at its height in the 1690s, the multicity maroon state of Palmares, in Brazil, consisted of perhaps eleven thousand people; according to Cartagena's governor, the province of Cartagena alone held "more than 20,000 blacks" in 1622.[14]

AS THE SHORT-LIVED extraction and exploitation industries of the early sixteenth century receded, Spain's Caribbean colonies to some extent moved back toward a version of the Portuguese *feitoria* (trading post) model, with two important differences. First, rather than collection points for gold acquired through trade with indigenous peoples (as in the case of São Jorge da Mina), circum-Caribbean ports became administrative centers, fortified naval bases, multipurpose transit points, and hubs for regional and long-distance commerce. A second major difference was that forced migrants from sub-Saharan Africa and their descendants soon replaced both coerced Amerindian workers and Iberian colonists. Less than a century after Columbus's voyages, Spanish Caribbean seaports had evolved into a

---

14. For Spanish Caribbean population estimates, see Appendix 1; Chapter Five, below, addresses Africans' demographic predominance within rural Caribbean workforces in detail. On slavery's function as a supplement to nonelite Iberian labor in early modern Portugal, see A. C. de C. M. Saunders, *A Social History of Black Slaves and Freedmen in Portugal, 1441–1555* (Cambridge, 1982), 84–85, 127, 131–132, 146–147. On the sizes of Palmares and Cartagena in the 1690s and 1620s respectively, see Stuart B. Schwartz, *Slaves, Peasants, and Rebels: Reconsidering Brazilian Slavery* (Urbana, Ill., 1992), 121; Don García Giron a S. M., Mar. 28, 1622, AGI-SF 38, r.6, n.176. I borrow the term "black majority" from Peter H. Wood, *Black Majority: Negroes in Colonial South Carolina from 1670 through the Stono Rebellion* (New York, 1975).

network of fortified port cities sustained in large part by African migrants. Their geopolitical functions, commercial activities, and demographic composition gradually made them less like São Jorge da Mina and more like Portuguese colonies such as the Cape Verde Islands, São Tomé, and Luanda. Widely accepted depictions of Portuguese outposts in Africa and elsewhere as "strategic maritime cities," "trading factories and slaving stations," and "pressure points of trade" that "dominat[ed] the sea-lanes" could equally be applied to the Spanish Caribbean after 1570. Such descriptions are far more apt than the notion that the region was merely a handful of failed mining colonies or undeveloped sugar islands.[15]

The colonial Spanish Caribbean did not merely resemble Portuguese colonies and trading stations in western Africa and the Atlantic Islands; the two regions were closely connected via the transatlantic slave trade throughout the late sixteenth and early seventeenth centuries. The imaginary line in the Atlantic Ocean that theoretically separated Spanish and Portuguese imperial spheres was especially blurred during the Iberian Union (1580–1640), when the same Hapsburg rulers governed both empires. Although sources used in Chapters 1 through 3 often deal with slave trafficking and slave traffickers, this is not a study of the slave trade per se. Rather, the first half of the book illustrates the degree to which Spanish Caribbean society during this period was an extension of the Luso-African Atlantic world, with emphasis on events and precedents in Upper Guinea and West Central Africa and continuities in the Spanish Caribbean.

Although Upper Guinea supplied the vast majority of captives arriving in the Spanish Americas for most of the sixteenth century, slave exports from Upper Guinea to the Caribbean were preceded by more than a century of interaction between Iberians, Capeverdeans, and diverse Upper Guinean communities; slave trafficking was just one component of much broader systems of commerce and politics. This prior history of trade, diplomacy, evangelization, and cross-cultural exchange is reflected in Spanish Caribbean sources that consistently demonstrate widespread recognition of specific Upper Guinean ethnolinguistic identities.

15. P. E. H. Hair, "Columbus from Guinea to America," *HA*, XVII (1990), 113–129; Kathleen Deagan and José María Cruxent, *Columbus's Outpost among the Taínos: Spain and America at La Isabela, 1493–1498* (New Haven, Conn., 2002), 1, 8–9, 12, 15–18; James Lockhart and Stuart B. Schwartz, *Early Latin America: A History of Colonial Spanish America and Brazil* (Cambridge, 1983), 29 (quotes)—compare with description of the Spanish Caribbean as "a backwater occasionally brought to life by the passage of the silver fleets" (65, 76). See also Elinor G. K. Melville, "Land Use and the Transformation of the Environment," in Bulmer-Thomas, Coatsworth, and Cortés Conde, eds., *Cambridge Economic Hisory of Latin America*, I, 125–126.

West Central Africans began to arrive in the Spanish Caribbean in significant numbers beginning in the 1590s, and, within the space of a quarter century, Angola would become the predominant African provenance zone for the entire transatlantic slave trade. Large-scale warfare associated with the expansion of Portuguese Angola was the major factor generating captives for export. Luanda elites' frequent participation in slaving voyages to the Caribbean provides ample evidence that Portugal's colonization of Angola and Spanish colonization of the Caribbean mutually reinforced one another during the early seventeenth century. The large numbers of children arriving on slave ships from Angola further distinguished West Central African migrants from the Upper Guineans who had preceded them.

In addition to captives, slave ships brought passengers and crew members who were already accustomed to overlapping Iberian and African worlds. Non-Hispanic Europeans were commonly permitted to reside and trade in Spanish America, providing they paid requisite fees and trade duties. Among them, the Portuguese were by far the most influential for the development of Spanish Caribbean society before 1640. Portugal's historic ties and geographical proximity to Spain (Castile)—further enhanced during the period of the Iberian Union—facilitated migration from Portugal and its overseas territories, and the spread of Portuguese commercial networks, on a vast scale. The slave trade served as a vehicle for both processes. Some who arrived as crew members or passengers on slave ships were *tangomãos,* Iberian or Capeverdean merchants who had spent considerable time in western Africa, acquiring knowledge of African peoples, languages, and cultural practices. Others were sub-Saharan Africans and people of African descent employed as sailors, pilots, or slave ship guardians; in African contexts such individuals were typically known as *grumetes.* The long-term presence of Luso-Africans and Iberians with extensive experience in Africa and the regular presence of African mariners familiar with the Iberian world provide tangible examples of cross-cultural exchanges and social relations forged in coastal western Africa extending to the Spanish Caribbean.[16]

Just as the book's first half focuses on aspects of African history that spilled over directly into the Caribbean, the second half of the book exam-

16. On Portuguese migrants' ambiguous legal status in the Spanish Americas before the 1640s, see Fernando Serrano Mangas, "La presencia portuguesa en la América española en la época de los Habsburgos (siglos XVI–XVII)," in Maria da Graça A. Mateus Ventura, coord., *A União Ibérica e o Mundo Atlântico* (Lisbon, 1997), 73–79; Mateus Ventura, *Portugueses no Peru ao tempo da União Ibérica: Mobilidade, cumplicidades e vivências* (Lisbon, 2005), vol. I, tomo 1, 65–84. For the observation that the Portuguese were probably no more foreign to sixteenth-century Castilians than Basques or Catalans, see James Lockhart, *Spanish Peru, 1532–1560: A Social History,* 2d ed. (Madison, Wis., 1994), 146; see

ines free and enslaved Africans' participatory roles as settlers or colonists in Spanish Caribbean seaports and their hinterlands. The social and occupational activities of Africans and people of African descent, like those of their contemporaries in western Africa, facilitated Iberian overseas expansion through settlement, rather than extraction or exploitation. Instead of immediately producing a strict racial hierarchy, coerced migration and slavery often blurred the boundaries separating slaves from settlers—and Africans from Spaniards. Of particular concern are the timing and circumstances under which first-generation African migrants and their offspring began to be considered pobladores and *vecinos* (propertied, permanent residents).

As seen from the vantage point of the African and Portuguese Atlantic world, some elements of colonial Spanish Caribbean society were adaptations of social relations that had long characterized Portuguese trade and expansion in Africa. Spanish sources typically identified the numerous free women of color who resided in Spanish Caribbean seaports as *morenas horras*. These African and African-descended women wielded less individual power and influence than female merchants known as *nharas* in coastal western Africa. Yet, they played similar roles on a broader scale, as propertyowners, as businesswomen, and as partners and spouses for Iberian men.

By the late sixteenth century, most rural lands in the Spanish circum-Caribbean were oriented toward agriculture and animal husbandry. Much like Portuguese settlements in São Tomé and Luanda, Spanish Caribbean ports and urban centers were sustained by farms and ranches operated almost entirely by Africans and people of African descent. In the rural and semirural hinterlands of Cartagena, Santo Domingo, Panama, and Havana, slaves and free people of color made up the overwhelming majority of the populace. Given the nature of their labor—essentially the same as that of agricultural and livestock workers in Iberia—rural slaves appear to have enjoyed a considerable degree of autonomy and mobility. Although most rural properties were owned by Iberians (who tended to concentrate in towns and cities, leaving their operation to overseers, slaves, and wage laborers), a surprising number of rural properties were owned by free men and women of color, including sub-Saharan African former slaves.

also Pablo E. Pérez-Mallaína, *Spain's Men of the Sea: Daily Life on the Indies Fleets in the Sixteenth Century,* trans. Carla Rahn Phillips (Baltimore, 1998), 56–58. On overlapping Iberian sea roads, see David Wheat, "Global Transit Points and Travel in the Iberian Maritime World, 1580–1640," in Peter C. Mancall and Carole Shammas, eds., *Governing the Sea in the Early Modern Era: Essays in Honor of Robert C. Ritchie* (San Marino, Calif., 2015), 253–274.

African migrants' adaptation to colonial Spanish Caribbean society relied heavily on African intermediaries. Like translators known as *chalonas* who facilitated commercial transactions in western Africa—but in far greater numbers—*ladino* or "Latinized" Africans throughout the Spanish Caribbean served as interpreters and godparents for other forced migrants of similar background. Free and enslaved Africans' regular appearance in these roles indicates that African acquisition of Iberian social and cultural mores was both rapid and widespread. Most significantly, Hispanicized Africans' presence and their interaction with newly arrived Africans—even as documented in official contexts—reveal ground-level social mechanisms through which Spain was able to exert control over colonial populations of largely non-Spanish origin.

In short, this is the story of sub-Saharan Africans becoming the colonists of the Spanish Caribbean. It imagines the postconquest Caribbean as an extension of an older, deeper, African and Iberian world. Violence, forced migration, and slavery shaped the region as much during the sixteenth and seventeenth as they would during the eighteenth and nineteenth centuries. Yet, the emphasis on industrial-scale sugar complexes and slave resistance in this later period fails to take account of the overlapping Iberian and African worlds that influenced the early phases of Spanish colonialism in the Caribbean. The extensive participation of Luso-Africans, Latinized Africans, and free people of color made possible Spain's colonization of the region; the consolidation of stark racial categories would not come until later. In defending Spanish rule and contributing to the social and economic development of Spanish Caribbean colonies, men and women like Pedro Yalonga were protecting settlements that were arguably just as much African as they were Spanish. Perhaps to an even greater extent than the tangomãos, nharas, grumetes, and chalonas who helped sustain an Iberian presence in western Africa, Africans and people of African descent played dynamic roles within early colonial Spanish Caribbean society. Their descendants would comprise the region's demographic core until well into the eighteenth century, sustaining urban population centers and rural economies based on ranching and farming, rather than sugar cultivation, long after the disruption of Iberian Atlantic slaving networks in 1640.

ONE

The Rivers of Guinea

Sailing from the Cape Verde Islands toward Cartagena de Indias, the slave ship *Nuestra Señora de la Concepción* wrecked off the coast of present-day Colombia near the mouth of the Magdalena River in 1593. The caravel's crew members and passengers, and most of its captives—those who had survived the transoceanic voyage—managed to swim ashore. Spanish American authorities based in the nearby town of Santa Marta immediately began to collect evidence to determine whether the shipwreck had been a genuine accident or merely a ploy to cover up the unauthorized disembarkation of enslaved Africans. With the help of the ship's crew, local officials soon located more than one hundred scattered in groups along the beach, a swamp, and an adjacent farm or ranch; some had already been taken directly to Santa Marta. An extensive investigation conducted over the following months generated nearly five hundred pages of documentation. Though authorities were primarily concerned with ascertaining how many captives had been on the ship at the time it reached the Magdalena River and on whose account they had been transported, their reports also include descriptions of more than twenty of the *Concepción*'s forced migrants.[1]

In addition to royal officials' observations, these portrayals incorporated testimonies provided by the individual Africans themselves, just hours after their arrival in the Americas. Although some spoke Portuguese or Spanish—there is no mention of a translator, and several identified themselves with Iberian names—the captives' self-descriptions convey an unequivocal awareness of their diverse and distinctive ethnolinguistic origins in Upper Guinea. One tall black man with filed teeth and a brand on the left side of his chest appeared to be around twenty years old; according to royal officials, "He himself said that he was of the Bran land." A stately woman with several filed teeth and scarifications extending from her stomach downward

---

1. "El fiscal de su magestad contra el capitán Valentin Velo," 1593, AGN-FNE Magdalena 4, hojas 19r–21v.

declared that "she was named Estaçia and that she was of the Mandinga nation." Another man gave his name as Gaspar, stating that he was "of the Caçanga land"; yet another "said he was named Marcos of the Biafara land." Several children identified themselves in similar terms as well: a seven- or eight-year-old black boy noted that "he is of the Bran nation," and a black girl "said she was Bañul."[2]

The "nations" and "lands" referred to by captives in Santa Marta in 1593 were diverse ethnonyms or ethnolinguistic identities associated with peoples from the region of West Africa known to early modern Iberians as the "Guinea of Cape Verde," or, more commonly in Spanish sources, "the Rivers of Guinea." Stretching approximately from the Senegal River to Cape Mount, with large tracts of submerged coastline and rivers, including the Gambia, Casamance, Cacheu, Gêba, Grande, Nunez, and others, the area roughly corresponds to the Upper Guinea coast, Senegambia, and Sierra Leone. Echoing medieval European texts, Spanish American sources occasionally refer to sub-Saharan Africa broadly as "Guinea," but, in the early colonial Spanish Caribbean, "Guinea" was nearly always shorthand for "the Rivers of Guinea." This geographical precision reflected contemporary Portuguese mariners' usage of the word: in 1535, one Portuguese pilot wrote of the "diverse provinces and countries" along western Africa's coastline, including "Guiné, the Malagueta coast, the Kingdom of Benim [Benin], and the Kingdom of Manicongo [Kongo]." In similar fashion, João Teixeira Albernaz's 1630 world map clearly labels the West African coast from just south of the "Çenaga" (Senegal) River to "Serra Lioa" as "Guiné."[3]

---

2. Ibid., hojas 19r–21v ("el mismo dijo ser de terra bran," hoja 19r, "dixo llamarse estaçia y ser de naçion mandinga," hoja 19v, "dijo llamarse gaspar ladino y ser de tierra caçanga," hoja 20r, "dixo llamarse Marcos de tierra biafara," hoja 20r, "dijo es de naçion bran," hoja 19v, "dijo ser bañul," hoja 21v).

3. [Anonymous Portuguese pilot], "Navegação de Lisboa à Ilha de São Tomé," [circa 1534–1563], in Luis de Albuquerque, dir., *A ilha de São Tomé nos séculos XV e XVI* (Lisbon, 1989), 14; João Teixeira Albernaz, "Taboas geraes de toda a navegação . . . ," 1630, Map 1 (World), Library of Congress Geography and Map Division, LC Luso-Hispanic World 8, accessed May 22, 2015, http://hdl.loc.gov/loc .gmd/g3200m.gct00052. For further discussion of Iberian usage of the term "Guinea" as shorthand for the Upper Guinea coast, see Linda A. Newson and Susie Minchin, *From Capture to Sale: The Portuguese Slave Trade to Spanish South America in the Early Seventeenth Century* (Leiden, 2007), 62–63. On change over time in Portuguese usage of the term, see Mariza de Carvalho Soares, *People of Faith: Slavery and African Catholics in Eighteenth-Century Rio de Janeiro*, trans. Jerry D. Metz (Durham, N.C., 2011), 19–39. On defining "the Rivers of Guinea," see José da Silva Horta, "Evidence for a Luso-African Identity in 'Portuguese' Accounts on 'Guinea of Cape Verde' (Sixteenth-Seventeenth Centuries)," *HA*, XXVII (2000), 99–130. See also Walter Rodney, *A History of the Upper Guinea Coast, 1545–1800* (New York, 1970), 1–5; Walter Hawthorne, *Planting Rice and Harvesting Slaves: Transformations along the Guinea-Bissau Coast, 1400–1900* (Portsmouth, N.H., 2003), 1–2, 29, 42; George E. Brooks, *Landlords and Strangers: Ecology, Society, and Trade in Western Africa, 1000–1630* (Boulder, Col., 1993), 14, 17, 19–23.

The phrase "Rivers of Guinea" also regularly appears in sixteenth- and early-seventeenth-century Spanish Caribbean sources and features very prominently in *De instauranda Aethiopum salute,* a treatise by the Spanish Jesuit Alonso de Sandoval (1577–1652). Initially published in Seville in 1627 and addressed to the superior general of the Society of Jesus, Sandoval's treatise sought to justify the Jesuit order's mission to evangelize enslaved sub-Saharan Africans in the Spanish Americas. Sandoval resided primarily in Cartagena de Indias from 1605 until his death in 1652. Along with his contemporary Pedro Claver, he led Jesuit efforts to proselytize enslaved Africans in Cartagena, at times even going aboard newly arrived slave ships. Drawing on his extensive first-hand experience of Africans—supplemented by conversations with slave traders and interpreters as well as correspondence with Jesuit colleagues based in Africa and elsewhere—Sandoval's text provides a wealth of information about Upper Guinea and Upper Guineans, including geography, climate, languages, ethnic identities, and commercial and political relationships. Sandoval observed that "the rivers that we commonly call of Guinea . . . begin on the mainland of Cape Verde," that is, near present-day Dakar, Senegal. His treatise addresses Africans and people of African descent throughout the continent and even across the Indian Ocean but frequently centers on various peoples living along the rivers and coast of Upper Guinea as far south as Sierra Leone, with careful attention to ethnic and linguistic identities.[4]

Although Sandoval's treatise is unparalleled for its attention to ethnographic detail, a host of lesser-known documents generated in the Caribbean during the same era likewise reproduce Upper Guinean identities

4. Alonso de Sandoval, *Un tratado sobre la esclavitud,* introduction and transcription by Enriqueta Vila Vilar (Madrid, 1987), 104–110. The original text was published as *De instauranda Aethiopum salute* (Seville, 1627); a revised and updated version was printed in Madrid in 1647. Copies of one or more tomes from the original manuscripts are in Colombia's Biblioteca Nacional, the British National Library, and in libraries at the Universidad de Sevilla (Spain), the Universidad de Granada (Spain), and the Università degli Studi di Cagliari (Italy). I have relied on the most readily available unabridged transcription by Vila Vilar, who used a copy of the 1627 original held at the Biblioteca Nacional de Colombia. For an earlier and more complete transcription that also reproduces Sandoval's citations and notes in the margins of the orginal text, see Alonso de Sandoval, *De instauranda Aethiopum salute: El mundo de la esclavitud negra en America,* transcription and introduction by Ángel Valtierra (Bogotá, 1956). For an abridged translation in English, see Sandoval, *Treatise on Slavery: Selections from "De instauranda Aethiopum salute,"* ed. and trans. Nicole von Germeten (Indianapolis, Ind., 2008). See also Margaret M. Olsen, *Slavery and Salvation in Colonial Cartagena de Indias* (Gainesville, Fla., 2004). On Sandoval's attention to ethnographic detail, his ideological position on slavery, and his cultural biases—as seen for instance in his references to Africans as "Ethiopans" and "gentiles" (terms associated with European attitudes towards the monstrous and Africans' supposed need for spiritual salvation)—see also Luz Adriana Maya Restrepo, *Brujería y reconstrucción de identidades entre los Africanos y sus descendientes en la Nueva Granada, siglo XVII* (Bogotá, 2005), 226–442.

with remarkable geographic and ethnolinguistic specificity. Unlike the enslaved Africans depicted in early modern English sources as undifferentiated "negroes" or "blacks," the captives who arrived in Santa Marta in 1593 are among thousands of Upper Guineans described in sixteenth- and early-seventeenth-century Spanish American sources whose origins can be identified with reasonable certainty. In part, this phenomenon can be explained by Upper Guinea's singular role in the sixteenth-century slave trade. For every decade from 1500 to 1580, Upper Guinea is estimated to have supplied anywhere from 75 to 100 percent of all captives embarked on transatlantic slaving vessels, gradually losing ground to Angola during the late 1500s and early 1600s. Although much larger numbers of enslaved Upper Guineans were transported to the Americas during the next two centuries, after the 1640s they never again constituted more than 12 percent of the total estimated number of captives embarked in any given decade. Like other Spanish Caribbean sources written during the late sixteenth and early seventeenth centuries, Sandoval's *De instauranda Aethiopum salute* displays an interest in the Rivers of Guinea that was directly proportionate to Upper Guineans' preponderance among African populations in the sixteenth-century Americas.[5]

A second, equally important factor explaining this detailed attention to Upper Guinean origins is that, by the mid-1500s, a century of sustained social, economic, and cultural exchange preceded Upper Guinean migrants' arrival in the Spanish Caribbean. In the Cape Verde Islands, relations of power between Iberians and captives acquired on the Upper Guinea coast were asymmetrical to be sure, but interaction between these groups spurred the formation of a creolized Luso-African society by the late 1400s. Upper Guinean identities also remained relevant in the Cape Verde Islands because they reflected political loyalties, cultural affinities, and market conditions on the nearby mainland. Iberian clergymen visited the Rivers of Guinea as missionaries and diplomats, and Portuguese and Luso-African traders integrated themselves into commercial networks geared toward

5. For change over time in the estimated volume of captives embarked in Upper Guinea, see *Voyages,* accessed May 23, 2015, http://slavevoyages.org/tast/assessment/estimates.faces?yearFrom =1501&yearTo=1866. Percentages supplied here combine estimates for "Senegambia and the offshore Atlantic" and "Sierra Leone." For evidence of Upper Guinea's continued importance in the slave trade to early-seventeenth-century Cartagena, see David Wheat, "The First Great Waves: African Provenance Zones for the Transatlantic Slave Trade to Cartagena de Indias, 1570–1640," *JAH,* LII (2011), 1–22. On concentrations of Upper Guinean forced migrants in eighteenth-century Maranhão, Brazil, see Daniel B. Domingues da Silva, "The Atlantic Slave Trade to Maranhão, 1680–1846: Volume, Routes, and Organisation," *SA,* XXIX (2008), 485–487; Walter Hawthorne, *From Africa to Brazil: Culture, Identity, and an Atlantic Slave Trade, 1600–1830* (Cambridge, 2010).

regional exchange, rather than large-scale slave production, all along the Upper Guinea coast. As late as the 1630s, Iberian merchants' acquisition of Upper Guinean captives for export remained merely one element in a broader system of trade that included the extensive participation of Luso-Africans and Africans of diverse status and the exchange of European commodities alongside local products such as millet and beeswax. The success or failure of these commercial, diplomatic, and evangelical ventures often depended on Iberians' capacity to understand and accommodate the diverse interests of specific Upper Guinean peoples. On slave ships departing from the Upper Guinea coast and Cape Verde Islands, captives, crew members, and passengers alike carried this legacy of exchange and interaction—including Iberian recognition of distinct Upper Guinean origins—with them to the Caribbean.[6]

By the 1700s, transatlantic slaving networks underpinned colonial American plantation and mining economies that bore little relation to earlier patterns of cross-cultural exchange in Upper Guinea and the Cape Verde Islands. With few exceptions, Upper Guineans would arrive in the eighteenth-century Americas not only as slaves but also as foreigners and as minorities in comparison to forced migrants from other African regions; by this time, rather than pinpointing specific lands or nations, European-language sources more commonly employed the term "Guinea" to refer to all West Africans, or even to all Africans. Historiographical emphasis on the slave trade and African diasporas during this later era obscures an earlier history in which Upper Guineans predominated among diasporic African populations and Iberians commonly recognized their distinctive political and ethnolinguistic identities. For Richard Reid, studies of ethnicity represent a prime example of "the hegemony of the recent past in African studies":

> [Their] basic argument is that, in precolonial Africa, 'ethnicity' was not clear-cut . . . rather, such identities were plural, overlapping, simultaneous, and characterized by considerable mobility. Professions of identification or loyalty were wholly contingent on context and current circumstances. Only during colonial rule was ethnicity in its modern rigid form 'invented'—first through the European creation

6. Maria Manuel Ferraz Torrão, "Actividade comercial externa de Cabo Verde: Organização, funcionamento, evolução," in Luís de Albuquerque and Maria Emília Madeira Santos, coords., *História geral de Cabo Verde* (Lisbon, 1991), I, 237–345; Brooks, *Landlords and Strangers,* 143–166; Toby Green, *The Rise of the Trans-Atlantic Slave Trade in Western Africa, 1300–1589* (New York, 2012); Linda A. Newson, "Africans and Luso-Africans in the Portuguese Slave Trade on the Upper Guinea Coast in the Early Seventeenth Century," *JAH,* LIII (2012), 1–24.

of 'tribes' . . . and then through African appropriation of such identities . . . this colonial 'imagining' . . . has blinded us to the very real possibilities of pre-modern links to the present, and to very real continuities in African identities from the precolonial past.

Despite, or in addition to, their geographical mobility, rapidly changing circumstances, and multiple or overlapping identities, Upper Guinean migrants to the sixteenth- and early-seventeenth-century Spanish Caribbean arrived with a strong sense of their ethnolinguistic origins, and these origins were widely recognized. Even a cursory examination of extant sources reveals identifications of Africans such as "Catalina Bañon," "María Biafara," "Sebastián Bioho," "Juan Bran," and "Gaspar Zape." These surnames were in fact ethnic markers that, like those in sources described by P. E. H. Hair nearly half a century ago, reflect strong continuities with modern and present-day populations living along the Upper Guinea coast.[7]

Spanish Caribbean sources also provide ample information regarding the experiences of diasporic West Central Africans and Lower Guineans, but the origins of Upper Guinean migrants are extraordinarily well documented. Indeed, Iberians in the early Spanish Americas viewed Upper Guineans' ethnolinguistic diversity as a characteristic that distinguished them from other sub-Saharan Africans. In 1622, royal officials in Bogotá wrote that "the black slaves brought to Cartagena and sold there are of three types: the first and most esteemed [are] those of the Rivers of Guinea . . . who have different names." Another seventeenth-century observer noted of slave ships arriving in Cartagena that, "if the ship was from the region of the Rivers," the captives onboard spoke "so many languages, that sometimes they numbered more than forty." Unlike captives exported from Luanda to the Spanish Americas during the sixteenth and seventeenth centuries, who were usually described as either "Angolas," "Congos," or "Enchicos," more

7. Richard Reid, "Past and Presentism: The 'Precolonial' and the Foreshortening of African History," *JAH*, LII (2011), 147–148; P. E. H. Hair, "Ethnolinguistic Continuity on the Guinea Coast," *JAH*, VIII (1967), 247–268; Hair, "Black African Slaves at Valencia, 1482–1516: An Onomastic Inquiry," *HA*, VII (1980), 119–139. See also Toby Green, "Building Slavery in the Atlantic World: Atlantic Connections and the Changing Institution of Slavery in Cabo Verde, Fifteenth–Sixteenth Centuries," *SA*, XXXII (2011), 227–245. For Upper Guinean ethnonyms that commonly appear in Spanish Caribbean sources, see Tables 7, 11, and 12, below. Compare with later usage of the descriptors "Guinea" or "Guiné" in Louisiana and Brazil, as discussed in Peter Caron, "'Of a Nation Which the Others Do Not Understand': Bambara Slaves and African Ethnicity in Colonial Louisiana, 1718–60," *SA*, XVIII, no. 1 (1997), 100–101; Mariza de Carvalho Soares, "Descobrindo a Guiné no Brasil colonial," *RIHGB*, a. 161, n. 407 (2000), 71–94; James H. Sweet, *Recreating Africa: Culture, Kinship, and Religion in the African-Portuguese World, 1441–1770* (Chapel Hill, N.C., 2003), 19–21.

than twenty different ethnonyms and toponyms were ascribed to those arriving from Upper Guinea directly or via the Cape Verde Islands (for a partial listing, see Table 1). Of these terms, at least ten—"Jolofo," "Mandinga," "Caçanga," "Bañon," "Folupo," "Biafara," "Nalu," "Bioho," "Bran," and "Zape"—regularly appear in baptismal records, notarial records, and other Spanish Caribbean sources for the same era.[8]

Iberians' greater familiarity with peoples from the Rivers of Guinea helps to explain why Upper Guineans frequently held higher status than other sub-Saharan Africans in early Spanish Caribbean society. As forced migrants from other African regions, especially West Central Africa, began to arrive in larger numbers, Iberians in the Spanish Caribbean described Upper Guineans as "top quality blacks" (*negros de ley*) and placed them in positions of relative autonomy or authority over other Africans. Around 1600, for example, Pedro Biafara was entrusted to carry documents from Havana across the island to El Cobre on behalf of his owner. Meanwhile, in Havana's foundry, "assistant blacksmith" Francisco Biafara worked alongside Antonio Angola *peon* (unskilled worker). Like Lima during the early seventeenth century, Upper Guineans' presence might have been most noticeable in Spanish Caribbean urban centers, where they lived and labored in proximity to Iberians. Thus, Upper Guineans predominated among the Africans listed in a 1605 census of Santiago de Cuba, whereas most enslaved laborers working in nearby mines just three years later were ascribed West Central African origins.[9]

But Upper Guineans could be found in rural and semirural areas too, often directing the labor of other Africans. On a farm near Cartagena in

8. Carta de Miguel Corcuera y Baltasar Perez Bernal, June 27, 1622, AGI-SF 52, n.172a, fol. 5r; Anna María Splendiani and Tulio Aristizábal Giraldo, eds. and trans., *Proceso de beatificación y canonización de San Pedro Claver, edición de 1696* (Bogotá, 2002), 86. For discussion of ethnonyms ascribed to West Central Africans in central Mexico and the province of Guatemala during the first half of the seventeenth century, see Frank "Trey" Proctor III, "African Diasporic Ethnicity in Mexico City to 1650," in Sherwin K. Bryant, Rachel Sarah O'Toole, and Ben Vinson III, eds., *Africans to Spanish America: Expanding the Diaspora* (Urbana, Ill., 2012), 50–72; Paul Lokken, "From the 'Kingdoms of Angola' to Santiago de Guatemala: The Portuguese Asientos and Spanish Central America, 1595–1640," *HAHR*, XCIII (2013), 193–196.

9. On "negros de ley," see Sandoval, *Un tratado sobre la esclavitud,* transcription Vila Vilar, 104, 122, 136, 139, 146; Carta de Miguel Corcuera y Baltasar Pérez Bernal, June 27, 1622, AGI-SF 52, n.172a, fol. 5r. For the enslaved courier Pedro Biafara and foundry workers Francisco Biafara and Antonio Angola, see "Oficiales reales Marcos de Valera Arçeo y Pedro de Redondo Villegas a S. M.," AGI-SD 119, s/n, June 30, 1603, fols. 27r, 54r. On Upper Guineans in Santiago de Cuba and West Central Africans in the nearby mines of El Cobre, see "Minuta y padrón de la gente y casas de la çiudad de Santiago de Cuba," Oct. 6, 1605, AGI-SD 150, r.2, n.33; María Elena Díaz, *The Virgin, the King, and the Royal Slaves of El Cobre: Negotiating Freedom in Colonial Cuba, 1670–1780* (Stanford, Calif., 2000), 42–45. See also Newson and Minchin, *From Capture to Sale,* 68.

1605, *capitán* (captain) Luis Bran supervised at least two West Central African fieldworkers; Antón Bañol oversaw seventeen enslaved men and women of diverse origins on another farm in Cartagena's province in 1622. A decade later, crew members of a boat that transported merchandise from Cartagena up the Magdalena River included one Spanish pilot and eleven Africans of various backgrounds; the enslaved mariners' "captain" was Pedro Folupo. Unlike the "Angolas" whom they often supervised, these Upper Guinean overseers and work crew leaders bore surnames indicating precise ethnolinguistic identities. In practice, Spain's reliance on African migrants in lieu of nonelite Iberian colonists meant that Upper Guineans—who were most likely to have had prior experience of the Iberian world and whom Iberians knew better than people from any other region of sub-Saharan Africa—were also most likely to work in proximity to Iberians and to exercise authority over other surrogate settlers.[10]

Throughout the sixteenth- and early-seventeenth-century Spanish Caribbean, Iberian cognizance of Upper Guinean origins reflected a prior legacy of cross-cultural exchange that included, but was not limited to, colonial expansion, slave trafficking, and the exploitation of slave labor. In addition to providing a means of ascertaining which peoples were forcibly transported from Upper Guinea to the Americas, Iberians' strikingly accurate assessment and consistent acknowledgement of Upper Guinean cultures reveals a level of engagement far beyond superficial observations that some Africans were reputed to work harder than others or that some were exceptionally prone to certain forms of slave resistance. The abundance of such ethnographic data, and its demonstrable correlation with contemporaneous events in Upper Guinea, indicates that, for Iberians and Upper Guineans alike, early Spanish Caribbean society constituted a vibrant extension of the Rivers of Guinea and the region's peoples.

Upper Guinean Ethnonyms in Slave Ship Rosters

During the sixteenth and early seventeenth centuries, the Spanish Caribbean represented the Americas' primary point of contact with Upper Guinea. Forced migrants from the Rivers of Guinea had a notable pres-

---

10. For Upper Guinean estancia overseers Luis Bran and Antón Bañol, see "Pleito entre Juan de Meneses y Francisco Camargo sobre un negro esclavo y sus jornales," 1608, AGN-FNE, Bolívar 6, hojas 10r, 68r–68v; Pedro Guiral con Joan de Arce y Juan de Acosta, 1622, AGI-Esc 632B, pieza 2, fols. 77r, 159v, 196r, 591v, 738v. For Pedro Folupo, see "Ynformaçion fecha çerca de la poblaçion que . . . el enemigo Yngles en la Ysla Santa Catalina," May 9, 1635, AGI-SF 223, n.34, fol. 8v.

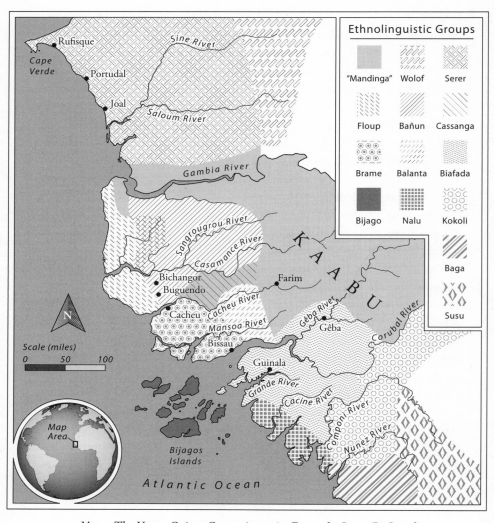

Ethnolinguistic Groups

"Mandinga" Wolof Serer

Floup Bañun Cassanga

Brame Balanta Biafada

Bijago Nalu Kokoli

Baga

Susu

Map 2 The Upper Guinea Coast, circa 1580. Drawn by James DeGrand.

Based on maps by Stephan Bühnen, in Bühnen, "Ethnic Origins of Peruvian Slaves (1548–1650): Figures for Upper Guinea," *Paideuma,* XXXIX (1993), 81, 102, and by Eugene Fleury, in Linda Newson and Susie Minchin, *From Capture to Sale: The Portuguese Slave Trade to Spanish South America in the Early Seventeenth Century* (Leiden, 2007), 53.

The location of ethnolinguistic groups depicted here are approximate, and, in reality, there was often considerable overlap. This map does not include every Upper Guinean ethnolinguistic group; Fula pastoralists, for example, spread across much of the region. "Mandinga" included ethnic Mandinkas but also possibly Soninkes, Senufos, and others. In addition to the Cassanga, many Biafada and Kokoli settlements appear to have been directly subject to Kaabu as client states and probably experienced significant "Mandinga" influence as well.

ence throughout much of the Spanish Americas in this era, but virtually all of them appear to have arrived via the Spanish Caribbean. Most passed through the port of Cartagena de Indias, by far the region's most important slaving hub and redistribution center for secondary slave markets. Cartagena and other Spanish Caribbean seaports maintained extensive maritime links to Upper Guinea and the Cape Verde Islands that generated a wealth of documentary evidence, including port entry records, slave ship inspections, and litigation regarding contraband slave trafficking. Notarial records, criminal records, and ecclesiastical sources describing Upper Guineans can be found not only in the Caribbean but also in Peru and elsewhere in the Spanish Americas.[11]

The long-standing assumption that the Spanish Americas drew heavily on slave exports from Upper Guinea during the sixteenth century and, later, from Angola during the seventeenth century, does appear to be, so far, fairly accurate. Cartagena port entry records show that ships departing from Upper Guinea and the Cape Verde Islands composed the majority of known transatlantic slaving voyages during the 1570s, 1580s, and early 1590s. Though slave traffic from Upper Guinea subsequently overlapped with slave exports from Lower Guinea and Angola and was eventually overshadowed by the latter, voyages from Upper Guinea continued to disembark captives in Spanish Caribbean ports well into the late 1630s.[12]

11. Philip D. Curtin, *The Atlantic Slave Trade: A Census* (Madison, Wis., 1969), 96–111; Frederick P. Bowser, *The African Slave in Colonial Peru, 1524–1650* (Stanford, Calif., 1974), 30–31, 40–42, 54, 72; Alejandro de la Fuente, "Denominaciones étnicas de los esclavos introducidos en Cuba, siglos XVI y XVII," *Anales del Caribe, Centro de Estudios del Caribe*, VI (1986), 75–96; Lolita Gutiérrez Brockington, *The Leverage of Labor: Managing the Cortés Haciendas in Tehuantepec, 1588–1688* (Durham, N.C., 1989), 128–130; Stephan Bühnen, "Ethnic Origins of Peruvian Slaves (1548–1650): Figures for Upper Guinea," *Paideuma*, XXXIX (1993), 57–110; Jean-Pierre Tardieu, "Origines des esclaves de la région de Lima, au Pérou, aux XVIe e XVIIe siècles," in Doudou Diene, dir., *La chaîne et le lien: Une vision de la traite négrière (Actes du Colloque de Ouidah)* (Paris, 1998), 81–94; Patrick James Carroll, *Blacks in Colonial Veracruz: Race, Ethnicity, and Regional Development*, 2d ed. (Austin, Tex., 2001), 158–159; Lourdes Mondragón Barrios, *Esclavos africanos en la Ciudad de México: El servicio doméstico durante el siglo XVI* (Mexico City, 1999), 36–39; Antonino Vidal Ortega, *Cartagena de Indias y la región histórica del Caribe, 1580–1640* (Seville, 2002), 119–122; María Cristina Navarrete, *Génesis y desarrollo de la esclavitud en Colombia, siglos XVI y XVII* (Cali, Colombia, 2005), 110; Rachel Sarah O'Toole, "From the Rivers of Guinea to the Valleys of Peru: Becoming a *Bran* Diaspora within Spanish Slavery," *Social Text*, XXV, no. 3 (Fall 2007), 19–36.

12. Curtin, *Atlantic Slave Trade*, 106–108; Enriqueta Vila Vilar, *Hispanoamérica y el comercio de esclavos: Los asientos portugueses* (Seville, 1977), 144–145; Newson and Minchin, *From Capture to Sale*, 66–67; Rafael M. Pérez García and Manuel F. Fernández Chaves, "Sevilla y la trata negrera atlántica: Envíos de esclavos desde Cabo Verde a la América española, 1569–1579," in León Carlos Álvarez Santaló, coord., *Estudios de historia moderna en homenaje al profesor Antonio García-Baquero* (Seville, 2009), 597–622; Wheat, "The First Great Waves," *JAH*, LII (2011), 1–22.

Spanish Caribbean customs officials occasionally compiled rosters of captives disembarked from slave ships; though irregular and not always complete, such lists provide exceptionally detailed evidence of the origins of Upper Guinean migrants. Table 1 below is a composite list of male and female captives disembarked from five slave ships arriving in the Spanish Caribbean from 1572 to 1634. Three voyages departed from the Cape Verde Islands, one sailed directly from Buguendo (in present-day Guinea Bissau), and one from an unknown port or ports on the Grande River. Royal officials in Havana and Santo Domingo carefully noted the "land" *(tierra)* of most captives disembarked from the *San Pedro* and *San Jorge,* arriving in 1572 and 1574 respectively. However, only partial records survive for the last three ships, since each of these voyages was allegedly disrupted by shipwreck or piracy. After the ship *Nuestra Señora de la Concepción* crashed near Santa Marta in 1593, at least 100 captives were recovered, but the subsequent investigation generated detailed information for only 26 individuals. After having been boarded by English pirates near Dominica, the *Santa María* disembarked at least 61 enslaved Africans in Puerto Rico in 1594; it is not clear how many were initially on board or how many actually arrived, and only 25 are listed by name and ethnonym. Ostensibly bound for the Canary Islands, mariners on the frigate *San Josephe* had purchased at least 128 captives in the "Rivers of Guinea" but were forced to change course because the ship was repeatedly threatened by "enemy sails." When the vessel finally arrived in Veracruz in 1634, royal officials' inspection of the ship revealed only 70 survivors; some were said to have died at sea, and others died shortly after arrival. Despite the imperfect nature of the data, the five slave ship rosters combined afford an invaluable glimpse of the sex and nations (or lands) of more than 500 Upper Guinean forced migrants disembarked in five discrete locations throughout the circum-Caribbean.[13]

Although most captives listed in Table 1 were acquired south of the Gambia River, several bore ethnonyms indicating Senegambian origins. The presence of individuals, albeit few, described as "Jolofo" on the *San*

13. On the ship *San Pedro,* see "Relación de los ciento y noventa y un esclavos de su magestad," Nov. 3, 1572, AGI-Ctdra 1174, n.6; Oficiales reales a S. M., Aug. 18, 1572, AGI-SD 118, r.2, n.100; Irene Aloha Wright, *Historia documentada de San Cristóbal de la Habana en el siglo XVI, basada en los documentos originales existentes en el Archivo General de Indias en Sevilla* (Havana, 1927), I, 58–59, 209–211. On the *San Jorge,* see "Contratadores de Cabo Verde y Guinea con Cristóbal Cayado y otros del reino de Portugal," 1582–1589, AGI-Esc 2A, pieza 2; Green, *Rise of the Trans-Atlantic Slave Trade,* 217, 250–255, 263, 274–275. On the *Concepción, Santa María,* and *San Josephe* respectively, see "El fiscal de su magestad contra el capitán Valentin Velo," 1593, AGN-FNE, Magdalena 4; "El fiscal con Enrique Suero," 1594, AGI-Esc 119A; "Arivada de Jorje Nuñez de Andrada," 1634–1636, AGI-Esc 295A, n.2.

Pedro, San Jorge, San Josephe, and the *Concepcion* and others described as "Berbesí" on the *San Pedro* and *San Josephe* reveals that the transatlantic slave trade from Upper Guinea and the Cape Verde Islands drew on slave catchment areas extending perhaps as far north as the Senegal River. One captive arriving in Havana on the *San Pedro* in 1572 was described as a black woman from Arguim ("Argui"), an island off the Mauritanian coast, even farther north. "Jolofo" (Wolof) is the Senegambian ethnonym most commonly found in Spanish Caribbean sources for this period; the term first appears in Spanish sources for Valencia in the 1450s as a vague geographical designation. Historians widely suspect that a century later, following the disintegration of the Jolof empire, its inhabitants might have been enslaved and transported to the Americas in substantial numbers.[14]

By the late sixteenth century, given the customary usage of a variety of Senegambian and Upper Guinean ethnonyms, it seems likely that "Jolofo" referred specifically to Wolofs, rather than serving as an umbrella category for Wolof, Serer, Fula, and Mandinka peoples from the Gambia River area. Moreover, the term "Figuine," as recorded in Havana in 1572, suggests that captives had some leeway in defining their own places or cultures of origin; for Wolof speakers, *fi Guiné* translates as "here, Guinea," a plausible response to the question, "Where are you from?" Not including the man from "Figuine," the six "Jolofo" captives on these voyages only slightly outnumbered two Serer men listed as "Berbesí," an ethnonym derived from the Wolof political title *Bur ba Siin,* meaning the "ruler of Siin." Like its neighbor Saloum, Siin was a Serer homeland that had been incorporated

---

14. Hair, "Black African Slaves," *HA,* VII (1980), 120; Curtin, *Atlantic Slave Trade,* 102; Philip D. Curtin, *Economic Change in Precolonial Africa: Senegambia in the Era of the Slave Trade* (Madison, Wis., 1975), 12–13, 61; Brooks, *Landlords and Strangers,* 125–127, 139, 146; Bühnen, "Ethnic Origins," *Paideuma,* XXXIX (1993), 75–77, 97; Ivana Elbl, "The Volume of the Early Atlantic Slave Trade, 1450–1521," *JAH,* XXXVIII (1997), 43–44; Green, *Rise of the Trans-Atlantic Slave Trade,* 81n, 203–206; Herbert S. Klein and Ben Vinson III, *African Slavery in Latin America and the Caribbean* (Oxford, 2007), 136. For discussion of the Upper Guinea coast as part of "Greater Senegambia," see Boubacar Barry, *Senegambia and the Atlantic Slave Trade,* trans. Ayi Kwei Armah (New York, 1998), xi–xii; Gwendolyn Midlo Hall, *Slavery and African Ethnicities in the Americas: Restoring the Links* (Chapel Hill, N.C., 2005), 80–100; Peter Mark and José da Silva Horta, *The Forgotten Diaspora: Jewish Communities in West Africa and the Making of the Atlantic World* (New York, 2011), 2–7, 205. Wolof people usually appear in Spanish Caribbean sources as "Jolofo" or "Jolofa"; the ethnonym closely resembles the name of the powerful Wolof state known as Jolof, or the Jolof empire, that splintered after 1549. Spanish Caribbean sources also identified Wolofs using other terms such as "Jalofo," "Xolofo," "Yolofo," "Jorofo," "Golofa," "Julufu," or "Gelofe"; see, for example, Sagrada Catedral de San Cristóbal de La Habana, "Libro de Barajas: Bautismos, 1590–1600" (CH-LB/B), fols. 10v, 42v, 66v, 95r, 103r–103v, 108r, 109r, 117v, 123r–124v, 137r, 140r–140v.

Table 1 Upper Guinean Captives on Five Voyages to the Spanish Caribbean by Ethnonym and Sex

Ethnonym	San Pedro (1572) Cape Verde Islands to Havana			San Jorge (1574–1575) Buguendo to Nizao			Concepción (1593) Cape Verde Islands to Santa Marta			Santa María (1594) Río Grande to Puerto Rico			San Josephe (1634) Cape Verde Islands to Veracruz			Total
	M	F	Total	M	F	Total	M	F	Total	M	F	Total	M	F	Total	
"Argui" (Arguim)	0	1	1	0	0	0	0	0	0	0	0	0	0	0	0	1
"Ariata" (Arriata)	0	0	0	1	0	1	0	0	0	0	0	0	0	0	0	1
Balanta	0	0	0	4	2	6	3	0	3	0	1	1	3	3	6	16
"Bañon" (Bañun)	2	1	3	12	3	15	1	1	2	0	1	1	1	4	5	26
"Baoyote" (Baiote)	0	0	0	0	0	0	0	0	0	0	0	0	0	1	1	1
"Berbesi" (Serer)	1	0	1	0	0	0	0	0	0	0	0	0	1	0	1	2
"Biafara" (Biafada)	29	11	40	18	17	35	2	1	3	1	1	2	2	2	4	84
"Bioho" (Bijago)	8	3	11	9	2	11	2	1	3	2	1	3	0	2	2	30
"Bran" (Brame)	34	17	51	60	21	81	5	0	5	3	1	4	6	3	9	150
Papel	0	0	0	2	1	3	0	0	0	0	0	0	0	0	0	3
"Casanga" (Cassanga)	6	4	10	4	3	7	1	0	1	4	2	6	4	2	6	30
"Figuine"	1	0	1	0	0	0	0	0	0	0	0	0	0	0	0	1
"Folupo" (Floup)	0	0	0	2	1	3	0	0	0	0	0	0	8	3	11	14
"Jolofo" (Wolof)	1	1	2	1	0	1	0	2	2	0	0	0	1	0	1	6
"Mandinga"	15	0	15	4	0	4	2	1	3	0	1	1	2	4	6	29
Nalu	4	2	6	10	3	13	3	0	3	0	0	0	0	0	0	22
"Oquali"	1	0	1	0	0	0	0	0	0	0	0	0	0	0	0	1

	San Pedro			San Jorge			Nuestra Señora de la Concepción			Santa María			San Josephe			TOTAL
"Zape"	15	21	36	4	2	6	0	0	0	0	1	1	3	6	9	52
Baga	0	0	0	1	0	1	0	0	0	0	0	0	2	0	2	3
"Cocolí" (Kokoli)	0	1	1	0	0	0	1	0	1	0	0	0	2	1	3	5
"Landima" (Landuma)	0	0	0	0	0	0	0	0	0	0	0	0	1	1	2	2
"Linba" (Limba)	8	2	10	0	0	0	0	0	0	0	0	0	0	0	0	10
"Soso" (Susu)	1	2	3	1	1	2	0	0	0	0	0	0	1	1	2	7
Unspecified	0	0	0	3	0	3	0	0	0	3	3	6	0	0	0	9
TOTAL	126	66	192	136	56	192	20	6	26	13	12	25	37	33	70	505

Sources: For the *San Pedro,* see "Relación de los ciento y noventa y un esclavos de su magestad," Nov. 3, 1572, AGI-Ctdra 1174, n.6, fols. 12v–16r; for the *San Jorge,* see "Contratadores de Cabo Verde y Guinea con Cristóbal Cayado y otros del reino de Portugal," 1582–1589, AGI-Esc 2A, pieza 2, fols. 493v–498r; for the *Nuestra Señora de la Concepción,* see "El fiscal de su magestad contra el capitán Valentín Velo," 1593, AGN-FNE Magdalena 4, hojas 19r–21v; for the *Santa María,* see "El fiscal con Enrique Suero," 1594, AGI-Esc 119A, fols. 200v–206r; for the *San Josephe,* see "Arivada de Jorje Nuñez de Andrada," 1634–1636, AGI-Esc 295A, n.2, fols. 551v–555r.

Note: One Biafada on the *San Jorge* identified only as an *una criatura* (nursing infant) is listed here, arbitrarily, as female. Ethnonyms with alternate spellings that appear in these sources include Balanta (Blanta, Planta, Valanta); Bañon (Bañol, Bañul, Banu); Berbesí (Berbeçi, Berbecin, Verbesí); Bioho (Biho, Bioxo, Bijojo, Bijocho, Bizogo, Bijago); Bran (Bram, Brame); Casanga (Caçanga); Jolofo (Gelofe); Zape (Çape, Sape); Baga (Bag); Cocolí (Cololi); Landima (Ladema); Linba (Lumba, Lemba); Soso (Soço, Zozo, Zojo). Though listed here as an ethnonym, "Argui" (Arguim) was a toponym.

into the former Jolof empire. Serers from both Siin and Saloum were known to Iberians as "Berbesí," "Berbecín," or "Barbacins."[15]

Although the twenty-nine "Mandingas" listed in Table 1 could have been ethnic Mandinka from the lower Gambia River area, it is also possible they originated much farther inland. Based on knowledge gleaned from his own research and more than a decade of extensive interaction with Africans in Cartagena, Sandoval wrote that "Mandingas" could be found in the Upper Guinean interior up the Gambia River and as far south as "the head of the river Ladigola" (presumably the Gêba River). Interestingly, he then noted that the term "Mandinga" was also commonly ascribed to people more accurately identified as "Soninkes" (or "Soniquies") and "Senfones" (Senufos). Historically residing on Senegambia's eastern fringes, Soninkes participated in various trade networks spreading across West Africa, notably as Wangara merchants who linked the empires of Mali and Songhay to gold-producing areas in Lower Guinea. Another important trade route operated by Soninke-speaking merchants known as Jahanke ran westward toward the Gambia River. Placing the Senufo near coastal Senegambia is more difficult; for the past two centuries they have primarily lived in what is today southern Mali and the northern Ivory Coast. If any of the "Mandingas" transported on these ships were in fact Senufo, as Sandoval suggests, then their presence on the Upper Guinea coast could provide a rare example of internal West African slave routes oriented toward the Iberian Atlantic.[16]

15. "Contratadores de Cabo Verde y Guinea con Cristóbal Cayado," 1582–1589, AGI-Esc 2A, pieza 2; "El fiscal de su magestad contra el capitán Valentin Velo," 1593, AGN-FNE, Magdalena 4; "Arivada de Jorje Nuñez de Andrada," 1634–1636, AGI-Esc 295A, n.2. I am grateful to Bala Saho for suggesting this interpretation for "Figuine" and to Assan Sarr for pointing me toward the etymology of "Berbesí." On the latter topic, see also G[onzalo] Aguirre Beltrán, "The Rivers of Guinea," *JNH,* XXXI (1946), 294–295; Hair, "Ethnolinguistic Continuity," *JAH,* VIII (1967), 249–250; Hair, "Black African Slaves," *HA,* VII (1980), 121, 132; Jean Boulègue, *Le grand Jolof, XIIIe–XVIe siècle* (Blois, France, 1987), 18, 129–130; Bühnen, "Ethnic Origins," *Paideuma,* XXXIX (1993), 80; Carlos Lopes, *Kaabunké: Espaço, território e poder na Guiné-Bissau, Gâmbia e Casamance pré-coloniais,* trans. Maria Augusta Júdice and Lurdes Júdice (Lisbon, 1999), 57.

16. Sandoval, *Un tratado sobre la esclavitud,* transcription Vila Vilar, 63, 106–108, 119; P. E. H. Hair, "Sources on Early Sierra Leone: (3) Sandoval (1627)," *ARB,* V, no. 2 (1975), 84; Brooks, *Landlords and Strangers,* 61, 68–69, 85–86, 266; Curtin, *Atlantic Slave Trade,* 97–98; Curtin, *Economic Change,* 7, 10, 20, 66–82, 276; Bühnen, "Ethnic Origins," *Paideuma,* XXXIX (1993), 81; Lopes, *Kaabunké,* trans. Júdice and Júdice, 90; Donald R. Wright, *The World and a Very Small Place in Africa: A History of Globalization in Niumi, the Gambia,* 3d ed. (Armonk, N.Y., 2010), 51–57, 69–70; Ivor Wilks, "A Medieval Trade-Route from the Niger to the Gulf of Guinea," *JAH,* III (1962), 337–341; Andreas W. Massing, "The Wangara, an Old Soninke Diaspora in West Africa?" *CEA,* XL (2000), 281–308; Dolores Richter, "Further Considerations of Caste in West Africa: The Senufo," *Africa: Journal of the International African Institute,* L (1980), 37–54.

If "Mandingas" originated in the West African interior, their appearance on the lists would suggest that the Upper Guinea coast served as an intermediary market, importing captives from distant centralized states in Islamic West Africa and then exporting them to the Spanish Americas. But this scenario is highly unlikely. For example, according to Española's royal officials in 1574, one captive arriving on the *San Jorge* was identified only as "a black man named Congoy." The name is phonetically similar to Kongay, a small town on the bank of the Niger River north of Gao—an area that was squarely within the heart of Songhay during the 1570s. Otherwise, Spanish Caribbean sources present little evidence to indicate that the Niger River was ever a major conduit for slave traffic from Songhay toward the Upper Guinea coast. The numbers of enslaved "Mandingas" who appear in known Spanish American sources are always few in comparison to coastal Upper Guinean groups, and these numbers do not increase noticeably after the fall of Songhay in 1591. Although slavery was widely practiced within the Islamic world, slave exports from the Islamic West African interior toward Atlantic markets were limited in scale and presumably remained so until the nineteenth century.[17]

In the sixteenth and early seventeenth centuries, scholars such as Makhlūf al-Balbālī and Ahmad Bābā formulated policies intended to prevent Muslims from enslaving fellow Muslims; both used ethnicity as a rudimentary means of identifying devout Muslim peoples whom they believed should not be enslaved. Sandoval's assertion that "Mandinga[s]" in the Spanish Americas were often Soninkes and Senufos (rather than ethnic Mandinkas) does not necessarily contradict Ahmad Bābā, who mentions neither group. Although some modern Senufo follow Islam, their ancestors only converted in the 1700s; the Soninke converted to Islam much earlier, in the eleventh century, but might have been viewed nonetheless by Ahmad Bābā as one of many peoples "whose Islamic practice was suspect and hence should not be protected against enslavement." Thus far, however, Sandoval's

17. "Contratadores de Cabo Verde y Guinea con Cristóbal Cayado," 1582–1589, AGI-Esc 2A, pieza 2, fols. 496v, 498r; Paul E. Lovejoy, "Islam, Slavery, and Political Transformation in West Africa: Constraints on the Trans-Atlantic Slave Trade," *Outre-Mers: Revue d'histoire,* LXXXIX (2002), 247–282; Jennifer Lofkrantz and Paul E. Lovejoy, "Maintaining Network Boundaries: Islamic Law and Commerce from Sahara to Guinea Shores," *SA,* XXXVI (2015), 211–232. See also Lansiné Kaba, "Archers, Musketeers, and Mosquitoes: The Moroccan Invasion of the Sudan and the Songhay Resistance (1591–1612)," *JAH,* XXII (1981), 457–475; John Hunwick, "Songhay, Borno, and the Hausaland in the Sixteenth Century," in J. F. A. Ajayi and Michael Crowder, eds., *History of West Africa,* 3d ed. (Bath, England, 1976), I, 323–371, and John Ralph Willis, "The Western Sudan from the Moroccan Invasion (1591) to the Death of al-Mukhtar al-Kunti (1811)," I, 531–576.

treatise remains the only early Spanish Caribbean source known to mention the Soninke or Senufos at all.[18]

The most important source of enslaved "Mandingas" transported to the early Spanish Caribbean was probably the federation of Mande states collectively known as Kaabu. Formed by Mandinka migration to Upper Guinea in approximately the thirteenth century, Kaabu might have constituted a western province of the Mali empire until the late fifteenth or early sixteenth century, when it grew powerful enough to claim autonomy. Sandoval's description of territories inhabited by Mandinkas and Soninkes in the Upper Guinean interior, stretching from the Gambia River southward to the head of the Gêba River, closely corresponds to Kaabu's geographical parameters during the sixteenth and seventeenth centuries. His reference to "Soninkes" in this region is also indirectly confirmed by knowledge that the Soninke later constituted an important segment of Kaabu's ruling elite. As the immediate hinterland for peoples living along the Upper Guinea coast south of the Gambia River, Kaabu appears to have operated as a predatory state that exploited its non-Mande neighbors on the coastal littoral. In addition to demanding tribute from conquered peoples, Kaabu supplied captives to visiting Luso-African traders or sold them indirectly to Portuguese merchants via intermediary markets nearer the coast. But decentralized coastal peoples fully participated in slaving, too, to strengthen their own communities. Some of the "Mandingas" listed in these slave ship rosters might have been captured and sold by coastal Upper Guinean peoples who resisted the encroachment of Kaabu and its vassal states. Others were likely enslaved in Kaabu or elsewhere because of debts or as a result of judicial proceedings, then sold to intermediaries and resold to Iberian merchants.[19]

18. The literature on this topic is substantial. For useful overviews, see John Hunwick, "Islamic Law and Polemics over Race and Slavery in North and West Africa (16th–19th Century)," *Princeton Papers: Interdisciplinary Journal of Middle Eastern Studies,* VII (1999), 43–68; Jean Boulègue and Zakari Dramani-Issifou, "La classification ethnique de deux lettrés (XIIIe–XVIIe siècle)," in Jean-Pierre Chrétien and Gérard Prunier, dirs., *Les ethnies ont une histoire,* 2d ed. (Paris, 2003), 33–48; Marta García Novo, "Islamic Law and Slavery in Premodern West Africa," *Entremons,* II (November 2011), 1–20; Chouki El-Hamel, *Black Morocco: A History of Slavery, Race, and Islam* (New York, 2013), 79–85. See also Paul E. Lovejoy, "The Context of Enslavement in West Africa: Ahmad Bābā and the Ethics of Slavery," in Jane G. Landers and Barry M. Robinson, eds., *Slaves, Subjects, and Subversives: Blacks in Colonial Latin America* (Albuquerque, N.Mex., 2006), 9–38. On conversion to Islam among southern Senufos during the eighteenth century, see James S. Olson, *The Peoples of Africa: An Ethnohistorical Dictionary* (Westport, Conn., 1996), 515.

19. Rodney, *History of the Upper Guinea Coast,* 81, 113; Hawthorne, *Planting Rice,* 2, 4, 29, 42, 56, 91–115, 203–210. See also Curtin, *Economic Change,* 8–13; Brooks, *Landlords and Strangers,* 68–69, 109–113, 227, 242, 251, 256–257; Wright, *World and a Very Small Place in Africa,* 69, 110; Barry, *Senegambia,* trans. Armah, 21–23; Lopes, *Kaabunké,* trans. Júdice and Júdice, 123–184; Philip J. Havik, *Silences and Sound-*

Although by all accounts the expansion of Kaabu was closely associated with ethnic conflict and slave production in sixteenth- and seventeenth-century Upper Guinea, Kaabu's outlying client states were often more directly implicated in the enslaving and trafficking of other Upper Guineans. Located inland between the Casamance and Cacheu Rivers, the former Bañun state of Casa was conquered by Mandinkas by the mid-fifteenth century and became a vassal state of Kaabu. Casa's highest political authority held the Mandinka title *Casa mansa* (the mansa, or ruler, of Casa) and governed from the fortified capital of Brucama on the Casamance River (the name is derived from Casa mansa). Though its population initially consisted of Bañuns and other coastal peoples, strong Mandinka influence distinguished Casa from its Bañun neighbors. By the sixteenth century, Iberians explicitly recognized Casa's residents as "Caçanga," or "Casanga," an ethnonym and language that have persisted into the modern era (Cassanga, Kasanga, Kassanké). Attempting to extend Mandinka power north, south, and west, Cassangas attacked nearby Bañun, Floup, Balanta, and Brame peoples, collecting steep annual tribute payments (primarily in the form of livestock) from those whom they subjected; some of these resources would then be forwarded as tribute to Kaabu. Warfare between Cassangas and Bañuns was particularly intense and often overlapped with competition for access to Atlantic markets. For instance, although Casa's cavalry had traditionally formed the basis of its military strength, Bañuns blockaded the Casamance River during much of the sixteenth century to prevent Portuguese and Capeverdean traders from supplying the Cassanga with horses. Yet, the Casa ruler Masatamba burned the Bañun port of Buguendo in circa 1574—possibly coinciding with the *San Jorge*'s departure—and by 1580 had opened direct trade with Portuguese and Luso-Africans at Sarar, a port farther upstream and only one day's journey away from Brucama.[20]

Many of the seventeen "Casanga[s]" transported to the Spanish Caribbean on the *San Pedro* and *San Jorge* might have been enslaved as a result of

bites: The Gendered Dynamics of Trade and Brokerage in the Pre-Colonial Guinea Bissau Region (Münster, Germany, 2004), 120–125; Newson and Minchin, *From Capture to Sale*, 53; Green, *Rise of the Trans-Atlantic Slave Trade*, 33, 46–60.

20. Rodney, *History of the Upper Guinea Coast*, 7, 89, 111; Hair, "Ethnolinguistic Continuity," *JAH*, VIII (1967), 251; Brooks, *Landlords and Strangers*, 93, 109–110, 172, 225–237; Robert M. Baum, *Shrines of the Slave Trade: Diola Religion and Society in Precolonial Senegambia* (New York, 1999), 65–68; Hawthorne, *Planting Rice*, 63–65, 93–95; Green, *Rise of the Trans-Atlantic Slave Trade*, 48, 53–55. For the argument that Iberians might have initially labeled Cassangas as "Mandingas," see Bühnen, "Ethnic Origins," *Paideuma*, XXXIX (1993), 77. Among the "Casangas" and "Bañuns" who arrived in Nizao as captives on the San Jorge in January 1575, none were described as wounded.

Cassanga-Bañun conflict in the early 1570s. It is also very likely that judicial enslavement within the Casa state was an important factor in producing Cassanga captives for Atlantic export. In the 1570s, Masatamba reportedly enslaved and sold the entire extended families of men who died falling from palm trees while tapping them for palm wine and were thus judged to have been "witch[es]." Sandoval's treatise also refers to an Upper Guinean man in Cartagena who had been enslaved and sold by order of "the King of Cazamanza." Little is known of Casa during the period Sandoval wrote. After Masatamba's death in the early 1580s, the Bañun recovered some of their lost territories, and Sarar was rapidly eclipsed by the Brame port of Cacheu on the southern bank of the Cacheu River. Some four decades later, Sandoval noted that "few ships" traded along the Casamance River and that most commerce in the area was conducted overland; Cacheu had become the premier maritime hub for Iberian commerce in Upper Guinea. Significantly, Sandoval also described the "King of Casamance Bulcama" (Brucama) as "Emperor of all the Banunes, of the Cafangas, and of some Mandingas," indicating that Casa might have remained powerful as late as circa 1620, despite reduced access to Ibero-Atlantic commerce. Regardless of changes in Casa's role in producing slaves for export, the rosters of captives disembarked from the ships *Concepción* and *Santa María* during the 1590s and from the frigate *San Josephe* in 1634 demonstrate that small numbers of Cassangas continued to arrive in the Spanish circum-Caribbean well into the seventeenth century.[21]

Despite the Mandinka conquest of Casa and subsequent warfare between Casa and other Bañun states, Bañuns maintained control over much of the territory between the Gambia and Cacheu Rivers throughout the sixteenth and early seventeenth centuries. The political, economic, and demographic importance of Bañun groups during this period presents a notable contrast with the modern Bañun (Banyun, Banhun, Bainounk), who are believed to have been gradually absorbed by neighboring peoples. West of Casa on the northern bank of the Cacheu River, the state of Buguendo (including the port of the same name) might have been the original Bañun homeland; other Bañun states such as Bichangor, Foni, Jase, and Jagra were located farther north. Bañun trade fairs in Buguendo attracted Brames from across the Cacheu River, and Bañuns often visited markets on the river's opposite shore. Bañuns also played a major role in one of Upper Guinea's most

21. Brooks, *Landlords and Strangers*, 235–241; Bühnen, "Ethnic Origins," *Paideuma*, XXXIX (1993), 98; Hawthorne, *Planting Rice*, 94–95; Sandoval, *Un tratado sobre la esclavitud*, transcription Vila Vilar, 63–64, 107, 137, 149.

important long-distance trade networks, with much of their commercial activity—and territorial expansion, if Buguendo was their ancestral homeland—directed northward. In collaboration with their Floup neighbors and Mandinka mariners who resided along the mouth of the Gambia River, the Bañun extended their "Banyun-Bak" trade route as far as the Senegal River and Cape Verde Islands.[22]

Since Bañuns typically outnumber Cassangas in colonial Spanish American sources, the presence of roughly equal numbers of Bañuns and Cassangas in Table 1 is somewhat surprising. Upon arriving in Havana in 1572, the *San Pedro* disembarked only three Bañuns and no less than ten Cassangas; in this case, the captives' ethnic composition might have simply reflected slave market conditions in the Cape Verde Islands. The majority of Bañuns listed in Table 1 arrived in Española less than three years later on the *San Jorge,* which had departed from the Bañun port of Buguendo. Evidence of Bañun captives exported from Buguendo lends support to Stephan Bühnen's hypothesis that, in Upper Guinea, judicial enslavement of members of one's own community might have sometimes been more important than conflict among rival groups in generating captives for export to the Americas. On the other hand, the *San Jorge's* departure from Buguendo possibly took place after Cassangas attacked and burned the port, presumably acquiring a number of Bañun captives in the process.[23]

Though less well documented than their long-term hostilities with Casa, Bañun conflict with their neighbors to the east and south—the Floup, Arriata, Brame, and even other Bañun—likewise generated Upper Guinean captives for transatlantic export. As highly decentralized communities, Bañun groups might at times have been tempted to ensure their own wellbeing at one another's expense; competition and internecine conflict, rather than judicial enslavement, could account for some Bañun captives sold to Iberian merchants. Sandoval distinguishes "pure" Bañun from "Banúnes Bootes" (Baiotes), whom he describes as a "very cruel people" sometimes mistakenly identified as "Fulupos." According to Sandoval, the Baiote "had

22. On the "Banyun-Bak network," see Brooks, *Landlords and Strangers,* 87–95, 111. Bak refers to a family of non-tonal languages spoken by various peoples in modern Guinea-Bissau and Senegal. Floups, Balantas, Brames, and perhaps Baiotes may be classified as speakers of Bak languages. See also Hair, "Ethnolinguistic Continuity," *JAH,* VIII (1967), 251; Rodney, *History of the Upper Guinea Coast,* 6–7; Havik, *Silences and Soundbites,* 99–103.

23. Bühnen, "Ethnic Origins," *Paideuma,* XXXIX (1993), 97, 106. Spanish American sources commonly identify individual Bañuns as "Bañon" or "Bañol" and, less frequently, "Banu." For examples of Bañuns outnumbering Cassangas, see Bowser, *African Slave in Colonial Peru,* 40–43; de la Fuente, "Denominaciones étnicas," *Anales del Caribe, Centro de Estudios del Caribe,* VI (1986), 95.

their kingdom between the Fulupos and Banunes" and were completely different from "pure" Bañuns, even though "if asked about their castes, both will answer that they are Banunes.┃ He portrays their languages as mutually unintelligible, noting that it was far more common for "pure" Bañuns to understand Cassangas (and to a lesser extent, Brames and "Mandingas"), while Baiotes commonly understood Floup. With the exception of Sandoval's comments, references to Baiotes are quite rare in known Spanish American sources; the only Baiote listed in Table 1 was a ten-year-old *muleca* (girl) named Madalena, "of the Baoyote caste," who arrived in Veracruz in 1634 on the *San Josephe,* alongside five Bañuns and eleven Floups.[24]

In modern times, both Baiotes and Floups are considered subgroups of the Diola (Jola), but Iberians apparently labeled Diolas in general as "Folupo" (Floup) during the sixteenth and seventeenth centuries. References to Diolas are also scarce in Spanish American sources for this period; no captive listed in Table 1, or in any other source consulted for this study, was identified as Diola. Sandoval only fleetingly mentions the kingdom of "Iola," providing somewhat better information on the "innumerable" Floup who inhabited the coastal area between the mouths of the Gambia and Cacheu Rivers. European travel accounts portray Floups as the victims of coastal raids by Cassangas and Mandinkas during the 1560s and 1570s and refer to Bañun "kings" making "frequent wars on rebellious Folupo subjects" and selling "great numbers to the Europeans" during the mid-seventeenth century. Peruvian sources support the theory that the "hostile Bañol-Folupo relations" described by Bühnen produced Floup captives for transatlantic export; Floups first appear in samplings of notarial records in 1595, reaching substantial numbers only during the early seventeenth century. Table 1 parallels this pattern, with only three Floups arriving in the 1570s and eleven arriving on one voyage in 1634. Among the captives disembarked from the *San Josephe* in Veracruz, Floups constituted the largest single group listed.[25]

24. Hawthorne, *Planting Rice,* 98–99; Sandoval, *Un tratado sobre la esclavitud,* transcription Vila Vilar, 63 ("Bootes," "Banúnes Bootes"), 137 ("Banum Boote, o Boyocho"); "Arivada de Jorje Nuñez de Andrada," 1634–1636, AGI-Esc 295A, n.2, fol. 552v. See also Rodney, *History of the Upper Guinea Coast,* 103; Brooks, *Landlords and Strangers,* 231; Bühnen, "Ethnic Origins," *Paideuma,* XXXIX (1993), 99.

25. Hair, "Ethnolinguistic Continuity," *JAH,* VIII (1967), 250–251; Rodney, *History of the Upper Guinea Coast,* 21, 105; Hawthorne, *Planting Rice,* 99; Bühnen, "Ethnic Origins," *Paideuma,* XXXIX (1993), 79n, 82, 99n; Baum, *Shrines of the Slave Trade,* 63; Havik, *Silences and Soundbites,* 89–95; Sandoval, *Un tratado sobre la esclavitud,* transcription Vila Vilar, 63, 106; Bowser, *African Slave in Colonial Peru,* 40–43. See also de la Fuente, "Denominaciones étnicas," *Anales del Caribe, Centro de Estudios del Caribe,* VI (1986), 95. Both the Baiote and the Floup are often associated with rice cultivation; Rodney notes that "Baiote" meant "men of the rice nursery" (21).

Like the Baiotes, Arriatas were closely associated with Floups and might have been enslaved by Bañuns and sold to Iberian merchants in Buguendo or elsewhere. References to Arriatas in Spanish American sources are extremely rare; even Sandoval makes no mention of them. Late-sixteenth-century Portuguese travelers described Arriatas as living near "Folupos," adding that both groups "understand each other." Arriatas' absence in known sources for later periods raises the possibility that they were in fact Floup and "may never have existed as a distinct group." However, the presence of "a black man from Ariata" as well as two men and a young woman "of the Falupo land" on a ship arriving in Española in early 1575 suggests that some distinction could be drawn between them and that the term "Ariata" bore some meaning that was lost after the sixteenth century.[26]

The "Beafares" and "Biafara" mentioned in early modern Iberian sources are far easier to identify as the modern Biafada (also spelled Beafada). Much like Casa, Biafada states along the Gêba, Corubal, and Grande Rivers were either directly or indirectly subject to Kaabu during the sixteenth and early seventeenth centuries. Commerce and the spread of Mandinka culture further linked the Biafada to Kaabu. Portuguese accounts portray Biafada societies as semidecentralized, with kings in Biguba, Guinala, and Bissegue ruling over lesser political authorities within those states. Based in Bruco, near the port of Guinala on the Rio Grande, the ruler of Guinala might have exerted some control over other Biafada states, including Bissegue, Mompara, and Bolola, though the extent of Guinala's influence was probably fairly limited. Furthermore, the positions of Biafada communities in relation to Kaabu were not uniform; whereas states such as Guinala were ruled by Biafadas who paid tribute to Kaabu, Mandinkas conquered the eastern Biafada state of Degola (including the port of Gêba), renamed it Badour, and placed it directly under Mandinka rule. According to Sandoval, the "kingdoms, and cities of the Biafara nation"—which numbered more than seventy—were "very diverse and spread out," but the same "more or less elegant" language was spoken in each. Confirming Kaabu's political

26. Olga F. Linares, "Deferring to Trade in Slaves: The Jola of Casamance, Senegal in Historical Perspective," *HA*, XIV (1987), 115–116, citing Peter Mark, *A Cultural, Economic, and Religious History of the Basse Casamance Since 1500* (Stuttgart, Germany, 1985), 20–22. For the observation that Floups and Arriatas "understand each other" (*se entendem os Arriatas com os Falupos*), see André Álvares d'Almada, *Tratado breve dos Rios de Guiné do Cabo Verde* (circa 1594), transcription, introduction, and notes by António Brásio (Lisbon, 1964), 60. For the arrival of three Floups and one Arriata in Española in 1575, see "Contratadores de Cabo Verde y Guinea con Cristóbal Cayado," 1582–1589, AGI-Esc 2A, pieza 2, fols. 494v, 495v, 496v, 498r. See also Bühnen, "Ethnic Origins," *Paideuma*, XXXIX (1993), 78n, 93n; Hawthorne, *Planting Rice*, 63, 99; Green, *Rise of the Trans-Atlantic Slave Trade*, 201.

sway over neighboring Biafada states, Sandoval pointed out that, at the head of the Gêba River, Biafadas lived not far from the "Emperor" known as Farincavo: the *farim,* or governor, of Kaabu.[27]

In addition to their connections to Kaabu, Biafada states traded heavily with Iberian merchants, and much of this commerce revolved around the transatlantic slave trade. "Biafada elites were notorious for selling captives into Atlantic slavery," and Portuguese and Luso-African traders in late-sixteenth-century Guinala could expect to purchase captives of diverse backgrounds, including "Biafada, Mandinka brought via Degola, Nalu, Bijago, and Papel." Although this commerce, combined with Biafadas' association with Kaabu, has been taken as evidence that the Biafada were aggressive slave raiders, the mechanisms Biafadas used to procure captives are less clear-cut. Biafadas held some political power over a few Brame communities, and both Biafadas and Brames likely raided each other for captives from time to time; however, at no point did relations between the two groups feature any type of long-term military conflict comparable to the hostilities between Cassangas and Bañuns during the sixteenth century.[28]

Instead, slave exports from Biafada territories might be characterized as one extension of a vast Biafada-"Zape" trade network in which Biafada merchants linked Mandinka trade routes to Nalu and "Zape" markets south of Biafada lands. Using "Zape" as a lingua franca, Biafadas headed south along the Atlantic coast in very large dugout canoes laden with iron, gold, and cotton, returning with kola, malaguetta peppers, and various other goods; the same vessels also brought back captives for reexport. Although Biafadas might have periodically raided Nalus for slaves, other sources indicate that Biafadas in Bissegue and Bolola acted as intermediaries for Iberians who desired to purchase Nalu captives, ivory, and mats but with whom the allegedly "wild" Nalu refused to trade. Sandoval described the Nalu as a "nation that is not interested in our commerce," noting that Iberian access to Nalu markets was restricted to trade conducted by the Nalu's immediate neighbors, "Biafaras Balolas."[29]

27. Hair, "Ethnolinguistic Continuity," *JAH,* VIII (1967), 252; Rodney, *History of the Upper Guinea Coast,* 26–30, 81, 232; Brooks, *Landlords and Strangers,* 84–86, 111, 265–267; Havik, *Silences and Soundbites,* 103–107; Sandoval, *Un tratado sobre la esclavitud,* transcription Vila Vilar, 63–64, 107–108, 138. "Farincavo" (that is, Farim Kaabu) is mistakenly transcribed by Vila Vilar as "Tarincavo." In addition to other Biafada groups, Sandoval mentions "Gulubalies," perhaps referring to a state known as "Gulubal" (Corubal). On "Carbali," see Brooks, *Landlords and Strangers,* 260.

28. Brooks, *Landlords and Strangers,* 86, 267, 271; Rodney, *History of the Upper Guinea Coast,* 104, 146; Hawthorne, *Planting Rice,* 104–107; Havik, *Silences and Soundbites,* 104–105, 109.

29. For discussion of the "Biafada-Sapi network," see Brooks, *Landlords and Strangers,* 80–87, 110–111, 251, 260–268, 276. On Biafada trade with Nalus, see Sandoval, *Un tratado sobre la esclavitud,*

As Table 1 indicates, Biafadas were also enslaved and exported to the Spanish Caribbean in relatively large numbers during the late sixteenth and early seventeenth centuries. Figuring most prominently among captives disembarked in the 1570s from the *San Pedro* and the *San Jorge,* Biafadas composed almost one-fifth of captives arriving on all five voyages combined. Peruvian notarial records confirm the importance of Biafadas among slave exports from Upper Guinea during this era, with Biafadas outnumbering all other Upper Guineans—and all other African forced migrants—in nearly every year sampled before 1595. The sale of Biafada captives in the port of Guinala suggests that judicial enslavement or conflict between Biafada groups might have been significant in producing enslaved Biafadas for transatlantic export. Contemporaneous Portuguese and Capeverdean accounts also refer to Biafadas enslaving other Biafadas through trickery and kidnapping. The early seventeenth century was an era of "Biafada social breakdown," wherein some Biafadas became bandits or "professional slave hunters" known as *gampisas,* raiding Biafada communities for captives to sell to Iberian merchants. In rare instances, contemporary Portuguese sources refer to Biafadas selling close kin or even selling themselves, ostensibly to exchange one ruler for another. However, the destabilization of Biafada society during the early 1600s might also be attributed to external factors, the most important being an unprecedented surge of slave raiding and violence launched from nearby islands by the Bijago.[30]

The Bijago (Bissago, Bidyogo) have long inhabited some twenty islands near the mouths of the Gêba and Grande Rivers; during the sixteenth and seventeenth centuries, Bijagos used their strategic geographical location to prey on regional maritime traffic and to launch raids on the nearby mainland, resulting in the enslavement and sale of Floups, Nalus, Brames, Balantas, and especially Biafadas. Sandoval described "Biojoes or Bijogoes" setting out in "canoes like those that navigate the Ma[g]dalena River, but so large that fifty blacks fit in each one." Sneaking ashore under cover of night, these heavily armed Bijago "pirates" and "corsairs" ambushed unsuspecting villages just before dawn. After seizing their victims, Bijago raiders would

---

transcription Vila Vilar, 64, 108. For description of the Nalu as "wild people" (*gente brava*), see Almada, *Tratado breve dos Rios de Guiné,* transcription Brásio, 111. See also Rodney, *History of the Upper Guinea Coast,* 105; Havik, *Silences and Soundbites,* 118–120; Edda L. Fields-Black, *Deep Roots: Rice Farmers in West Africa and the African Diaspora* (Bloomington, Ind., 2008), 33–34.

30. Bowser, *African Slave in Colonial Peru,* 40–41; Brooks, *Landlords and Strangers,* 268; Rodney, *History of the Upper Guinea Coast,* 106; Hawthorne, *Planting Rice,* 105–107; Bühnen, "Ethnic Origins," *Paideuma,* XXXIX (1993), 97, 100–101.

"tie them up and carry them back to their own lands," where captives would then be sold to waiting Portuguese ships. Iberian merchants thus acquired "innumerable blacks" in "the port of the Bijogoes." Those most affected by Bijago raids at the time Sandoval wrote (circa 1620) were "principally Biafaras, whose kingdoms they have destroyed."[31]

During the same period, Bijagos also appear as slaves in various Spanish American sources, commonly identified as "Bioho." In the 1570s, as Table 1 demonstrates, the *San Pedro,* departing from the Cape Verde Islands, and the *San Jorge,* departing from the Bañun port of Buguendo, each carried at least eleven enslaved "Bioho[s]" onboard, with male captives predominating. The presence of Bijagos in these slave ship rosters—coupled with evidence that Bijagos could also be purchased in the Biafada port of Guinala—points to Bijagos as victims as well as predators. Sandoval's observation that the Bijagos spoke "only two languages [that are] somewhat diverse" suggests that it might be inaccurate to portray them as a single "ethnic group." The Bijago were highly decentralized, and captives were sometimes produced by conflict between different Bijago groups. Echoing earlier Portuguese-language sources, Sandoval describes a ceremony conducted before Bijago slaving expeditions: after sacrificing wine and an animal to honor their ancestors, raiding party members were "obliged to fight, and capture whomever they might encounter," even should they happen upon "their relatives, their friends or acquaintances," or others "from the same islands." Despite this tradition of interisland conflict, presumably influenced by the steady Iberian demand for captives, Bijagos from different islands carried out coordinated attacks on the Upper Guinean mainland during the early seventeenth century, most notably capturing the Biafada ports of Biguba and Guinala in 1607 and 1609.[32]

The Upper Guinean ethnonym most frequently found in early colonial Spanish Caribbean sources is "Bran" (Brame); the term was used interchangeably with "Papel" and might have also included speakers of the Manjaku (Mandyak) and Mankañe (Mancanha) languages. Together, these closely related groups compose more than 12 percent of the population of

31. Rodney, *History of the Upper Guinea Coast,* 103–104; Brooks, *Landlords and Strangers,* 261–264, 272–273; Hawthorne, *Planting Rice,* 92, 101–104, 169–170; Havik, *Silences and Soundbites,* 114–118; Sandoval, *Un tratado sobre la esclavitud,* transcription Vila Vilar, 64, 108, 138, 146–147.

32. Sandoval, *Un tratado sobre la esclavitud,* transcription Vila Vilar, 138 ("some call themselves Biojoes, and others add [that they are] Biojoes Bizcainos"), 146–147; Rodney, *History of the Upper Guinea Coast,* 103–104; Brooks, *Landlords and Strangers,* 263, 272–273; Hawthorne, *Planting Rice,* 103; Hawthorne, *From Africa to Brazil,* 92–95. For the observation that Bijagos might have made up multiple ethnolinguistic groups, see, especially, Green, *Rise of the Trans-Atlantic Slave Trade,* 48.

present-day Guinea-Bissau. Directly facing the Atlantic Ocean and straddling the Mansoa River, Brame lands during the sixteenth and seventeenth centuries were bounded by the Cacheu River to the north and the Gêba River to the south. Encompassing only about four thousand square kilometers, the region was probably densely populated. Although Iberian sources for the era use "Bran" and "Papel" interchangeably (and historians of precolonial Africa have largely done the same, opting for one or the other), the term "Bran" is far more common in Spanish American records. The *San Jorge* slave roster is unusual in describing three captives disembarked in Española as "Papel," in addition to more than eighty listed as "Bran." Even so, one of the enslaved Papels was described as "a black woman of the Papel land, which is Bran" (*una negra de tierra papel que es bran*). Writing half a century later, Sandoval affirms that Iberians referred to Papels as "Bran," adding that the term encompassed several more specific identities; most referred to islands, regions, or towns within Brame territory. "When asked what caste they are," he states, "the Brans . . . answer with one or another of these names: Cacheo, Basserral, Bojola[,] Papel, Pessis"—elsewhere he also mentions "Bisaos"—"and it is the same as saying I am of the Bran caste." He goes on to explain that Brames spoke variations of the same language, all of which were mutually intelligible. According to Sandoval, Brames also commonly spoke many other languages, including those of the Bañun, Floup, Balanta, "Mandinga," and Biafada.[33]

The Brame played a pivotal role in regional and long-distance commerce on the Upper Guinea coast during the sixteenth and seventeenth centuries, linking Bañun commercial networks that spread north of the Cacheu River to Biafada trade networks that extended from the Gêba River southward. The hospitality of Brame communities toward Portuguese and Luso-African merchants amplified this role, particularly with regard to the transatlantic slave trade. The ruler of Bissau, a southern Brame state facing the Gêba River, was traditionally a strong ally of the Portuguese, and the

33. "Contratadores de Cabo Verde y Guinea con Cristóbal Cayado," 1582–1589, AGI-Esc 2A, pieza 2, fol. 494r; Sandoval, *Un tratado sobre la esclavitud,* transcription Vila Vilar, 64, 107, 136, 137 ("aunque estos diferencian algo en las lenguas . . . todos se catechizan con cualquiera dellas"); Brooks, *Landlords and Strangers,* 232–233; Bühnen, "Ethnic Origins," *Paideuma,* XXXIX (1993), 101, 104–105; Hair, "Ethnolinguistic Continuity," *JAH,* VIII (1967), 251; Havik, *Silences and Soundbites,* 107–114; O'Toole, "From the Rivers," *Social Text,* XXV, no. 3 (Fall 2007), 24–25; Green, *Rise of the Trans-Atlantic Slave Trade,* 48. Brames from Pecixe Island appear as "Busio" or "Buji" in "Juan Rodriguez de Mesa . . . con Diego de Morales Olivera," Sept. 6, 1632, AGN-FNE, Bolívar 3, hojas 639r–639v. For a late-sixteenth-century observation that Brames and Papels were the same ("Buramos, chamados por outro nome Papéis"), see Almada, *Tratado breve dos Rios de Guiné,* transcription Brásio, 74.

powerful king of Pecixe (Bussis) Island, at the mouth of the Mansoa River, traded extensively with Iberian and Capeverdean merchants. Cacheu, on the banks of the Cacheu River in the northern Brame state of Cacanda, became the major port linking Bañun and Biafada trade routes—facilitating Iberian access to both—during the early seventeenth century. Sailing south from Cacheu along a Biafada-"Zape" trade route, Capeverdean "kola fleets" carried cloth, gold, and other goods to Sierra Leone, returning laden with kola, ivory, mats, and captives. The 1616 itinerary of António Nunes da Costa, a Portuguese merchant based in Cacheu, provides a similar example of Iberian penetration of regional markets using Cacheu as a commercial hub. Traveling north and east up the Gambia River, roughly following trade routes associated with the Bañun-Bak network, he offered beads, European and Asian cloth, iron, wine, and kola to Upper Guinean communities in exchange for captives, beeswax, locally produced cloth, and provisions. As each of these examples suggests, captives were funneled toward Cacheu from multiple directions along with diverse regional commodities. By the early 1600s, the Brame port of Cacheu had become the first Portuguese outpost on the Upper Guinea coast to receive official recognition from Lisbon and the single most important slaving port in the Rivers of Guinea, with slave exports rivaling those of the Cape Verde Islands. This slave traffic based in Cacheu also relied on a localized trade in captives that supplemented regional commercial networks. As Iberians and Luso-Africans based in Cacheu tapped Bañun and Biafada trade routes, Brames acquired captives for reexport from their Floup and Balanta neighbors, who were less connected to Atlantic markets. Brames also generated captives through judicial enslavement and by means of occasional raids on nearby Biafadas, Nalus, and Balantas.[34]

Iberian slave ships carried Brames to the Americas in larger numbers than any other Upper Guinean group during the late sixteenth and early seventeenth centuries, but the principal factors driving this Brame diaspora remain unclear. The presence of Portuguese at Cacheu might have been responsible for a spike in Brame captives arriving in Peru between 1580

34. Sandoval, Un tratado sobre la esclavitud, transcription Vila Vilar, 107; Rodney, History of the Upper Guinea Coast, 8, 21, 30–32, 82, 85, 91–93, 104–105, 123–124, 129, 142, 150–158, 181, 206; Brooks, Landlords and Strangers, 23, 86–87, 91–93, 228–230, 237–244, 264, 271–272; Maria Manuel Ferraz Torrão, "Rotas comerciais, agentes económicos, meios de pagamento," in Maria Emília Madeira Santos, coord., História geral de Cabo Verde (Lisbon, 1995), II, 17–18; Hawthorne, Planting Rice, 43, 57, 63–66, 98–100, 107–109; Havik, Silences and Soundbites, 95–99, 108–110; Newson, "Africans and Luso-Africans," JAH, LIII (2012), 1–24.

and 1600; Sandoval relates that one slave trader he spoke with "was certain that there would not be half as many wars between the blacks, if they knew that the Spanish would not come to trade with them for blacks." On the other hand, if internal conflict and judicial enslavement were primary mechanisms of Brame slave production, then the availability of Brame captives could have drawn the Portuguese to settle at Cacheu in the first place. But Brames were also captured and sold by Bijagos, Biafadas, Bañuns, and Cassangas, and, as Table 1 reveals, Brames were already being exported in substantial numbers from the Cape Verde Islands and Buguendo—a Bañun port—in the early 1570s. Cacheu's rise to prominence during the early 1600s illustrates how Upper Guinean coastal peoples' ethnolinguistic diversity and political decentralization enabled Iberian and Luso-African slave merchants to respond to changing local conditions, shifting from one slave market to another along the Cacheu River, all the while maintaining access to long-distance regional networks. Iberian and Capeverdean traders' own participation in the Bañun-Bak and Biafada-"Zape" trade routes probably offset any temporary downturn in regional trade caused by moving an Atlantic slaving hub from one site to another.[35]

On the *San Pedro*, which sailed from the Cape Verde Islands, "Bran[s]" were the largest group represented, with fifty-one captives. Their ratio of exactly two men for every woman corresponds to sex ratios stipulated in Iberian slave trade legislation, perhaps attesting to the availability of enslaved Brames in the Cape Verde Islands in 1572. Arriving in Española from the Bañun port of Buguendo less than three years later, the *San Jorge* disembarked no less than eighty-one Brames, constituting more than 40 percent of all captives transported on this voyage. More than twenty captives arriving on the *San Jorge*—including ten described as "Bran" or "Papel"—carried visible wounds or scars, perhaps results of violence associated with their enslavement. One Brame boy had "two lance wounds, one above the belly and the other on his right side." A tall Brame man had been cut by a blade on his right shoulder; another Brame bore a knife wound *(cuchillada)* on his left cheek, and a man listed as Papel had been "cut across his belly lengthwise." Five other Brame men bore wounds on their arms, shoulders, stomach, abdomen, or temple, always on the right side of

35. Sandoval, *Un tratado sobre la esclavitud*, transcription Vila Vilar, 147 ("tenia por cierto no abria entre los negros la mitad de las guerras que avia, si supiesen no avian de ir los españoles a rescatarles negros"); Bühnen, "Ethnic Origins," *Paideuma*, XXXIX (1993), 97, 101, 103; Rodney, *History of the Upper Guinea Coast*, 104; Brooks, *Landlords and Strangers*, 261–263; Hawthorne, *Planting Rice*, 92, 94, 98.

their bodies—possibly indicating a defensive posture. Two Brame women bore injuries that suggest they might have been attempting to flee: one was wounded on the left side of her back, the other on her lower back. Some of these injuries could have been inflicted by crew members, while others that healed during the five-week journey would have gone unmentioned. But some of the wounds listed here were serious ones that likely reflected the violence some captives experienced during their initial enslavement. On this voyage, Brames, in particular, had probably been captured by their Bañun neighbors via raids or localized warfare; among eighty-one Brames, at least ten (12 percent) bore physical signs of violence. By comparison, the fifteen Bañuns who disembarked from the *San Jorge* were almost certainly enslaved as a form of judicial punishment or as the result of internal conflict among Bañuns. None were described as wounded.[36]

Although "Bran" was the most common ethnonym among forced migrants listed in Table 1, the number of captives described as "Zape" nearly equaled that of Brames disembarked from the *San Pedro* in 1572, if "Zape" subgroups are taken into account. Among the captives known to have arrived in Veracruz on the *San Josephe* in 1634, "Zapes" fully doubled the smaller number of Brames disembarked. During the sixteenth and seventeenth centuries, Iberians used the ethnonym "Zape" (or "Çape") as an umbrella term for diverse peoples inhabiting the Sierra Leone region, including the modern Sapi. Unlike "Mandinga," another ethnonym that functioned as a rubric encompassing multiple West African peoples, "Zape" was frequently accompanied in Spanish Caribbean sources with additional, secondary ethnonyms. According to Sandoval, "Zapes" comprised an "innumerable diversity of castes," though "all say that they are Zapes." He divided "Zapes" into four main subgroups, the first being "pure Zape," which might have referred to the modern Sapi, or perhaps the Temne. The other main subgroups were the Baga, the "Cocolí" (Kokoli) or "Landima" (Landuma), and the "Yalonga" (Yalunka) or "Zozo" (Susu). Though he deemed them less important, Sandoval also listed other "Zape" subgroups that can be matched with historical and present-day peoples in Sierra Leone, Guinea, and northern Liberia, including the "Boulone" (Bullom), Limba, "Logo" (Loko), and "Peli Coya" (Kpelle Kquoja). Additional "Zape" groups men-

36. "Contratadores de Cabo Verde y Guinea con Cristóbal Cayado," 1582–1589, AGI-Esc 2A, pieza 2, fols. 493v–498r. Others bearing injuries included seven men wounded on their chest, stomach, arms, or face (three Biafadas, two "Mandingas," one Nalu, one "Zape"); a Balanta woman "with the mark of a wound on her left cheek"; a "Bioho" girl wounded on her left shoulder; a "Bioho" man wounded on the nape of his neck; and an Arriata with a stab wound in his lower back.

tioned by Sandoval include the "Mane," "Boloncho," "Baca," "Lindagoza," and "Burga."[37]

Sandoval's observation that the "Zape" encompassed a "great diversity of languages and nations" and "do not always understand one another" contradicts well-known descriptions of the Upper Guinea coast written during the 1590s and 1620s. The Capeverdean authors André Alvares d'Almada and André Donelha each asserted that the various "Zape" groups "understand each another" (se entendem). Faced with divergent sources, historians disagree over the extent to which peoples known to early modern Iberians as "Zapes" spoke mutually intelligible languages, but most argue in favor of at least some broadly shared cultural traits. Although it remains unclear whether "Zape" migrants in the early Spanish Caribbean were able to communicate with one another in a shared language other than Spanish or Portuguese, the development of "Zape" confraternities in colonial Española, Mexico, and Peru suggests there must have been some initial basis for collective action and cohesion among the various peoples described as "Zape."[38]

37. Sandoval, Un tratado sobre la esclavitud, transcription Vila Vilar, 64–65, 108–109, 136–139, 600–601. For the suggestion that Sandoval's "pure Zape" were Temne, see Bühnen, "Ethnic Origins," Paideuma, XXXIX (1993), 80. See also Christopher Fyfe, A History of Sierra Leone (London, 1962), 1–7; Hair, "Ethnolinguistic Continuity," JAH, VIII (1967), 253–256; Hair, "An Ethnolinguistic Inventory of the Lower Guinea Coast before 1700: Part I," African Language Review, VII (1968), 47–73; Hair, "The History of the Baga in Early Written Sources," HA, XXIV (1997), 381–391; Rodney, History of the Upper Guinea Coast, 39–70; Adam Jones, "Who Were the Vai?" JAH, XXII (1981), 159–178; Jones, "The Kquoja Kingdom: A Forest State in Seventeenth Century West Africa," Paideuma, XXIX (1983), 23–43; Brooks, Landlords and Strangers, 274–319; Fields-Black, Deep Roots, 81.

38. Sandoval, Un tratado sobre la esclavitud, transcription Vila Vilar, 138, 600–601; compare with Almada, Tratado breve dos Rios de Guiné, transcription Brásio, 113, 116, 118 ("se entendem e se comunicam"), 125; André Donelha, Descrição da Serra Leoa e dos rios de Guiné do Cabo Verde (1625) / Description de la Serra Leoa et des Rios de Guiné du Cabo Verde (1625), eds. Avelino Teixeira da Mota and P. E. H. Hair, trans. Léon Bourdon (Lisbon, 1977), 98–99, 238n–241n. Extrapolating from Almada's account, Rodney characterizes peoples who "went under the generic name of 'Sape'" as "a virtually homogeneous society"; see Rodney, History of the Upper Guinea Coast, 32–33. At the other extreme, Hair rejects Capeverdean sources' claims that "all the Sape peoples 'understood each other'" and surmises that even Sandoval's mention of "Zapes Manes" was "surely an error," since "all other sources contrasted the Sapes and the Manes"; see, for example, Hair, "Ethnolinguistic Continuity," JAH, VIII (1967), 254n; Hair, "Sources on Early Sierra Leone," ARB, V, no. 2 (1975), 91. See also Bühnen, "Ethnic Origins," Paideuma, XXXIX (1993), 58n; Brooks, Landlords and Strangers, 66, 82; Green, Rise of the Trans-Atlantic Slave Trade, 235. On "Zape" confraternities in Spanish America, see Nicole von Germeten, Black Blood Brothers: Confraternities and Social Mobility for Afro-Mexicans (Gainesville, Fla., 2006); Karen B. Graubart, "'So color de una cofradía': Catholic Confraternities and the Development of Afro-Peruvian Ethnicities in Early Colonial Peru," SA, XXXIII (2012), 43–64. On the evolution of diasporic African identities in a late colonial Brazilian confraternity, see Soares, People of Faith, trans. Metz, 85–92.

If "Zape" cultural unity or diversity remains open to interpretation, even less is known of slave production in sixteenth-century Sierra Leone, with one exception. A Mande group known as the Mane (or Mani) migrated to Sierra Leone during the mid-sixteenth century, conquering or displacing "Zape" communities. At least one wave of Mane migrants incorporated local Upper Guinean allies known as the "Sumba" (rather than an ethnolinguistic designation, the term likely referred to Upper Guineans of various origins who joined the Mane, perhaps after having been defeated by them). By approximately 1560, the Mane and Sumba held control over "Zape" groups in much of Sierra Leone. Though Iberians helped some "Zape" refugees resettle in the Cape Verde Islands and Cacheu, they also evidently took advantage of the sudden availability of "Zape" captives. Iberian slave exports from Sierra Leone probably surged during the 1550s, 1560s, and 1570s, with Portuguese merchants competing with English, French, and Spanish slaving fleets during the 1560s.[39]

Another interpretation of the Mane invasions holds that they occurred in multiple stages over a longer period of time, taking the form of gradual colonization. This possibility would create room for large-scale, multigenerational interactions between the "Zape" and Mane migrants. Yet, even if the Mane invasion occurred within a relatively short period of time (circa 1545 to 1560), cross-cultural interaction along the same lines could have taken place during the following decades. Sandoval's allusions to "Zapes Manes" can be interpreted to mean that "by the 1620s the Manes had settled in relative peace and indeed adopted many Sape customs." Among the seventy captives arriving in Veracruz on the *San Josephe* in 1634 (Table 1), nine were identified as "Zape," ranging in age from an eight-year-old muleca to a forty-year-old man. Although other captives were listed as Baga, "Linba" (Limba), "Soso" (Susu), and "Cocolí" (Kokoli), none were identified as "Mane" (or "Sumba"). Perhaps, nearly a century after the Mane invasion, Manes had blended with "Zapes" to the point that Iberians ceased to dis-

39. P. E. H. Hair, "Sources on Early Sierra Leone: (15) Marmol 1573," *ARB*, IX, no. 3 (1979), 77–78; Brooks, *Landlords and Strangers*, 293–294; Bühnen, "Ethnic Origins," *Paideuma*, XXXIX (1993), 98; Green, *Rise of the Trans-Atlantic Slave Trade*, 23–25, 236–239, 253. Historical interpretations of the Mane invasion(s) vary considerably. Walter Rodney argues that a single Mane invasion from the south took place between roughly 1545 and 1560; see Rodney, *History of the Upper Guinea Coast*, 39–70. For the suggestion that this invasion was preceded by an earlier one approximately a century earlier, see Yves Person, "Ethnic Movements and Acculturation in Upper Guinea Since the Fifteenth Century," *African Historical Studies*, IV, (1971), 675–686. Adam Jones posits that a gradual increase in Mane trade, intermarriage, and settlement among coastal peoples might have been exaggerated in European accounts as an invasion; see Jones, "Who Were the Vai?" *JAH*, XXII (1981), 175.

tinguish between them. Or perhaps Mane elites and their descendants were simply less likely to be enslaved.[40]

The historiography of Sierra Leone emphasizes the Mane invasion(s) of "Zape" lands as a primary engine of slave production during the sixteenth century, but there are several other ways "Zape" captives might have been generated for sale to Iberian markets. First, Mane migration resulted in the establishment of at least four Mane states in the region, with each ruled by a farim; an early-seventeenth-century Portuguese missionary report mentions wars within and between these states, as well as judicial enslavement, each resulting in the sale of captives to Portuguese buyers. Secondly, some unconquered "Zape" groups such as the Limba continued to resist the Mane and their allies long after the era of the Mane invasions. Sandoval wrote in the 1620s that the Limba were "continually at war" with the "Logos" (Loko), one of several groups conquered by the Mane. If captives were taken and sold to merchants based in the Cape Verde Islands, then Limba-Loko military conflict could plausibly explain the presence of ten enslaved "Linba" among those disembarked from the *San Pedro* in Havana in 1572 (Table 1). The Susu and Yalunka—two Mande peoples originating in Upper Guinea's Futa Jalon highlands, so closely related that they are often treated by scholars as a single group before the modern era—were not conquered by the Mane either and might have even enslaved and exported the Mane or their subjects. Before the arrival of the Mane, Susu/Yalunka caravans had long provided Fula (Fulani, Peul, Fulbe) pastoralists in the Upper Guinean interior with salt produced by Bagas along the mouth of the Nunez River; the Baga, in return, obtained Fula cloth, cattle, gold, and iron from the Susu/Yalunka. With the arrival of the Mane, the Susu/Yalunka were forced to divert their traditional caravan routes, but they were not conquered. Rather, they roundly defeated the Mane with the aid of Fula cavalry, taking many prisoners who might have been sold to Iberian merchants. Although some hostility toward the Mane remained, by the early 1600s the Susu/Yalunka had reopened their trade routes. Given their position as intermediaries linking coastal peoples to others in the highlands farther inland, in diasporic contexts the Susu/Yalunka might have been just as likely to associate with fellow Mande peoples (including non-"Zapes") as with "Zape" groups such as the Baga who were not of Mande origin.[41]

40. Andreas W. Massing, "The Mane, the Decline of Mali, and Mandinka Expansion towards the South Windward Coast," *CEA*, XXV (1985), 21–55; Green, *Rise of the Trans-Atlantic Slave Trade*, 236; Sandoval, *Un tratado sobre la esclavitud*, transcription Vila Vilar, 65, 109.

41. P. E. H. Hair, "Sources on Early Sierra Leone: (6) Barreira on Just Enslavement, 1606," *ARB*,

Long-distance commercial routes associated with the Nunez River area represent a third way Iberians might have obtained "Zape" captives for overseas export. At the same time that it fueled Susu / Yalunka trade with the interior, the Nunez River area played an important role in the Biafada-"Zape" trade network discussed above. The "Cocolí" resided south of Biafada lands and inland behind the Nalu. Twenty leagues up the Nunez, at the Kokoli port of Kagandy (Kakundy), Iberians traded for indigo dye, ivory, gold, wax, and presumably kola, in addition to captives. Thus far, very little is known of Iberian slave trafficking in Sierra Leone before the late eighteenth century, but, according to Sandoval, Kagandy was "the main port of the Spanish" and a slave trading hub frequented by Portuguese merchants who acquired captives from the Kokoli and indigo dye from the Susu / Yalunka.[42]

Although the source and identity of captives produced by the Kokolis remain unclear, the Kokoli appear to have been major slave producers alongside other Mande or Mande-influenced groups. Both the Kokoli and Susu / Yalunka were of Mande origin, and both maintained Mande-style political hierarchies like those of the Cassanga (and to some extent the Biafada) in relation to Kaabu. For example, a Portuguese account written in 1606 mentions that Massacanda, ruler of seven kingdoms within the Susu / Yalunka state of Bena, was in turn subject to a more powerful ruler named Farim Concho; Sandoval likewise describes the "Zozo" as a "corrupted caste of the Mandinga," governed by an "Emperor named Concho." Sandoval and other sources also refer to a "Farinlandama" or "Farim Cocali." The terms "Cocolí," "Landima," "Soso," and "Yalonga" can thus be used to infer some diasporic Africans' positions in relation to centralized Mande states. However, the appearance of these ethnonyms in Iberian

VI (1975), 65–66; Sandoval, *Un tratado sobre la esclavitud,* transcription Vila Vilar, 109. See also Fyfe, *History of Sierra Leone,* 1; Rodney, *History of the Upper Guinea Coast,* 10–11, 20, 46, 62, 111–112, 226; Hair, "Ethnolinguistic Continuity," *JAH,* VIII (1967), 255; Brooks, *Landlords and Strangers,* 113–114, 276–280, 292, 299, 303–304; Bühnen, "Ethnic Origins," *Paideuma,* XXXIX (1993), 78–79; Fields-Black, *Deep Roots,* 148.

42. Sandoval, *Un tratado sobre la esclavitud,* transcription Vila Vilar, 108; Rodney, *History of the Upper Guinea Coast,* 6, 33, 111–113, 154; Hair, "Ethnolinguistic Continuity," *JAH,* VIII (1967), 253; Brooks, *Landlords and Strangers,* 80, 82, 111, 260, 275–276; Bühnen, "Ethnic Origins," *Paideuma,* XXXIX (1993), 79–80. Kokoli and Landuma are generally viewed as interchangeable names for the same people. Note, however, that three captives disembarked from the *San Josephe* in 1634 are listed as "Cocolí," while two other forced migrants arriving on the same voyage are described as "Landima" (Table 1). The earliest Iberian voyage currently listed as having embarked captives in Sierra Leone took place in 1767; see *Voyages,* accessed May 25, 2015, http://slavevoyages.org/tast/database/search.faces?yearFrom =1514&yearTo=1866&mjbyptimp=60200&natinimp=3.6.

slave ship rosters confirms that slave exports from Upper Guinea were not merely the result of powerful Mande states preying on decentralized coastal peoples.[43]

The Upper Guinean ethnic markers documented in Iberian slave ship rosters are fragmentary reflections of a complex world defined not only by Mande expansion at coastal peoples' expense but also by specific conflicts and political alliances, by trade routes linking coastal communities to one another and to the interior, and by varying levels of engagement with the Iberian Atlantic world. Spanish Caribbean sources' frequent reference to nations and lands that directly corresponded to specific peoples and places in Upper Guinea echoes an earlier history of cross-cultural exchange that included but was not limited to slave trafficking. Iberians' knowledge of diverse Upper Guinean peoples was transferred to the Spanish Caribbean, where Iberian colonists would continue to interact with and recognize Upper Guinean migrants as individuals based on their distinct ethnolinguistic origins.

Upper Guinean Maroons, Miners, and Royal Slaves

As the preceding discussion of Upper Guinean ethnonyms attests, depictions of sub-Saharan Africans in early Spanish Caribbean source materials are consistently at odds with their portrayals in an African diaspora historiography that focuses on racialized societies dominated by slave-based plantation and mining economies. These models tend to place African motives, experiences, and systems of meaning in fundamental opposition to those of Iberians. However, the entrenched colonial structures of eighteenth-century Brazil, or the European colonialist impulses of the nineteenth century—or, for that matter, twentieth-century race relations—cannot be retrofitted onto the Spanish Caribbean hundreds of years earlier. To assume that diasporic Africans possessed fluid, malleable identities that changed over time requires a similar understanding that Iberian attitudes and the

---

43. Rodney, *History of the Upper Guinea Coast,* 26, 81, 111–113; Sandoval, *Un tratado sobre la esclavitud,* transcription Vila Vilar, 108, 138; Brooks, *Landlords and Strangers,* 111, 309–312. Although Rodney's overarching vision of coastal Upper Guinean peoples surrounded by powerful Mande groups and their client states remains influential, Hawthorne has shown that decentralized coastal groups also adapted to slave trafficking rather than merely becoming the victims of Mande raiders and European slavers; see Hawthorne, *Planting Rice.* For discussion of cultural diffusion that accompanied the spread of Mande power beginning in the 1300s, see Green, *Rise of the Trans-Atlantic Slave Trade,* 46–62, 231–234.

colonial systems they devised also adjusted with evolving circumstances, altered geographical locations, and shifting social contexts.[44]

For Iberians in Africa and residents of the early Spanish Caribbean, the distinctions between Upper Guinean peoples were legible and significant. Excepting the umbrella terms "Mandinga" and "Zape," which appear to have functioned as general designations encompassing various peoples from regions less familiar to Iberians—and which later might have taken on new meanings in diasporic settings as composite ethnonyms—most of the Upper Guinean nations reproduced in early Spanish Caribbean sources reflect eth-nolinguistic and geographical origins with considerable accuracy. Sando-val's writings and scattered slave ship rosters indicate that Upper Guineans were commonly given the opportunity to identify themselves. However, by the late 1500s, after more than a century of sustained Iberian presence in Upper Guinea and the Cape Verde Islands, Upper Guineans arriving in the Spanish Caribbean might not even have needed to do so, since some Iberians and Luso-Africans would have recognized where they were from. Certainly, the ethnonyms commonly used in the Spanish Caribbean might have selectively compressed Upper Guinean identities, prioritizing ethno-linguistic affiliations rather than other aspects such as lineage or relations to kin. Yet, even so, Upper Guineans knew how to portray themselves in terms that Iberians recognized. Spanish Caribbean settlements inherited a mutual understanding that was the fruit of earlier cross-cultural exchanges in Upper Guinea and the Cape Verde Islands. Iberians' and Upper Guin-eans' prior experiences of one another made it possible to create and sustain Spanish colonial settlements peopled by Iberians and Africans on a larger scale in the Caribbean.[45]

Extant documents recounting the breakup of Bayano (or Ballano), a ma-roon federation in sixteenth-century Panama, confirm that ethnolinguistic identities played important social functions for diasporic Upper Guineans. Following diplomatic overtures initiated by maroon leaders, and fearing

44. For analysis of African ethnonyms in eighteenth-century Brazil as group identities creatively transformed in response to alienation, colonial oppression, and varying social conditions, see, for example, Soares, *People of Faith,* trans. Metz, 88; James H. Sweet, "Mistaken Identities? Olaudah Equiano, Domingos Álvares, and the Methodological Challenges of Studying the African Diaspora," *AHR,* CXIV (2009), 283. On the probable importance of lineage and kinship as opposed to "proto-ethnic" identities on the Upper Guinea coast during the fourteenth and fifteenth centuries, see Green, *Rise of the Trans-Atlantic Slave Trade,* 62–68.

45. On the authenticity of Upper Guinean ethnonyms recorded in colonial Latin American sources, see also Bühnen, "Ethnic Origins," *Paideuma,* XXXIX (1993), 60; Hawthorne, *From Africa to Brazil,* 8–9, 11–12, 178. For discussion of Iberians who possessed extensive experience living and working in western Africa before moving to the Spanish Caribbean, see Chapter 3, below.

that maroons might again ally with Sir Francis Drake or some other European enemy, in the early 1580s Spanish authorities in Panama gladly made peace. The former maroons agreed to "reduce themselves" *(reducirse)* and relocate to two towns newly established for this purpose (Santa Cruz la Real and Santiago del Príncipe), pledging their allegiance to the Spanish crown in exchange for formal acknowledgement of their freedom. Spanish magistrates attempted to account for every former resident of Bayano, even interviewing ex-maroon leaders in hopes of learning about the small splinter groups that remained at large. The officials also drew up a series of rosters naming every individual transported from Bayano to one of the new settlements. Within these rosters, sub-Saharan Africans were almost invariably listed by name and ethnonym; others were ascribed racial designations such as *criollos del monte* (Afrocreoles born free in Bayano), *yndios* (Amerindians), and *zambaigos* (people of mixed African and Amerindian ancestry).[46]

Though most of these rosters simply enumerate the ex-maroons as they arrived from Bayano, grouped by the Spanish general or officer who escorted them, a subset of lists sheds light on Bayano's internal organization along ethnolinguistic lines. In early April 1582, Spanish officials and ex-maroons enacted a ceremony in the plaza of Santa Cruz la Real in which the latter laid down their arms, prostrating themselves before the high-ranking magistrate Doctor Alonso Criado de Castilla. Simultaneously creating a census of the new town and a list of ex-maroons whose former owners would no longer have any claim over them, Criado then recorded the names of each of Santa Cruz la Real's new residents—nearly 250 men, women, and children—divided into six groups according to the leaders they had followed in Bayano. Thus, for example, Spanish officials observed that "these people are of the company of captain Juan Jolofo whom he brought under his charge[,] and with him they reduced themselves" (that is, swore fealty

---

46. "Reduçion y poblaçion de los negros de Ballano," Panamá, 1580–1582, AGI-Patronato 234, r.6, bloque 1, fols. 207r–526v, bloque 2, fols. 527r–667v. Testimonies provided by ex-maroon leaders appear in bloque 2, fols. 570r–580v. The best discussion of this source and the context in which it was generated is Jean-Pierre Tardieu, *Cimarrones de Panamá: La forja de una identidad afroamericana en el siglo XVI* (Madrid, 2009), esp. 204–221. Tardieu acknowledges a strong tendency toward ethnic cohesion within Bayano (212–213) but places greater emphasis on factors that might have contributed to the early formation of pan-ethnic racial identities, including Bayano's political centralization, cross-cultural sexual unions, and Afrocreole children born free to maroon parents (20, 50, 94, 212–214, 234–235). Note that the figures in Tardieu's chart (215–216) are slightly larger than those given here in Table 2; Tardieu includes analysis of general rosters that listed ex-maroons and their Amerindian captives or allies as they arrived from Bayano (bloque 1, fols. 416v–420r, 425r–426v, 431v–434r, 550v–554r, 558v–561v, 566r–569r), in addition to the rosters that associated them with specific Bayano leaders.

to Spanish authorities). Likewise, they noted, "now entering [the plaza] are the people under the charge of Antón Mandinga who came to reduce themselves with him." Beginning with their leaders, the names and ethnonyms ascribed to members of each group indicate that these associations coalesced largely on the basis of common ethnolinguistic backgrounds, with Upper Guineans predominating in four of the six groups. The groups appear to have been organized by their male members' African origins in particular (the more diverse origins ascribed to women and children within each group rules out the possibility that Iberian officials had organized the ex-maroons based on perceived ethnolinguistic identities). Although these communities were formed beyond the reach of Spanish Caribbean authorities, the groups that consisted primarily of Upper Guineans expressed their ethnic compositions in terms of the same lands and nations commonly ascribed to Upper Guineans within Spanish Caribbean society (Table 2).[47]

In the smallest Upper Guinean group, led by Juan Jolofo, "leader of all the blacks" (cabeza e mayoral de todos los negros), all eight African men were described as either "Jolofo" or "Berbesí." That these forced migrants chose to associate with one another when given the opportunity echoed the social and geographical proximity of their Senegambian homelands. As noted above, the Serer states of Siin and Saloum had both previously formed part of the Jolof empire. If by the late sixteenth century Siin was "relatively small and homogeneously Sereer," neighboring Saloum was ethnically diverse, inhabited by Serers, Wolofs, Mandinkas, and others. Such Senegambian precedents facilitated interaction between the Wolof and Serer who formed the backbone of this group. In fact, no man in any other group was identified as "Jolofo" or "Berbesí," and, among all the Bayano maroons listed in this source, only two women in Juan Jolofo's group were described as "Jalofa." "Berbesí" women are somewhat more evenly distributed, with one in each of three Upper Guinean groups. If the slave trade from the

47. "Lista de la gente reduzida," Apr. 4, 1582, AGI-Patronato 234, r.6, bloque 1, fols. 447v–456v (repeated in bloque 2, fols. 585r–592r). Bayano leaders Antón Mandinga, Pedro Ubala, Antón Tigre, Juan Angola, and Pedro Çape are listed in Juan Jalofo's group, in addition to their own groups, presumably indicating his authority over the other captains. To avoid repetition, Table 2 does not list these leaders in Juan Jalofo's group (Group I). Though no lists of Juan Caçanga's or Juan Nalu's followers appear in this source, both men are also excluded from Juan Jalofo's group in Table 2 since they, too, are described as captains. For the ex-maroons' ceremonial laying down of arms, see bloque 2, fol. 549r. For similar evidence of maroons pledging loyalty to the Spanish crown—while remaining under the immediate supervision of their own leaders—see Jane G. Landers, "Cimarrón and Citizen: African Ethnicity, Corporate Identity, and the Evolution of Free Black Towns in the Spanish Circum-Caribbean," in Landers and Barry M. Robinson, eds., Slaves, Subjects, and Subversives: Blacks in Colonial Latin America (Albuquerque, N.Mex., 2006), 127, 134.

Rivers of Guinea brought captives of diverse origins together in ports such as Santiago de Cabo Verde and Cartagena, the Wolofs and Serers who found themselves in Bayano managed to undo this process, associating with other migrants of similar or familiar backgrounds. Although Juan Jolofo is often described as the leader of all the Bayano maroons who agreed to treat with the Spanish, he was also the leader of a smaller number of men and women whose ethnolinguistic and geographical origins most closely corresponded to his own.[48]

Numbering thirty-five men, twenty women, and eleven children, the largest Upper Guinean maroon group led by Pedro Ubala follows the same pattern. At least twenty-two Biafada men composed an ethnolinguistic nucleus (Pedro Ubala was likely Biafada as well). This male core was supported by smaller numbers of men from societies well known to the Biafada, in this case four Nalus and one "Bioho." Strikingly, Pedro Ubala's group appears to have incorporated virtually all of the Biafada, Nalu, and Bijago men known to have resided in Bayano. This pattern of heavy ethnic concentration is typical for the African men in each of the four groups controlled by Upper Guineans. Women under Pedro Ubala's leadership were somewhat more diverse; in addition to eight "Biafaras" and five women listed by other Upper Guinean ethnonyms, there were also three *"Indias* married to blacks" and three women of African-Amerindian descent *(zambaigas)*. Analyzed in terms of ethnic composition, the Bayano rosters reveal a pattern of maroon community formation in which enslaved men escaped, congregating with other men—and when possible, women—of similar background. Some likely planned and carried out their initial escape together. Over time, each group would incorporate additional members drawn from diverse backgrounds, most noticeably in the case of women, which is not surprising given the likelihood that each group initially faced severely imbalanced sex ratios. This dynamic explains the presence of seven Amerindian women, twelve adults and several children identified as zambaigos, and the complete absence of Amerindian men.[49]

48. See Curtin, *Economic Change,* 12. Sandoval expressed admiration for Serer horsemanship and Wolof and Serer women's manner of dress; he also commented that their languages differed little from one another—he refers to the Serer as "Iolofos Berbefies"—and notes that Wolofs, Serers, Fulas, and "Mandingas" could generally understand one another; see Sandoval, *Un tratado sobre la esclavitud,* transcription Vila Vilar, 63, 105–106, 111–113, 118, 136. Among the African interpreters who aided Sandoval's colleague Pedro Claver, one man named Francisco Yolofo spoke not only "the Yolofa language" and Portuguese but also "the Mandinga and Verdesí [Berbesí]" languages; see Splendiani and Aristizábal, eds. and trans., *Proceso de beatificación,* 310–311.

49. Additional Nalu, Biafada, and Bijago men might have been concentrated in the group led by captain Juan Nalu. Though he is named as captain in Juan Jolofo's group and provides testimony

Table 2 Six Bayano Maroon Groups by Leader, Ethnonym, and Sex, Panama, 1582

Ethnonym	I. Juan Jolofo		II. Pedro Ubala		III. Anton Mandinga		IV. Pedro Zape		V. Juan Angola		VI. Anton Tigre		Total (M/F)		Total (M + F)
	M	F	M	F	M	F	M	F	M	F	M	F	M	F	
UPPER GUINEA															
"Bañon" (Bañun)	0	0	0	2	0	0	0	0	0	0	0	0	0	2	2
"Berbesi" (Serer)	4	1	0	1	0	1	0	0	0	0	0	0	4	3	7
"Biafara" (Biafada)	0	0	22	8	0	2	0	1	0	0	0	0	22	11	33
"Bioho" (Bijago)	0	1	1	0	0	0	0	0	0	0	0	0	1	1	2
"Bran" (Brame)	0	0	0	0	8	4	0	0	0	0	0	1	8	5	13
"Casanga" (Cassanga)	0	0	0	0	5	2	0	0	0	0	0	0	5	2	7
"Jolofo" (Wolof)	4	2	0	0	0	0	0	0	0	0	0	0	4	2	6
"Mandinga"	0	0	0	1	8	4	0	0	0	0	0	0	8	5	13
Nalu	0	0	4	0	0	1	0	0	0	0	0	0	4	1	5
"Zape"	0	1	0	1	0	2	19	7	0	2	0	0	19	13	32
"Yalonga"[a] (Yalunka)	0	0	0	0	3	0	0	0	0	1	0	0	3	1	4
OTHER AFRICA															
"Terranoba"	0	0	0	0	0	0	1	1	0	0	0	0	1	1	2
"Congo"	0	1	0	0	0	1	0	0	3	2	2	2	5	6	11
"Angola"	0	0	0	0	0	0	0	0	5	2	0	0	5	2	7
"Enchico" (Ansiku)	0	0	0	0	0	0	0	0	1	0	0	0	1	0	1
"Moçanga"	0	0	0	0	0	0	0	0	1	0	1	1	2	1	3
"Maçanbique"	0	0	0	0	0	0	0	0	2	0	2	0	4	0	4

OTHER

OTHER														
Criollo	2	4	4	0	0	7	1	2	0	4	0	0	7	17	24
Havana	1	0	0	0	0	0	0	0	0	0	0	0	1	0	1
Campeche	0	0	2	0	0	0	0	0	0	0	0	0	2	0	2
Zambaigo	0	0	0	3	1	1	0	0	4	2	1	0	6	6	12
India	0	0	0	3	0	1	0	0	0	2	0	1	0	7	7
Portuguesa	0	0	0	0	0	0	0	0	0	1	0	0	0	1	1
Unspecified	1	0	2	1	0	0	0	0	6	0	1	0	10	1	11
TOTAL	12	10	35	20	24	26	22	11	22	14	7	7	122	88	210

Source: "Reduçion y Poblaçion de los negros de Ballano," 1580–1582, AGI-Patronato 234, r.6, bloque 1, fols. 450r–455v.

Note: In Group VI, a woman named "María Moçanga" is also identified as "María Conga." One "Angola" in Group V is described as a *muchacho* (boy). Thirty-seven additional children (not listed above) were also spread among these groups. Children in Group I included two boys, named Perico de Ortega and Alo[n]sillo, and Catalina Bioho's nursing infant, Anica. Children in Group II included two boys, named Andresico, and others, named Manuel, Juanico Zanbahigo, Antonico Criollo, Juan Galan, Françisquillo Criollo, and Pedro criollo as well as Inesica, Mariquita, and Juanico, nursing infants born to Catalina Biafara, Bitoria Biafara, and Ana Bañol, respectively. The children listed in Group III were María Bran's son Francisco, María Biafara's daughter Isabelica, Bitoria Cazanga's daughter Felipa, Catalina Criolla's daughter Justa, Isabel Criolla's children Diego and Inesica, Elena Criolla's daughter Mariquita, Juana Mandinga's son Françisquito, and her nursing infant Sebastián as well as other children named Hernandico, Mariquita, and Juanica. Group IV included Catalina Çape's daughter Mariquita and Leonor Çape's daughter Antonica. The children who appear in Group V were four boys, named Diego Canpillo, Francisco, Dominguillo, and Cristóbal; Isabel Angola's daughters Juanica and Madalena; and Gerónima Criolla's son Martinico. Additional members of Group VI were Isabel Bran's daughter Elvira and Francisca Zanbahiga's daughter Mariquita.

A third group under Antón Mandinga featured a male core divided among "Mandinga," "Bran," "Casanga," and "Yalonga." Like the contingents led by captains Juan Jolofo and Pedro Ubala, this group was defined by its ethnic composition. Rather than being scattered throughout Bayano, all the "Mandinga," Brame, Cassanga, and Yalunka men listed in Table 2 were gathered in this single group, constituting its entire adult male membership. Although adult female members included ten non-Upper Guineans (mostly Afrocreoles), roughly two-thirds were Upper Guineans bearing seven different ethnonyms. Yet, some ethnolinguistic concentration is noticeable among women, too; this group included four of the five Brame women listed in this source, four of five "Mandinga" women, and both Cassanga women. Compared with the other Upper Guinean maroon groups, Antón Mandinga's followers included a wider mix of Upper Guinean nations. Social conditions surely influenced the formation of this relatively multiethnic group, but social, cultural, and political relationships forged in Upper Guinea, rather than in Panama, appear to have been of primary importance. Although Upper Guineans shared basic cultural affinities, the limited data for these six Bayano maroon groups indicates that, among diasporic Upper Guineans, some interethnic alliances were quicker to form than others. The main ethnic components of Antón Mandinga's group—twelve "Mandinga," seven Cassanga, and three Yalunka—were all either Mande or Mande-influenced. Only the notable presence of twelve Brames disrupts what appears to be an otherwise straightforward example of Mande solidarity. According to Sandoval, Brames commonly spoke Mandinka, among other languages, which might help explain their presence. Alternately, if ethnic origins corresponded to social hierarchies within the group, Brames might have initially held subservient status.[50]

The remaining Upper Guinean group, captained by Pedro Zape, appears to have been more recently established; it was heavily male and almost entirely composed of "Zapes." The only other sub-Saharan Africans in the group were one Biafada woman and a man and woman each described as

---

regarding the number and whereabouts of Bayano maroons who had not yet laid down their arms, Juan Nalu's followers are not listed as a discrete group in the "Lista de gente reduzida" composed in Santa Cruz la Real in early April 1582. For Juan Nalu's testimony, see "Reduçion y poblaçion de los negros de Ballano," 1580–1582, AGI-Patronato 234, r.6, bloque 2, fols. 578r–578v; Tardieu, *Cimarrones de Panamá*, 211.

50. For analysis of widely shared religious, culinary, and parenting traditions that might have served as the basis for a "common Guinean identity" in slave trade bulking centers, on slave ships, and on plantations in eighteenth-century Maranhão, see Hawthorne, *From Africa to Brazil*, 108–109, 133, 178, 183, 209–212.

"Terranoba" (that is, Lucumí). The twenty-six "Zape" led by Pedro Zape might have considered themselves Sapi, Baga, Kokoli, Limba, or any of the various peoples that Iberians viewed as subcategories of this umbrella term. The formation of a group consisting almost exclusively of "Zapes" obviously suggests some degree of regional identity or ethnolinguistic commonality. Although three "Yalonga" men were listed in Antón Mandinga's group, no Susu / Yalunka were mentioned among Pedro Zape's followers despite their being one of four main castes among the "Zape." These sixteenth-century Yalunka men were an example of diasporic Africans who had the option of choosing from among multiple identities (Yalunka, Mande, "Zape"); for them, such group relationships might have been fluid and subject to change depending on their immediate circumstances. Yet, regardless of whether the Yalunka joined maroon groups that were primarily Mande or primarily "Zape," either choice likely was grounded in prior political developments and social, economic, and cultural exchange in precolonial Upper Guinea and Sierra Leone.[51]

Although the precise circumstances in which each maroon group was formed remain unknown, the 1582 Bayano roster clearly depicts diasporic Upper Guineans gravitating toward others of similar ethnolinguistic background or relying on alliances previously established in Upper Guinea. One implication of this pattern of organization was probably the continued use of Upper Guinean languages within each group. Fascinatingly, the Bayano roster lists several maroons by names that would have been meaningful primarily for people familiar with specific Upper Guinean languages or regions. As previously noted, the largest Bayano maroon group was led by a man identified as captain "Pedro Ubala." Although the name resembles Ubalá, a town in the Colombian Andes that might have derived its name from Amerindian traditions, it seems most likely that "Ubala" in this case was a term of Upper Guinean origin that would be known to the Biafada men and women who constituted the nucleus of this group. The name of another maroon provides a more concrete example of Biafada vocabulary employed in sixteenth-century Panama. Though he does not appear in any of the groups discussed above, former maroon Antón Canpisa was one of the porters accompanying a Spanish mission to find the last remain-

51. Captain Pedro Zape could be the same person described fourteen years later as Don Pedro Zape, "maestre de campo de los soldados" (field marshal) in Santiago del Príncipe, the other town settled by ex-Bayano maroons. See "Pedro Yalonga esclavo sobre q se le de livertad por lo q ha servido," May 24–June 12, 1596, AGI-Panamá 44, n.56 (2), fols. 7v–8v.

ing Bayano maroons and to persuade them to join the others. *Canpisa*—or gampisa—was a Biafada term for bandit or slave trafficker. As an ex-maroon himself, Antón Canpisa could have acquired his surname in Panama after helping recruit involuntary members for a maroon group like the one led by Pedro Ubala; alternately, if he had previously worked as a slave catcher in the Spanish Caribbean, other Upper Guineans might have ascribed him this nickname. However, it is also entirely possible that Antón Canpisa had once been a member of a renegade group that kidnapped and sold other Biafadas in Upper Guinea, before being enslaved and sold to Iberians himself. If so, his continued identification in the Spanish Caribbean as Antón Canpisa (rather than Antón Biafada) might be viewed as an extension of the "Biafada social breakdown" occurring in precolonial Upper Guinea.[52]

A final Bayano maroon group, which Antón Canpisa's party eventually located, apparently resembled other Upper Guinean groups listed in Table 2. By the time they entered Panama City in September 1582, known members included Cassanga, Bañun, and "Zape" men, a "Zape" woman, and two Afrocreole *(criolla)* women. The group's leader was Alonzo Cazanga, also known as "Maçatamba" (alternately spelled Mazatamba or Masatamba). The history of late-sixteenth-century Upper Guinea provides context to his name. With his ostensible ethnolinguistic origins as Alonzo "Cazanga" (Cassanga), the name "Maçatamba" would immediately resonate with forced migrants from the Mandinka-ruled former Bañun state of Casa, or from neighboring areas. Continually at war with the Bañun, Casa was at the height of its power during the 1570s; during this decade, the Cassanga burned the Bañun port of Buguendo, drawing Iberian Atlantic trade toward Sarar, a Cassanga port near their capital. These military successes were achieved under the rule of Masatamba, the same "King of Cazamanza" who was widely feared for enslaving and exporting his own subjects. That maroon leader Alonzo Cazanga took the name "Masatamba" in late-sixteenth-century Panama is no accident; he was a direct contemporary of the Casa ruler Masatamba in Upper Guinea and might have had firsthand experience of the Casa mansa's power over the lives of his subjects. In Panama, Alonzo Cazanga enhanced his own stature among Upper Guineans (and probably

---

52. "Lista de la gente reduzida," Mar. 29, 1582, AGI-Patronato 234, r.6, bloque 1, fol. 448v. Sandoval refers to the Biafada state of Bissegue as "Ubissegue" in Sandoval, *Un tratado sobre la esclavitud,* transcription Vila Vilar, 138. On "u-" as a singular class prefix in modern Biafada, see W. A. A. Wilson, "An Outline Description of Biafada," *Journal of West African Languages,* XXIII, no. 2 (1993), 63. For relevant vocabulary, see Havik, *Silences and Soundbites,* 103–105.

some Iberians) by appropriating a name that in the Rivers of Guinea connoted supreme authority backed by military force.[53]

Upper Guinean maroons in Panama drew distinctions among themselves in ways that closely correspond to ethnonyms ascribed to them in slave ship rosters; the same nations or lands—occasionally accompanied by more specific terms—also regularly appear in more common colonial-era documents such as slave sales. Ethnonyms and toponyms recorded in a list of nearly fifty enslaved men and women purchased in 1570 in Mariquita, in the New Kingdom of Granada, provide an exceptionally revealing example of this type of source. Ostensibly to be employed mining for gold, all but two bear Upper Guinean ethnonyms that are virtually identical to those discussed above. Fifteen "Zape" and fifteen "Biafara" made up most of the group. The remaining captives included three "Jolofo" (also "Bulufo," "Golofo"), two "Mandingas," two "Bran," two "Gelonga" (Yalunka), and four individuals described as "Nalu," "Bañon," "Balanta," and "Caçanga," respectively. An additional female captive was listed as criolla, and, for another, no ethnonym is provided.[54]

Although most captives listed in this bill of sale are identified with Iberian first names ("Lucas Mandinga," "Ana Caçanga," and so forth), many bear given names that are distinctly non-Iberian. Two "Zape" men appear as "Manca Çape"; two women appear as "Comata Çape" and "Ensebo Çape." Among "Biafara" captives, no less than eight men or boys are listed with first names such as "Fabara," "Buruco," "Enbaba," "Sara," "Solbia," "Oyama," "Tenguerengue," and "Begre" (Figure 1). Several of these names appear to be toponyms representing specific towns located in or near Biafada lands. "Buruco Biafara['s]" name referred to Bruco, a port and an important center of political authority in the Biafada state of Guinala, on the Grande River. Likewise, the name "Enbaba Biafara" might refer to Enpada, a sector in present-day Guinea-Bissau along the southern bank of the Grande (the same region appears in sixteenth-century European sources as

---

53. "Lista de la gente reduzida," Mar. 29, 1582, AGI-Patronato 234, r.6, bloque 1, fols. 448v–449r, 495r–525r (Masatamba's testimony appears on fols. 520v–521v; for Luis Çape's assertion that he had been with Alonzo Cazanga in Panama for more than twelve years—thus indicating that he was not the real Masatamba—see fol. 522r). However, the two men might have been of the same generation; in 1582—roughly the same time that Masatamba, the ruler of Casa, is believed to have died—Spanish officials estimated Alonzo Cazanga "Maçatamba" to be approximately seventy years old. See also Carol F. Jopling, comp., *Indios y negros en Panamá en los siglos XVI y XVII: Selecciones de los documentos del Archivo General de Indias* (Antigua, Guatemala, 1994), 382–383; Tardieu, *Cimarrones de Panamá*, 210–212, 221, 232.
54. "Obligacion que hizo Alonso de Olalla," 1570, AGI-Ctdra 1380, n.1, fols. 98r–104r.

"Bissegue"). The name "Sara Biafara" could refer to Sarar, a Mande port on a creek off the Cacheu River conquered by Masatamba during the 1560s—a conflict that might explain Sara Biafara's presence in Mariquita in 1570. Rather than alluding to any specific place, "Fabara" could have been a name or nickname that carried special meaning for Biafadas far from home; in modern Biafada, the phrase *faa bwara* means "where are you off to?"[55]

Similar sources generated in Havana further confirm that, even within Spanish Caribbean society, precolonial Upper Guinean naming practices, political identities, and social categories continued to influence the way diasporic Upper Guineans identified themselves and one another. Captives disembarked from the *San Pedro* in 1572 (see Table 1) were intended to serve as royal slaves working on Havana's fortifications; some died of illness soon after arrival, and others were sent elsewhere. However, a list composed eleven years later suggests that many might have remained in Havana. Of 125 royal slaves listed in 1583, all but 9 bore Upper Guinean ethnonyms. In addition to Iberian given names and Upper Guinean ethnonyms or surnames, several men bore what appear to be nicknames (Luis Bran "Lion," Pedro Biafara "Magellan"). Other names included occupational designations, such as Francisco "Pilot" Çape. Whereas the more specific ethnolinguistic backgrounds of other "Zape" royal slaves in this list remain unknown, at least one person's name included a compound ethnonym: "Anton Jojo Çape" was almost certainly Susu ("Jojo" is an alternate spelling of "Zozo"). The appearance of names such as "Bartolome Zape Quiçani," "Juanico Brati Biafara," and "Pedro Bran Çamaca" indicate that, long after arriving in the Spanish Caribbean, at least a few enslaved Upper Guineans continued to be identified in Upper Guinean terms, even in official reports addressed to the Spanish crown.[56]

55. Ibid., fols. 98r–99r; Brooks, *Landlords and Strangers,* 92, 233, 242, 265–266; Wilson, "Outline Description," *Journal of West African Languages,* XXIII, no. 2 (1983), 81. "Tenguerengue" also appears in Lynne A. Guitar, "Cultural Genesis: Relationships among Indians, Africans, and Spaniards in Rural Hispaniola, First Half of the Sixteenth Century" (Ph.D. diss., Vanderbilt University, 1998), 443, as the name of an enslaved livestock worker on a sugar estate near Azua, Española, in 1547.

56. Wright, *Historia documentada,* I, 58–59, 211–213; "Memoria y lista de los negros de Su Magestad," Oct. 3, 1583, AGI-Ctdra 1088, n.3, fols. 129r–130v. Most royal slaves listed here were either "Zape" (thirty men, seventeen women), "Biafara" (fifteen men, twelve women), or "Bran" (seventeen men, seven women). Others were Nalu (five men, two women), "Bioho" (six men), "Casanga" (two men), "Mandinga" (one man, one woman), and "Jolofo" (one woman). Among the remaining captives, three were children; these included Catalina Biafara's ten- or eleven-year-old daughter "Francisca Criolla *boba* [mentally disabled]," Domynga Gelofo's daughter Martica (around one year old), and Guiomar Bran's son Nicolás (around two years old). See also Alejandro de la Fuente, with César García del Pino and Bernardo Iglesias Delgado, *Havana and the Atlantic in the Sixteenth Century* (Chapel Hill, N.C., 2008), 252n.

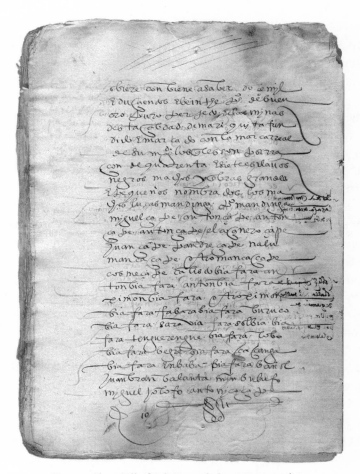

Figure 1 Slave Bill of Sale Recorded in Mariquita (New Kingdom of Granada), Featuring African Names and Ethnonyms, circa 1570. España. Ministerio de Educación, Cultura y Deporte. Archivo General de Indias. Contaduría 1380, Caja de Cartagena, Cuentas de Real Hacienda (1570–1577), n.1, fol. 98v

As with Antón Canpisa and Alonzo Cazanga alias "Maçatamba," African history provides reasonable interpretations for the names of Havana royal slaves "Francisco Çape Maçabuey" and "Hernando Çape Mazacu." Closely related to the Mande word *mansa* (ruler), *masa (maça, maza)* means "king" in the Susu language. Maçabuey and Mazacu are very similar to Massacanda, Massaiare, and Massacaeta; all were names of Susu, Temne, and Bullom leaders during the early 1600s. The Massaquoi were a powerful family in Sierra Leone for centuries before the colonial period. It seems likely that

Francisco Zape Maçabuey and Hernando Zape Mazacu were associated—or deliberately associated themselves—with rulers or families known as "Massabuey" and "Massacu." Although these references to people or polities in Sierra Leone are today obscure, they could have carried special significance for other "Zape" in sixteenth-century Havana.[57]

In the case of another royal slave, the ethnonym "Zape" was accompanied by at least one occupational designation. As confirmed by separate accounting records, "Francisco More Herrero Çape" was a blacksmith (*herrero*). In 1582, he was given three hundred Castilian pounds (three *quintales*) of iron and instructed to fashion chained cannon balls (*balas de cadena*) for artillery mounted in Havana's fortress. Given his level of skill, Francisco More (or, in some sources, Mori) quite likely was a blacksmith before arriving in the Caribbean. Sandoval wrote that, among Upper Guineans, "one finds a great number of blacksmiths, in the manner of the gypsies in Spain." Sandoval also notes that the *maestros* (possibly, "imams" or "muezzins") of mosques in Upper Guinea were known as *mores*. In Upper Guinea, blacksmiths were widely respected as ritual specialists and authority figures; a possible association with Islam could have contributed to Francisco More's reputation in sixteenth-century Havana. Furthermore, he was probably Susu, since among "Zape" peoples only the Susu were known for iron smelting and smithing.[58]

EARLY SPANISH CARIBBEAN SOURCES reveal the effects of social conditions in transforming or redefining diasporic African identities; yet they also present an opportunity to explore the roles African identities played in the formation of colonial social conditions, rather than vice versa. This is particularly true for Upper Guineans, whose regularly attributed ethnonyms reflected precise ethnolinguistic origins. Terms such as "Bañon,"

57. "Memoria y lista de los negros de Su Magestad," Oct. 3, 1583, AGI-Ctdra 1088, n.3, fol. 129v; Fyfe, *History of Sierra Leone*, 10, 156; P. E. H. Hair, "Hamlet in an Afro-Portuguese Setting: New Perspectives on Sierra Leone in 1607," *HA*, V (1978), 37–38; Brooks, *Landlords and Strangers*, 309–312; Manuel Álvares, *Ethiopia Minor and a Geographical Account of the Province of Sierra Leone (c.1615)* (Liverpool, England, 1990), part II, Chapter 3.

58. "Memoria y lista de los negros de Su Magestad," Oct. 3, 1583, AGI-Ctdra 1088, n.3, fol. 129r; "Gastos de herramientas y barcos de la fortaleza," 1583, AGI-Ctdra 1088, n.2, fol. 36r; Marriage of Ximon Congo and Madalena Çape, Oct. 6, 1585, CH-LB/M, fol. 5r ("Francisco Mori negro del rrey" was *padrino*, or godfather, at the wedding); Sandoval, *Un tratado sobre la esclavitud*, transcription Vila Vilar, 111, 120; Rodney, *History of the Upper Guinea Coast*, 64–65; Brooks, *Landlords and Strangers*, 33–47, 65–77, 99–105, 110, 173, 217, 263–265, 279–280; Fields-Black, *Deep Roots*, 145. See also Bowser, *African Slave in Colonial Peru*, 132. My thanks to Walter Hawthorne for suggesting that "more" could indicate a possible association with Islam.

"Biafara," "Bran," "Folupo," "Nalu," and "Balanta" represented processes of group identity formation and negotiation preceding Upper Guineans' enslavement and transportation to the early Spanish Caribbean. The same might be said of "Zape" subcategories such as "Baga," "Cocolí," and "Soso" or "Yalonga." These ethnonyms were used on both sides of the Iberian Atlantic during the sixteenth and early seventeenth centuries, and some remain in use today. Their appearance in early colonial Spanish Caribbean sources reveals far more about Upper Guineans' relationships to one another and to Iberians in the Rivers of Guinea and the Cape Verde Islands—and the circumstances of Upper Guineans' enslavement and forced migration—than about strategies for resisting European colonialist ideologies or ethnogenesis within the confines of racialized slave societies in the western hemisphere.

TWO

The Kingdoms of Angola

In January 1590, black ranch hands found eleven half-starved African men wandering across westernmost Cuba, near Cabo San Antón. Though one was too ill to make the sixty-league journey to Havana, the others were soon brought before the island's royal officials. To learn of the circumstances behind their arrival, officials conscripted "Mariana of the Angola nation," a *ladina* (Latinized) domestic servant "who knows the language of these blacks." Instructed to "speak to them in their language and to ask them what she was commanded," Mariana began to pose questions to "one of the blacks who seemed most capable of answering." His responses constitute one of the earliest known accounts of the Middle Passage as told by one of its survivors:

> [He] said that he is from [the] Angola land and the others are from nearby regions and that they all understand one another. . . . [He] said that a Portuguese man [bought them] by *resgate* [barter] and [he] does not know [the man's name] and [he] said that he was going with them to Santo Domingo. . . . The ship was large and came very full of male and female slaves [so full] that no more would fit and [he] does not know how many they would have been all together. . . . [For] ten days they traveled navigating at sea and at the end of that time a French ship happened upon them and overtook them. . . . The one ship fought with the other and the French killed five Portuguese people and among them the owner of the blacks . . . and they took control of the Portuguese ship. . . . The French took it to São Tomé where they left it with half of the blacks and all of the white people who came aboard it. . . . Many of the blacks died [at sea] and the French [ship] came with the [blacks] who remained to these parts[,] and in this land where they were found [the French] left ashore eleven [blacks] and another one who died and many blacks remained in the ship. . . . They were put ashore because of the great lack of food and drink. . . . One month [had passed since

then,] and in this time they ate *palmichos* [palm hearts] and meat they killed[;] the French gave them an axe and flint. . . . Later after leaving [the blacks] ashore they made sail.[1]

The interrogation from which this narrative is drawn represents a compromise of sorts, between Africans who sought to tell the story of their journey from Angola as they had experienced it and royal officials intent on determining who would be entitled to own or sell them. Rather than a straightforward narrative told in the first person, the original document is a series of responses to specific questions asked by royal officials, mediated by the interpreter Mariana, and recorded in Spanish by a scribe. It is not clear whether the individual who testified was chosen by royal officials, by Mariana, or by his fellow migrants. Despite these multiple filters, his testimony includes considerable information that was not solicited by Havana's officials, representing details that help to explain the transatlantic voyage from the forced migrants' points of view. Royal officials never queried how these men were acquired by the Portuguese merchant who first embarked them on a transatlantic slave ship, but the deponent noted that they had been purchased through resgate (or, *rescate*), though he does not explain how they were initially enslaved. Nor did the officials inquire as to how the African men survived for a month in western Cuba before being discovered; the information was given without any prompting. When asked about their origins, the deponent replied that he was from "the Angola land" and his companions were from neighboring areas *(circunvezinos)* but added that they "all understand one another." Regardless of how the ten men possibly identified themselves, they all appear as "Angolas"—and newly baptized royal slaves—in Havana's baptismal register in May and June 1590.[2]

Unlike their Upper Guinean counterparts, whose presence in the Spanish Americas built on more than a century of cross-cultural exchange in western Africa and the Cape Verde Islands, forced migrants from Angola arrived in the early Spanish Caribbean during the late sixteenth and early

1. Oficiales reales de la Habana a S. M. sobre "onze pieças de esclavos boçales," Jan. 31–Mar. 24, 1590, AGI-SD 118, r.5, n.215, fols. 2v–4r.

2. Ibid., fol. 3r ("dijo que el es de tierra Angola y los demas son çircunvezinos e que se entiende todos unos a otros"); Baptisms of royal slaves Sebastián Angola, Francisco Angola, Pedro Angola, Francisco Angola, Mateo Angola, Antón Angola, Cristóbal Angola, Manuel negro Angola, Gaspar Angola, May 6–June 10, 1590, CH-LB/B, fols. 5r–6r. On dialects of Kimbundu spoken in Angola's interior before the late sixteenth century and the spread of a standardized form of the language during the following century, see Jan Vansina, "Portuguese vs Kimbundu: Language Use in the Colony of Angola (1575–c.1845)," *Bulletin des seances: Academie Royale des Sciences d'Outre-Mer,* XLVII (2001), 267–281, esp. 273–274.

seventeenth centuries under very different circumstances. Chronologically, Spanish colonization of the Caribbean preceded Portuguese colonization of Angola, but the founding and growth of the latter held major implications for the expansion of Spanish Caribbean society. Although small numbers of "Angolas" appear in Caribbean sources as early as the 1560s, arriving via São Tomé, the first slaving voyages known to have sailed directly from Angola to the Spanish Caribbean took place during the 1580s, corresponding to the founding of Luanda in late 1575 and the earliest phase of Portuguese expansion in Angola, which lasted from roughly 1579 to the early 1590s. The colonization of Angola differed significantly from Portuguese and Luso-African activities in Upper Guinea and in the nearby Kingdom of Kongo. Rather than merchants and missionaries dependent on the goodwill of their African hosts and trading partners, the Portuguese came to the region they called Angola to conquer and rule its inhabitants.[3]

Angola's colonial state apparatus played a major role in generating captives for export, with colonial authorities heavily involved in slave trafficking. As in Upper Guinean ports, Portuguese and Luso-African merchants based in Luanda relied on slave markets and long-distance trading networks to acquire captives (indeed, the men testifying in Cuba in 1590 claimed to have been bartered). But diplomatic relations between the Portuguese colony and the neighboring kingdom of Ndongo rapidly deteriorated, and, by 1580—just five years after Luanda was founded—the two powers were openly at war. Aided by powerful armies of Imbangala mercenaries, Portuguese colonists in Angola used military force, and the threat of force, to produce captives for export on an unprecedented scale over the next half century. In Havana, the ten or eleven newcomers from "the Angola land" in 1590 preceded the arrival of larger numbers of enslaved West Central Africans during the second half of the same decade. Among more than 400 enslaved Africans baptized in Havana during the 1590s, more than half (221) are listed as "Angolas," with the vast majority (174) baptized between 1595 and 1599. West Central Africans' sudden prominence in western Cuba, particularly after 1595, was a visible result of this increase in slave traffic from

3. Beatrix Heintze, "The Angolan Vassal Tributes of the 17th Century," *RHES*, VI (1980), 57. For an excellent overview of social life in seventeenth-century Luanda, see Arlindo Manuel Caldeira, "Luanda in the 17th Century: Diversity and Cultural Interaction in the Process of Forming an Afro-Atlantic City," *Nordic Journal of African Studies*, XXII (2013), 72–104; see also Catarina Madeira Santos, "Luanda: A Colonial City between Africa and the Atlantic, Seventeenth and Eighteenth Centuries," in Liam Matthew Brockey, ed., *Portuguese Colonial Cities in the Early Modern World* (Burlington, Vt., 2008), 249–272.

Angola and can be matched with specific periods of intensified warfare and tribute exacted from conquered Mbundu populations.[4]

Although Brazil, more than any other region of colonial Latin America, had the most enduring connections to West Central Africa, the Spanish Caribbean was also very strongly linked to Angola during this early period. The colonization of Portuguese America was predicated on warfare and enslavement: the "continual construction of Brazil" and the "constant destruction of Angola" were two sides of the same coin. A vibrant Lusophone South Atlantic paradigm has brought out the diverse West Central African influences on Brazilian society and vice versa, especially during the eighteenth and nineteenth centuries. However, events in Angola reverberated far beyond Brazil; during the Iberian Union (1580–1640), forced migration from West Central Africa fundamentally reshaped much of the Iberian Atlantic world. Warfare in West Central Africa fueled transatlantic slaving networks that disembarked captives not only in Brazil but also in São Tomé, the Canary Islands, Spain, the Río de la Plata, and the Spanish circum-Caribbean, with the latter trajectories rivaling and at times surpassing the slave trade to Brazil.[5]

4. Jan Vansina, *Kingdoms of the Savanna: A History of Central African States until European Occupation* (Madison, Wis., 1966), 124–130; David Birmingham, *Trade and Conflict in Angola: The Mbundu and Their Neighbours under the Influence of the Portuguese, 1483–1790* (Oxford, 1966), 17n, 78–100; Beatrix Heintze, "Angola nas garras do tráfico de escravos: As guerras do Ndongo (1611–1630)," *RIEA*, no. 1 (January / June 1984), 11–60; Joseph C. Miller, *Way of Death: Merchant Capitalism and the Angolan Slave Trade, 1730–1830* (Madison, Wis., 1988), 105–139; John K. Thornton, *Warfare in Atlantic Africa, 1500–1800* (London, 1999), 99–125; Ilídio do Amaral, *O consulado de Paulo Dias de Novais: Angola no último quartel do século XVI e primeiro do século XVII* (Lisbon, 2000), 117–128. For people described as "Angola" (also "Anguola," "Engola," "Enguola") in Havana's baptismal register, see CH-LB/B, fols. 1r, 2r–3r, 5r–6v, 9r, 14r–14v, 20v, 23r–23v, 24v, 25v, 27r, 29r, 37r, 39r, 40r, 41v–42r, 45r–45v, 47r–47v, 48v, 51v, 52v–53r, 56v, 59r, 60v, 62r–62v, 63v–66r, 70v–71v, 72v–73r, 74v, 75v, 77v, 78v, 80r–80v, 82v, 83v, 84v–86r, 87r, 88r, 89r, 90v–92r, 93v, 94v, 95v–96r, 97v–101r, 102r–102v, 103v, 104v–105v, 106v, 107v–108r, 109r–109v, 111r–111v, 112v–113v, 114v–115v, 117r–117v, 120r–121r, 122r, 123r–124v, 125v–127r, 128v–130r, 131r–131v, 137v, 138v–139r, 140r–141r, 144r, 149v, 150v, 152v–153r, 154r, 155r–157r. For previous studies that document the growing presence of West Central Africans in Cuba during the late sixteenth century, see Alejandro de la Fuente García, "Denominaciones étnicas de los esclavos introducidos en Cuba, siglos XVI y XVII," *Anales del Caribe, Centro de Estudios del Caribe*, VI (1986), 75–96; de la Fuente García, "Esclavos africanos en La Habana: Zonas de procedencia y denominaciones étnicas, 1570–1699," *Revista española de antropología americana*, XX (1990), 135–160.

5. Luiz Felipe de Alencastro, *O trato dos viventes: Formação do Brasil no Atlântico Sul, séculos XVI e XVII* (São Paulo, Brazil, 2000), 325 (quote). For additional studies illustrating the utility of a South Atlantic paradigm, see, for example, Marina de Mello e Souza, *Reis negros no Brasil escravista: História da festa de coroação de rei Congo* (Belo Horizonte, Brazil, 2002); James H. Sweet, *Recreating Africa: Culture, Kinship, and Religion in the African-Portuguese World, 1441–1770* (Chapel Hill, N.C., 2003); Estevam Costa Thompson, "Negreiros nos mares do Sul: Famílias traficantes nas rotas entre Angola e Brasil em fins do século XVIII" (M.A. thesis, Universidade de Brasília, 2006); Kalle Kananoja, "Central African Identities and Religiosity in Colonial Minas Gerais" (Ph.D. diss., Åbo Akademi University, 2012); Roquinaldo Amaral Ferreira, *Cross-Cultural Exchange in the Atlantic World: Angola*

Portugal's colonization of Angola and Spain's colonization of the Americas mutually reinforced one another. The early seventeenth century saw a tremendous surge in coerced migration from Angola to the Spanish Caribbean, an "Angola wave" that came to dominate the slave trade to the Americas by the 1620s. Government officials and administrators, religious authorities, Iberian and Luso-African merchants, and other colonists residing in Luanda routinely participated in many of these slaving voyages. Some sent enslaved Africans to be sold on their behalf; others personally traveled to the Caribbean as slave ship passengers or as captains of their own vessels. Portuguese and Luso-African slave merchants' physical presence in the Caribbean was far from unusual, but Luanda elites differed from other transatlantic slave traffickers in that they were far more directly involved in the very processes that generated captives for export.[6]

Forced migrants arriving on slave ships from Angola included exceptionally large numbers of children—a phenomenon generally associated with the eighteenth- and nineteenth-century slave trade—representing another distinctive characteristic of Angola's influence on early Spanish Caribbean society. Whereas children and young adolescents were also commonly exported from Upper Guinea and the Cape Verde Islands, ships arriving from Angola in the early seventeenth century appear to have carried larger numbers of children, including very young children, corresponding with changes in metropolitan legislation regulating the slave trade and with new systems for expressing enslaved Africans' market values for taxation purposes. Rather than a function of Iberian demand in the Americas, the arrival of enslaved children from Angola seems to have resulted from conditions of slave production in West Central Africa, including the mass enslavement of entire communities, the payment of children as tribute, and a preference among Imbangala mercenaries to retain adolescent and young adult captives but to sell small children.

In short, just as the histories of early colonial Brazil and Angola take on new dimensions when viewed within a broader South Atlantic framework,

and Brazil during the Era of the Slave Trade (Cambridge, 2012); Mariana P. Candido, *An African Slaving Port and the Atlantic World: Benguela and Its Hinterland* (New York, 2013). For Angola's connections to Buenos Aires (often through Brazil), see, especially, Kara D. Schultz, "'The Kingdom of Angola Is Not Very Far from Here': The South Atlantic Slave Port of Buenos Aires, 1585–1640," *SA,* XXXVI (2015), 424–444.

6. On the "Angola wave," see Linda M. Heywood and John K. Thornton, *Central Africans, Atlantic Creoles, and the Foundation of the Americas, 1585–1660* (Cambridge, 2007), ix, 39–41. For further discussion of Portuguese and Luso-African mariners' and merchants' regular presence in Spanish Caribbean settlements, see Chapter 3, below.

the evolving conditions of slave production in Angola and West Central African captives' arrival in the Spanish Caribbean were complementary aspects of a single, unified history. The slaving networks that connected Angola to the Spanish Caribbean from roughly 1590 to 1640 reveal a scenario even more complex than Brazilian colonial formations counterbalanced with Portuguese / Imbangala wars in Angola or bidirectional exchanges between Portuguese colonies in the South Atlantic. The effects of warfare and enslavement in Angola rippled outward across much of the early modern Iberian Atlantic, with exiled women, men, and children arriving en masse in both Brazil and Spanish America; the colonization of both regions contributed to Portuguese Angola's expansion at the expense of West Central African states and communities.[7]

Warfare and the Angola Wave, circa 1590–1640

Luanda is now believed to have exported roughly 1.3 million captives, more than any other African port, over the duration of the entire transatlantic slave trade. This direct slave traffic from Angola to the Americas began some ninety years after the initial Spanish colonization of the Caribbean; the quality and abundance of documentation generated in circum-Caribbean ports during the early seventeenth century in particular provides a window on the rise of the Angola trade that is not available for older branches of the slave trade, whose origins remain obscure. For most of the sixteenth century, transatlantic slave traffic from Angola was oriented primarily toward São Tomé, with Brazil becoming an important destination at some point in the second half of the century. The Caribbean followed soon afterward, though the few "Angolas" who appeared preceding the late 1580s probably arrived via São Tomé. Yet, by 1622, royal officials in Bogotá characterized

7. For an exceptional overview of slave traffic from Angola to both Spanish America and Brazil, see Arlindo Manuel Caldeira, "Angola and the Seventeenth-Century South Atlantic Slave Trade," in David Richardson and Filipa Ribeiro da Silva, eds., *Networks and Trans-Cultural Exchange: Slave Trading in the South Atlantic, 1590–1867* (Leiden, 2015), 101–142. Though the transatlantic slave trade to Brazil was already underway by the mid-sixteenth century, at present only fifteen Iberian slaving voyages with a Brazilian port as their main destination are known to have been completed before the 1640s. For Iberian slave ships arriving in Brazil in 1574–1576, 1582, 1611, 1624, 1627, 1630, 1633, 1636, and 1639, see *Voyages,* accessed May 23, 2015, http://slavevoyages.org/tast/database/search.faces ?yearFrom=1514&yearTo=1640&natinimp=3.6&mjslptimp=50000&fate2=1. Most of these voyages are only known through Dutch sources. See also Daniel Barros Domingues da Silva and David Eltis, "The Slave Trade to Pernambuco, 1561–1851," in Eltis and David Richardson, eds., *Extending the Frontiers: Essays on the New Transatlantic Slave Trade Database* (New Haven, Conn., 2008), 96–97, Alexandre Vieira Ribeiro, "The Transatlantic Slave Trade to Bahia, 1582–1851," 130–131.

the "Angolas and Congos" regularly disembarked in Cartagena as "infinitely numerous." West Central African migrants might well have seemed infinite in number to contemporary observers in the circum-Caribbean; with nearly four hundred Iberian voyages from Angola arriving between 1593 and 1640, forced migration from West Central Africa surely surpassed any other Old World migration to the Caribbean during the same decades.[8]

One of the first Iberian colonies devoted to sugar cultivation, São Tomé was also a slave trade bulking center that ultimately helped shape the earliest West Central African diasporas in the Americas. Originally uninhabited, the island was encountered by Portuguese mariners around 1470, and its colonization began during the 1490s. With or without royal backing, Portuguese and Luso-Africans residing in São Tomé played key roles in Portuguese expansion in West Central Africa, including lands south of the Kingdom of Kongo. According to the anonymous author of the "Relação da Costa da Guiné" (1607), Portuguese commerce with "Angola" was established "during the era of King João II," that is, during the 1480s or 1490s, "though with little frequency." Voyages from São Tomé to territories under the control of the *ngola* (ruler) of Ndongo were probably common soon afterward. As early as the 1550s—a full quarter century before the founding of Luanda—a Portuguese factor and clerk were posted in the region to coordinate slave traffic that, at that time, was oriented toward São Tomé and Lisbon.[9]

Alongside Lower Guineans and locally born creoles, West Central Africans must have constituted an important segment of São Tomé's enslaved population during the 1500s. Maroon communities that formed on the island during the mid-sixteenth century became recognized as *Angolares*, though the term appears to have originated in eighteenth-century sources.

8. David Eltis, "A Brief Overview of the Trans-Atlantic Slave Trade," *Voyages*, accessed May 19, 2014, http://www.slavevoyages.org/tast/assessment/essays-intro-01.faces; Heywood and Thornton, *Central Africans*, 39; Carta de Miguel Corcuera y Baltasar Perez Bernal, June 27, 1622, AGI-SF 52, n.172a, fol. 5r ("angolas y congos de que ay infinitos en sus tierras"). For known voyages from Angola to the circum-Caribbean, see *Voyages*, accessed May 19, 2014, http://slavevoyages.org/tast/database/search.faces?yearFrom=1593&yearTo=1640&fate2=1&mjbyptimp=60700&mjslptimp=31100.31200.31300.31400.35100.35400.41200.

9. Robert Garfield, *A History of São Tomé Island, 1470–1655: The Key to Guinea* (San Francisco, Calif., 1992); Cristina Maria Seuanes Serafim, *As ilhas de São Tomé no século XVII* (Lisbon, 2000), 15–19; "Relação da Costa da Guiné," 1607, in António Brásio, *MMA* (1), V, 387–388; Vansina, *Kingdoms of the Savanna*, 37–69, 125–126, 130, 139; Birmingham, *Trade and Conflict*, 30–33, 42–48, 56; Anne Hilton, *The Kingdom of Kongo* (Oxford, 1985), 50–141; Amaral, *O consulado*, 118, 138, 188–194, 254; Joseph C. Miller, "Central Africa during the Era of the Slave Trade, c.1490s–1850s," in Linda M. Heywood, ed., *Central Africans and Cultural Transformations in the American Diaspora* (Cambridge, 2002), 21–70; Heywood and Thornton, *Central Africans*, 51, 79–80.

The first known transatlantic slave trade voyage possibly carried some Mbundu captives from São Tomé to Española in 1525, but currently the earliest documented voyage to have transported "Angolas" to the Caribbean (or anywhere in the Americas) took place fifty years later. Sailing from São Tomé, the *San Antonio* arrived in Santo Domingo in 1575, disembarking at least 243 enslaved men, women, and children. Royal officials carefully recorded the sale of each captive over the next six months; almost all were described as being "from the Angola land." The only exceptions were a boy from "the land of Manicongo," that is, the Kingdom of Kongo, and another "who said he was from the land of the River Anche," perhaps referring to either the Nke River in present-day Gabon or Nké in the Pool region of present-day Congo.[10]

Despite the occurrence of transatlantic migration from "the Angola land" via São Tomé during the mid-1570s, captives exported from the Portuguese colony of Angola remained relatively unknown in Cartagena de Indias—a city that was fast becoming the Spanish Caribbean's primary slaving port—more than ten years later. In January 1588, having departed from São Tomé, a slave ship overshot Cartagena and wrecked on the nearby island of Baru. After four days without food or water, 279 surviving captives were espied by the crew of a passing frigate and were brought to the city. The voyage generated far less tax revenue than expected. The captives' perceived value was affected not only by their weakened physical condition, royal officials explained, but also because they were "Congos and Angolas[,] a type which in these parts has no reputation or value whatsoever." Furthermore, since two slave ships from Upper Guinea were expected to arrive soon, few prospective buyers in Cartagena were interested in the West Central Africans.[11]

Consistent with such observations, and with contemporary descriptions of African populations in early colonial Mexico and Peru, "Angolas" appear only sporadically in Spanish Caribbean records before the very late

10. Birmingham, *Trade and Conflict*, 25; John Vogt, *Portuguese Rule on the Gold Coast, 1469–1682* (Athens, Ga., 1979), 71–72; Miller, *Way of Death*, 116–117; Garfield, *History of São Tomé*, 178–181; Serafim, *As ilhas de São Tomé*, 285; Gerhard Seibert, "Castaways, Autochthons, or Maroons? The Debate on the Angolares of São Tomé Island," in Philip J. Havik and Malyn Newitt, eds., *Creole Societies in the Portuguese Colonial Empire* (Bristol, England, 2007), 105–126; Gerardo A. Lorenzino, "Linguistic, Historical, and Ethnographic Evidence on the Formation of the *Angolares*, a Maroon-Descendant Community in São Tomé (West Africa)," *Portuguese Studies Review*, XV (2007), 193–226; *Voyages*, accessed May 19, 2014, voyage 46473; Proceso contra Pedro de Esplugas et al., 1578–1590, AGI-Esc 1A, pieza 4, fols. 274v–327r (for references to "un negrito de tierra Manicongo" and "un negrito que dixo hera de tierra ryo anche," see fols. 282r, 306r).

11. Oficiales reales a S. M., Feb. 10, 1588, AGI-SF 72, n.75, fols. 1v–2r.

sixteenth century. Until nearly 1590, forced migrants described as "Angolas" were few even in comparison to other West Central Africans and Lower Guineans exported from São Tomé (all of whom were usually outnumbered by Upper Guineans). Some, however, did arrive earlier. In Santo Domingo in 1570, following the arrival of an unregistered caravel from São Tomé several months before, "Silvestre Angola" was sold alongside captives "Pedro Manicongo" and Juana "of the Beni land." By 1577, a free black man named "Francisco Engola" owned a home in Havana and successfully petitioned the town council for land to raise livestock. Between 1578 and 1588 in Havana, 35 "Angola[s]" or "Engola[s]" were sold to new owners, listed in last wills, given in dowry, or designated as collateral. Likewise, when the maroon state of Bayano was disbanded in 1582, rosters of its members enumerated several "Angolas" among nearly 250 former maroons (see Table 2). Within Bayano, the group led by Juan Angola evidently had the largest concentration of Central Africans, with 16 people identified as either "Angola," "Congo," "Enchico," "Maçanbique," or "Moçanga." Of these, only 7, including its captain, were "Angolas."[12]

After 1595, the frequency of slave trade voyages arriving from Angola and the numbers of enslaved West Central Africans transported directly from Luanda to the Caribbean greatly surpassed those associated with the slave trade from São Tomé. By this time, São Tomé had experienced a severe economic decline, with far fewer captives being imported for local use. In 1609, royal officials wistfully evoked the island's sixteenth-century glory days, when colonists operated "many sugar mills" with "an abundance of slaves who came there from Congo and Angola." As they recalled, "each month there arrived at the factory a ship with 500 [or] 600 *peças* [that is, slaves]," not counting others imported by private traders. By contrast, they noted, "today there are very few *emgenhos* [mills] that are populated" with slaves. Despite the collapse of the island's sugar industry and its decreasing importance as a slaving entrepôt, São Tomé continued to play a part

12. Caja de Santo Domingo, "Quentas que se tomaron," AGI-Ctdra 1052, n.1 (1570–1571), fol. 21r; Emilio Roig de Leuchsenring, ed., *Actas capitulares del ayuntamiento de La Habana* (Havana, 1937–1946), III, 109, 194; María Teresa de Rojas, "Algunos datos sobre los negros esclavos y horros en la Habana del siglo XVI," in *Miscelánea de estudios dedicados a Fernando Ortiz* (Havana, 1956), II, 1283; Rojas, [ed.], *Índice y extractos del archivo de protocolos de la Habana*, 3 vols. (Havana, 1947–1957), I, 148–149, 370–389, II, 17, 21, 52, 83, 94–96, 108, 212, 258, 284, 302, 322, 360, 376–377, 394, 408, III, 18, 29, 70, 75, 188; "Lista de la gente reduzida," Mar. 29, 1582, AGI-Patronato 234, r.6, bloque 1, fols. 447v–456v. Notarial records and hacienda inventories for Lima and Mexico City reveal similar patterns. See Frederick P. Bowser, *The African Slave in Colonial Peru, 1524–1650* (Stanford, Calif., 1974), 40–43; Lourdes Mondragón Barrios, *Esclavos africanos en la Ciudad de México: El servicio doméstico durante el siglo XVI* (Mexico City, 1999), 36–39.

in the transatlantic slave trade. Between 1597 and 1628, at least twenty-five voyages transported captives from São Tomé to ports in the Americas. At a rate of less than one voyage per year, all arrived in the circum-Caribbean, with most docking in Cartagena. Concomitant with the surge in slave traffic from Angola during the early seventeenth century, São Tomé might have also taken on a supporting role as a place to plan and prepare for slaving voyages from West Central Africa. In 1613, when the slave ship *Santiago* made an unscheduled landing and disembarked its captives in Havana, the city's authorities were sent to investigate. One of the witnesses, the priest Francisco Pinto de Azevedo, reported that in San Antonio on the island of Príncipe the ship's captain, Pedro Navarro, had told him he was preparing for an upcoming voyage to Angola.[13]

The first Iberian slaving voyages to sail directly from Angola to the Caribbean—foreshadowing the massive Angola wave—probably took place in the mid-1580s, beginning with the disembarkation of 164 captives in Santo Domingo, Española, in 1585 and another 168 captives in La Guaira, on the Venezuelan coast north of Caracas, in 1587. Both vessels were allegedly en route to Brazil, indicating that an Angola-Brazil slave traffic was already in existence. The third documented slave trade voyage from Angola to the Caribbean arrived in Cartagena with nearly 250 captives in August 1588; in a list of thirty-six slave ships that disembarked enslaved Africans in the city between 1585 and 1590, the voyage in question was the sole vessel described as having departed from Angola rather than Upper Guinea or the Cape Verde Islands. Additional slave ships from Angola followed, arriving in Cartagena in 1591, 1593, and 1594. Other early voyages from Angola to the Caribbean, including unregistered voyages and even non-Iberian voyages, were likely. For example, a French ship landed at least 150 "Angolan blacks" in Spanish Jamaica in 1588. Like the French vessel that left 11 West Central African men ashore in Cuba the following year, this earlier ship might have also captured a Portuguese slave ship en route from Angola or São Tomé to the Caribbean. But, as a general rule, forced migrants described as "Angolas" appear to have reached the Caribbean only in small numbers, primarily on Iberian slave ships arriving from São Tomé, until the end of the sixteenth century.[14]

13. Carta do Conselho da India sobre os oficiaes da camara da ilha de São Thome, June 7, 1610, AHU-ST cx.1, n.17, fol. 1r; Proceso contra Pedro Navarro, 1613, AGI-Esc 38B, pieza 1, fols. 141v–142r. For slaving voyages departing São Tomé, see *Voyages*, accessed May 19, 2014, http://slavevoyages.org/tast/database/search.faces?yearFrom=1595&yearTo=1640&mjbyptimp=60673.60676.

14. Caja de Santo Domingo, "Relación de cargo y data del año 1586," AGI-Ctdra 1053, n.7, pliego 7; Caja de Santo Domingo, Cuentas del año 1586, AGI-Ctdra 1058, fol. 41r; Eduardo Arcila Farias, dir.,

In terms of sheer volume and the frequency and chronological distribution of slaving voyages, the Angola wave hit Caribbean shores during the final decade of the sixteenth century and lasted through the first four decades of the seventeenth century, reaching a peak around 1621 when at least twenty-nine vessels departing from Angola disembarked captives in the Spanish Americas alone. Although slave ships continued to arrive from Upper Guinea throughout this period, this older branch of the transatlantic slave trade was relatively feeble by the late 1620s; Angola's dominance in the slave trade to the Spanish Americas was most pronounced during the years 1626 to 1640. For many slaving voyages during this period, little or no information on the actual number of captives disembarked survives. However, for voyages from Angola arriving in the single port of Cartagena de Indias between 1588 and 1640, at least 32,341 captives were either declared by slave ship crews or discovered by royal officials. This figure is the absolute minimum number of West Central African captives landed in Cartagena; the actual number was certainly much larger.[15]

Throughout the first half of the seventeenth century, wars waged against Ndongo and neighboring peoples fueled slave traffic to the Spanish Caribbean. Though warfare contributed to the expansion of the Portuguese colony of Angola, territorial gain was not the principal motive for conflict. Angola's governors repeatedly authorized military incursions for the express purpose of producing captives for export, a departure from the previous century, when Portuguese and Luso-African merchants primarily obtained captives through long-established slave markets. Abetted by notoriously destructive armies of Imbangala mercenaries, the warfare dur-

Hacienda y comercio de Venezuela en el siglo XVI (Caracas, 1983), 149; Carta de Don Pedro de Lodeña, Sept. 6, 1591, AGI-SF 37, r.6, n.103a/b, fol. 3r; María del Carmen Borrego Plá, *Cartagena de Indias en el siglo XVI* (Seville, 1983), 58; Caja de Cartagena, Cuenta tomada del año de 1591, AGI-Ctdra 1384, n.3, r.5, fols. 51r–54r; Caja de Cartagena, Cuentas del año 1594, AGI-Ctdra 1385, n.2, fols. 38r–39r, 48r–49v; Juan de Ybarra al gobernador de Jamaica, July 10, 1612, AGI-SF 73, n.17d; Oficiales reales a S. M., July 21, 1613, AGI-SF 73, n.26; Caja de Cartagena, Cuentas del año 1605, AGI-Ctdra 1385, n.12, pliego 6. For an earlier slaving voyage from Angola arriving in Bahia in 1582, see *Voyages*, accessed May 19, 2014, voyage 49522; "Certidão ao capitão André Dias," 1582, in Brásio, *MMA* (1), IV, 346–347; Schultz, "'The Kingdom of Angola,'" *SA*, XXXVI (2015), 424–444.

15. David Wheat, "The First Great Waves: African Provenance Zones for the Transatlantic Slave Trade to Cartagena de Indias, 1570–1640," *JAH*, LII (2011), 1–22; Wheat, "The Afro-Portuguese Maritime World and the Foundations of Spanish Caribbean Society, 1570–1640" (Ph.D. diss., Vanderbilt University, 2009), 255–256. On contraband slaving from Angola during the same era, see Nikolaus Böttcher, "Negreros portugueses y la Inquisición: Cartagena de Indias, siglo XVII," *Memoria*, IX (2003), 38–55; Paul Lokken, "From the 'Kingdoms of Angola' to Santiago de Guatemala: The Portuguese Asientos and Spanish Central America, 1595–1640," *HAHR*, XCIII (2013), 171–203; Marc Eagle, "Chasing the *Avença*: An Investigation of Illicit Slave Trading in Santo Domingo at the End of the Portuguese *Asiento* Period," *SA*, XXXV (2014), 99–120.

ing the 1590s through the 1630s correlated exactly with the wave of forced migrants from Angola to the Spanish Caribbean. This violence generated so many captives that the traditional slave fairs ceased to operate, and, by 1620, Portuguese and Luso-African merchants were more likely to purchase war captives from allied or independent Imbangala groups.[16]

Within the broader Angola wave, surges in the slave trade were connected to campaigns led by specific governors of Angola. Direct slave exports from Luanda to Cartagena and Veracruz first began to rival exports from Upper Guinea during the years 1593–1601. Although the slave trade asiento held by Pedro Gomez Reynel (or Reinel) gave Portuguese and Luanda merchants greater access to Spanish American markets beginning in 1595, the actions taken by Portuguese authorities in Angola were most directly responsible for a rapid acceleration in the numbers of captives embarked. João Furtado de Mendonça served as governor of Angola from 1594 to 1602, precisely during the years that the colony's slave exports to the Caribbean reached significant numbers for the first time. His brutal offensive inland from Luanda along the Bengo River between 1596 and 1598 resulted in the enslavement of thousands of West Central Africans, including some with little or no connection to Portugal's ostensible adversary, the kingdom of Ndongo. In fact, Spanish American shipping records reveal that during the years 1594–1602, more than eighty ships from Angola arrived in Cartagena, Veracruz, Buenos Aires, Santo Domingo, La Guaira, Jamaica, and other ports, disembarking nearly fifteen thousand declared captives. Most were likely enslaved or paid in tribute as a result of the military expeditions organized by Furtado de Mendonça.[17]

16. Vansina, *Kingdoms of the Savanna,* 126–128; Beatrix Heintze, "Traite de 'pièces' en Angola: Ce qui n'est pas dit dans nos sources," in Serge Daget, ed., *De la traite à l'esclavage: Actes du colloque international sur la traite des noirs, Nantes 1985* (Paris, 1988), I, 147–172; Heintze, "Angola nas garras," *RIEA,* no. 1 (January / June 1984), 20–21; Heywood and Thornton, *Central Africans,* 78–95, 114–124; Alonso de Sandoval, *Un tratado sobre la esclavitud,* introduction and transcription by Enriqueta Vila Vilar (Madrid, 1987), 144–146. The extent to which Imbalangas were associated with people identified as "Jagas" in Portuguese sources has been a subject of debate among historians of precolonial West Central Africa for the past half century. For recaps of influential interpretations, see John Thornton, "The African Experience of the '20. and Odd Negroes' Arriving in Virginia in 1619," *WMQ,* 3d Ser., LV (1998), 425–426; Miller, "Central Africa," in Heywood, ed., *Central Africans,* 43; Beatrix Heintze, "The Extraordinary Journey of the Jaga through the Centuries: Critical Approaches to Precolonial Angolan Historical Sources," trans. Katja Rieck, *HA,* XXXIV (2007), 67–101. On Buenos Aires, see Schultz, "'The Kingdom of Angola,'" *SA,* XXXVI (2015), 424–444.

17. On Furtado de Mendonça's campaign during the late 1590s, see Thornton, "African Experience," *WMQ,* LV (1998), 422–432; Heywood and Thornton, *Central Africans,* 90–91. For slaving voyages to Spanish America during the Pedro Gomez Reynel asiento (1595–1601), see Henri Lapeyre, "Le trafic négrier avec l'amérique espagnole," in *Homenaje a Jaime Vicens Vives* (Barcelona, 1967), II, 285–306; Enriqueta Vila Vilar, *Hispanoamérica y el comercio de esclavos: Los asientos portugueses* (Seville,

Warfare unleashed by Portuguese authorities in Angola was also a root cause of a second wave of coerced migration from western Africa to the Spanish Caribbean. Portuguese military campaigns launched during Luis Mendes de Vasconcelos's governorship of Angola (1617–1621) correspond to the initial years of this second increase in slave exports. Between 1617 and 1625, more than 150 ships from Angola landed a minimum of thirty thousand captives in Cartagena, Veracruz, Santo Domingo, La Guaira, Puerto Rico, Jamaica, Buenos Aires, and elsewhere. Voyages from Angola had comprised the bulk of transatlantic slave traffic to Veracruz since the late 1590s; during this nine-year period, Angola definitively surpassed Upper Guinea as the main provenance zone for slaving voyages to Cartagena as well. By around 1620, Angola had become the Spanish Americas' most important source of enslaved sub-Saharan Africans—a role it would retain until the Iberian Union came to an end in 1640.[18]

Though many people shipped from Angola to the early-seventeenth-century Spanish Caribbean were enslaved during the course of military campaigns, Portuguese attacks on Ndongo and other West Central African states also contributed to slave production by forcing conquered populations to pay tribute in the form of captives. After successful battles or intimidation of Mbundu populations, Portuguese interlopers assumed jurisdiction over local political authorities known as *sobas* and, by extension, the communities they governed (*sobados*). A 1587 list of nearly fifty "captains" who had been awarded sobados reveals several who held more than one; some individuals were known to have possessed as many as fifteen or twenty. During the following decades, colonists and Jesuits vied for the sobados until finally, in 1607, the crown claimed authority over any sobadas who had submitted to Portuguese rule.[19]

Much like colonial governors' capacity both to enslave West Central Africans through warfare and to export them overseas, Portuguese subjugation of sobados enabled colonial expansion and provided enslaved people

---

1977), 23–38, 244–255. Figures for ships arriving and captives landed in the Spanish Americas are from David Wheat, "All Known Slaving Voyages to Spanish America, 1525–1640," an unpublished data set based on published sources and archival materials drawn primarily from the AGI.

18. Spanish Caribbean sources resoundingly confirm that "it was Mendes de Vasconcelos's campaigns that would flood the Spanish Indies with captives," as stated in Heywood and Thornton, *Central Africans*, 116. See also Heintze, "Angola nas garras," *RIEA*, no. 1 (January/June 1984), 21; Thornton, "African Experience," *WMQ*, LV (1998), 422–432; Wheat, "First Great Waves," *JAH*, LII (2011), 15, 18–19. Figures for voyages from Angola to the Spanish Americas are from Wheat, "All Known Slaving Voyages" (unpublished data set).

19. Amaral, *O consulado*, 225–237; Heintze, "Angolan Vassal Tributes," *RHES*, VI (1980), 11–60.

for transatlantic markets, regardless of whether initial profits accrued to Portuguese colonists, Jesuits, or the crown. Thus, during the governorship of Bento Banho Cardoso, following a Portuguese and Imbangala offensive against Ndongo in 1611, about eighty sobas were obliged to support the colonial Angolan state by providing slaves as a form of annual tribute. Likewise, campaigns led by Governor Mendes de Vasconcelos between 1617 and 1621 generated large numbers of captives for immediate export and also ensured a continual supply, with nearly two hundred sobas forced to become tribute-paying vassals. This aspect of slave production in Angola bore closer resemblance to repartimientos and encomiendas in Spanish America than to mechanisms for procuring coerced laborers in other regions of Atlantic Africa.[20]

Luanda Elites and the Spanish Caribbean

Contact between Angola and the Spanish Caribbean flourished during the first half of the seventeenth century, with Luanda colonists routinely participating in slaving voyages to the Caribbean as investors, passengers, and masters of their own slave ships. In this era of the Angola wave, when Luanda emerged as Atlantic Africa's foremost slaving port, the transatlantic trade to the Spanish Caribbean was just as robust as that to Brazil; the reports for the years 1624 to 1626 show near parity in the numbers of captives transported from Luanda to the Spanish and Portuguese empires. Strong maritime ties, based largely on the slave trade, connected Luanda to various Spanish Caribbean port cities. Although Luanda's upper echelons were most heavily implicated in this trade, the Portuguese and Luso-Africans who invested in trafficking slaves to the circum-Caribbean included a wide cross section of colonial Luanda society: government officials, ecclesiastical authorities, military leaders, notaries, lawyers, physicians, landowners, merchants, and other long-term residents. Angolan colonists' economic and physical presence in Caribbean ports reveals a common history shared by both regions during the Iberian Union. Angola's orientation toward the Caribbean points to the existence of a multilateral web of commercial associations linking Luanda to Iberia, São Tomé, the Canary Islands, Spanish

20. Heintze, "Angola nas garras," *RIEA*, no. 1 (January / June 1984), 15, 20–21. For discussion of Portuguese interest in developing some version of the Spanish encomienda system in their own colonies, see Sanjay Subrahmanyam, "Holding the World in Balance: The Connected Histories of the Iberian Overseas Empires, 1500–1640," *AHR*, CXII (2007), 1359–1385.

America, and Brazil, all founded on the transportation and sale of enslaved West Central Africans.[21]

Writing to his Lisbon-based employer, Luanda factor Francisco de Mar detailed a bustling slave trade in Angola during the years 1609 to 1611, often mentioning transatlantic slave ship captains and local merchants by name. Though he also dealt with other types of merchandise, de Mar was mainly involved in slave trafficking. His most important duty was to ensure that ship captains were able to procure captives at the best possible price and without excessive delay. He had difficulty simultaneously gathering enslaved Africans for multiple slaving voyages: "I cannot gather ten *piesas* (captives) for Antonio Luis, and another twelve for Pedro Fernandez, and . . . ten for Juan Vicente Carnero." All three hoped to depart Luanda within the following week, as did Enrique Freire, who "already has two hundred piesas." At least two of these men steered their ships toward the Spanish Caribbean. Evidently departing Luanda in late July 1609 as planned, Juan Vicente Carnero disembarked nearly two hundred captives in Veracruz two months later; Freire set sail for Cartagena, though his actual itinerary remains unknown.[22]

De Mar would have preferred to match ship captains with local slave merchants, but he apparently had trouble making such connections and was forced to procure captives himself. Luanda's residents, he wrote, "do not want to work for me." This helps to explain his colorful complaints about other merchants based in Luanda (such as, "His son is as fit for trading with white men as I am for the papacy"). Although de Mar does not appear to have been successful in forming local alliances, he clearly respected Senhora Isabel de Oliveira Corte Real, the widow of a Spanish *capitão-mor* (captain-major) in Angola. She was a "shrewd negotiator," he noted, who at one point cornered the entire Luanda slave market, buying up all the

21. From 1624 to 1626, according to Angola's governor, thirty-one ships transported 9,400 peças (captives) to "the Indies and other parts of Castile"; thirty-seven ships carried 7,933 peças toward Brazil; and eleven ships took 1,184 peças and *moleques* (younger captives) to São Tomé and Lisbon. See Cartas do gov. Fernão de Sousa e escrivão Estevão do Carvalhal, July 16–Dec. 31, 1626, AHU-Angola, cx. 2, n.103 and 108; Bowser, *African Slave in Colonial Peru,* 39; Heintze, "Angola nas garras," *RIEA,* no. 1 (January / June 1984), 33.

22. Francisco de Mar a Joan de Argomedo, July 23, 1609, AHU-Angola, cx.1, n.4A; Governador D. Manuel Pereira a João de Argomedo, Mar. 13, 1611, AHU-Angola, cx.1, n.13. Both of Francisco de Mar's letters are written in Spanish. For further information on the slaving voyages of Juan Vicente Carnero and Enrique Freire, see Vila Vilar, *Hispanoamérica,* 256–257; *Voyages,* accessed May 19, 2014, voyage 29877. In addition to salt and shell money (*zimbo*) used locally, commodities exported from Angola during the same period included various *panos* or textiles (*pintados, songas, exfulas, ensacas*), ivory, elephant tails (*xingas*), and dyewood (*tacula*); see Bento Banha Cardoso's "Informasão," Aug. 10, 1611, Brásio, *MMA* (1), VI, 18–20, "Alvitre de Pedro Sardinha," circa 1611, 52–56.

best captives available and promptly reselling them to slave ship captains—some of whom, presumably, were bound for ports in the Caribbean. The most successful slave merchants in Luanda, like Isabel de Oliveira, were able to draw on personal connections established through marriage and family networks, military service, and long periods of residence in Angola. Isabel de Oliveira must have acquired extensive contacts during her deceased husband's military career. Like their Spanish father, her sons were wealthy merchants, infantry captains, and landowners in Angola. By the 1620s, they served as Luanda city council members and magistrates, and all three married the daughters of high-ranking military officers (one of whom was also Spanish). De Oliveira's daughter married Gaspar Borges de Madureira, another landowner and infantry captain who eventually became captain-major of Angola himself. De Mar evidently had no such network of personal contacts in Luanda.[23]

Although slaving voyages from Luanda to the Spanish Caribbean often carried large numbers of captives owned by just one or two primary *armadores* (investors or voyage backers), factors and slave ship captains in Luanda also commonly acquired small lots of captives from multiple individuals. Jointly or separately, several Angolan colonists or officials could be stakeholders in a single slaving voyage. Some of these collaborative ventures involved the transportation of commodities in addition to forced migrants. The ship *Nuestra Señora del Espineyro* sailed from São Tomé to Riohacha and Cartagena in 1629 with sugar, cotton, and at least forty enslaved Africans. Most of the latter were owned by crew members, but the sugar belonged to the "governor of Angola" (at that time, Fernão de Sousa). Eight young captives described as *muleques* were sold in Riohacha on behalf of Father Bento Ferraz, vicar of Angola. Ferraz, who had previously been canon in Sergipe, in the See of Bahia, was also the ship's owner.[24]

23. Francisco de Mar a Joan de Argomedo, Apr. 22, 1611, AHU-Angola, cx.1, n.14; De Mar a De Argomedo, July 23, 1609, AHU-Angola, cx.1, n.4A, pliegos 2, 5. On Isabel de Oliveira Corte Real, her husband João de Vilória Pinto, sons Duarte Mendes de Oliveira, Francisco Vilória Pinto, and António Ribeiro Pinto, her daughter and son-in-law Gaspar Borges de Madureira, and the São Miguel and Bruto families (whose daughters married de Oliveira's sons), see Beatrix Heintze, with Maria Adélia de Carvalho Mendes, *Fontes para a história de Angola de século XVII*, I, *Memórias, relações e outros manuscritos da colectânea documental de Fernão de Sousa, 1622–1635* (Stuttgart, Germany, 1985), 76–77, 96–97, 100–101, 103–104, II, *Cartas e documentos oficiais da colectânea documental de Fernão de Sousa, 1624–1635* (Stuttgart, Germany, 1988), 57, 59, 91, 108, 135, 195, 210, 233–234, 297–298, 312, 358n–359n, 364–367, 369–375.

24. Caja de Cartagena, Cuentas de los años 1628 y 1629, AGI-Ctdra 1398, n.1, pliegos 94, 110–111 ("padre Benito Forraez bicario de Angola dueño del dho navio"); Heintze, *Fontes*, I, 88–89, 225, II, 199, 205n, 210n, 211, 213n, 254–256, 409.

In other cases of cooperation between Luanda colonists, each lot of captives transported on the same voyage could be financed in a different fashion. On December 24, 1599, before setting sail for Cuba, slave ship captain Gonzalo Prieto acquired groups of enslaved West Central Africans from several Luanda colonists and officials. Some of these captives were sent directly between factors on either side of the Atlantic; Antonio Enriques, probably working on behalf of *asentista* (asiento holder) Pedro Gomez Reynel, sent four captives to be delivered to Reynel's factor in Havana. Slave sales in Luanda more typically involved transfers of currency or credit. In the latter case, monies owed to Luanda slave vendors could be deposited with factors in the Caribbean after the captives had been sold. At the time of his departure from Luanda, Prieto owed 380,000 *reis* to Juan Gomez, *"vecino* [permanent resident] of Angola," who sold him fifteen enslaved Africans. In January 1601, some nine months after his arrival in Cuba, Prieto settled this debt by paying the equivalent value (9,500 Castilian *reales*) to the slave trade factor in Havana. Thus, Luanda residents participated in diffuse slaving networks, splitting the risks and profits with one another and with slave ship crews. One way or another, all could expect to eventually receive shares of income generated by slave sales in Spanish Caribbean ports.[25]

Prieto's voyage from Luanda to Havana at the dawn of the seventeenth century also illustrates how slave trafficking reinforced both Portugal's colonization of Angola and Spain's colonization of the Caribbean at the same time that it enriched those who invested in the trade. Among the various residents of Luanda who had stakes in this voyage, royally appointed slave trade factor Antonio Machado entrusted Prieto with eight captives to be transported on behalf of the crown. As royal slaves in Havana, these individuals would almost certainly work on the city's fortifications and on other projects deemed important by royal officials in Cuba. Another Luanda resident named Gaspar Álvares supplied Prieto with at least ten of the captives he would transport to Havana. Originally from Lisbon, Álvares was described by one of Angola's governors as "the greatest merchant that is or [ever] will be in this Ethiopia." In addition to renting out houses and slave barracoons, Álvares collected taxes on captives exported from Luanda,

25. Cartas de pago y recibos otorgados por Antonio Gonzalez mercader y Gonzalo Prieto, Jan. 27, 1601, ANC-PN (Regueyra/J. B. Guilisasti), mfn 68066806–68116811; Vila Vilar, *Hispanoamérica,* 254–255. On factor Antonio Gonzalez, who operated a "public store" in Havana and was authorized to confiscate captives brought illegally from São Tomé or Angola, see Oficiales reales a S. M., Aug. 4, 1597, AGI-SD 118, r.5, n.238; Georges Scelle, *La traite négrière aux Indes de Castille, contrats et traités d'assiento* (Paris, 1906), 381.

applying the funds to public works. Complementing West Central Africans' labor, the tax revenues generated by their passage from one port to another shored up defenses and infrastructure in both Luanda and in Spanish Caribbean settlements alike.[26]

In collaboration with other Luanda elites, government officials ensured that Portuguese colonial rule and territorial expansion went hand in hand with slave production. Angola's governors in particular fomented wars to produce captives, all the while participating in the slave traffic themselves, including the slave trade "from the Kingdom of Angola to the Indies of Castile." As they established contacts with local merchants, long-term residents, factors, and slave ship captains, governors and administrators in Luanda inserted themselves into the very networks of trust and information that made the slave trade possible. The double motives of Angolan authorities during the early seventeenth century were obvious. Most famously, João Rodrigues Coutinho successfully obtained an asiento with the Spanish crown to supply slaves to the Americas at the same time he served as governor of Angola (1602–1603). As governor, he would receive thirteen *ducados* for each captive exported from Luanda; as asentista, he was entitled to another twenty-seven ducados for each captive disembarked in the Americas. Although his tenure as governor was brief, Rodrigues Coutinho managed to use his position, and the connections that it facilitated, as a vehicle for his own personal enrichment and that of his family and associates through the transatlantic slave trade.[27]

One of Rodrigues Coutinho's successors, João Correia de Sousa, was another governor who exploited his position to generate captives for export to the Americas. As governor of Angola from 1621 to 1623, Correia de Sousa is perhaps best known for establishing diplomatic relations with Queen Nzinga. Despite the disapproval of other Luanda officials, he openly waged war against nearby Cassanze in late 1622, acquiring "a great quantity" of captives, including "sobas" and "free blacks." Some of the illegally enslaved captives were sent to Brazil, while the governor himself, to escape punish-

26. Cartas de pago y recibos otorgados por Antonio Gonzalez mercader y Gonzalo Prieto, Jan. 27, 1601, ANC-PN (Regueyra / J. B. Guilisasti), mfn 68076807, 68106810; Heintze, *Fontes*, I, 69, 267, II, 151–152, 387; Alencastro, *O trato*, 106. For a list of sixteen newly purchased royal slaves described as "Angola[s]" in Havana three decades later—each branded on the right side of their chest with a crown ("marcados todos con la Corona en la tetilla derecha")—see "Lista por abecedario de los esclavos y forzados, 1636–1638," Dec. 20, 1638, AGI-Ctdra 1118, n.2 (A), pliegos 3–4.

27. Amaral, *O consulado*, 201–202; Scelle, *La traite négrière*, 383–391, 811–812; Frédéric Mauro, *Le Portugal et l'Atlantique au XVIIe siècle, 1570–1670: Étude économique* (Paris, 1960), 157–162; Vila Vilar, *Hispanoamérica*, 38–42, 106–108; Alencastro, *O trato*, 80–81. Although João Rodrigues Coutinho's asiento was supposed to last from 1601 until 1609, he fell ill and died in Angola in July 1603.

ment, abruptly abdicated his duties and fled the colony in early 1623. He was accompanied by an official *(ouvidor)* and an unspecified number of slaves.[28]

Though the early stages of his transatlantic voyage are unclear, Correia de Sousa sailed from Luanda, or perhaps São Tomé, to Cartagena de Indias and from there to Spain. As a passenger on a slave ship, he would have had the opportunity to bring at least a small group of captives to sell in the Caribbean en route to Spain or Portugal. He probably stood to make greater profits on the larger numbers of enslaved West Central Africans he sent to Brazil but would have had to wait longer to receive payment; slave sales in Cartagena were much more likely to involve the exchange of currency or precious metals—that is, *plata corriente* (common or unassayed silver)—as opposed to credit. In Cartagena, he booked passage on the galleon *San Antonio,* which would stop in Havana en route to Seville. As the ship's captain later testified, Correia de Sousa was an elite passenger who appeared to be a loyal servant of the crown, traveling to Iberia to report on his governorship in Angola. Before leaving Havana, Correia de Sousa evidently spoke with the city's governor, urging him to arrest "a magistrate from Angola" who happened to be in Havana at the time. (Presumably the magistrate was among those who had objected to Correia de Sousa's invasion of Cassanze). The *San Antonio* reached Sanlúcar de Barrameda, on the southwestern coast of Spain, on May 22, 1624; in the middle of the night, an oared boat pulled alongside the galleon. Leaving behind his personal slaves and servants—including two black midgets, an albino, and an "Indian woman who says she is free"—Correia de Sousa escaped with most of his possessions. After crossing the Atlantic twice, sailing from Luanda to the Caribbean to the mouth of the Guadalquivir, he quietly stepped ashore on the beach at Huelva and disappeared from the historical record. No less than his chance encounter with an adversary in Havana, Correia de Sousa's multistage voyage illustrates the interconnectedness of Iberian Atlantic seaports during the early seventeenth century and the geographical mobility that slaving circuits afforded to officials, merchants, and mariners alike.[29]

28. Heywood and Thornton, *Central Africans,* 156–157, 197; Cartas sobre "João Corea de Sousa governador que foy do reino de Angola," 1623–1624, AHU-Angola, cx.2, ns.13–15, 18, 20 ("muita quantidade de escravos"), 27 ("sovas e negros livres"); Heintze, "Angola nas garras," *RIEA,* no. 1 (January/June 1984), 22–24; Amaral, *O consulado,* 121–125.

29. "Proceso criminal . . . sobre la fuga de Juan Correa de Sossa governador de Angola," 1624, AGI-Esc 1080A, n.5. Though several of his accomplices were fined or jailed, according to this Spanish source Correia de Sousa was never apprehended; the case remained unresolved in 1639. For a rather different outcome, see Alencastro, *O trato,* 106 ("upon disembarking in Lisbon, the governor was imprisoned, and died in chains"). On the accumulation and exchange of precious metals in Cartagena, see Antonino Vidal Ortega, *Cartagena de Indias y la región histórica del Caribe, 1580–1640* (Seville, 2002),

Angolan colonist Garcia Mendes de Castelo Branco perhaps best exemplifies the integrated enterprises of colonial administration, self-aggrandizement, and the pursuit of commercial interests. As a leading participant in the initial Portuguese conquest of Angola, Castelo Branco undoubtedly appropriated one or more sobados. Arriving with Angola's first governor in 1575, Castelo Branco lived in Angola for forty-six years, holding various military titles and serving as a judge in Luanda. Drawing on insights gleaned from his long residence in the colony, by 1620, he had gathered chorographical information and formulated plans for strengthening Iberian rule in Angola that, if enacted, would also benefit himself. He appeared before the Spanish crown in Madrid that year with several reports containing detailed descriptions of West Central Africa's flora, fauna, geography, and political structures. He also proposed to "free" roughly two hundred sobas from crown authority by allotting them as before to Portuguese overseers, who would make annual payments in exchange for this privilege. At the same time, he offered to finance and supervise construction of a fortress in Anzele, between the Cuanza and Bengo Rivers several leagues inland, to better defend Luanda. In return, he requested that the crown "give me the soba Caculo Quehacango, with all his clan" to be held in perpetuity by him and his heirs. This soba, he noted, had authority in the region where the proposed fort would be built. These plans never came to fruition, since Castelo Branco died in Angola shortly after his return in 1621. However, he had found other ways to profit from his time residing in the slave-trading entrepôt of Luanda.[30]

Though his own writings neglect to address his maritime enterprises, Castelo Branco traveled to the Caribbean as a slave ship captain at least three times before his death in 1621. His first known slaving voyage took place in 1599 (though his probable absence from Luanda in 1587 invites further speculation). As registered shipmaster of the slave ship *Nuestra Señora del Rosario,* he must have been aboard the vessel when it departed Lisbon, sailing toward Luanda. After embarking an unknown number of enslaved

59–68. For further discussion of trans-imperial maritime travel during the Iberian Union, see David Wheat, "Global Transit Points and Travel in the Iberian Maritime World, 1580–1640," in Peter C. Mancall and Carole Shammas, eds., *Governing the Sea in the Early Modern Era: Essays in Honor of Robert C. Ritchie* (San Marino, Calif., 2015), 253–274.

30. "Relação de Garcia Mendes Castelo Branco," Jan. 1, 1620, Brásio, *MMA* (1), VI, 437–478; Heintze, *Fontes,* I, 82, 146, 265; Amaral, *O consulado,* 21–22, 74–75, 92, 108–117, 126–128, 227–228; 243–247; Heintze, "Angolan Vassal Tributes," *RHES,* VI (1980), 62. Though his name does not appear in the 1587 list of colonists awarded sobados, Amaral notes that Castelo Branco's absence from the list is strange and suggests that he was one of two people who controlled sobados but were not present when the list was composed (227–228).

West Central Africans, the vessel crossed the Atlantic only to wreck near Riohacha, where some captives appear to have drowned—though they might have been clandestinely set ashore. After the shipwreck, 226 captives were transported to Cartagena on smaller frigates. More than a decade later, "Garciméndez de Castellobranco" reappears in Spanish Caribbean sources as captain of the slave ship *San Agustín,* sailing from Angola toward Veracruz. As in his previous voyage, the ship allegedly wrecked in Havana, where six Africans were sold. Upon arriving in Veracruz in late 1612, only 94 captives disembarked, though at least 160 had boarded in Angola. Some had been concealed; the *San Agustín* landed additional captives in Jamaica two months later in January 1613, including 50 subsequently transported from Jamaica back to Havana for resale. Five years later, "Garci Méndez Castello Branco" made a third slaving voyage, this time on the ship *Santa Catalina.* Departing from Luanda with 189 captives onboard, the ship landed only 140 in Veracruz in 1618; royal officials reported that 49 had died during the voyage. If this voyage resembled the previous two, however, it seems likely that one-fourth of the ship's captives were sold elsewhere rather than dying at sea. Though many details of this 1618 voyage remain unknown, clearly this was an intermediate stage in a roughly circular route that took Castelo Branco from Angola to Lisbon and back with authorization to undertake a slaving voyage; from Luanda to Veracruz with slaves; from Veracruz to Madrid, where he gave his reports to the Spanish crown in 1620; and from Madrid back to Angola, where he died soon afterward.[31]

Castelo Branco was not the only Luanda elite to personally transport captives to the Caribbean during the early seventeenth century. Paio de Araújo de Azevedo, another member of Luanda's elite, traveled to the Spanish Caribbean under similar circumstances. Arriving in Angola in approximately 1602, Azevedo went on to exercise a variety of military and administrative positions in the Portuguese colony over the following four decades (cavalry captain, auditor, judge, and landowner) and was described by governor Fernão de Sousa at one point as "the most honorable *morador* [inhabitant] of Luanda." As capitão-mor, Azevedo led the Portuguese campaign against Queen Nzinga in 1628 and succeeded in capturing two of her

---

31. Lapeyre, "Le trafic négrier," in *Homenaje a Jaime Vicens Vives,* II, 294–295; Vila Vilar, *Hispanoamérica,* 248–249, 258–261; Proceso contra Pedro Navarro, 1613, AGI-Esc 38B, pieza 2, fols. 427r–427v. Like many other Iberian slaving voyages that wrecked or ran aground at sites far from their registered destinations, Castelo Branco's shipwrecks in 1599 and circa 1612 incurred the suspicion of royal officials but provided a reasonable excuse for stopping in an unauthorized port—probably to disembark unregistered slaves and passengers—before resuming his journey.

sisters the following year. In 1617, ship master Antonio Bravo sailed from Iberia to Angola, ostensibly bound for New Spain. Most of the West Central Africans he took aboard his ship in Luanda were supplied by none other than "Pedro Araujo de Azevedo, captain-major of the cavalry of the kingdoms of Angola." Perhaps intending to safeguard his investment, Azevedo embarked on the ship as well and was present when it arrived in Española (allegedly blown off course) with more than two hundred captives onboard. Although royal officials temporarily detained Azevedo, Bravo continued on to Cartagena with more than ninety captives on a second caravel that wrecked near the mouth of the Magdalena River. The whole affair resulted in an extensive investigation—more than one thousand pages of legal wrangling and testimonies—conducted in both Santo Domingo and Cartagena.[32]

Several captains and passengers on slave ships arriving in the Spanish Caribbean were *procuradores* (lawyers or representatives) in Luanda. Appointed procurador in Angola in 1624, *licenciado* (licenciate) João Mendes de Carvalho was master of a ship that disembarked at least 135 captives in Santo Domingo in 1626. Although procurador Fernando Barbosa represented Angola's governor Fernão de Sousa in the early 1630s, he had previously embarked enslaved West Central Africans on a slave ship bound for Cartagena, taking part in the voyage himself as a passenger. A third Luanda procurador named Gonçalo Nunes de Sepulveda had also been a slave trade factor; some sources indicate that he died in Luanda, with his widow taking over his position as the local representative for a metropolitan asiento holder. Yet, other sources suggest that Sepulveda actually moved to Madrid in the late 1620s, eventually becoming one of several Portuguese New Christian bankers who served the Spanish crown. The procurador / slave trade factor and royal banker might have been the same person. According to Cartagena officials, a man identified as "Gonçalo Nuñez de Sepulveda" arrived in the port in September 1628 as master of the ship *Nuestra Señora de Buen Viaje,* disembarking at least 170 captives. At roughly the same time he was alleged to have died in Luanda, Sepulveda might have sailed to Cartagena, then Madrid. For procuradores like Sepulveda, transatlantic slaving circuits passing through the Spanish Caribbean presented opportunities for both

32. Heintze, *Fontes,* I, 73–74, II, 133, 140, 200–207, 217, 230–236, 243, 282–288, 306–314, 365. As with Castelo Branco, Spanish Caribbean sources add a new dimension to Azevedo's career as a leading colonist in Angola; see "Benito Jimenez guarda mayor . . . sobre el descamino de negros esclavos," 1617, AGN-FNE, Bolívar 7, hojas 1r–550v; Oficiales reales a S. M., Aug. 17, 1618, AGI-SF 73, n.37, fol. 1v; "Certificaçion de los negros que han entrado en Cartaxena," Mar. 28, 1623, AGI-SF 74, n.6, fol. 6v; Vila Vilar, *Hispanoamérica,* 171n.

Table 3 Luanda Elites and Colonists as Slave Merchants in Spanish American Ports, circa 1600–1640

Name	Years active in Angola	Social rank or occupation in Angola	Date(s) of arrival in Spanish America	Port(s) of disembarkation	Role or rank aboard ship	Captives disembarked
Garcia Mendes de Castelo Branco	1575–1621	*fidalgo*, lieutenant, captain-major, judge, etc.	1599	Riohacha / Cartagena	shipmaster	226
			1612–1613	Havana / Veracruz / Jamaica	shipmaster	150
			1618	Veracruz	shipmaster	140
Baltazar Rodrigues Serpa	?–1619	captain, factor (mines)	1605	Buenos Aires	shipowner, captain	278
			1617	Cartagena	shipmaster	24
Miguel de Horta	1584–circa 1617	merchant	1613	Puerto Rico	shipmaster	—
			1622	Santo Domingo	shipmaster	—
Manuel Castaño	1620s	landowner	1616	Cartagena	shipmaster	25
Paio de Araújo de Azevedo	1602–1640s	captain-major, judge, cavalry captain, etc.	1617	Santo Domingo	*armador*, passenger	250
João Mendes de Carvalho	1620s	legal representative	1626	Santo Domingo	shipmaster	135
Gonçalo Nunes de Sepulveda	1600s–circa 1626	slave trade factor	1628	Cartagena	shipmaster	170

Roque Camelo	1620s	landowner	Havana	1628	passenger	25
Francisco Barbosa	1630s	legal representative	Cartagena	1630	*cargador*, passenger	15
Gaspar de Matos	1620s	physician	Cartagena	1638	shipmaster	61

Sources: Brásio, *MMA* (1), VI, 437–478; Beatrix Heintze, with Maria Adélia de Carvalho Mendes, *Fontes para a história de Angola de século XVII*, I, *Memórias, relações, e outros manuscritos da colectânea documental de Fernão de Sousa, 1622–1635* (Stuttgart, Germany, 1985) I, 73–75, 79, 81–82, 98, 106, 140, 146, 265, 362, II, *Cartas e documentos oficiais da colectânea documental de Fernão de Sousa, 1624–1635* (Stuttgart, Germany, 1988), II, 60, 97, 120, 133, 140, 148, 160, 200–207, 210, 214, 217, 230–236, 243, 282–288, 297, 306–314, 334, 355–356, 365–366, 371; Heintze, "The Angolan Vassal Tributes of the 17th Century," *RHES*, VI (1980), 62; José Gonçalves Salvador, *Os magnatas do tráfico negreiro: Séculos XVI e XVII* (São Paulo, Brazil, 1981), 42, 74, 101, 131; Henri Lapeyre, "Le trafic négrier avec l'amérique espagnole," in *Homenaje a Jaime Vicens Vives* (Barcelona, 1967), II, 294–295; Enriqueta Vila Vilar, *Hispanoamérica y el comercio de esclavos: Los asientos portugueses* (Seville, 1977), 171n, 248–249, 258–261, 270–275, 278–279; Ilídio do Amaral, *O consulado de Paulo Dias de Novais: Angola no último quartel do século XVI e primeiro do século XVII* (Lisbon, 2000), 21–22, 74–75, 92, 108–117, 126–128, 227–228, 243–247; Proceso contra Pedro Navarro, 1613, AGI-Esc 38B, pieza 2, fols. 427r–427v; "Benito Jimenez guarda mayor . . . sobre el descamino de negros esclavos," 1617, AGN-FNE, Bolívar 7, hojas 1r–55ov; Oficiales reales a S. M., Aug. 17, 1618, AGI-SF 73, fol. 1v; "Certificaçion de los negros que han entrado en Cartaxena," Mar. 28, 1623, AGI-SF 74, n.6, fol. 6v; Caja de Santo Domingo, Relación de los oficiales reales, 1624–1629, AGI-Ctdra 1057, n.1, fols. 20v–21r; Caja de Cartagena, Cuentas, AGI-Ctdra 1397, n.3 (1627–1628), pliegos 28, 30; Caja de Cartagena, Cuentas, AGI-Ctdra 1397, n.5 (1630–1631), pliegos 29–30; "Relaçion y abecedario de los estrangeros que se hallaron en la çiudad de Cartagena, 1630," May 13, 1631, AGI-SF 56B, n.73a, fols. 9v–10r; "Certificazion de los esclavos que entraron en Buenos Ayres desde el año de 97 asta el de 607," June 12, 1682, AGI-Charcas 123, s/n, fols. 13v–14r; "Certificaçion de los negros que han entrado en Cartaxena," Mar. 28, 1623, AGI-SF 74, n.6, fols. 3r–3v, 17v–18r; "Autos sobre la arribada del navío San Pedro," 1628–1631, AGI-SD 119, s/n; *Voyages*, accessed May 19, 2014, voyages 28129, 28131, 28154, 29369, 29388, 29437, 29473, 29568, 29579.

Note: A slave voyage *cargador*—often a resident of an African port—acquired captives to be embarked on the slave ship before its departure from the African coast. A slave ship *armador* might also provide captives but played a more important role as financial backer or organizer of the entire voyage. Rather than serving as crew members, neither cargadores nor armadores necessarily traveled aboard slave ships; when they did, it was typically as passengers overseeing their investments.

geographical mobility and for socioeconomic advancement in Luanda and beyond.[33]

Slaving voyages made by other Luanda colonists further attest to the regularity of commercial ties between Angola and the Spanish Caribbean during the early seventeenth century. Originally from Spain, the merchant Miguel de Horta moved to Angola in 1584 and resided there for more than three decades; he appeared in the Spanish Caribbean as the *maestre* (ship master or cargo master) of slave ships arriving in Puerto Rico and Santo Domingo in 1613 and 1622. In Angola, Baltazar Rodrigues Serpa was a military captain and factor who oversaw copper mines; before his death in 1619, he made at least one voyage to Buenos Aires as the owner and captain of a slave ship in 1605 and another voyage to Cartagena in 1617 as a slave ship maestre. A notary or scribe in Luanda during the 1620s, Sebastião de Carvalho had previously transported enslaved Africans to Veracruz; as late as 1621, residents of the Gulf coast port were still making payments for captives purchased from "captain Sebastián de Carballo" and an associate, both described as "vecinos of Angola." Other Angola colonists known to have participated in slaving voyages to the Caribbean include Angola landowners Manuel Castaño (slave ship captain, Cartagena, 1616) and Roque Camelo (slave ship passenger, Havana, 1628). Licenciado Gaspar de Matos, a physician who had studied medicine in Salamanca and Coimbra, was also a landowner in Angola. Though he initially begged to be excused from such duties, in 1628, Governor Fernão de Sousa compelled him to travel to Benguela to minister to the needs of wounded Portuguese soldiers. A decade later, Matos surfaced in Cartagena as maestre of the slave ship *Nuestra Señora de los Remedios y San Antonio,* recently arrived from Angola.[34]

33. Heintze, *Fontes,* I, 75, 81, 106, II, 60, 97, 120, 160, 210, 214, 334, 355–356; Caja de Santo Domingo, Relación de los oficiales reales, 1624–1629, AGI-Ctdra 1057, n.1, fols. 20v–21r; Caja de Cartagena, Cuentas, AGI-Ctdra 1397, n.3 (1627–1628), pliegos 28, 30; Caja de Cartagena, Cuentas, AGI-Ctdra 1397, n.5 (1630–1631), pliegos 29–30; "Relaçion y abecedario de los estrangeros," May 13, 1631, AGI-SF 56B, n.73a, fols. 9v–10r; Vila Vilar, *Hispanoamérica,* 270–273, 278–279; James C. Boyajian, *Portuguese Bankers at the Court of Spain, 1626–1650* (New Brunswick, N.J., 1983), 51–53, 114; Alencastro, *O trato,* 82; *Voyages,* accessed May 19, 2014, voyages 29369, 29388, 29473, 40690.

34. Heintze, *Fontes,* I, 79, 98, 140, 146, 265, 292, 313, 362, II, 148, 297, 365–366, 371; "Certificazion de los esclavos que entraron en Buenos Ayres desde el año de 97 asta el de 607," June 12, 1682, AGI-Charcas 123, s/n, fols. 13v–14r; "Certificaçion de los negros que han entrado en Cartaxena," Mar. 28, 1623, AGI-SF 74, n.6, fols. 3r–3v, 17v–18r; Obligación de Francisco Hernández de la Higuera, Aug. 6, 1621, ANUV protocolos, años 1617–1631, n.5, fols. 347–347v (clave: 27_1617_2876), accessed Aug. 20, 2013, http://www.uv.mx/bnotarial/; "Autos sobre la arribada del navío San Pedro," 1628–1631, AGI-SD 119, s/n; José Gonçalves Salvador, *Os magnatas do tráfico negreiro: Séculos XVI e XVII* (São Paulo, Brazil, 1981), 42, 74, 101, 131; Vila Vilar, *Hispanoamérica,* 274–275; *Voyages,* accessed Aug. 20, 2013, voyages 28129, 28131, 28154, 29437, 29521, 29568, 29579. Several slave ship masters arriving in Cartagena in 1598–1599 (Gaspar Manso, Francisco de Acuña, Prospero Diaz Lobo, Duarte Lopez, Juan Gallego, and

These extensive connections between Luanda and port cities such as Havana, Cartagena, and Santo Domingo provide information on who was being enslaved and exported (or not) from Angola and thus a fuller understanding of the roles played by West Central Africans in early-seventeenth-century Spanish Caribbean society. Although slave ships commonly disembarked "males and females, children and adults" (*varones y hembras, chicos y grandes*), women and particularly children often comprised a surprisingly large percentage of forced migrants arriving from Angola. During the late sixteenth and early seventeenth centuries, therefore, the Spanish Caribbean's diverse African-born population probably included a disproportionate number of West Central African children.[35]

In terms of sex and age, the structure of forced migration from Angola presents a notable contrast with known slave traffic from Upper Guinea. If, by the 1570s, captives exported from Upper Guinea to the Spanish Caribbean were predominantly adult males (for example two-thirds males and two-thirds to three-fourths adults), then a third slaving voyage during the same period contradicts this pattern. Departing from São Tomé, the ship *San Antonio* arrived in Española in late 1575. Royal officials accused pilot and owner Francisco Rebolo of transporting captives with no registration other than licenses that had already been used for an earlier voyage. Their subsequent investigation produced a list of 243 captives disembarked from the *San Antonio* and sold in Santo Domingo between December 1575 and mid-1576. These slave sales described each captive in gender-specific terms that reflect their approximate age. Though the vessel's African port of

Alvaro Nuñez de Acosta) were also each described as a "vezino del rreyno de Angola"; see El fiscal con Juan Rodrigues Coutinho, 1602, AGI-Esc 1012A, pieza 5, fols. 28r–28v, 29v, 34r; *Voyages*, accessed May 19, 2014, voyages 29071, 29073, 29074, 29079, 29081, 29113.

35. Women and children also figured prominently among those enslaved in West Central Africa during the eighteenth century, but, with the exception of older, male children—who constituted an increasingly large segment of captives exported overseas—they were usually retained for local markets; see Miller, *Way of Death*, xii–xiii, 67n, 99, 346–348, 387–389, 566–567, 666; David Eltis, *The Rise of African Slavery in the Americas* (Cambridge, 2000), 285–292. For evidence that slavers evaded taxes in Angola during the late 1600s by claiming that adults were children, see Caldeira, "Angola and the Seventeenth-Century South Atlantic Slave Trade," in Richardson and Rebeiro da Silva, eds., *Networks and Trans-Cultural Exchange*, 132. In the early Spanish Caribbean, this ploy would have required the collusion of officials responsible for evaluating captives upon arrival. However, several voyages from Angola arrived with large numbers of children before the enactment of legislation exempting them from taxation. For similarly large percentages of women and children among West Central African captives arriving in Buenos Aires, see Schultz, "'The Kingdom of Angola,'" *SA*, XXXVI (2015), 424–444.

departure was São Tomé, all but a handful were "from the Angola land." Unlike contemporary voyages from the Cape Verde Islands and Buguendo that disembarked "a third part females," nearly half of these West Central African forced migrants—about 42 percent—were females. Furthermore, adolescents and children comprised roughly one-third of the captives. One black boy (*negrito muchacho*) was said to have been between twelve and fourteen years old, and a *negrita* was estimated at ten years old. If these terms were used consistently, the *San Antonio* disembarked no less than 50 ten-year-old children described as negritos or negritas, evenly split between males and females. Eleven were listed as muchachos or *muchachas* (approximately twelve to fourteen years old), and 13 captives were smaller children described as *negrillos* or *negrillas*. Including 1 infant (*criatura*) and 1 adolescent girl (*moça*), these 76 child captives comprised 31 percent of all captives on board the *San Antonio*. No known voyage from Upper Guinea during the sixteenth or seventeenth centuries features a comparable percentage of child captives.[36]

Though multiple factors surely influenced the sex and age distribution of captives exported to the Spanish Caribbean, no single external factor adequately explains the apparent long-term trend toward the sale of children from Luanda. Buyer preference and metropolitan legislation might have influenced the composition of Upper Guinean and West Central African slave exports, particularly for those departing from the Cape Verde Islands or São Tomé. Voyages departing from these bulking centers conceivably drew on multiple shipments of captives, perhaps supplemented by very small numbers of locally born creoles. To the extent that slave merchants could select captives for reexport from slave trade hubs, captives on voyages arriving from São Tomé or the Cape Verde Islands might not accurately reflect the age or sex structure of enslaved Africans brought from the mainland. This could explain, for example, why virtually every captive transported from the Cape Verde Islands to Havana on the *San Pedro* in 1572

36. Proceso contra Francisco Rebolo, 1578–1590, AGI-Esc 1A, pieza 4, fols. 274v–327r. See also "Las quentas que se thomaron," 1575, AGI-Ctdra 1052, n.1 (1575), fols. 13r, 32r–33r; "Quentas del año de 1577," AGI-Ctdra 1052, n.1 (1577), fol. 18v. Sixteenth-century Iberian slave trade legislation frequently specified ideal sex ratios of captives to be embarked; beginning in the 1560s, the ratio was nearly always two-thirds males and "a third part females" (*la tercia parte hembras*); see Scelle, *La traite négrière*, 223, 773, 780–781, 785, 795. For analysis of two ships sailing from Arguim to Lisbon in 1510 and 1514, in which more than half the captives on both ships were women and one-fifth were eighteen years old or younger, see António de Almeida Mendes, "Portugal e o tráfico de escravos na primeira metade do séc. XVI," *Africana Studia*, no. 7 (December 2004), 13–30; Mendes, "Child Slaves in the Early North Atlantic Trade in the Fifteenth and Sixteenth Centuries," in Gwyn Campbell, Suzanne Miers, Joseph C. Miller, eds., *Children in Slavery through the Ages* (Athens, Oh., 2009), 19–34.

was eighteen or older while almost a quarter of the captives transported from Buguendo to Española on the *San Jorge* in 1575 were adolescents and children (though most were listed as either *moços* or muchachos, probably between the ages of roughly twelve and eighteen years old). Yet, the ages and sexes of West Central Africans sold in the Caribbean were perhaps not determined by their buyers anyway; Iberian contemporaries regularly categorized captives from Upper Guinea as "top quality" (*de ley*) and those from Angola as "the worst"; their respective age upon arrival might have been one of the factors contributing to this stereotype.[37]

More than any external factor, transformations in the nature of warfare and slave production in West Central Africa were primarily responsible for the enslavement and sale of large numbers of women and children to transatlantic markets during the early seventeenth century. When Portuguese and Luso-African merchants based in São Tomé purchased captives from the ngola of Ndongo in the 1570s, they most likely acquired war captives and individuals who had been judicially enslaved. But slave production in the region transformed rapidly with the onset and escalation of violence between Ndongo and the Portuguese colony of Angola, resulting in as many as fifty thousand captives exported from Luanda between 1579 and 1592. During the early seventeenth century, Portuguese and Imbangala campaigns involved all-out military assaults on towns, as opposed to isolated raids. In cases such as Correia de Sousa's war against Cassanze, entire communities were subject to capture, and those least able to flee their homes ran the greatest risk of being enslaved.

The scale of warfare between massed armies—sometimes including tens of thousands of combatants on both sides—was a second major aspect of conflict in seventeenth-century Angola that contributed to the enslavement of large numbers of women and children. Baggage trains, or *kikumba,* composed of women, conscripts, and other noncombatants who transported the foodstuffs and provisions necessary to sustain large armies, were among the

37. For Upper Guinean captives disembarked from the *San Pedro* and the *San Jorge,* see "Relación de los ciento y noventa y un esclavos de su magestad," Nov. 3, 1572, AGI-Ctdra 1174, n.6, fols. 12v–16r; "Contratadores de Cabo Verde y Guinea con Cristóbal Cayado y otros del reino de Portugal," 1582–1589, AGI-Esc 2A, pieza 2, fols. 493v–498r; Table 1. On captives from Angola being described as inferior to Upper Guineans, see, for example, "Diego de Azambuja, vecino de Lisboa, con Juan de Tejeda, governador de La Habana," 1598–1603, AGI-Esc 1011B, fol. 75v; Carta de Miguel Corcuera y Baltasar Pérez, June 27, 1622, AGI-SF 52, n.172a, fols. 1r, 5r. Another factor that surely influenced Iberian evaluations of West Central African captives stemmed from their poorer physical condition after having traveled a greater distance; see Vila Vilar, *Hispanoamérica,* 137, 147–153; Linda A. Newson and Susie Minchin, *From Capture to Sale: The Portuguese Slave Trade to Spanish South America in the Early Seventeenth Century* (Leiden, 2007), 29, 82, 103, 106–110.

most desirable spoils of war. If soldiers were defeated or fled to regroup, leaving their baggage train defenseless, then large numbers of women and children could be enslaved en masse. Routed armies sometimes even sought to minimize their losses by abandoning their baggage train to be looted—and soldiers' wives and children to be enslaved—while they escaped.[38]

Imbangala mercenaries' military organization and social practices probably further contributed to the export of large numbers of women and children from West Central Africa. Portuguese described Imbangala bands as cannibals, "enemies of all living things," and "thieves in any land they enter." In 1617, one of Angola's governors wrote that the Imbangala had been used like "dogs of war" to generate captives. During this era, the Imbangala were not yet an ethnic group; according to an account attributed to Andrew Battell—an English sailor who spent more than a year among one Imbangala group in 1600 and 1601—the Imbangala were a multiethnic group who killed ("buried quick") any children born to women in their camps. Rather than reproducing naturally, Imbangala bands grew exponentially by capturing or recruiting, and then training, adolescent captives or young adults. Initially numbering only around five hundred people, within less than two years the Imbangala band that Battell joined had grown in size to sixteen thousand people, by his estimation.[39]

Yet, the relative numbers of adolescents in their early teens incorporated by the Imbangala, as opposed to twenty-year-old adults, are not clear. Nor are the disproportionate ratios of male to female captives taken: did the sixteen thousand Imbangala mentioned by Battell really include only "fourteen or fifteen women"? Or only "fourteen or fifteen women" whom he considered "natural" Imbangalas? These expansive Imbangala groups took thousands of captives who would be either killed, incorporated, or sold. Even Imbangala bands that never allied with the Portuguese sold war captives to Luanda-based merchants. If the Imbangala primarily absorbed young men, it stands to reason that most captives they sold to the Portuguese included significant numbers of women and small children. That the

38. John Thornton's work clearly demonstrates the logistical and tactical importance of baggage trains. See Heywood and Thornton, *Central Africans*, 78, 95; John K. Thornton, "The Art of War in Angola, 1575–1680," *Comparative Studies in Society and History*, XXX (1988), 370–371. See also Thornton's discussion of noncombatant roles in Thornton, "African Experience," *WMQ*, LV (1998), 429–431; Thornton, *Warfare in Atlantic Africa*, 119–120.

39. "Carta do governador de Angola a El-Rei," Aug. 28, 1617, in Brásio, *MMA* (1), VI, 283–285; E. G. Ravenstein, ed., *The Strange Adventures of Andrew Battell of Leigh, in Angola and the Adjoining Regions* (1625) (London, 1901), 32; Thornton, "African Experience," *WMQ*, LV (1998), 426; Heintze, "Extraordinary Journey," trans. Rieck, *HA*, XXXIV (2007), 78.

Imbangala retained captives they deemed most promising for their own purposes further explains why the West Central Africans disembarked in the Spanish Caribbean during the same period were regularly described by Iberians as "the worst."[40]

Although Portuguese administrators and clerics rarely referred specifically to the enslavement of women or children in West Central Africa, captives arriving in the Spanish Caribbean from Angola definitively included both women and children. The forced migration of children is especially evident. During the late 1610s and early 1620s, slaving voyages from Angola commonly included large numbers of children described as muleques, muchachos, and *crías de pecho* (nursing infants). Of the 173 captives Azevedo embarked at the outset of his 1617 voyage to Santo Domingo, 42 were identified as muleques, including more than 30 children between the ages of five and nine years old. Children were even more prominent on other slaving voyages from Angola during the same era. Sailing from Luanda three years later, the ship *Nuestra Señora de Rocha* disembarked a total of 280 captives in Cumaná, in eastern Venezuela. Among the captives who had survived the voyage, 49 were considered muleques and muchachas; another 45 were nursing infants. This coerced migration of children from West Central Africa was by no means limited to Española and Venezuela. Ships sailing from Angola to Veracruz in 1622 also carried significant numbers of child captives. The *San Francisco* landed a total of 349 captives, including 80 muleques and 34 nursing infants. The caravel *Santa Ursula* disembarked another 239 captives, of whom 72 were considered muleques. On each of these voyages, small children constituted roughly one-third of the captives.[41]

Among slaving voyages from Angola known to have carried substantial numbers of children, the common practice seems to have been disembarking and selling younger captives in secondary ports before arriving in the

40. Ravenstein, ed., *Strange Adventures,* 32–33, 85; for the observation that captives taken by the Imbangala are described as thirteen or fourteen years old in one passage but anywhere from ten to twenty years old in another, see Heywood and Thornton, *Central Africans,* 93n. Various aspects of Battell's account seem contradictory, which is perhaps unsurprising given the complicated nature of this source and its various editions. The original version was authored by Samuel Purchas (who interviewed Battell) and published in 1613; an expanded version written by an anonymous author, then edited by Purchas, was published in 1625 and served as the basis for Ravenstein's 1901 edition. For a close comparison of the 1613 and 1625 texts, see Jan Vansina, "On Ravenstein's Edition of Battell's Adventures in Angola and Loango," *HA,* XXXIV (January 2007), 321–347.

41. "Benito Jimenez guarda mayor . . . sobre el descamino de negros esclavos," 1617, AGN-FNE, Bolívar 7, hojas 293r–295v; Ermila Troconis de Veracoechea, ed., *Documentos para el estudio de los esclavos negros en Venezuela* (Caracas, 1969), 146–190; Vila Vilar, *Hispanoamérica,* 264–265. For references to the capture of women and children within West Central Africa, see Amaral, *O consulado,* 133–135, 156; "Representação de Manuel Cerveira Pereira," July 2, 1618, in Brásio, *MMA* (1), VI, 315–319.

voyage's primary destination. Having departed from Angola with 350 captives, in 1619, the *San Juan Bautista* arrived in Veracruz with only 123 captives after having allegedly been "robbed by Englishmen." According to the ship's crew, they had also sold 24 muleques in Jamaica. Also sailing from Angola, crew members of the ship *La Trinidad y Concepción* claimed to have sold 31 muleques in Santo Domingo before arriving in Veracruz with 134 captives in 1638. En route from Angola to Cartagena, the ship *San Antonio y Nuestra Señora de la Esperanza* also put into port in Santo Domingo in September 1631, where 30 captives—7 adults and 23 "negritos and negritas" between the ages of three and ten years old—were sold to pay for repairs. The ship then continued on to Cartagena, arriving in October 1631 with 142 captives. For each of these voyages, the number of children among the remaining captives disembarked in each voyage's final port or intended port of call remains unknown. These preliminary stops involving the sale of children might have been a means of saving the most valuable (adult) captives for the most distant markets, where they could be sold for higher prices. Furthermore, the young were likely most vulnerable to disease or malnourishment, which would be important considerations by the time a vessel reached the Caribbean, given the length of the transatlantic journey.[42]

A roughly contemporary voyage from Angola to Cádiz, Spain, appears to have followed a similar trajectory. From December 1625 through early March 1626, several dozen captives arriving from Luanda on the ship *Nuestra Señora de la Muela* were sold in Cádiz. Among the sixty-four captives listed, no less than forty-seven were females, ranging in age from seven to twenty-two years old; among the sixty-two captives for whom estimated ages were recorded, the average age was slightly more than fourteen years old. If the ship carried larger numbers of adult males, they were evidently reserved for sale elsewhere.[43]

42. Caja de Santo Domingo, Cuenta de los oficiales Reales, 1631, AGI-Ctdra 1057, n.4, pliegos 5, 8; Caja de Cartagena, Cuentas, 1631–1633, AGI-Ctdra 1397, n.6, pliegos 37–38; Caja de Cartagena, Cuentas, 1631–1633, AGI-Ctdra 1398, n.3, pliego 106; Vila Vilar, *Hispanoamérica,* 262–263, 266–267, 272–273.

43. Ventas de esclavos y cartas de poder, Dec. 23, 1625–Mar. 7, 1626, AHPC-Cádiz 319, notaria 2 (Juan de Castro), fols. 1771r, 1773r, 1775r, 1777r, 1779r, AHPC-Cádiz 320, notaria 2 (Juan de Castro), fols. 22v, 24v, 26r, 28r, 45r, 51r, 54r, 56r, 67r, 127r, 172v, 175r, AHPC-Cádiz 2089, notaria 11 (Melchor Escobar Ibáñez), fols. 1r, 8v, 10v, 51r, 53r, 91r, 187r, AHPC-Cádiz 3030, notaria 14 (Diego Prieto de Alcázar), fols. 568r, 570r, AHPC-Cádiz 3031, notaria 14 (Diego Prieto de Alcázar), fols. 4v, 9v, 14r, 20r, 25v, 29r, 33v, 38v, 45v, 115r, 171r, AHPC-Cádiz 4373, notaria 19 (Diego de Soto Castellanos), fols. 1476v, 1482v, 1486r, 1488r, 1490r, 1492r, 1494r, 1506v, 1510v, 1512v, 1514v, 1516v, 1518r, 1520r, 1522r, 1526r, 1530r, 1532r, 1534r, 1537r, 1539r, 1541r, 1545v. A sixteen-year-old girl described as a "bosal [unacculturated slave] de Angola" and four boys between the ages of nine and thirteen, likewise from Angola, were also sold in Cádiz in January and March 1626 and could have arrived on the same ship. See AHPC-Cádiz 3031, notaria 14 (Diego Prieto de Alcázar), fols. 27v–29r, 164–166r, 179r–181r.

Table 4 Child Captives on Slaving Voyages from Angola, 1619–1639

Year	Ship	Port(s) of disembarkation	Captives landed	Children among captives landed	Children as % of captives landed
1619	*San Juan Bautista*	Jamaica; Veracruz	147	24 *muleques* (young captives, probably older children) (Jamaica only)	16.3
1620	*Nuestra Señora de la Rocha*	Cumaná	280	45 infants, 49 muleques and *muchachas* (girls)	33.6
1621	*Espiritu Santo*	Cartagena	290	45 *muchachos* (boys) and muchachas	15.5
1622	*San Francisco*	Veracruz	349	80 muleques, 34 *crías de pecho* (nursing infants)	32.7
1622	*Santa Ursula*	Veracruz	239	72 muleques	30.1
1625	*Nuestra Señora de la Muela*	Cádiz (Spain)	64	37 captives aged 7–14 years	57.8
1628	*Nuestra Señora del Rosario y San Antonio*	Cartagena	207	54 *crías y bambos muy pequeños* (very small children)	26.1
1628	*San Pedro*	Havana	230	166 *cañengues* (children), crias, and bambos	72.2
1631	*San Antonio y Nuestra Señora de la Esperanza*	Santo Domingo; Cartagena	172	23 *negritos* and *negritas* aged 3–10 years (Santo Domingo only)	13.4
1638	*Trinidad y Concepcion*	Santo Domingo; Veracruz	165	31 muleques (Santo Domingo only)	18.8
1639	*Nuestra Señora del Juncal*	Havana	310	80 *niños de pecho* and bambos	25.8

Sources: Enriqueta Vila Vilar, *Hispanoamérica y el comercio de esclavos: Los asientos portugueses* (Seville, 1977), 171n, 264–273; Ermila Troconis de Veracoechea, ed., *Documentos para el estudio de los esclavos negros en Venezuela* (Caracas, Venezuela, 1969), 146–190; Pedro Guiral, "Autos sobre lo tocante a negros esclavos Boçales," Nov. 9, 1621, AGI-SF 73, n.71a, fols. 10v–11v; El fiscal de S. M. con Salvador Rodriguez, 1623, AGI-Esc 291A; Ventas de esclavos y cartas de poder, Dec. 23, 1625–Mar. 7, 1626, AHPC-Cádiz 319, notaria 2 (Juan de Castro), fols. 1771r, 1773r, 1775r, 1777r, 1779r; AHPC-Cádiz 320, notaria 2 (Juan de Castro), fols. 22v, 24v, 26r, 28r, 45r, 51r, 54r, 56r, 67r, 127r, 172v, 175r; AHPC-Cádiz 2089, notaria 11 (Melchor Escobar Ibáñez), fols. 1r, 8v, 10v, 51r, 53r, 91r, 187r; AHPC-Cádiz 3030, notaria 14 (Diego Prieto de Alcázar), fols. 568r, 570r; AHPC-Cádiz 3031, notaria 14 (Diego Prieto de Alcázar), fols. 4v, 9v, 14r, 20r, 25v, 29r, 33v, 38v, 45v, 115r, 171r; AHPC-Cádiz 4373, notaria 19 (Diego de Soto Castellanos), fols. 1476v, 1482v, 1486r, 1488r, 1490r, 1492r, 1494r, 1506v, 1510v, 1512v, 1514v, 1516v, 1518r, 1520r, 1522r, 1526r, 1530r, 1532r, 1534r, 1537r, 1539r, 1541r, 1545v; Caja de Cartagena, Cuentas, 1628–1629, AGI-Ctdra 1397, n.4, pliegos 42, 47; Caja de Cartagena, Cuentas, 1628–1629, AGI-Ctdra 1398, n.1, pliegos 114–115, 142, 147; "Autos sobre la arribada del navío San Pedro," 1628–1631, AGI-SD 119, s/n; Caja de Cartagena, Cuentas, 1631–1633, AGI-Ctdra 1397, n.6, pliegos 37–38; Caja de Cartagena, Cuentas, 1631–1633, AGI-Ctdra 1398, n.3, pliego 106; Caja de Santo Domingo, Cuenta de los oficiales reales, 1631, AGI-Ctdra 1057, n.4, pliegos 5, 8; Leví Marrero, *Cuba: Economía y Sociedad: El siglo XVII (I)* (Madrid, 1975), III, 40.

Following the *Santa Ursula's* arrival in New Spain in 1622, Veracruz's royal officials attempted to levy import taxes on all children and adults disembarked; this practice appears to have been customary in circum-Caribbean ports throughout the previous century (with exceptions, perhaps, for newborns). But the ship's owner and armador Salvador Rodriguez protested, initiating a legal suit that eventually resulted in the passage of new metropolitan legislation that acknowledged and encouraged the traffic in enslaved children. According to a royal decree issued in Madrid on July 12, 1624, import fees owed to the crown would no longer be collected on "muleques less than seven years old." Rodriguez's case, and the exact date and wording of the royal decree, were specifically cited on at least two occasions soon afterward. The frigate *Nuestra Señora del Rosario y San Antonio* sailed from Angola to Cartagena in 1628, landing a total of 207 enslaved West Central Africans. More than one-quarter of the captives disembarked were *"crías y bambos,"* infants and children who were certainly under the age of seven. Citing the decree issued in response to Rodriguez's complaints six years earlier, the frigate's captain claimed that they were exempt from taxation. Also traveling from Angola, the *San Pedro* arrived in Cartagena in 1629. Though the total number of captives disembarked is unknown, it was carrying 88 unregistered captives, including 5 crías and bambos. Presenting a copy of the same royal decree, the ship's captain was able to avoid paying extra fees on the 5 small children who were landed in excess of the ship's registration. Information on the trafficking of children exists for only a handful of the 165 voyages from Angola known to have arrived in Spanish America after the passage of this legislation in 1624. The declared numbers of enslaved people disembarked from these ships more than likely do not include a substantial number of small children. Since captives under the age of seven were no longer taxed by the crown, royal officials had no reason to report them.[44]

The passage of legislation favoring the coerced migration of children under the age of seven helps to explain the increasing use of terms such as "cría," "bambo," and *cañengue* to describe children transported from Angola during the 1620s and 1630s. Regardless of whether the new decree fueled the traffic in children, or simply acknowledged a long-standing pattern in the slave trade from Luanda, it ensured that West Central African children

44. El fiscal de S. M. con Salvador Rodriguez, 1623, AGI-Esc 291A; Caja de Cartagena, Cuentas, 1628–1629, AGI-Ctdra 1398, n.1, pliegos 114–115; Caja de Cartagena, Cuentas, 1630–1631, AGI-Ctdra 1398, n.2, pliego 78. On voyages from Angola reaching Spanish America after July 12, 1624, see Wheat, "All Known Slaving Voyages" (unpublished data set).

were more likely to be recorded as such in the Spanish Caribbean after 1624. Sailing from "the kingdoms of Angola" in 1628, another slave ship named *San Pedro* was allegedly bound for Veracruz but dropped anchor instead in Havana. Several captives died of illness after the ship's arrival, and, among those who remained to be sold, three-quarters were estimated to be under the age of fifteen. Thirty-seven were nursing infants who arrived with their mothers; nearly fifty were small children from approximately four to six years old, identified as "cañengues *de muy poca edad.*" The earliest known appearance of the term "cañengue" in Spanish Caribbean sources dates to 1622. In a roster of enslaved Africans employed on a farm near Cartagena at that time, one was identified as "Francisco cañengue" or "Francisco Angola, who they call the cañengue." Best known as an early form of tango, the word *canyengue* has been linked to various purported West Central African origins. The word's appearance in seventeenth-century Havana and Cartagena confirms the link to West Central Africa but also reveals a much deeper history. Three hundred years ago, "cañengue" referred to children. This definition is consistent with usage of the terms *kanengue* in twentieth-century Minas Gerais and *kandengue* in present-day Angola, both of which signify "child."[45]

The *San Pedro's* 1628 voyage also reveals a second important linguistic development related to the traffic of West Central African children during the early 1600s. Since the 1560s, if not earlier, in the Spanish Caribbean the terms *pieza* (piece or unit) and *pieza de esclavo* (piece or unit of slaves) referred to one enslaved person, regardless of sex, age, health, or provenance. The terms were used interchangeably with "negro," "esclavo," "licencia," "pieza de negro," and "licencia de esclavo." But over the course of the seventeenth century, in the context of the slave trade, the term "pieza" evolved in a way that enabled royal officials to tax enslaved children at adjustable rates based on the value of one healthy, adult captive. Echoing earlier developments in Portuguese and African contexts, in the Spanish Caribbean "pieza" became *pieza de pago* (unit of payment) during the era of the Angolan wave and eventually *pieza de Indias* (piece of the Indies), though this better-known term appears infrequently in Spanish American records until the late seventeenth century.[46]

45. "Autos sobre la arribada del navío San Pedro," 1628–1631, AGI-SD 119, s/n; Visita de Pedro Guiral, 1622, AGI-Esc 632B, pieza 2, fols. 159v, 196r, 591r–591v, 738v; Robert Farris Thompson, *Tango: The Art History of Love* (New York, 2005), 150–167; Amanda Sônia López de Oliveira, *Palavra Africana em Minas Gerais* (Belo Horizonte, Brazil, 2006), 53; Mike Stead and Sean Rorison, *Angola* (Chalfont St. Peter, England, 2009), 261.

46. See Gonzalo Aguirre Beltrán, *La población negra de México, 1519–1810: Estudio etnohistórico*

The first known use of "pieza" in Spanish-language sources that differentiates between adults and children occurred in Luanda in 1611. The factor de Mar reported that although "piezas" were scarce, *"muleques* and *mulecas"* were even scarcer. By the mid-1620s, enslaved Africans disembarked in Caribbean ports were commonly measured in such fashion. The captives landed in Havana in 1628 on the *San Pedro* numbered 230 piezas de esclavos but were evaluated as 142 *piessas de pago*. Most were young boys and girls whose value was estimated to be two-thirds or one-half that of an adult; mothers and infants were assessed jointly as 1 pieza de pago. Likewise, when a slave ship disembarked 16 "young and old" West Central Africans in Santo Domingo in 1631, they were evaluated as 10.5 piezas. Another ship arriving in Cuba in 1639 similarly landed 310 captives, evaluated as 175.5 piezas; among them were 80 captives described as bambos or nursing infants for whom no import fees were paid. Following the arrival of a different slave ship in Santo Domingo from Angola in 1633, the shipmaster's legal representative argued that the voyage did not bring any more captives than his registration papers specified, if their numbers were "reduced to piezas de Indias, as is customary." This practice was indeed customary by the 1630s, though usage of the term "pieza de Indias" itself does not yet appear to have been widespread. It seems no coincidence that this shift in terminology took place precisely during the era of an Angola wave that entailed a substantial traffic in children.[47]

(Mexico City, 1946), 38; Bowser, *African Slave in Colonial Peru*, 39; Vila Vilar, *Hispanoamérica*, 186–193; Maria da Graça A. Mateus Ventura, *Negreiros Portugueses na rota das Índias de Castela, 1541–1556* (Lisbon, 1999), 63; María Cristina Navarrete, *Génesis y desarrollo de la esclavitud en Colombia, siglos XVI y XVII* (Cali, Colombia, 2005), 140n; António de Almeida Mendes, "The Foundations of the System: A Reassessment of the Slave Trade to the Spanish Americas in the Sixteenth and Seventeenth Centuries," in Eltis and Richardson, eds., *Extending the Frontiers*, 91n. According to Portuguese sources describing slave trafficking during the 1520s, one "peça" was a unit of value equal to that of one slave between the ages of fifteen and forty; see Mendes, "Uma contribuição para a história da escravatura no Benim: O livro de armação do navio Sao João (1526)," *Africana Studia*, no. 5 (2002), 32n. On use of the term *peça de Indias* in Angola during the late 1630s and afterwards, see Heintze, "Angolan Vassal Tributes," *RHES*, VI (1980), 64–65, 65n. For an example of the terms "negro," "esclavo," "licencia," and "pieza de negro," all being used interchangeably in Cartagena during the 1580s, see Carta de Don Pedro de Lodeña, Sept. 6, 1591, AGI-SF 37, r.6, n.103a/b.

47. Francisco de Mar a Joan de Argomedo, Apr. 22, 1611, AHU-Angola, cx.1, n.14, fol. 3r ("El tiempo esta muy esteril de piezas y mas de muleques y mulecas por donde no me a ssido pussible juntar mas que cossa de 30"); "Autos sobre la arribada del navío San Pedro," 1628–1631, AGI-SD 119, s/n, pieza 1, fols. 66r–66v ("piessas de pago"); Caja de Santo Domingo, Cuenta de los oficiales reales, 1631, AGI-Ctdra 1057, n.4, pliegos 4–5 ("chicos y grandes"); Leví Marrero, *Cuba: Economía y Sociedad: El siglo XVII (I)* (Madrid, 1975), III, 40; Isabelo Macías Domínguez, *Cuba en la primera mitad del siglo XVII* (Seville, 1978), 431; "Autos seguidos por Miguel Fernández de Fonseca," 1633, AGI-Esc 4, n.12, pieza 1, fols. 6or ("Reduciendose como se acostumbra los dhos esclabos a piesas de yndias"), 67v–68r.

THE SIGNIFICANT NUMBER of children on transatlantic slaving voyages from Luanda was a function not only of the production of captives but also a marker of the qualitative nature of forced migration from Angola to the Caribbean. A possible consequence was that West Central Africans' experiences of slavery in the early-seventeenth-century Spanish Caribbean might have differed from those of forced migrants from other African regions. If "Angolas" comprised a disproportionately large share of the enslaved children in the early Spanish Caribbean populations, their relative youth might help to explain why West Central Africans, unlike Upper Guineans, only rarely identified themselves to Iberians using more specific ethnonyms or toponyms. The strong presence of children among the West Central Africans arriving in the Caribbean during the era of the Angola wave also correlates with the infrequency of slave revolts on ships sailing from Angola to the Caribbean, unlike on the ships carrying captives from Upper Guinea. That "Angolas" sometimes labored under the direction of Upper Guinean overseers, while the opposite was rarely, if ever, the case, could also be attributed to the difference in age groups. Finally, the prominence of children among West Central African captives would have contributed to the speed with which coerced migrants from Angola appear to have adapted to Spanish Caribbean society, notably in terms of language acquisition.

If the early Spanish Caribbean comprised an extension of prior Iberian interactions with Upper Guineans, the maintenance and growth of Spanish Caribbean society was facilitated by Iberian expansion in Angola and the transatlantic slave trade from Luanda. Though Spanish settlement of the Caribbean preceded Portuguese expansion in Angola, throughout the early seventeenth century these Iberian colonization projects mutually reinforced one another. The Angola wave stretching from the mid-1590s to 1640 directly paralleled the spread of large-scale conflict instigated by Portuguese and Imbangala forces at Ndongo's expense and the tribute that Portuguese colonists imposed on subjugated populations. Luanda colonists' regular appearance in circum-Caribbean ports as slave ship captains and passengers reflects the intricate connections of these histories; their presence also suggests that Spanish Caribbean markets played a major role in Luanda's growth and provided an economic impetus for the slave wars that generated West Central African captives throughout the early seventeenth century.

THREE

Tangomãos and Luso-Africans

Departing the port of Buguendo on Christmas Eve 1574, the caravel *San Jorge* followed the São Domingos River until it emptied into the larger Cacheu River, a direct passage to the Atlantic Ocean. As its crew and passengers later testified, they were bound for the nearby Cape Verde Islands. They expected their journey to last only four days, but a storm severely damaged the vessel on their third day at sea. Strong winds prevented them from sailing north or east. They were left with no choice, they claimed, other than to sail west toward "the Indies," a well-known route traveled by dozens of other ships leaving the Upper Guinea coast and Cape Verde Islands during the late sixteenth century. Near the end of January 1575, after five weeks at sea, the *San Jorge* reached Nizao, near Santo Domingo, on the southern coast of Española. The island's royal officials correctly guessed that the voyage had never been registered with the House of Trade in Seville and proceeded to carry out a meticulous inspection. In addition to cloth, porcelain, beeswax, soap, and ivory, the *San Jorge* was found to be carrying nearly two hundred African captives and a number of passengers. Its crew members included several free people of color and enslaved mariners.[1]

To avoid paying steep taxes on the captives they disembarked, nine of the *San Jorge's* passengers identified themselves as *tangomãos*—Iberian or Cape-verdean merchants who had spent considerable time in Upper Guinea—and claimed to be exempt from paying taxes on slaves, since they had already paid very high taxes to the Portuguese crown upon departing the Upper Guinea coast. In Santo Domingo, Española, deponents were soon called

1. "Contratadores de Cabo Verde y Guinea con Cristóbal Cayado y otros del reino de Portugal," 1582–1589, AGI-Esc 2A. For discussion of Buguendo's rise and fall as an important sixteenth-century slaving port, see George E. Brooks, *Landlords and Strangers: Ecology, Society, and Trade in Western Africa, 1000–1630* (Boulder, Col., 1993), 92, 226–244. On voyages from the Cape Verde Islands to the Spanish Americas during the 1570s, see Rafael M. Pérez García and Manuel F. Fernández Chaves, "Sevilla y la trata negrera atlántica: Envíos de esclavos desde Cabo Verde a la América española, 1569–1579," in León Carlos Álvarez Santaló, coord., *Estudios de historia moderna en homenaje al profesor Antonio García-Baquero* (Seville, 2009), 597–622.

forth to provide testimony based on their personal knowledge of events in western Africa. Several affirmed that anyone "who went to the Rivers of Guinea to trade for slaves, and resided there for longer than a year and a day," was afterward commonly known as a "tangomão" or *"lançado."* Deponent Fernan Diaz, for example, had been a slave trade factor in São Tomé before becoming a *vecino* (permanent resident) of Santo Domingo. Claiming to have brought "a great quantity of blacks" from the Cape Verde Islands himself "several times," deponent Francisco Rebolo had also been the captain of a slave ship arriving from São Tomé earlier the same year, a complicated voyage of questionable legality that generated an extensive investigation of its own. Others had actually known the tangomãos in question in the "Rivers of Guinea." In March 1576, a Portuguese man named Vicente de Vis testified that he had known Francisco de Vitoria in Buguendo "for many years, and knows that he is a tangomão." Citing his own experience as a slave ship captain, another Portuguese resident of Santo Domingo named Pedro Alvarez de Silva claimed that he, too, had seen Vitoria, Juan Gonçales, Alfonso Lopez, Nicolas Fernandes, Diego Gomez, and Rodrigo Alvarez trading for slaves in the Rivers of Guinea. In short, the tangomãos' voyage from Buguendo to the Spanish Caribbean during the 1570s was not unique, and their presence in Española was probably not even unusual. These Portuguese men interviewed in Santo Domingo were able to provide eyewitness testimony of the workings of the slave trade in Lisbon, Upper Guinea, the Cape Verde Islands, and São Tomé because most had been associated with the slave trade themselves.[2]

Portuguese often outnumbered other non-Hispanic Europeans in the Spanish Caribbean (and indeed throughout the Spanish Americas) during the sixteenth and early seventeenth centuries. Their legal status in Spain's overseas territories as quasi foreigners was poorly defined, contradictory, and inconsistently enforced. With the exception of Portuguese migrants native to the Algarve, who were entitled to the same rights as Castilians, Portuguese migrants were not supposed to own encomiendas or hold high government positions in the Spanish colonies; during the seventeenth century in particular, they were often viewed as smugglers or crypto-Jews. Yet,

2. "Contratadores de Cabo Verde y Guinea con Cristóbal Cayado," 1582–1589, AGI-Esc 2A, pieza 2, fols. 65r–80v, 519v–530r. For another voyage that had been "going from the island of Terceira to the island of Santiago de Cabo Verde, with people from the island of Cabo Verde" onboard but landed in Puerto Rico instead, see Diego Rodriguez de Castellano a S. M., Oct. 15, 1603, AGI-SD 166, r.3, fols. 386–387. On Francisco Rebolo's voyage from São Tomé, see Proceso contra Pedro de Esplugas et al., 1578–1590, AGI-Esc 1A, pieza 4.

the Spanish crown and its representatives on both sides of the Atlantic made frequent use of Portuguese settlers, merchants, soldiers, sailors, and pilots before and during the Iberian Union. Most of the 1,522 foreigners who received authorization to emigrate to Spanish America during the sixteenth century were from Portugal. Others, like clandestine migrants from Spain, enlisted as mariners on the Indies fleets then jumped ship upon arrival in ports such as Cartagena, Veracruz, and Havana. The transatlantic slave trade further facilitated Portuguese migration to the Spanish Americas. With an average of fifteen to twenty crew members on each slaving voyage, as many as twenty thousand seamen arrived in the Caribbean on slave ships alone. Slave ship passengers and mariners of all ranks commonly disembarked in Caribbean ports and often ended up becoming long-term or permanent residents. These practices were expressly prohibited by the crown, but such regulations were difficult, if not impossible, to enforce.[3]

Iberian and Luso-African migration from Africa to the early colonial Caribbean on slave ships produced a heterogeneous mix of mariners, travelers, and passengers that included but was not limited to merely slave traders. Nor were all Portuguese migrants to the early Spanish Caribbean bound in a deep-seated, collective identity. In 1603, Cartagena's governor observed that slave ship captains were "poor men, usually, who do not work on their own behalf, but in the name of other great, wealthy men in Lisbon." Though ultimately directed, perhaps, by a handful of powerful men in western Europe, or by affluent merchants who owned multiple ships, extravagant homes, and hundreds of slaves, Iberian slaving networks depended on much larger numbers of mid-level and lower-level agents. Far away from the headquarters of bankers and *asentistas* (asiento holders) in

3. Fernando Serrano Mangas, "La presencia portuguesa en la América española en la época de los Habsburgos (siglos XVI–XVII)," in Maria da Graça M. Ventura, ed., *A União Ibérica e o Mundo Atlântico* (Lisbon, 1997), 73–79; Ventura, *Portugueses no Peru ao Tempo da União Ibérica: Mobilidade, cumplicidades e vivências* (Lisbon, 2005), vol. I, tomo 1, 65–84; Peter Boyd-Bowman, "Patterns of Spanish Emigration to the Indies until 1600," *HAHR*, LVI (1976), 585, 588, 596–597, 599; Ida Altman, "Marriage, Family, and Ethnicity in the Early Spanish Caribbean," *WMQ*, 3d Ser., LXX (2013), 238; Auke Pieter Jacobs, "Legal and Illegal Emigration from Seville, 1550–1650," in Ida Altman and James Horn, eds., *"To Make America": European Emigration in the Early Modern Period* (Berkeley, Calif., 1991), 59–84; Pablo E. Pérez-Mallaína, *Spain's Men of the Sea: Daily Life on the Indies Fleets in the Sixteenth Century*, trans. Carla Rahn Phillips (Baltimore, 1998), 54–62. On Portuguese migration via African ports, see Henry H. Keith, "New World Interlopers: The Portuguese in the Spanish West Indies from the Discovery to 1640," *Americas*, XXV (1969), 360–371; Enriqueta Vila Vilar, "Extranjeros en Cartagena (1593–1630)," *JGSWGL*, XVI (December 1979), 147–184. See also Vila Vilar, *Hispanoamérica y el comercio de esclavos: Los asientos portugueses* (Seville, 1977), 99–103, 134–137; Linda A. Newson and Susie Minchin, *From Capture to Sale: The Portuguese Slave Trade to Spanish South America in the Early Seventeenth Century* (Leiden, 2007), 140; Daviken Studnicki-Gizbert, *A Nation upon the Ocean Sea: Portugal's Atlantic Diaspora and the Crisis of the Spanish Empire, 1492–1640* (Oxford, 2007), 60–61.

Iberian capitals and the fabulous mansions of elite merchants in Spanish American viceroyalties, Caribbean ports hosted a substantially wider cast of characters. Rather than being confined to slave ship holds, some sub-Saharan Africans crossed the Atlantic as sailors, domestic slaves, or servants on slaving voyages. Other slave ship travelers were Luso-Africans: individuals of Iberian ancestry who were born or lived for extended periods in western Africa or people of African or African-Iberian descent born or raised in Iberian societies in Africa. The latter were usually described as "Portuguese blacks," "Portuguese *mulatos*," "black creoles of Cape Verde," or "black creoles of São Tomé."[4]

Among the Portuguese traveling to the Spanish Caribbean on slave ships, even those who were not Luso-Africans very likely had prior experience residing in sub-Saharan Africa or in the Atlantic islands off the African coast. By the early 1600s, slave ship crews commonly remained in Upper Guinea for periods of time ranging from eight months to a year, purchasing captives and engaging in other types of trade. Merchants like the tangomãos who testified in Española in the 1570s had resided in western Africa for even longer periods of time. Furthermore, they were accompanied by sailors, servants, domestic slaves, and family members who were themselves products of a syncretic African-Iberian world and who might have been leaving Atlantic Africa for the first time. In addition to their knowledge of slave trade ports and the ground-level workings of the slave trade, such individuals possessed firsthand knowledge of African identities, languages, cuisines, and cultural practices that would have been completely unfamiliar to most Castilian migrants to the Americas. In 1612, two "Portuguese" bystanders defused a plot because they "knew the language of Angola" and overheard several Africans and Afrocreoles allegedly discussing plans for fomenting a rebellion among Mexico City's black and mulato population. When one of Cartagena's wealthier Portuguese residents Luis Gomez Barreto was tried by the Inquisition in 1636, his wife sent an Upper Guinean slave to deliver "a pot of stewed chicken and a dozen kola nuts" to his cell to make his incarceration less unpleasant. Although deeply implicated in the commodification and trafficking of enslaved Africans, Portuguese

4. Jerónimo de Zuazo a S. M., Aug. 1, 1603, AGI-SF 38, r.2, n.55, fol. 1v. On the term "Luso-African," see Peter Mark, "The Evolution of 'Portuguese' Identity: Luso-Africans on the Upper Guinea Coast from the Sixteenth to the Early Nineteenth Century," *JAH*, XL (1999), 173–191; José da Silva Horta, "Evidence for a Luso-African Identity in 'Portuguese' Accounts on 'Guinea of Cape Verde' (Sixteenth–Seventeenth Centuries)," *HA*, XXVII (2000), 99–130. For emphasis on merchant houses as the "animating core" of a collective Portuguese "nation" in diaspora, see Studnicki-Gizbert, *Nation upon the Ocean Sea*, 43, 56–57, 66–67.

and Luso-African migrants also selectively adopted sub-Saharan African customs more thoroughly than any other segment of Spanish Caribbean society excepting sub-Saharan Africans themselves.[5]

Like the go-betweens who facilitated Iberian interaction with Brazil's indigenous populations during the same era, Portuguese and Luso-African intermediaries played an ambiguous yet significant role in the colonization of the Spanish Caribbean. In addition to cross-cultural exchange in Upper Guinea preceding Spanish colonization of the Caribbean and Portuguese colonization of Angola reinforcing Spanish expansion in the Americas, the presence of tangomãos and Luso-Africans in the Spanish Caribbean reveals that the social order taking shape there during the late sixteenth and early seventeenth centuries was in many ways an extension of earlier patterns and contemporary events in Atlantic Africa, not a violent clash of cultures or a tense encounter negotiated by Europeans and Africans who knew little about each other beforehand.[6]

Portuguese Foreigners on Spanish Caribbean Shores

Portuguese presence in the Caribbean was noticeable from very early in the colonial period. In the 1580s, less than a century after Santo Domingo was founded, visiting officials and city council members claimed that more than half of all free men on the entire island of Española were Portuguese and that they dominated local commerce to the detriment of Spanish merchants. On Margarita Island, Portuguese also allegedly outnumbered Spanish residents, while in Cartagena, too, royal officials complained of Portuguese slave traders monopolizing the city's revenues.[7]

---

5. Newson and Minchin, *From Capture to Sale,* 100; Luis Querol y Roso, "Negros y mulatos de Nueva España (Historia de su alzamiento en Méjico en 1612)," in *Separado de los anales de la Universidad de Valencia, año XII, cuad. 90* (Valencia, Spain, 1935), 15; María Cristina Navarrete, *Historia social del negro en la colonia: Cartagena, siglo XVII* (Cali, Colombia, 1995), 65; Renée Soulodre–La France and Paul E. Lovejoy, "Intercambios transatlánticos, sociedad esclavista e Inquisición en la Cartagena del siglo XVII," trans. Óscar Grandio, in Claudia Mosquera, Mauricio Pardo, and Odile Hoffman, eds., *Afrodescendientes en las Américas: Trayectorias sociales e identitarias* (Bogotá, 2002), 195–211. See also J. H. Elliott, "A Europe of Composite Monarchies," *Past and Present,* no. 137 (November 1992), 48–71.

6. On "go-betweens" in sixteenth-century Brazil, see Alida C. Metcalf, *Go-Betweens and the Colonization of Brazil, 1500–1600* (Austin, Tex., 2005).

7. Luis de Guzman y Alonso de Tapia a S. M., July 4, 1590, AGI-SF 72, n.81, fol. 3r; Kenneth R. Andrews, *The Spanish Caribbean: Trade and Plunder, 1530–1630* (New Haven, Conn., 1978), 37–38; Fernando Serrano Mangas, *La encrucijada portuguesa: Esplendor y quiebra de la Unión Ibérica en las Indias de Castilla (1600–1668),* 2d ed. (Badajoz, Spain, 2001), 15–16; Henry Kamen, *Empire: How Spain Became a World Power, 1492–1763* (New York, 2003), 134–135; Genaro Rodríguez Morel, *Orígenes de la economía de plantación de La Española* (Santo Domingo, Dominican Republic, 2012), 88–91.

In each of these cases, local interest groups sought to weaken their competition by manipulating anxieties over the presence of foreigners in the Spanish empire. By approximately 1600, metropolitan authorities had come to view Portuguese settlers in the Americas as suspicious and potentially subversive. Encouraged by mercantilist political advisors and an influential lobby of Sevillian merchants, the crown issued a series of decrees in the late sixteenth and early seventeenth centuries designed to control transatlantic commerce and travel. Like other foreigners and undesirables—and like Spanish migrants and merchants themselves—the Portuguese were prohibited from traveling to the Spanish Americas without express permission. Such policies had always been difficult to implement and were perhaps even more so during the Iberian Union (1580–1640). Whereas in theory the same monarchs ruled the crowns of Castile and Portugal as separate kingdoms, along with their own respective empires, in reality transatlantic slaving networks made it almost as easy to cross from Portuguese to Spanish colonies as it was to cross the land border between Spain and Portugal. But comprehensive attempts to shore up Spain's mercantilist system—and to repress those perceived as threatening it—were intensified in the Caribbean during the first decade of the seventeenth century. Though these efforts failed in other respects, they were successful in generating a great deal of information on Portuguese migrants to the Caribbean, including many who had initially arrived on slave ships as mariners or passengers without authorization to stay.[8]

Although royal decrees aimed at regulating immigration and commerce refer broadly to "the Indies," the stakes were often highest, and the repercussions of royal policy most pronounced, in the Caribbean. If strategically positioned ports were to protect Spain's maritime lifelines from northern European trespassers, then the unauthorized presence of foreigners within those seaports was considered a potential flaw in the system. The very plausible threat of an English or Dutch invasion was to be aided, it was suspected, by foreigners and slaves, domestic populations of questionable loyalties. Most importantly, Portuguese persons residing in the Caribbean were assumed to be heavily involved in *rescate,* a term that can be loosely translated as "trade" or "barter." Though blatantly illegal for any resident

8. Joseph de Veitia Linage, *Norte de la contratación de las Indias ocidentales* (Seville, 1672), I, 236–244. Sevillian merchants' animosity toward their Portuguese competitors was at least partly a reaction against the latter's predominance in Seville's slave trade market during the late sixteenth century; see Rafael M. Pérez García and Manuel F. Fernández Chaves, "Las redes de la trata negrera: Mercaderes portugueses y tráfico de esclavos en Sevilla (c.1560–1580)," in Aurelia Martín Casares and Margarita García Barranco, comps., *La esclavitud negroafricana en la historia de España, siglos XVI y XVII* (Granada, Spain, 2010), 5–34.

of the Spanish colonies, the practice was widespread: instead of restricting their purchases to goods delivered on fleets dispatched periodically from Seville, Spanish Caribbean inhabitants—clergy and appointed officials included—traded with French, English, Dutch, and Portuguese interlopers, representing a major blow to Seville's merchant monopoly and a drain on royal tax revenues. Rescate involved the exchange of local products (such as hides, tobacco, and cacao) for imported merchandise and enslaved Africans. Well-founded accusations of endemic contraband led the crown to order the depopulation of several towns in northern and western Española in 1603, with inhabitants forcibly relocated to settlements closer to Santo Domingo in 1605 and 1606.[9]

In 1606, the cultivation of tobacco, a commodity much appreciated by non-Hispanic merchants, was prohibited for the space of ten years in Venezuela, Margarita Island, Española, Cuba, and Puerto Rico. A royal cedula issued the following year decreed the death penalty for captains or pilots of any rank who brought unlicensed passengers to the Americas. Another 1608 cedula stipulated that all Portuguese persons residing in the Spanish Americas were to abstain from conducting any form of trade until they received special permission. Finally, the asiento system regulating the slave trade—increasingly operated by Portuguese contractors and considered a vehicle for both contraband trade and clandestine migration—was also suspended from 1609 to 1615. Individually licensed slaving voyages were still permitted, but control over the traffic was temporarily concentrated in the hands of Sevillian merchants.[10]

One of the most drastic measures taken in response to rescate was a deliberate program for the deportation of Portuguese and all other foreigners from the Caribbean. Though not unrelated to the xenophobia that led to

9. I. A. Wright, "Rescates: With Special Reference to Cuba, 1599–1610," *HAHR,* III (1920), 333–361; Concepción Hernández Tapia, "Despoblaciones de la isla de Santo Domingo en el siglo XVII," *AEA,* XXVII (1970), 281–319; Andrews, *Spanish Caribbean,* 37–39, 72–80, 113–122, 131–132, 194–197, 208–216; Alejandro de la Fuente, "Introducción al estudio de la trata en Cuba, siglos XVI y XVII," *Santiago,* LXI (March 1986), 174–184; Juana Gil-Bermejo García, *La Española: Anotaciones históricas (1600–1650)* (Seville, 1983), 3–42; Roberto Cassá, *História social y económica de la República Dominicana* (Santo Domingo, Dominican Republic, 1983), I, 87, 90–95; Carlos Esteban Deive, *Tangomangos: Contrabando y piratería en Santo Domingo, 1522–1606* (Santo Domingo, Dominican Republic, 1996), 82–84, 207–243; Elsa Gelpí Baíz, *Siglo en blanco: Estudio de la economía azucarera en el Puerto Rico del siglo XVI (1540–1612)* (San Juan, Puerto Rico, 2000), 99–106.

10. Veitia Linage, *Norte de la contratación,* I, 221; Georges Scelle, *La traite négrière aux Indes de Castille, contrats et traités d'assiento* (Paris, 1906), 412; Andrews, *Spanish Caribbean,* 214–216; Vila Vilar, *Hispanoamérica,* 24, 42–45; Frank Moya Pons, "The Establishment of Primary Centres and Primary Plantations," in P. C. Emmer and German Carrera Damas, eds., *General History of the Caribbean,* II, *New Societies: The Caribbean in the Long Sixteenth Century* (London, 1999), 76–77.

the 1609–1615 expulsion of Spanish *moriscos* (Iberians of Muslim ancestry), this plan was primarily intended to eliminate reliance on foreign merchants and manufactures, in keeping with the purely mercantilist approaches espoused by merchants based in Seville and a subset of the early modern Spanish policy advocates known as *arbitristas*. Between 1605 and 1607, by royal edict, officials throughout the Spanish Caribbean took stock of the foreigners residing in their jurisdictions. Their subsequent reports to the crown were followed by royal decrees demanding the expulsion of Portuguese residents. Only those who had lived in the region for ten years or more were to be exempt. Portuguese migrants had long resided, for example, in Havana; a 1582 roster of the town's military effectives listed three temporary residents and sixteen vecinos described as Portuguese. In 1602, Cuba's newly arrived governor, Pedro de Valdes, estimated that "more than two-thirds of those who reside on this island are of different nations, and most of them Portuguese." Initially arriving on ships as mariners, he wrote, "all of them end up settling in the ports of this and other islands." He described the Portuguese as especially prone to engaging in unauthorized trade with non-Hispanic intruders, thus generating personal wealth at the crown's expense. As commanded by the crown, Valdes dutifully conducted a survey of foreign residents that was forwarded to Spain. In response, on January 24, 1608, the crown issued a royal cedula calling for the expulsion of the entire island's Portuguese population. Havana's Portuguese inhabitants were notified in June 1608, following Valdes's receipt of the decree, that, regardless of their socioeconomic status, they had exactly one day to provide collateral as insurance that they would embark with their households and families on the next galleons departing for Spain.[11]

In the years leading up to 1608, officials throughout the Caribbean had received instructions to conduct censuses of Portuguese and other foreigners in their jurisdictions, but not all authorities were eager to comply. After

---

11. Carta de Don Pedro de Valdes a S. M., Sept. 25, 1602, AGI-SD 100, r.2, n.14, fols. 4v–5r; Wright, "Rescates," *HAHR*, III (1920), 344–353; Levi Marrero, *Cuba: Economía y sociedad: Siglo XVI: La economía* (Madrid, 1974), II, 332–334; Isabelo Macías Domínguez, *Cuba en la primera mitad del siglo XVII* (Seville, 1978), 30–32, 48, 57–58, 327; Alejandro de la Fuente, with César García del Pino and Bernardo Iglesias Delgado, *Havana and the Atlantic in the Sixteenth Century* (Chapel Hill, N.C., 2008), 93–101. For the 1608 order, see "Ynformacion de Simon Fernandez Leyton," Aug. 24, 1608, AGI-SD 119, r.2, s/n. For a classic depiction of arbitristas, see J. H. Elliott, "Self-Perception and Decline in Early Seventeenth-Centry Spain," *Past and Present*, no. 74 (February 1977), 41–61. Among other things, Elliot criticizes a "stockade mentality" that saw "Spain as surrounded by foreign enemies and in imminent danger of subversion by the enemy within" (60–61). For an overview of this historiographically weighty topic with emphasis on currency and coinage, see Elena María García Guerra, *Moneda y arbitrios: Consideraciones del siglo XVII* (Madrid, 2003).

five years in Havana, even Valdes was no longer certain whether or not Portuguese inhabitants should be classified as "foreigners." In 1606, Puerto Rico's governor wrote that "a great quantity" of Portuguese and Italians had resided on the island for some time. However, he reported, he "did not dare" follow through with royal instructions, since the Portuguese alone made up nearly one-fifth of the island's population. Officials in Puerto Rico and elsewhere were probably reluctant to deport a population of considerable size that included individuals who could bring trade to the island in any form. The same Caribbean administrators might have been ensconced in commercial networks of dubious legality themselves.[12]

Other colonial officials were apparently no less reluctant to lose their Portuguese residents. Despite various accounts describing Portuguese numerical prominence and participation in foreign trade networks in Española during the late sixteenth century, a 1606 census of more than six hundred households in Santo Domingo listed only six vecinos as "Portuguese." Perhaps the city council's complaints about Portuguese settlers during the 1580s had been exaggerated, or, perhaps Española's significant Portuguese population vanished—or became "Spanish"—over the following decades. More likely, however, the paucity of numbers reflected contemporary views of the island's Portuguese inhabitants as central agents in the widespread rescate that led to the crown's drastic decision to uproot settlements on the western side of the island and forcibly relocate them closer to Santo Domingo. These events unfolded at the same time the census was conducted; in fact, the same governor, Antonio Osorio, was ultimately responsible for overseeing both processes. Though intended to eliminate contraband that was considered detrimental to metropolitan agendas, within a local context the depopulation of western Española might have been understood as an opportunity to transfer lucrative non-Hispanic trade networks to the island's capital. Santo Domingo officials' apparent willingness to understate the numbers of Portuguese inhabitants was shrewd, if patently dishonest: their successors continued to debate the presence of Portuguese on the island as late as the 1640s and 1650s, even after the end of the Iberian Union.[13]

A 1605 census of more than seventy households in Santiago de Cuba like-

12. Sancho Ochoa de Castro a S. M., Jan. 18, 1606, AGI-SD 155, r.15, n.177; Wright, "Rescates," *HAHR*, III (1920), 349–353; Gelpí Baíz, *Siglo en blanco*, 13–14, 26.

13. "Testimonio de quantos lugares ay en esta ysla," Oct. 2, 1606, AGI-SD 83, r.2, s/n, fols. 33–69, transcribed in E[milio] Rodríguez Demorizi, comp., *Relaciones históricas de Santo Domingo* (Ciudad Trujillo [Santo Domingo], Dominican Republic, 1945), II, 374–403. Compare with Marcel Bataillon, "Santo Domingo 'Era Portugal,'" in *Historia y sociedad en el mundo de habla español* (Mexico City, 1970),

Figure 2 "Pintura de la costa de Cartaxena" (Drawing of the coast of Cartagena),
1629. España. Ministerio de Educación, Cultura y Deporte. Archivo General de Indias.
Mapas y Planos, Panamá 264, Mapa de la costa septentrional de América del Sur,
desde la Península de Araya, en Venezuela, hasta Portobelo, en Panamá

wise failed to label anyone as Portuguese, despite its inclusion of numerous names suggesting Portuguese origins, such as "Bartolomé de Silba" (da
Silva), "Leonor Cuello" (Coelho), and "Rodrigo de Noroña" (Noronha).
Soon after the general census was taken, Santiago's governor apparently
conducted a more specific census of foreigners; he also warned that the
town harbored many wealthy Portuguese merchants, including two accused
of contraband slave trading. But, following the governor's death in late 1612,
his temporary replacement—Captain Francisco Sanchez de Moya, who had
already resided in eastern Cuba for some time—dismissed such claims as
unfounded, arguing that Santiago's Portuguese residents were in fact quite
poor and would probably be glad to move elsewhere if given the chance.

113–120; Juan José Ponce Vázquez, "Social and Political Survival at the Edge of Empire: Spanish
Local Elites in Hispaniola, 1580–1697" (Ph.D. diss., University of Pennsylvania, 2011), 33–37; Marc
Eagle, "The Audiencia of Santo Domingo in the Seventeenth Century" (Ph.D. diss., Tulane Univer-
sity, 2005), 66; Eagle, "Beard-Pulling and Furniture-Rearranging: Conflict within the Seventeenth-
Century Audiencia of Santo Domingo," *Americas*, LXVIII (2012), 479n.

Like the mestizos who had been incorporated into Spanish Caribbean society during the early 1500s, migrants from Portugal and the Lusophone Atlantic world contributed to the formation of stable colonial populations as extensions of nominally Spanish households and social networks. At the same time, as these opposing characterizations of Portuguese persons residing in Santiago de Cuba illustrate, their experiences differed from those of mestizos a century earlier in that their presence was also the subject of metropolitan concerns over transimperial smuggling in defiance of mercantilistic legal strictures.[14]

Spanish authorities' efforts to distinguish Portuguese settlers from clandestine migrants and potential smugglers are manifested in censuses conducted in Santa Marta, Venezuela, and Havana in 1606 and 1607. Compiled in secret (presumably to avoid alarming culpable parties who might otherwise flee or go into hiding), the censuses provided information used to determine which Portuguese inhabitants in the circum-Caribbean would be allowed to remain in face of forthcoming royal expulsion orders. A duplicate of the 1606 list of Portuguese and other foreigners residing in the province of Santa Marta includes crown officials' comments indicating who would be forced to leave and who could stay. For slightly more than half of the forty-one Portuguese men residing in Santa Marta, Riohacha, Tenerife, and Valledupar, the initial verdict was *fuera* (out). Those permitted to remain had become entrenched in their communities. They either had paid fees to establish themselves as vecinos, had lived in the region ten years or more, or had "put down roots" by marrying locally, raising families, and establishing households with properties including houses, livestock, farms, or mills. In 1607, Venezuelan officials produced a larger census of the same nature, listing more than one hundred Portuguese persons residing in Caracas, Coro, Carora, Tocuyo, Guanaguanare, Trujillo, Valencia, and Barquisiméto. As noted above, Governor Valdes conducted a similar census in Havana later that year. Of the three documents, only the Havana census mentions women, who made up eight of the forty-nine Portuguese residents listed. Officials' attention to migrants' wealth and status in each of these censuses indicates that metropolitan authorities in the early 1600s

14. "Minuta y padrón de la gente y cassas de la çiudad de Santiago de Cuba," Oct. 6, 1605, AGI-SD 150, r.2, n.33; I. A. Wright, *Santiago de Cuba and Its District (1607–1640)* (Madrid, 1918), 33–34, 101–103. On mestizos' incorporation into Spanish Caribbean society during the early sixteenth century, see Stuart B. Schwartz, "Spaniards, *Pardos,* and the Missing Mestizos: Identities and Racial Categories in the Early Hispanic Caribbean," *NWIG,* LXXI (1997), 5–19; Altman, "Marriage, Family, and Ethnicity," *WMQ,* LXX (2013), 225–250.

were most favorably disposed toward Portuguese who could supplement or augment the ranks of elite Spanish or Spanish American colonists. Most could not hope to match this ideal.[15]

The 1606–1607 censuses for Havana, Santa Marta, and Venezuela together contain descriptions of 202 Portuguese migrants. More than 140 are listed by roughly thirty different occupations, ranging from mariners to miners and from muleteers to silversmiths. Although several are described only as "working for a living" (*vive de su trabajo*) or as "poor," others were merchants, clergymen, and physicians "licensed . . . in medicine." For all but 16, the censuses also estimate how long each person had lived in the region. The periods ranged from as little as two months to "more than fifty years"; the average was approximately eight years. If the Santa Marta census is indicative of broader royal policy, more than half of those listed in the Venezuela and Havana censuses were commanded to depart for Spain with their families and possessions. Havana's governor later claimed to have deported 92 Portuguese and other foreigners, a figure suggesting either the incomplete nature of the city's 1607 census or the pace at which new migrants arrived. Yet, even among those deported, some individuals were able to appeal or otherwise evade their sentence, and those unable to muster a legal defense might have slipped away off the Portuguese coast before the fleets' arrival in Seville. In the case of Havana, at least, very few Portuguese inhabitants appear to have been permanently expelled.[16]

The Portuguese migrants most favored by royal policy and local authorities alike included thirteen men in Venezuela and another five in Santa Marta identified as encomenderos. Nearly all had married in the Spanish Americas. Among those residing in Venezuela, several had been there for less than a decade, but others had been present for "many years." Portuguese encomendero Cristóbal Suarez Brito is described as "ancient in the land," and Andrés Gonzalez is listed as a founding settler of Caracas. Baltazar

15. "Ynforme el gobernador de Santa Marta los estrangeros que ay," Dec. 20, 1606, AGI-SF 49, r.14, n.60a; "Relaçion de los estrangeros," circa June 15, 1607, AGI-SD 193, r.15, n.50b; Pedro de Valdes a S. M., Aug. 12, 1607, AGI-SD 100, r.2, n.58.

16. "Relaçion de los estrangeros," circa June 15, 1607, AGI-SD 193, r.15, n.50b, fols. 1r, 2v–3r; "Ynforme el gobernador de Santa Marta los estrangeros que ay," Dec. 20, 1606, AGI-SF 49, r.14, n.60a, fol. 1v. On Portuguese who managed to avoid deportation from Cuba, see Wright, "Rescates," *HAHR*, III (1920), 352–353. The Indies fleets' trajectory almost invariably ended in Seville or adjacent Spanish ports, where deportees likely feared they would face bureaucratic inconveniences, unwanted expenses, and possibly further punishment. Absenting themselves from the Indies fleet at the first opportunity might have placed some deportees in a better position to return quickly to the Caribbean or another destination of their choosing. For a high-profile escape along similar lines in 1624, see discussion of João Correia de Sousa, former governor of Angola, in Chapter 2, above.

Passana had lived in Caracas for twenty-eight years and was "married to the granddaughter of a conquistador." Since all five Portuguese encomenderos in Santa Marta had resided in the region for ten to twenty years and all had duly paid fees required of foreign residents, they were allowed to stay, though metropolitan authorities requested further information explaining how, precisely, these Portuguese men came to possess encomiendas. Among them only Passana, as a native of the Algarve in southern Portugal, theoretically enjoyed the same rights as Castilians—including the right to hold an encomienda. Though Havana had no Portuguese encomenderos, other prosperous, long-term residents received similar consideration. Hernán Rodriguez Tavares, owner of houses and a sugar mill and patriarch of a large extended family, was considered an "ancient" resident; another "very ancient" resident was Sebastián Fernandez Pacheco, described as the wealthiest man in Havana.[17]

The majority of Portuguese enumerated in the three censuses had spent considerably fewer years in the region. Among merchants and vendors, who constituted nearly one-fifth of all those specified by occupation, most had been in the Caribbean for less than ten years. Judging by the Santa Marta census, nearly all probably had to leave. Mateo Andres, the only merchant authorized to remain in Santa Marta, had lived there for "more than twenty years." As of 1607, two *pulperos* (grocers) had lived in Caracas for five years and eight years respectively; a trader *(tratante)* in the same city had been there only a year. Of those in Havana, two were merchants, and seven were shopkeepers. An additional six wine vendors who did not own a shop or store of their own included two men, two women, and the married couple Duarte de Acuña and his wife ("a black woman, also Portuguese"). All fifteen had been in the city for eight years or less. Only Milicia de Castro, a Portuguese woman who "sells food on the beach" and whose unnamed husband was a Portuguese mariner typically working in the Indies fleets, had lived in Havana for longer than ten years. Most Portuguese tailors and cobblers were in a similar position. Among the twelve listed in the censuses, one tailor and two cobblers had been in Venezuela for sixteen years or more, and one cobbler in Havana had been there for ten; but none of the others had been around longer than six years. Inhabitants employed in construction and the building trades were often even more recent arrivals.

17. "Ynforme el gobernador de Santa Marta los estrangeros que ay," Dec. 20, 1606, AGI-SF 49, r.14, n.60a, fols. 1r, 2r; "Relaçion de los estrangeros," circa June 15, 1607, AGI-SD 193, r.15, n.50b, fols. 1r–3r; Pedro de Valdes a S. M., Aug. 12, 1607, AGI-SD 100, r.2, n.58, fols. 2r–2v. See also Miguel Acosta Saignes, *Historia de los Portugueses en Venezuela* (Caracas, 1977), 79; de la Fuente, *Havana*, 96–98.

Out of seventeen men identified as carpenters, caulkers, bricklayers, and masons, all but five had been in Cuba or Venezuela for four years or less. The main exception was a carpenter named Correa who had lived in Cuba for twelve years and had previously served as a soldier in the city's forts. His experience is consistent with that of two Portuguese soldiers in Venezuela, likewise forced to "work for a living." Other Portuguese migrants had several occupations; in Havana, a baker rented out houses to guests, and a pilot ran a small store.[18]

At least one-fifth of the Portuguese sojourners in the Havana, Santa Marta, and Venezuela censuses owned or labored on farms (estancias) or pearl fisheries, both scenarios in which they were likely to command or work alongside enslaved Africans. Those associated with estancias included two rural landowners and eleven men who "serve in the countryside" in Venezuela, four farm overseers (mayordomos de estancia) in Santa Marta, and two estancia workers in Havana. Since all four overseers in Santa Marta had been present for six years or less, all four were to be expelled. In Venezuela, the two relatively prosperous "men of the countryside" (hombres del campo) and five long-term residents who "served in the countryside" were probably allowed to stay. Another eight farmworkers in Venezuela and Havana had been in the region for six years or less. Since none were married or propertied, they most likely had to leave. The Havana census reveals that rural labor was an option for newly arrived Portuguese and for people unable to find work in their chosen professions. One farmworker had been in Havana for two years but was still described as a "passenger." Another was a book vendor who, "for lack of work in his profession, works on an estancia." Much like farmworkers, those Portuguese involved with pearl fishing—another occupation that relied heavily on African labor—were often fairly recent arrivals. In the Santa Marta census, nine Portuguese men "served as canoeros," or canoe overseers, in Riohacha's pearl fisheries. Six were to be expelled; the other three had married women in Riohacha or Spain and paid fees to establish themselves as resident foreigners. Two had lived in the region for fifteen years or more. Julián Perez, "owner of a canoe of blacks," was also permitted to stay. Naturalized by royal decree, Perez had lived in Riohacha for thirty years, marrying a local woman and raising children who were themselves "married to Spaniards." His possession of enslaved pearl divers meant less to officials than other markers of stabil-

18. "Ynforme el gobernador de Santa Marta los estrangeros que ay," Dec. 20, 1606, AGI-SF 49, r.14, n.60a, fol. 1v; "Relaçion de los estrangeros," circa June 15, 1607, AGI-SD 193, r.15, n.50b, fols. 1r–1v, 3r; Pedro de Valdes a S. M., Aug. 12, 1607, AGI-SD 100, r.2, n.58, fols. 1v, 2v.

ity that would distinguish him as a loyal vecino, most notably his period of residency and his close association with Spanish families through two generations of intermarriage. But, in owning or supervising sub-Saharan African workers, Perez and other canoeros and estancia overseers played roles within early Spanish Caribbean society that strongly echoed Spanish colonies' reliance on Portuguese agents to procure enslaved Africans in the first place.[19]

Tangomãos *and* Grumetes *in Española*

Before their arrival in the Spanish Caribbean, many Portuguese and Luso-African migrants had acquired experience from time spent in Africa or neighboring Atlantic islands. Their extensive cultural exposure and contacts from living in western Africa emerge from the detailed investigation conducted after the *San Jorge*'s arrival in Española in 1575. Nearly half of all enslaved Africans transported on the *San Jorge* were owned by nine passengers repeatedly identified as tangomãos, sometimes rendered in Spanish as *tangomangos*. (Española officials used the word interchangeably with "lançados," a more disparaging Portuguese term for traders who "threw themselves *[lançavam-se]* among the blacks" on the Upper Guinea coast). Spending extended periods of time well beyond the reach of Iberian authorities, tangomãos often maintained long-term partnerships with African women, contributing to the formation of syncretic Luso-African societies. Their main economic activity was *resgate,* meaning "to exchange, or barter"; the term could refer to "trade in male and female slaves" as well as gold and other merchandise. Just as tangomãos in Upper Guinea practiced "resgate," tangomangos in the sixteenth-century Caribbean engaged in "rescate," with both terms describing the acquisition of African captives. "Resgate" in western Africa and "rescate" in the Spanish Caribbean were not merely linguistic parallels or mirror images of one another. The voyage of nine tangomãos from Buguendo to Española on the *San Jorge* reveals that developments in both contexts were directly connected. Such individu-

19. "Relaçion de los estrangeros," circa June 15, 1607, AGI-SD 193, r.15, n.50b, fols. 1r–1v, 2v; "Ynforme el gobernador de Santa Marta los estrangeros que ay," Dec. 20, 1606, AGI-SF 49, r.14, n.60a, fols. 1r–1v; Pedro de Valdes a S. M., Aug. 12, 1607, AGI-SD 100, r.2, n.58, fols. 1r–2r. On canoeros and pearl divers, see Trinidad Miranda Vázquez, *La gobernación de Santa Marta (1570–1670)* (Seville, 1976), 64–68; Acosta Saignes, *Historia de los Portugueses,* 58; Jean-Pierre Tardieu, "Perlas y piel de azabache: El negro en las pesquerías de las Indias Occidentales," *AEA,* LXV, no. 2 (July–December 2008), 91–124; Molly A. Warsh, "Enslaved Pearl Divers in the Sixteenth Century Caribbean," *SA,* XXXI (2010), 345–362.

als greatly facilitated transatlantic commerce, including slave trafficking, but their questionable loyalties—and in Upper Guinea, their temporary or permanent adoption of their hosts' cultures—incurred the suspicion of the Spanish and Portuguese crowns alike.[20]

Of the tangomãos who disembarked in Española in early 1575, at least five originated in Iberia and at least six lived in Portugal, Spain, or the Cape Verde Islands before their extended stay in the Rivers of Guinea. Each left Buguendo with captives intended for resale, and several were business partners. Francisco de Vitoria, formerly of Lisbon, embarked thirty-eight captives in collaboration with his partner Rodrigo Alvarez; apparently only twenty-five had survived by the time the ship reached Española. In addition to "trade captives" *(negros del trato)*, two free Africans traveled with Vitoria as his domestic servants. He claimed to be exempt from paying customs duties on one of them, Guiomar Bran, not only because she was free but also because she would be sailing back to Iberia with him when he left.[21]

Not all tangomãos originated in Portugal or the Portuguese empire; Diego Gomez was originally from "Xerez de Badajoz" (Jerez de los Caballeros), a small town in southwestern Spain located near the Portuguese border but better known as the birthplace of explorers and conquistadors. At some point before his travels in Upper Guinea, Gomez became a vecino of Santiago, in the Cape Verde Islands. He arrived in Española in possession of five black slaves, including three adult men identified as "Jolofo" (Wolof), "Bioho" (Bijago), and "Bran" (Brame). He also owned a tall Wolof woman and a fourteen-year-old black girl from Santiago; the latter were probably domestic slaves rather than trade captives.[22]

20. António Carreira, *Os Portuguêses nos rios de Guiné, 1500–1900* (Lisbon, 1984), 18–23; Jean Boulègue, *Les Luso-Africains de Sénégambie, XVIe–XIXe siècles* (Lisbon, 1989), 11–14; George E. Brooks, *Eurafricans in Western Africa: Commerce, Social Status, Gender, and Religious Observance from the Sixteenth to the Eighteenth Century* (Athens, Oh., 2003), 68–101. On resgate, see P. E. H. Hair, "Portuguese Documents on Africa and Some Problems of Translation," *HA*, XXVII (2000), 91–97; António Carreira, "Tratos e resgates dos Portugueses nos rios de Guiné e ilhas de Cabo Verde nos começos do século XVII," *RHES*, no. 2 (July–December 1978), 91–103; Maria Manuel Ferraz Torrão, "Rotas comerciais, agentes económicos, meios de pagamento," in Maria Emília Madeira Santos, coord., *História Geral de Cabo Verde* (Lisbon, 1995), II, 19–27. For an overview of the evolution of "rescate" on both sides of the Iberian Atlantic, see Enrique Otte, *Las perlas del Caribe: Nueva Cádiz de Cubagua* (Caracas, 1977), 98–100. On tangomangos as Caribbean smugglers, see Deive, *Tangomangos*, 82–84, 234.

21. "Contratadores de Cabo Verde y Guinea con Cristóbal Cayado," 1582–1589, AGI-Esc 2A, pieza 2, fols. 39v–40r, 67r, 72v, 113r–117r, 493v–497v, 553v–554r. For further analysis of this source, with emphasis on developments in Upper Guinea, see Toby Green, *The Rise of the Trans-Atlantic Slave Trade in Western Africa, 1300–1589* (New York, 2012), 25, 216–217, 225, 247, 250–251, 255, 258, 263, 266–267, 272–275.

22. "Contratadores de Cabo Verde y Guinea con Cristóbal Cayado," 1582–1589, AGI-Esc 2A, pieza 2, fols. 108v–112v, 494r–497v.

Table 5 *Tangomãos* and Passengers on the Slave Ship *San Jorge,* with Their Servants, Domestic Slaves, and Trade Captives, Española, 1575

Name and description	Place of Origin	*Vecino* of	Free servants	Domestic slaves	Trade captives
Francisco de Vitoria, tangomão	Portugal	Lisbon, Portugal	Guiomar Bran	A "Bran" (Brame) boy	25*
Rodrigo Alvarez, tangomão	—	—	—	—	
Ruy Lopez, tangomão	Portugal	"Los Alcazeres," Portugal	—	—	26*
Melchor Gomez, tangomão	—	—	—	—	
Alfonso Lopez, tangomão	Portugal	—	—	Leonor Bran; a young mulato boy	15*
Juan Gonçales, tangomão	Portugal	—	—	—	
Nicolao Fernandes, tangomão	—	—	—	—	12
Luisa Reja *mujer prieta* (black woman), tangomanga	—	Santiago, Cape Verde Islands	—	A "Bañol" (Bañun) man	5
Diego Gomez, tangomão	Jerez de los Caballeros, Spain	Santiago, Cape Verde Islands	—	A "Jolofa" (Wolof) woman; a Capeverdean girl	3
António Perez *portugues,* passenger	—	Santiago, Cape Verde Islands	—	Esperanza *criolla de Cabo Verde;* Antonyo negro	10
Francisco Lopez *negro horro,* passenger	—	—	—	—	—

Source: "Contratadores de Cabo Verde y Guinea con Cristóbal Cayado y otros del reino de Portugal," 1582–1589, AGI-Esc 2A, pieza 2, fols. 30r–54v, 493v–500r.

Note: Though not listed here, Luisa Reja was also accompanied by her seven-year-old daughter, Dominga. The asterisk (*) indicates groups of trade captives jointly owned by two tangomãos.

Among the *San Jorge*'s nine passengers described as tangomãos, the only female—and the only person of notable African ancestry—was Luisa Reja, a free woman of color. Her origins are not specified, but, like Gomez, Reja was considered a *"vecina* of the Cape Verde Islands." On the voyage to the Caribbean, she was accompanied by her seven-year-old daughter, "a little black girl named Dominga." She also brought six captives, one of whom died during the ocean crossing. Another—a black man "of the Bañol [Bañun] land"—was likely her domestic slave. The other five, presumably intended for sale, included two enslaved Brames listed by the Iberian names Felipa and Nicolau. In addition to her daughter, one domestic slave, and five trade captives, Reja brought a quintal (about one hundred pounds) of Upper Guinean beeswax.[23]

Following the *San Jorge*'s arrival in Española, one of the main reasons for litigation was that Spanish Caribbean officials believed that all captives disembarked should be either confiscated as unregistered contraband or at least taxed in accordance with standard procedures for incoming slave traffic. The tangomãos countered that their voyage was completely unintentional and swore they had already paid steep customs fees on the Upper Guinea coast. Under Portuguese law, anyone living in the "Rivers of Guinea" for more than "a year and a day" would thereafter be considered a lançado or tangomão and, as such, would automatically forfeit one-half of all their wealth. Thus, when tangomãos left Upper Guinea, they were obliged to surrender half of their captives (or an equivalent monetary value) to agents of the Portuguese crown. Furthermore, a ten *ducado* exit fee was required for each captive exported to the Spanish Americas; the tangomãos argued they had already paid this fee, too, in the form of *paños*—valuable textiles probably woven in the Cape Verde Islands—at a rate of twenty-four paños (worth ten ducados total) per captive.[24]

Other passengers arriving on the *San Jorge* were not described as tangomãos. António Perez, another Portuguese vecino of Santiago in the Cape Verde Islands, brought ten trade captives and two domestic slaves. One of the latter, a Capeverdean woman named Esperanza, evidently passed into the service of the ship's captain—and from slavery to freedom—at some point during the five-week voyage. Perez had much in common with several

23. Ibid., fols. 54v, 108v, 116r, 496v–499v.
24. Ibid., fols. 540r–541v. On Cape Verdean *panos*, see António Carreira, *Panaria Cabo-Verdiano-Guineense: Aspectos históricos e sócio-económicos* (Lisbon, 1969); Linda A. Newson, "The Slave-Trading Accounts of Manoel Batista Peres, 1613–1619: Double-Entry Bookkeeping in Cloth Money," *Accounting History*, XVIII (2013), 343–365.

of the tangomãos; like them, he normally resided in the Cape Verde Islands and had traveled to Buguendo to trade for slaves. But, unlike his fellow passengers designated as tangomãos or lançados, Perez spent only a short amount of time on the Upper Guinea coast. The free black man Francisco Lopez was also identified as a passenger but not as a tangomão. As he did not bring any captives on his own account, he appears to have been simply traveling between Buguendo and the Cape Verde Islands, if that was his intended destination, or from Buguendo to Española, if he knew the ship would ultimately sail toward the Caribbean.[25]

During the year after their arrival in Española, most of the *San Jorge*'s tangomãos and passengers sold their captives and merchandise to buyers in Santo Domingo, reinvesting in local commodities such as hides, tobacco, ginger, sugar, and other "fruits of the land." Although some money or bills of exchange likely changed hands, the African captives might have been traded directly for local products, a classic resgate / rescate scenario that would have been familiar to all parties involved. As of March 1576, several tangomãos had already left the island for parts unknown; those who remained in Española declared their intentions to depart with their newly acquired goods on the next fleet bound for Spain, then return to their respective homes. For tangomãos like Gomez and Reja, this would mean eventually returning to the Cape Verde Islands, where they had established themselves as vecinos. At least one tangomão, however, intended to remain. Alfonso Lopez married a woman in Santo Domingo soon after his arrival; numerous inhabitants of Santo Domingo testified that he had established a permanent household and "put down roots" in the city.[26]

In addition to trade captives, the *San Jorge*'s passengers and crew members brought Luso-African domestic slaves and servants, including several free, sub-Saharan Africans who bore Iberian given names and surnames. The vessel's captain and owner, Cristóbal Cayado, was also heavily invested in the voyage as the owner of sixty-three trade captives. Above deck, Cayado employed two free black maidservants: a Wolof woman named Felipa Martin and Esperanza, the Capeverdean woman. The ship's pilot Alfonso Yanes, who brought six captives for sale, also employed a free black servant of Capeverdean origin named Manuel. Two women onboard were apparently concubines for passengers or crew members, dependents whose

25. "Contratadores de Cabo Verde y Guinea con Cristóbal Cayado," 1582–1589, AGI-Esc 2A, pieza 2, fols. 74r–75v, 493v, 500r.

26. Ibid., fols. 67r–67v, 69v, 72v–73r, 74r, 75v–76r, 78v–79r, 80r–80v.

legal status as free or enslaved was fairly ambiguous. The free Papel woman Catalina Hernandez arrived in Española "with two mulato infants at her breasts." Another woman named Leonor Bran was accompanied by a "little mulatto boy." When the *San Jorge* was first inspected, Portuguese tangomão Alfonso Lopez stated that Leonor Bran was free; a few days later, however, he appeared before Española's royal officials to claim that he had lied and that in truth she was his slave. He might originally have been trying to avoid paying customs fees. Or, if he was the mulato boy's father, he might have been attempting to protect her and their son.[27]

According to the testimony of tangomão Ruy Lopez, the *San Jorge* carried at least eight free black *grumetes,* or apprentice seamen. Antónyo Gomez "of the Zape land" is identified as a grumete and a free man. Other free black men who were probably grumetes included another "Zape" man named Hernando; Amador Lopez and Atanácio Cardosso, both raised in the Cape Verde Islands; and Antónyo Sorrobero, *algarabio* (from the Algarve in southern Portugal). Several people of African descent on the *San Jorge* traveled or worked as enslaved sailors on behalf of absentee owners. Julián Gomez, "captain" of the ship's enslaved mariners, was owned by a man "who is in Lisbon." An enslaved, black Capeverdean named Bastián Botello was a grumete on the *San Jorge;* his owner presumably lived in the Cape Verde Islands, where Botello resided. A black man named Martin Vaez was owned by a scribe who also lived in the Cape Verde Islands.[28]

In the early modern Spanish maritime world, grumetes were apprentice seamen, not yet full-fledged sailors (*marineros*) but higher in rank and status than mere cabin boys (*pajes*). Meanwhile, in Portuguese, by the late fifteenth century the term came to hold entirely new meanings, particularly along the coasts and rivers of western Africa. Though it continued to be associated with maritime contexts, the term "grumete" designated sub-Saharan Africans and Luso-Africans who performed a wide range of tasks on behalf of Portuguese and Capeverdean merchants, mariners, and tangomãos. On the Upper Guinea coast, grumetes served as local pilots, interpreters, and commercial go-betweens and helped build and repair watercraft. On slave ships like the *San Jorge,* the term might have also referred to guardians who maintained control over larger numbers of trade captives. In early-seventeenth-century Cartagena, Jesuit missionary Alonso

27. Ibid., fols. 108v, 493r–493v, 499v–500v, 513r–513v.
28. Ibid., fols. 108v, 497v–500r, 513r.

de Sandoval mentioned a slave ship arriving with "twelve or fourteen . . . *ladinos* [Latinized Africans] who came guarding the rest."[29]

Although rarely specifying the types of labor actually performed, Iberian port departure records commonly refer to black grumetes and pajes on Iberian slave ships. Slave ship captains were obliged to provide assurances they would not sell their enslaved mariners in the Americas. Upon departing the Canary Islands in 1592, one shipmaster pledged one hundred thousand *maravedís* as collateral for two slaves serving as pajes on his ship, each described as "tall," "about twenty years old," and in good physical condition. They might have been sold anyway; one minor form of contraband slave trafficking consisted of enrolling slaves as sailors and selling them in the Americas, then claiming they had died during the voyage (in the early seventeenth century, for example, black grumetes appear to have died with surprising frequency en route to Veracruz).[30]

In some cases, little effort was made to conceal this type of illicit slave trafficking. For instance, sailing from Brazil and allegedly bound for Lisbon, mariners on the caravel *San Juan Bautista* apparently sold six enslaved crew members while stopping in Puerto Rico in 1607. But the assumption that black grumetes were merely trade captives in disguise ignores the critical roles grumetes played in African contexts. Caribbean officials might have been quick to associate African grumetes with trade captives but ultimately recognized that some black sailors, whether free or enslaved, were not for

29. Juan Manuel Pacheco, *Los jesuitas en Colombia* (Bogotá, 1959), I, 253. This source supports Stephanie E. Smallwood's argument that early modern Iberian slave ships regularly employed African guardians; see Smallwood, "African Guardians, European Slave Ships, and the Changing Dynamics of Power in the Early Modern Atlantic," *WMQ*, LXIV (2007), 686. For further discussion of ladinos, see Chapter 6, below. On Spanish grumetes, see Carla Rahn Phillips, *Six Galleons for the King of Spain: Imperial Defense in the Early Seventeenth Century* (Baltimore, 1986), 143–144; Pérez-Mallaína, *Spain's Men of the Sea*, trans. Phillips, 29, 75–79. For Luso-African contexts, see Brooks, *Landlords and Strangers*, 124, 136–137, 181, 194–195; Philip J. Havik, *Silences and Soundbites: The Gendered Dynamics of Trade and Brokerage in the Pre-Colonial Guinea Bissau Region* (Münster, Germany, 2004), 129–145.

30. "Registros despachados para las Yndias con sclavos desde la ysla d Teneriffe," 1592, AGI-Cttn 2875, n.6, r.6, fols. 110r–112r; Scelle, *La traite négrière*, 373–374, 809–810; Rozendo Sampaio Garcia, "Contribuição ao estudo do aprovisionamento de escravos negros na América Espanhola," *Anais do Museu Paulista*, XVI (1962), 92–93; Vila Vilar, *Hispanoamérica*, 137, 168–169. See also Mariana P. Candido, "Different Slave Journeys: Enslaved African Seamen on Board of Portuguese Ships, c.1760–1820s," *SA*, XXXI (2010), 395–409. Black grumetes and pajes appear in various slave ship crew rosters in "Registros de esclavos," 1584–1599, AGI-Cttn 2875. For examples of enslaved crew members allegedly dying near Veracruz, see "Autos sobre el sueldo de Juan Ventura," 1632, AGI-Cttn 533B, n.2, r.77; "Autos sobre los sueldos de Lorenzo Arfián," 1632, AGI-Cttn 533B, n.2, r.122; "Información sobre la muerte en Veracruz de Antón Sardina," 1608, AGI-Cttn 941B, n.32; "Gastos de entierro de Baltasar de Reyes," 1620, AGI-Cttn 5709, n.211, r.24; "Gastos de entierro de Pedro de la Torre," 1621, AGI-Cttn 5709, n.218, r.27.

sale. In 1595, they recorded the caravel *Nuestra Señora de la Concepción*'s arrival from Angola with at least two black grumetes on board. Likewise, when the caravel *San Antonio* arrived from Cacheu in 1628, royal officials noted that "among [the blacks] was one named Marçial" who claimed to be free and would provide written proof.[31]

The *San Jorge*'s voyage to Española provides another example of a readily discernable Luso-African presence in the early Spanish Caribbean: several free and enslaved people of color on the ship were natives of the Cape Verde Islands, especially the island of Santiago de Cabo Verde. Among the black mariners arriving in Española on the *San Jorge* in 1575, a number were originally born or raised in the Cape Verde Islands. The enslaved grumete Bastián Botello was a "creole from Cape Verde," and the free black grumete Amador Lopez was "raised on the island of Santiago." Likewise, at least two servants employed by officers and passengers were from the same islands; as noted above, Captain Cayado's servant Esperanza was a "black creole from Cape Verde," and tangomão Diego Gomez brought a *negrita muchacha* (little black girl) from "the island of Santiago."[32]

Although early colonial Spanish Caribbean sources mention African "lands" and "nations" with much greater frequency, references to African-descended creoles from the Cape Verde Islands (*criollos de Cabo Verde*) and São Tomé (*criollos de San Tomé*) are not uncommon. For example, twenty-four-year-old Francisca, "a creole from Cabo Verde," was sold in Havana during the late 1570s. An enslaved black woman named "Francisca de Cabo Verde" (possibly the same person) had her newborn son baptized in Havana in 1593. Two enslaved women identified as "Antona de San Tomé" and "Maria de San Tomé" served as godmothers for newly baptized African women during the same decade. Capeverdeans and São Tomeans of African descent also lived in Cartagena. A "creole from San Tomé" named Juliana was an enslaved black woman in her late twenties, owned by the city's Discalced Carmelite convent. She and her husband Gerónimo Angola both gave testimony in an investigation conducted in 1609. In his treatise on slavery, Sandoval devoted several lines to creoles from the Cape Verde Islands and São Tomé, and, during the mid-seventeenth century, enslaved deponents "Manuel de Cabo Verde" and "Mariana de Cabo Verde" testified

---

31. Vila Vilar, *Hispanoamérica*, 170n; Caja de Cartagena, Cuentas, 1595, AGI-Ctdra 1385, n.3, pliego 10; Caja de Cartagena, Cuentas de los años 1628 y 1629, AGI-Ctdra 1398, n.1, pliego 106.

32. "Contratadores de Cabo Verde y Guinea con Cristóbal Cayado," 1582–1589, AGI-Esc 2A, pieza 2, fols. 493v, 497v, 500r.

to the charitable and miraculous deeds performed by Sandoval's colleague, Pedro Claver.[33]

Afro-Iberians—people of African descent born or raised in Iberia—were similar to creoles of the Cape Verde Islands and São Tomé in that both groups arrived in the Spanish Caribbean with prior experience of interaction between Africans and Iberians. Afro-Iberians' familiarity with peninsular Spanish and Portuguese cultures also mirrored Portuguese and Capeverdean tangomãos' immersion in Upper Guinean societies, with the difference that the former's presence in Lisbon, Seville, and other areas of southwestern Iberia, where they comprised as much as 10 percent of the population, was largely involuntary. Although "Spanish blacks" are occasionally mentioned, most Afro-Iberians in the early colonial Spanish Caribbean were described as "Portuguese." Thus, in the late 1570s, two enslaved men sold in Havana were each described as a "black slave" and as "Portuguese." In Cartagena, "Anton Portugues" was one of more than twenty slaves employed on an estancia outside the city in 1622 (see Table 11). At the same time, Afro-Iberians were more likely than sub-Saharan Africans to arrive in the Spanish Caribbean as free people of color. Among the free black grumetes arriving in Española on the *San Jorge* in 1575, Antónyo Sorrobero was from the Algarve, in southern Portugal. Another free black man from Touro, Portugal, named Antón de Contreras was a witness in legal proceedings in Cartagena in 1583. Two decades later in Havana, "Matheo *moreno español*" (Matheo, Spanish black), who was not identified as a slave, and "Juan Portuguese moreno *horro*" (Juan free black Portuguese) each served as godfathers at the baptisms of enslaved women. Much like Capeverdean and São Tomean creoles, these Afro-Iberians embodied cross-cultural exchanges and forced migrations that had linked Africa to the Iberian world before Spanish colonization of the Caribbean.[34]

Despite their ostensible origins in Portugal, such men might have traveled to the Spanish Caribbean via Africa as mariners or servants on slave

33. María Teresa de Rojas, [ed.], *Índice y extractos del Archivo de protocolos de la Habana, 1578–1588,* 3 vols. (Havana, 1947–1957), I, 202; Baptisms of Francisca Bioho (Jan. 24, 1593), Domingo negro (Dec. 11, 1593), Lucresia Angola (Jan. 24, 1599), CH-LB/B, fols. 24v, 36v, 139r; "Autos del capitán Pedro de Murguia," 1609, AGI-Cttn 772, n.13, fols. 25r–26r; Alonso de Sandoval, *Un tratado sobre la esclavitud,* introduction and transcription by Enriqueta Vila Vilar (Madrid, 1987), 139–140; Anna María Splendiani and Tulio Aristizábal, eds. and trans., *Proceso de beatificación y canonización de san Pedro Claver, edición de 1696* (Bogotá, 2002), 110, 379–380, 397, 422, 463–464, 513–516; for the enslaved cook "Margarita de Cabo Verde," see also 437–438.

34. "Contratadores de Cabo Verde y Guinea con Cristóbal Cayado," 1582–1589, AGI-Esc 2A, pieza 2, fol. 500r; "Memorial y testimonio de autos de la ciudad y provincia de Cartagena sobre los abusos y delitos que contra aquellos vecinos cometen los soldados de las galeras y flotas," May 11, 1583, AGI-SF

ships. Cristóbal Mayorga, a free black man from Portimão in the Algarve, provides one such example. Though Mayorga ultimately became a merchant residing in Santiago de Cuba, he first reached the island on a slave ship as "a pilot of the Angola trade." In some cases, the term "Portuguese black" was probably used to designate African-descended people from any region of the Portuguese empire, including parts of western Africa. For example, although Manuel Lopez, who had traveled to Cartagena in 1629 on a slave ship as the captain's servant, was described by Cartagena officials the following year as a "mulato[,] native of Cacheu in Guinea," less discriminating observers might have just referred to him as Portuguese. Within the Spanish Caribbean, usage of the term "Portuguese" as shorthand for passers-through and migrants from all over the Luso-Atlantic world made sense given the highly diverse origins of the mariners, traders, and travelers who arrived aboard slave ships.[35]

Slave Ship Migrants in Cartagena de Indias

Perhaps more than anywhere else in the circum-Caribbean, Portuguese and Luso-Africans were firmly entrenched in Cartagena de Indias. Clearly aware of royal policies forbidding unauthorized travel to the Spanish Americas and of metropolitan authorities' particular concern over non-Hispanic migration, as early as 1586, the city's governor Pedro de Lodeña informed the Spanish crown of "the tremendous number of foreigners and Portuguese who for days and even years have resided in this city." This influx of non-Castilians was frequently attributed to the arrival of Portuguese merchants, seamen, and passengers on slave ships. Displaying an acute awareness of the profits generated by slave trafficking (derived in no small part from personal experience), Cartagena's royal officials complained in 1590 that "the great quantity of Portuguese who have arrived via Guinea and the Barlovento islands are gathering up all the money of this city and

---

62, n.28, fols. 30v–31v; Rojas, ed., *Índice y extractos,* I, 9, 241–242; Baptisms of María Angola (Jan. 30, 1594), Mariana esclava (Dec. 28, 1595), Graçia Bioho (Dec. 28, 1595), CH-LB/B, fols. 39r, 70r; Pedro Guiral con Joan de Arce y Juan de Acosta, 1622, AGI-Esc 632B, pieza 2, fols. 196r, 591r, 738v. See also Leo J. Garofalo, "The Shape of a Diaspora: The Movement of Afro-Iberians to Colonial Spanish America," in Sherwin K. Bryant et al., eds., *Africans to Spanish America: Expanding the Diaspora* (Urbana, Ill., 2012), 27–49. On the demographic presence of Africans and people of African origin in early modern Iberia, see A. C. de C. M. Saunders, *A Social History of Black Slaves and Freedmen in Portugal, 1441–1555* (Cambridge, 1982), 59; Pérez García and Fernández Chaves, "Sevilla y la trata," in Álvarez Santaló, coord., *Estudios de historia moderna,* 600–602.

35. De la Fuente, *Havana,* 99, 244n; "Relaçion y abecedario de los estrangeros," May 13, 1631, AGI-SF 56B, n.73a, fol. 22r; Vila Vilar, "Extranjeros," *JGSWGL,* XVI (December 1979), 181.

province through slave trading." Governor Lodeña's letter to the crown the same year also mentioned the potentially "inconvenient" fact that slave ships disembarked large numbers of Portuguese migrants throughout the region. Apparently on his own initiative, fifteen years before similar censuses were conducted in Santa Marta, Venezuela, and Havana, Lodeña appointed Portuguese vecino Luis de Santa Maria to compose a census of all Portuguese persons residing in Cartagena. Though the resulting list has not been found, Lodeña wrote the crown that it contained information on 164 people and awaited further orders on what to do with them. Like officials in Cuba and Española ten years later, Lodeña's assessment of Portuguese in Cartagena appears to have evolved rapidly, becoming more nuanced if not sympathetic in the space of just a few years. In 1592, still uncertain how to proceed, Lodeña again requested clarification on the status of Portuguese residents. This time, however, he reminded the crown that they included both long-term vecinos who had married into local families and licensed slave ship captains, "some of whom remain here for two or three years."[36]

By the dawn of the seventeenth century, following an unprecedented surge in transatlantic slave trafficking during the 1590s, Cartagena's highest-ranking authorities had come to view the slave trade as the city's primary source of income. In response to royal directives to purge the city of all "foreign" elements, especially Portuguese "Judaizers," Cartagena's city council and governor alike sought to protect those Portuguese associated with the slave trade, portraying them as key allies in maintaining the city's fragile prosperity. In 1602, Cartagena's city council requested that the crown reconsider its demand to expel the Portuguese, noting that "the city's conservation and growth depends on trade and commerce . . . most of which is administered by foreigners serving as factors for their [own] countrymen." Cartagena administrators' abrupt change of opinion regarding the Portuguese reflected their evolving responses to the conflicting economic agendas projected onto the city. Whereas newly arrived officials often attempted to enforce policies that backed the interests of the Spanish crown and merchants based in Seville, the intensification of the slave trade and the concomitant growth of Cartagena during the 1590s convinced local officials that it was in the city's best interests—and, presumably, their own—to

36. Cartas de Pedro de Lodeña a S. M., Aug. 13, 1586, AGI-SF 37, r.6, n.69, July 6, 1590, n.95, Sept. 15, 1592, n.107; Luis de Guzman y Alonso de Tapia a S. M., July 4, 1590, AGI-SF 72, n.81, fol. 3r; Vila Vilar, *Hispanoamérica,* 99–103, 118–22; Antonino Vidal Ortega, *Cartagena de Indias y la región histórica del Caribe, 1580–1640* (Seville, 2002), 76–79, 109, 122–149.

cultivate the Luso-Atlantic networks that had transformed Cartagena into the most important slaving hub in seventeenth-century Spanish America.[37]

New governor Jerónimo de Zuazo went further than royal officials, specifically addressing metropolitan concerns that disloyal, Portuguese crypto-Jews would contaminate local Indian populations with their religious beliefs and brazenly trade with Northern European interlopers. In a letter dated 1603, Zuazo informed the crown that there was "not a single house of Indians" in the city of Cartagena; in fact, "they are all in the interior and the closest Indian pueblo is six leagues away." Furthermore, the city's residents rarely dealt with Indians on account of "the land's roughness[,] the trail's discomforts[,] and other reasons." In self-congratulatory fashion, Zuazo also noted that thanks to the diligence of Cartagena's galleys (under his command), "enemy" merchant ships had not been seen in the area for quite some time. Echoing the city council, he wrote that "the largest and most important commerce of this city is that of the slaves who come from Guinea and Angola[,] and since these are provinces of the Portuguese Crown[,] everyone or nearly everyone involved is Portuguese." If Cartagena's Portuguese residents were expelled, he cautioned, this "fattest and best" commerce would be lost, along with the entire province's future labor supply. The royal treasury would forfeit not only revenues garnered from lucrative slave trade licenses but also local taxes on slave imports which, at twenty-six *reales* per captive, represented the primary source of income for maintaining Cartagena's fortifications.[38]

For Cartagena's governor and royal officials, revenues derived from the slave trade guaranteed the city's economic health and a steady flow of income for royal coffers, thus providing justification for tolerating and even encouraging a Portuguese presence in the Caribbean. According to Zuazo, without "relatives or friends of the same nation in Cartagena[,] people of credit who can take charge of newly arrived slaves," Lisbon elites would hesitate to invest in the slave trade. For many of the Caribbean's long-term Portuguese and Luso-African residents, however, the slave traffic was ultimately a mechanism for migration. Portuguese migrants in the 1605–1607 censuses for Havana, Santa Marta, and Venezuela had integrated themselves into Spanish Caribbean economies under diverse circumstances; many

37. Vidal Ortega, *Cartagena,* 79; Carta del cabildo secular de Cartagena, Aug. 14, 1602, AGI-SF 62, n.83; Jerónimo de Zuazo a S. M., Aug. 1, 1603, AGI-SF 38, r.2, n.55. Council members later blamed an economic downturn on a temporary lull in the slave trade; see Carta del cabildo secular de Cartagena, Aug. 18, 1606, AGI-SF 62, n.90.

38. Jerónimo de Zuazo a S. M., Aug. 1, 1603, AGI-SF 38, r.2, n.55; Vidal Ortega, *Cartagena,* 78–79.

likely arrived on slave ships. Such was the case for Coro resident Diego Lopez, who "came with a boatload of blacks." Among the slave ship pilots, mariners, and passengers who chose to remain in the Caribbean, some continued to exercise professions directly linked to the slave trade or to one of many subsidiary occupations that supported the slave trade and the Indies fleets. Or, like the Portuguese merchants who used their access to African ports and slave-trafficking networks as a means of establishing themselves in Seville, or those who entered Spanish American markets by selling enslaved Africans and then later switched to trading textiles, other nonelite Portuguese men who first arrived in the Spanish Caribbean on slave ships often came to exercise professions not directly related to the slave trade.[39]

In Cartagena, the flow of Portuguese migrants apparently never abated during the early seventeenth century; a second slave trade surge lasting from the late 1610s through the first half of the 1620s brought even larger numbers of Portuguese and Luso-Africans to the city. Pressure from the crown, the Council of the Indies, and Sevillian merchants to staunch this unauthorized migratory stream continued as before, with the difference that new, specially appointed officials (who were less beholden to Luso-Atlantic commercial networks and local social ties than Cartagena's governors and administrators) were sent from Spain. A detailed roster of nearly two hundred foreigners in urban Cartagena, taken by special commission in 1630, reveals slave ship passengers' and mariners' subsequent experiences in Spanish Caribbean society. More than 150 Portuguese men of varied background and social status provided brief autobiographies in response to questions posed by general inspector Don Antonio Rodriguez de San Isidro Manrique and his subordinates. As might be expected in Cartagena in 1630, these included a number of prosperous slave merchants. Indeed, several of Cartagena's prominent Portuguese elites owed their fortunes to this commerce. Among them were Juan Rodriguez de Mesa and Luis Gomez Barreto. Although each would later be accused of crypto-Jewish practices and judged by the Inquisition, in 1630, both were able to produce letters documenting their naturalization as Spanish subjects drawn up in Madrid and "signed by his Majesty's royal hand." Among other wealthy Portuguese

39. Jerónimo de Zuazo a S. M., Aug. 1, 1603, AGI-SF 38, r.2, n.55, fol. 1v; "Relaçion de los estrangeros," circa June 15, 1607, AGI-SD 193, r.15, n.50b, fol. 1v. On Havana's service economy, see de la Fuente, *Havana*, 51–67, 153–155. On slave trafficking as a mechanism for Portuguese entry into Spanish and Spanish American markets, see Manuel F. Fernández Chaves and Rafael M. Pérez García, "La penetración económica Portuguesa en la Sevilla del siglo XVI," *Espacio, tiempo y forma: Serie IV, historia moderna*, no. 25 (2012), 199–222; J. I. Israel, "The Portuguese in Seventeenth-Century Mexico," *JGSWGL*, XI (1974), 23–24.

men likewise accused of crypto-Jewish practices, at least four are known to have initially arrived on slave ships departing from Angola, São Tomé, and "Guinea." One was a surgeon; the others are each described as traders or merchants.[40]

According to his own testimony, Bernardo Drago first arrived in the Americas in 1619 on a slave ship sailing from Angola. Upon reaching Cartagena, his entire shipload of slaves was confiscated by Cartagena's royal officials. In the account he gave in 1630, more than a decade later, Drago neglected to mention several significant details. First, his voyage was completely unauthorized, thus explaining why all ninety-nine captives found onboard were confiscated. Secondly, before entering Cartagena's port, he had concealed an additional seventy captives on the nearby island of Baru. These were also confiscated as contraband, though only fifty-nine remained alive by the time port authorities discovered them. Despite this setback, Drago had eventually become quite successful as a commercial agent transporting "blacks and other kinds of merchandise" between Cartagena and Lima.[41]

Unlike Drago and other merchants whose experiences illustrate the substantial wealth that stood to be gained by trafficking enslaved Africans in the early modern Iberian world, most of the Portuguese men and women who participated in the transatlantic slave trade never became wealthy or powerful. Some of the slave ship pilots, sailors, deckhands, cabin boys, doctors, barbers, and passengers who appear in the 1630 report had arrived in Cartagena only recently and would soon depart for Iberia again, rather than pay the fees required to establish themselves as resident foreigners. Some likely never intended to stay; a Luanda-born slave ship passenger Lorenço Correa de Leon claimed to be traveling to Spain "to study at the University of Salamanca." Others had already resided in Cartagena, or elsewhere in the Caribbean, for years. Some found employment in maritime labors that might have resembled their activities as mariners on slave trade voyages. Others learned to practice new occupations or returned to professions they

40. "Relaçion y abecedario de los estrangeros que se hallaron en la çiudad de Cartagena, 1630," May 13, 1631, AGI-SF 56B, n.73a, fols. 16r, 17r, 19r. The pioneering study of this source is Vila Vilar, "Extranjeros," *JGSWGL*, XVI (December 1979), 160–165. See also Ventura, *Portugueses no Peru,* vol. I, tomo 1, 100–105, vol. II, 31–77; Ricardo Escobar Quevedo, *Inquisición y judaizantes en América española (siglos XVI–XVII)* (Bogotá, 2008), 246–256.

41. "Relaçion y abecedario de los estrangeros que se hallaron en la çiudad de Cartagena, 1630," May 13, 1631, AGI-SF 56B, n.73a, fols. 4v–5r; Vila Vilar, "Extranjeros," *JGSWGL,* XVI (December 1979), 180; Ventura, *Portugueses no Peru,* vol. II, 39–40; "Certificaçion de los negros que han entrado en Cartaxena," Mar. 28, 1623, AGI-SF 74, n.6, fol. 19v.

had known before crossing the Atlantic on slave ships. António de Rivero arrived in Cartagena as a cabin boy on a slave ship from Angola when he was nine years old. Thirty years later, he was married to a locally born woman and worked as an employee on an estancia outside Cartagena. Similarly, Domingo Diaz arrived in Cartagena on a slave ship sailing from the Cape Verde Islands in approximately 1600. Following his arrival, he served as a soldier for twelve or thirteen years and eventually started a small business transporting clothing and food supplies between Cartagena and Maracaibo. António Nuñez, a native of Terceira in the Azores, was forty years old in 1630. Like the other mariners mentioned here, he had departed from Angola as an assistant or apprentice sailor twenty years earlier on a slave ship that was bound for New Spain but landed at Margarita Island instead. After laboring as a sailor on many subsequent voyages throughout the region, he finally settled in Cartagena in 1623. There, he married a woman who was also from the Azores. They soon had two children, and he started a business buying and selling boats. At nineteen years old, Ignácio de Acosta arrived in Cartagena on a slave ship from São Tomé in 1627 and found work in the city as a goldsmith within three years. Taken together, such narratives provide insight into a historical process that facilitated Portuguese access to the Spanish Caribbean, bypassing the challenging (and for many, impossible) requirements necessary to procure travel authorization and passage on a vessel departing from Seville. Slave ships were a major conduit not only for Portuguese and Luso-Africans but also for the knowledge and diverse experiences of Africa and Africans that these migrants carried with them, largely resulting from their own participation in the transatlantic slave trade.[42]

Luso-African Knowledge of Africa and Africans

Although their perspectives were diverse, each of the mariners, merchants, and passengers who traveled to the early colonial Spanish Caribbean on slave ships brought some degree of knowledge of transatlantic slave trafficking. Some had extensive experience living in sub-Saharan African and Luso-African societies. In Cartagena during the first decade of the seven-

---

42. "Relaçion y abecedario de los estrangeros que se hallaron en la çiudad de Cartagena, 1630," May 13, 1631, AGI-SF 56B, n.73a, fols. 2v, 4r, 7r, 18r, 27r; Vila Vilar, "Extranjeros," *JGSWGL*, XVI (December 1979), 178–179, 182. For the various obstacles that would-be migrants had to overcome to travel legally from Seville to the Spanish Americas, see Jacobs, "Legal and Illegal Emigration," in Altman and Horn, eds., *"To Make America,"* 59–84.

teenth century, legal proceedings over the identity and ownership of an enslaved African led to Portuguese migrants' articulating their knowledge of Africa and of Africans. In 1607, standing before Spanish authorities in Cartagena, the scribe Juan de Meneses claimed that, five or six years earlier, he had purchased a black *bozal* (unacculturated) slave named Luis "of the Congo land." Though he was immediately put to work on Meneses's farm, Luis soon ran away and disappeared. In 1607, Meneses sent a frigate up the Magdalena River to Mompox, a town not far from Cartagena. On this trip, Meneses's enslaved sailor named Juan Angola encountered his old acquaintance Luis and spoke with him. Luis related that his new owner was Francisco Camargo, the most powerful man in Mompox. Rather than performing agricultural labor, Luis mainly served alongside other Africans who paddled Camargo's canoes, transporting merchandise up and down the river. When Meneses learned of Luis's whereabouts, he immediately drew up legal documents, demanding that Camargo return his long absent slave. In response, Camargo sent notice from Mompox that this was a case of mistaken identity: rather than Luis Congo, the African in question was a man named "Francisco Anchico," whom he had legally purchased several years earlier. As proof, Camargo enclosed a bill of sale. Evidently, he believed that his own power—or, perhaps, the vague understanding of West Central African ethnicities that prevailed in the Spanish Americas at that time—would suffice to support his argument.[43]

Such litigation over the ownership of enslaved women and men was quite common, yet this case is remarkable for its attention to the ethnolinguistic background of a West Central African man identified alternately by a variety of witnesses as Luis negro, Luis Congo, Francisco Anchico, Luis Angola, and Francisco Angola. Instead of focusing on whether his proper Spanish name was Luis or Francisco, the case's outcome hinged on determining his actual place and culture of origin. This was no easy task given that most inhabitants of the Spanish Caribbean had a very limited grasp of West Central African identities; even West Central Africans who spoke Spanish fluently were hard pressed to explain their own backgrounds for an audience of Spanish Caribbean colonists. The three ethnonyms most commonly ascribed to West Central Africans in the Caribbean were "Congo," "Angola," and "Anchico." If judged to be "Congo" or "Angola," Luis would be returned to Meneses in Cartagena; if he should prove to be "Anchico"

---

43. "Pleito entre Juan de Meneses y Francisco Camargo sobre un negro esclavo y sus jornales," 1608, AGN-FNE, Bolívar 6.

(Ansiku)—an ethnic group whose kingdom lay immediately north of the Kingdom of Kongo—he would remain in Mompox, employed by Camargo. To prove ownership of the man he referred to as Luis Congo, Meneses argued that the individual in question was clearly not the "Anchico" slave described in Camargo's bill of sale. "The black man Francisco Enxico listed in the bill of sale was a tall black with a poor body . . . and in conformity with his Anxico nation his entire forehead was painted and scarred above the eyebrows." Furthermore, Meneses noted: "My Francisco who previously was called Luis is a black man whom I purchased here in this city[,] recently arrived from Angola. . . . [He] is a black man of medium stature with no markings whatsoever on his forehead[,] and is not Anxico but rather Congo." Again, Meneses reiterated that Luis was not "painted above his eyebrows as are all of the Anchico blacks[,] who are known by those signs by all of the knowledgeable people in these parts."[44]

Subsequently, Meneses produced several witnesses who offered the same criteria for distinguishing "Anchicos" from "Congos." A vecino named Melchior de Marin was Cartagena's *corredor de lonja,* an official in charge of monitoring commercial transactions. Claiming to have conducted numerous slave sales in Cartagena, Panama, and Nombre de Dios, Marin stated that he knew

> for certain and without doubt that Luis negro . . . is of the Congo nation and not the Anxico nation . . . because all the Anxico negros brought to this city and other parts . . . arrive with markings on their forehead . . . and the *negras* arrive with the same[.] The other nations have their own *señales* [markings or scarifications ;] only Congos arrive with no markings whatsoever[,] and in this manner they are known and sold and bought[,] and this is certain and something that is known among the people who deal with the merchants that bring the aforementioned blacks.

Like Meneses, he argued that Luis Congo could not possibly be "Anchico," since he did not bear the characteristic scarifications. Other deponents gave similar testimony on behalf of Meneses, arguing for example that Luis "is not Anxico because all the Anxico blacks that this witness has seen up until now have their faces marked[,] and by this sign they are known[;] and the

---

44. Ibid., hojas 45v–47r, 67r. "Anchico," "Anxico," "Anzico," and "Enchico" are used interchangeably in Spanish-language sources. On the history of the Ansiku (also called Tyo or Teke), see Jan Vansina, *Kingdoms of the Savanna: A History of Central African States until European Occupation* (Madison, Wis., 1966), 28, 37–43, 52–54, 59, 64, 98–109, 123, 131.

Angolas and Congos have no markings whatsoever." One deponent also noted that "Luis says and declares he is of the Congo nation[,] and so he appears to be."[45]

The most significant aspect of Meneses's argument, supported by several witnesses, was his claim that "all the knowledgeable people in this region" could distinguish "Anchicos" from other West Central Africans using the criteria of scarification patterns. The testimony of an enslaved Upper Guinean woman—who probably saw few, if any, West Central Africans before her arrival in the Spanish Caribbean—further indicates that such knowledge was widespread in Cartagena. Antonia Balanta personally knew the Francisco Anchico mentioned in Camargo's bill of sale; for a time they had shared the same owner. Having seen Luis, the enslaved man at the heart of this litigation, she commented that the two men were obviously not the same person. According to Antonia Balanta, Francisco Anchico was "a black man of good stature with markings on his forehead and eyebrows[,] which are the signs of the blacks of that nation." The black man "Luis Congo," she stated, "is very different in person and body and markings and age from Francisco Anchico," being shorter in stature and "of the Congo land." Instead of bearing scarifications, his face was "clean."[46]

Presented as "evidence" before more than thirty witnesses, Luis was also asked to provide his own testimony. Interestingly, when asked to state his name, Luis replied that "in the city of Cartagena he was called Luis Angola"—rather than "Congo" or "Anchico"—and that, since moving to sites along the Magdalena River, he had been known as "Francisco Angola." He testified that previously he had indeed been owned by Meneses but ran away from Meneses's farm because the overseer, an Upper Guinean man named Luis Bran, whipped him too much. After some time hiding in a swamp, he was picked up in a boat by men he did not know; they took him upriver to Mompox, where he was imprisoned until claimed by Camargo. Since that time, he had paddled Camargo's canoes alongside other Africans, making trips to the mining settlement of Zaragoza and to the river port Honda. In Honda, he was baptized by a priest, who gave him his new name, Francisco.[47]

As further witnesses, Meneses presented two enslaved Africans who arrived in Cartagena along with Luis on the same slave ship. Despite their

45. "Pleito entre Juan de Meneses y Francisco Camargo sobre un negro esclavo y sus jornales," 1608, AGN-FNE, Bolívar 6, hojas 144r–145r, 146v–150r.
46. Ibid., hojas 82r–83r.
47. Ibid., hojas 9r–12v.

own origins in West Central Africa and their common experience crossing the Atlantic on the same vessel, they could confirm only that Luis was not "Anxico"; each had differing opinions as to whether he was "Congo" or "Angola." Like Luis, both María Antona "of the Angola land" and Francisco Congo were brought from "the Kingdoms of Angola" to Cartagena on a Portuguese slave ship captained by Pasqual Carvalho. Other sources corroborate their testimony; all three must have been among the 226 captives disembarked from the ship *San Francisco* in Cartagena on February 15, 1601. Like the sailor Juan Angola mentioned earlier, witness María Antona "of the Angola land" identified Luis as "Luis negro of the Congo land." Though she was now owned by Meneses's mother-in-law, María Antona had initially been purchased by Meneses along with another woman and three men, including Luis. One of the other men in this small group, Francisco Congo, was more specific when interviewed, stating that "about six years ago more or less this witness came from the kingdoms of Angola to this city [Cartagena] in the company of four others[,] two males and two females[,] brought by a Portuguese man." Francisco Congo also recognized Luis and identified him as "Luis Angola."[48]

Thus, while both María Antona and the sailor Juan Angola identified Luis as "Congo," both Luis himself and Francisco Congo identified him as "Angola." On one hand, these testimonies raise questions regarding the roles West Central Africans played in defining their own ethnicities or nations. On the other hand, a multitude of African identities were probably compressed into broader, homogenous categories such as "Congo" and "Angola," categories which could be more easily incorporated into Iberian systems of meanings. If so, then enslaved West Central Africans might have been subject to the same limitations as Iberians in Cartagena regarding their abilities to identify other enslaved Africans, even those ostensibly from the same region as themselves. Also Africans might have found it difficult to translate familiar concepts of West Central African identity into Spanish terms for a Spanish Caribbean audience.[49]

Several other Portuguese witnesses who testified on behalf of Meneses

48. Ibid., hojas 34r–38r, 50r–51r. On the *maestre* (shipmaster) of the ship *San Francisco* Pasqual Carvalho, see "Copia de la Relasion de Cartagena de los negros q Alli han entrado desde primero de Mayo de 1600," July 27, 1601, AGI-SF 72, n.105, fol. 24v; El fiscal con Juan Rodrigues Coutinho, 1602, AGI-Esc 1012A, pieza 3, fol. 13r; Vila Vilar, *Hispanoamérica*, 250–251.

49. See "Autos seguidos por Miguel Fernández de Fonseca," 1633, AGI-Esc 4, n.12, pieza 1, fols. 146r–152v for a rare list of 115 West Central African captives ascribed dozens of distinct ethnonyms shortly after their arrival in Española, including "Ambuyla" (Mbwela), "Banba" (Mbamba), "Benbe" (Mbembe), Bondo, "Chengue" (Kenge), "Dongo" (Ndongo), "Ganguela" (Ngangela), "Lanba"

concurred that "Anchicos" stood out because of their distinctive scarifications; their familiarity with western Africa allowed them to explain in greater detail. According to Andrés Lopez Morato, the enslaved man in question was "of the Congo nation, and not Anxico, because if he were Anxico his forehead would be worked [labrada] like all the others of that nation that this witness has seen." This was the same argument offered by several witnesses including Meneses himself, but Morato added further weight to this assertion. He knew about African scarifications "because he has been in Guinea and Cabo Verde and many other parts of that land, and has dealt in blacks and has knowledge of those nations." Furthermore, Morato made it clear that he was not the only person to understand the differences between "Anchicos" and "Congos." In his words, "any witness who might have said [that] Luis negro . . . is of the Anxico nation" has "committed perjury and spoken contrary to the truth[,] for the most part having no knowledge of those nations and being creoles of the land." With the latter phrase, Morato appears to dismiss local Spanish Americans as ignorant of the larger Atlantic world.[50]

Another Portuguese deponent identified as Captain Pedro Gonçales de Caceres goes into greater detail. Whether he had traveled to Africa or not, his title suggests authority in a maritime context, perhaps as ship captain or owner. Caceres claimed to have been active in Cartagena "for more than fifty years," having "bought, viewed, and dealt with blacks of all nations[:] of the Rivers[,] Banus, Biafaras, Sapes, [Co]colies, Falupos, Branes or Cacangas[;] Angolas, Congos, Anxicos[;] and [blacks] of other castes." He knew "the nations of these blacks," he explained, "by the señales among them," that is, by their scarifications. As examples, he noted that "Nalus have lines on their foreheads[;] the Capes have their teeth filed." Among "the Banus"—the Bañun—"the women's faces [are] marked and they are known by their language." In addition to these Upper Guinean groups, Caceres remarked that "the Congos have no markings whatsoever on their face." The "Anchicos," who "have some marks (berrugas) between their eyebrows on their forehead" could be identified by these markings as

---

(Lemba?), Lumbo, "Maonba" (Yombe), "Moncholo" (Monjolo), "Quisama" (Kisama), "Quiseque" (Soke?), "Robolo" (Libolo), "Tisongo" (Songo?), Unba, and "Onba" (Wambu?), among many others. See also Paul Lokken, "From the 'Kingdoms of Angola' to Santiago de Guatemala: The Portuguese Asientos and Spanish Central America, 1595–1640," HAHR, XCIII (2013), 195–196; de la Fuente, "Introducción," Santiago, LXI (March 1986), 205–208.

50. "Pleito entre Juan de Meneses y Francisco Camargo sobre un negro esclavo y sus jornales," 1608, AGN-FNE, Bolívar 6, hojas 142v–144r.

well as "by their languages." In summary, "the blacks [are] very different from one another." As his closing observation, Caceres added that Luis's "own language is Congo[,] and if he speaks or has spoken Anxico [it] is because of the communication that the ones have with the others." Though Caceres's own African background is unclear, he demonstrated considerable understanding of interactions between inhabitants of the neighboring West Central African polities of Kongo and Tyo (Ansiku).[51]

By general consensus, Luis's lack of facial scarifications established that he was not "Anchico"; yet his actual West Central African background remained uncertain until another Portuguese witness provided additional information. According to Paulo Correa de Silva,

> Luis negro[,] who was presented to this witness and to whom this witness spoke in his language[,] is neither of the Anxico nation nor has anything to do with it[.] Rather this witness knows that [he] is from a nation they call Mosi Obandos[,] which is between the provinces of Angola and Congo[,] and [that] Luis negro's ruler is subject to the King of Congo[.] The witness knows this because [he] knows the language of these nations[,] having lived among the aforementioned nations for more than twenty years.

Like a number of other deponents residing in Cartagena in 1607, Silva could easily distinguish Ansikus from other West Central Africans; he knew that Luis was not "Anchico" because he lacked the corresponding scarifications. Unlike the other individuals who gave testimony on behalf of Meneses, however, Silva had previously lived in West Central Africa for half his life (he was forty at the time he testified). Furthermore, he was able to communicate with Luis in Luis's own native language, probably Kikongo or Kimbundu. Not even the enslaved West Central African witnesses who crossed the Atlantic with Luis on the same slave ship could declare, as Silva did, that Luis was "not Anchico but rather of the Vando nation between Angola and Congo."[52]

---

51. Ibid., hojas 145r–146r. According to Caja de Cartagena, Cuentas (1624–1627), AGI-Ctdra 1397, n.2, pliego 78, a voyage captained by "Pedro Gonzalez" disembarked captives from Upper Guinea in Cartagena in 1623. These might be different people, however, since Pedro Gonçales de Caceres claimed to be more than seventy years old in 1607. On interactions between Tyo and Kongo, see Vansina, *Kingdoms of the Savanna*, 54–64, 98–109, 131.

52. "Pleito entre Juan de Meneses y Francisco Camargo sobre un negro esclavo y sus jornales," 1608, AGN-FNE, Bolívar 6, hojas 146r–146v ("Luis negro que se le [h]a mostrado a quien este t[estigo] [h]a hablado en su lengua no es de nacion anxico ni tiene q[ue] ver con ella antes sabe este t[estigo] quel susod[ic]ho es de una nacion que llaman mosi obandos questa entre las probincias de angola e congo

The European term "Vando nation" and the West Central African term "Mosi Ovando"—the people of Ovando—were two different ways of identifying the residents of Wandu, a southeastern province of the Kingdom of Kongo. A mountainous region with a series of fortified villages and a capital of the same name, Wandu (Mbanza Wandu) was one of several relatively independent provinces that typically elected its own rulers, rather than having them imposed by elites in Kongo's capital, São Salvador (Mbanza Kongo). Despite its tributary status as a province of Kongo, the town of Wandu began to trade directly with Luanda during the early seventeenth century, providing Angolan markets access to slave-producing areas northeast of Kongo. Before the mid-seventeenth century, when the province was visited by Capuchins and repeatedly invaded by Queen Nzinga, Wandu's main importance was its location as a border town along the only land route between the Kingdom of Kongo and the Portuguese colony of Angola. This route led northward from Angola through Mbwila, and then through Wandu, before finally entering Kongo's central provinces; the only other options were to either travel along the Atlantic coast or to attempt to pass over the mountains. Silva's ability to identify a man from Wandu in Cartagena de Indias during the first decade of the seventeenth century might be best explained by Wandu's position along this route. Having lived in West Central Africa for more than twenty years, Silva might have passed through Wandu while traveling overland from Angola to Kongo or vice versa. Though most witnesses did not have the experience to differentiate between West Central Africans who lacked highly visible scarifications, some Portuguese and Luso-African merchants had developed understandings of the region's kingdoms through long experience trading there. Luckily for Meneses—who won his case, regaining custody of the enslaved man who had fled six years earlier—men like Caceres and Silva brought their knowledge, along with forced migrants like Luis, from West Central Africa to the Spanish Caribbean.[53]

---

y el señor del d[ic]ho Luis negro es subjeto al Rey de congo lo qual sabe este t[estigo] porque sabe la lengua de las d[ic]has naciones por [h]aver andado entre las d[ic]has naciones mas de veynte a[ños] a esta parte. . . . El susod[ic]ho no es Anxico sino de la d[ic]ha nacion vando entre angola e congo.").

53. On Wandu, see John K. Thornton, *The Kingdom of Kongo: Civil War and Transition, 1641–1718* (Madison, Wis., 1983), 5–7, 40–44, 54, 70, 100, 105, 114; Anne Hilton, *The Kingdom of Kongo* (Oxford, 1985), 2, 4, 29, 33, 40, 49, 61, 77, 94, 110, 130, 140, 177–179, 193–196; Linda M. Heywood and John K. Thornton, *Central Africans, Atlantic Creoles, and the Foundation of the Americas, 1585–1660* (Cambridge, 2007), 50, 133, 150–152, 171, 202–203. I am grateful to Thornton for identifying Ovando as Wandu and "Mosi Ovando" as "the people of Wandu" by personal communication on June 12, 2008.

The same vessels that transported African captives simultaneously carried mariners, merchants, and passengers with extensive experience of West African and West Central African peoples and their cultures. Some were Iberians like Silva, who had resided for twenty years in sub-Saharan Africa and found himself living in Cartagena during the first decade of the seventeenth century. Others were people of African or mixed African-Iberian ancestry born or raised within Portuguese colonial settings, like the Capeverdean *tangomã* Luisa Reja, who sailed from Buguendo to Española in 1575. Still others were sub-Saharan Africans born outside the realm of Portuguese sovereignty but who acquired extensive knowledge of Iberian language and practices long before disembarking in a Caribbean port, as wage laborers, servants, or domestic slaves for Iberian and Luso-African employers and owners. Clearly the motives of Iberians, Luso-Africans, and sub-Saharan Africans who traveled or worked on slave ships did not necessarily overlap with the best interests of enslaved Africans transported on the same vessels. Yet, although sub-Saharan Africa and the Spanish Caribbean were primarily linked by the transatlantic slave trade, the production and export of captives were not the only results of this system. For the most part, Portuguese and Luso-African slave trade operatives were less central to the formations of Spanish Caribbean society than African trade captives themselves. However, their migration paths created discernable continuities between Atlantic Africa and the early colonial Caribbean with important implications for understanding the experiences of all parties involved, willingly or unwillingly.

Tangomãos and Luso-Africans in the early colonial Spanish Caribbean continued to interact with Africans and people of African descent in diverse ways, usually with far greater liberty than most sub-Saharan Africans themselves. As both short-term residents and long-term migrants, the merchants, passengers, mariners, servants, and slaves who arrived on Iberian slave ships mediated the integration of a relatively rapid influx of enslaved Africans. Despite—and in large part because of—their direct participation in the enslavement and displacement of African captives, tangomãos and Luso-Africans entered the Caribbean having experienced social proximity to Africans and cultural exchange that would have been foreign to most passengers arriving directly from Iberia on Indies fleets. Although much of their knowledge was used to further their own interests, even Portuguese and Luso-African migrants who grew wealthy through slave trafficking continued to show signs of their familiarity with Africans and African cultures. In settlements throughout the Spanish Caribbean, individuals described as Portuguese blacks or Afro-Portuguese creoles worked alongside diasporic Africans as fellow slaves and free people of color. Others—also described as Portuguese—supervised African laborers as overseers on farms and on pearl-fishing canoes. And some lived on terms of greater intimacy, becoming godparents, sexual partners, or spouses for first-generation African migrants and their children.

FOUR

Nharas and *Morenas Horras*

In 1583, Cartagena's city council sent a petition to the Spanish crown in hopes of obtaining assurance that soldiers, sailors, and Indies fleet passengers would have to abide by local laws while in port, rather than answering exclusively to their own commanding officers or other maritime authorities. A set of testimonies appended to the petition provides a fascinating glimpse of daily life during the late sixteenth century in a Spanish Caribbean seaport that regularly hosted large floating populations. Several witnesses described the sufferings of Cartagena's residents at the hands of unruly passers-through, beginning with the story of the *criada* (servant) Isabel Baez, a Spanish *donzella* (maiden) of eighteen or nineteen who was in the service of one of Cartagena's elite families. Much to her employers' dismay, shortly after her arrival in Cartagena Baez developed a sexual relationship with a man who had been a fellow passenger on the ship from Spain. The couple had absconded to an inn owned by María de Torres, a *mulata* who eventually made inquiries and reported the young woman to local authorities. Other deponents then described a second scandal involving a galley soldier's physical abuse of an unnamed mulata in her own home. At the time, one eyewitness to the incident had been in an adjacent house belonging to another mulata named Ana Enriquez. In a third account, a gambling dispute ended abruptly when a friar in disguise was stabbed to death by three soldiers and a sailor known only by his nickname, "Guinea." The murder took place in a garden or orchard owned by a West African woman identified as "María Xolofa."[1]

Though primarily intended to bolster the authority of local elites, these accounts of violence and disruption in Cartagena portray a backdrop of everyday social interaction in which free women of color described as *morenas horras* and *mulatas libres* regularly appear as permanent residents

---

1. "Memorial y testimonio de autos de la ciudad y provincia de Cartagena sobre los abusos y delitos que contra aquellos vecinos cometen los soldados de las galeras y flotas," May 11, 1583, AGI-SF 62, n.28, fols. 16r–24r, 28v–35r, 36r–45v.

and independent propertyowners. Late-sixteenth-century and early-seventeenth-century Spanish Caribbean populations included sizeable numbers of free people of color, reaching well into the hundreds in several ports, and women were usually disproportionately represented among them (see Appendix 5). María de Torres, Ana Enriquez, and María Xolofa were not unusual in their social and economic roles as free African and African-descended women who owned houses, plots of land, or small businesses such as inns, taverns, shops, and bakeries in Cartagena. Free women of color could be found engaged in similar occupations throughout the Spanish Caribbean, often associated with seaport hostelry and service economies.[2]

Sixteenth-century Havana's free black community is perhaps better documented than that of any other site in the early colonial Spanish Americas. By the mid-1560s, people of African descent comprised 10 or 15 percent of Havana's total free population. Estimates half a century later, recorded near the beginning of the seventeenth century, suggest that the city's free black community grew at the same rate as the rest of the city and perhaps even faster. According to one of Havana's bishops, the city was home to less than five hundred Iberian *vecinos* (permanent residents, or heads of household) in 1608, not including soldiers, though there were always temporary visitors, and *"negros* and *mulatos."* Six months later, other residents conjectured that Havana's free population consisted of "more than 600" or "more than 800" vecinos. Although these approximations were imprecise, a difference of one to three hundred vecinos might be explained by the bishop's exclusion of "negros and mulatos" from his earlier assessment. If so, this would indicate that, by around 1610, free people of color comprised at least 15 percent of Havana's free inhabitants and possibly as much as one-third. These estimates are supported by Havana's baptismal register for the 1590s, which lists more than twenty men and as many as ninety woman as either *horro* (freed) or *libre* (free) (see Appendix 4).[3]

Among communities of free people of color in early Spanish Caribbean

2. Alejandro de la Fuente, with César García del Pino and Bernardo Iglesias Delgado, *Havana and the Atlantic in the Sixteenth Century* (Chapel Hill, N.C., 2008), 153–161, 173.

3. Obispo de Cuba a S. M., Sept. 22, 1608, AGI-SD 150, r.2, n.48, fol. 1r; "Petición de la çiudad de Havana," Mar. 9, 1609 (seen in Madrid on Nov. 14, 1611), AGI-SD 116, r.3, n.124; "Papers Bearing on the Negroes of Cuba in the Seventeenth Century," *JNH,* XII (1927), 89–90, 92, 94; María Teresa de Rojas, "Algunos datos sobre los negros esclavos y horros en la Habana del siglo XVI," in *Miscelánea de estudios dedicados a Fernando Ortiz* (Havana, 1956), II, 1281; Isabelo Macías Domínguez, *Cuba en la primera mitad del siglo XVII* (Seville, 1978), 18–20, 36–37; de la Fuente, *Havana,* 107, 174–175. The higher estimate of one-third is not implausible: "non-whites made up nearly forty per cent of the free population" in Panama City during the first decade of the seventeenth-century; see Kenneth R. Andrews, *The Spanish Caribbean: Trade and Plunder, 1530–1630* (New Haven, Conn., 1978), 35.

settlements, women were especially prominent. The importance of their position becomes more readily apparent if understood within the context of the broader early modern Iberian world—particularly in comparison to other regions where Iberians came into extensive contact with Africans and people of African descent. Long before African and African-descended women hosted transient Iberians in port cities such as Cartagena and Havana, Portuguese expansion in western Africa brought African women into sustained contact with Iberian society and vice versa. One transformation in women's socioeconomic roles wrought by early modern overseas expansion was the rapid incorporation of African and African-descended women into Lusophone maritime contexts, both in Portugal and abroad. In western Africa, sexual unions between Portuguese sailors and African women were commonplace by the fifteenth century.[4]

For societies in Upper Guinea, such relationships fit within a broader category of reciprocal interaction between "landlords" and "strangers," a deeply rooted custom that proved mutually beneficial for both African hosts and European travelers. African landlords provided protection, aid, and sustenance for European strangers, who in turn were expected to submit to their hosts' authority, abiding by established rules of conduct. In the early seventeenth century, as one aspect of this traditional practice of hospitality toward visiting merchants and mariners, African hosts often provided wives or concubines—probably kinless captives or subordinate members of large clans—for Portuguese guests. Such contacts between Portuguese strangers and African women took a variety of forms, ranging from mutual interest to obligation to straightforward coercion; furthermore, these interactions were not limited to the Upper Guinea coast. Priests residing at São Jorge da Mina bitterly complained that enslaved African women were employed as prostitutes inside the fortress. On the islands of Santiago de Cabo Verde and São Tomé, clergymen themselves maintained long-standing sexual unions with black and mulata women, and Portuguese soldiers stationed in São Jorge da Mina and colonists in Luanda were known to have married local African women.[5]

4. A. C. de C. M. Saunders, *A Social History of Black Slaves and Freedmen in Portugal, 1441–1555* (Cambridge, 1982), 145; María Cristina Navarrete, *Génesis y desarrollo de la esclavitud en Colombia siglos XVI y XVII* (Cali, Colombia, 2005), 39; Ivana Elbl, "'Men without Wives': Sexual Arrangements in the Early Portuguese Expansion in West Africa," in Jacqueline Murray and Konrad Eisenbichler, eds., *Desire and Discipline: Sex and Sexuality in the Premodern West* (Toronto, 1996), 61–86. See also Darlene Abreu-Ferreira, "Fishmongers and Shipowners: Women in Maritime Communities of Early Modern Portugal," *Sixteenth Century Journal*, XXXI (2000), 7–23.

5. Philip D. Curtin, *Economic Change in Precolonial Africa: Senegambia in the Era of the Slave Trade*

African and Luso-African merchant women known as *nharas* (also *senhoras* or *signares*) on the Upper Guinea coast and as *donas* in West Central Africa often acted as power brokers and commercial agents in Upper Guinea. They invested in the slave trade and formed long-term sexual unions—commonly recognized as legitimate marriages, if not necessarily marriages officially endorsed by church authorities—with Portuguese men and, in the seventeenth through the nineteenth centuries, with French, Dutch, English, and Danish traders as well, among others. For these outsiders, nharas and donas represented conduits to local and internal trading networks that likely included their own associates and extended family members. Although foreign merchants' presence in African ports was often temporary or relatively brief, close association with one of these well-connected businesswomen conferred immediate status and credibility in the eyes of other long-term residents. As business partners, sexual companions, and go-betweens facilitating communication and social interaction, these African and Luso-African women took full advantage of their pivotal positions to benefit themselves and their children.[6]

In the late sixteenth and early seventeenth centuries, small numbers of African and African-descended women in the Spanish Caribbean's major seaports occupied ambiguous, intermediate positions that in some ways mirror those of nharas in western Africa during the same era. Though obvi-

(Madison, Wis., 1975), 298–299; Bruce L. Mouser, "Accommodation and Assimilation in the Landlord-Stranger Relationship," in B. K. Swartz Jr. and Raymond E. Dumett, eds., *West African Culture Dynamics: Archaeological and Historical Perspectives* (New York, 1980), 495–514; George E. Brooks, *Eurafricans in Western Africa: Commerce, Social Status, Gender, and Religious Observance from the Sixteenth to the Eighteenth Century* (Athens, Oh., 2003), 50–58, 122–160, 176; John Vogt, *Portuguese Rule on the Gold Coast, 1469–1682* (Athens, Ga., 1979), 121, 154, 182; Iva Cabral, "Ribeira Grande: Vida urbana, gente, mercancia, estagnação," in Maria Emília Madeira Santos, coord., *História geral de Cabo Verde* (Lisbon, 1995), II, 254–255; Arlindo Manuel Caldeira, *Mulheres, sexualidade e casamento em São Tomé e Príncipe, séculos XV–XVIII*, 2d ed. (Lisbon, 1999), 121–128, 205–212; Jan Vansina, "Portuguese vs Kimbundu: Language Use in the Colony of Angola (1575–c.1845)," *Bulletin des seances: Academie Royale des Sciences d'Outre-Mer*, XLVII (2001), 267–281; Roquinaldo Amaral Ferreira, "Transforming Atlantic Slaving: Trade, Warfare, and Territorial Control in Angola, 1650–1800" (Ph.D. diss., University of California, Los Angeles, 2003), 159–171; Peter Mark and José da Silva Horta, *The Forgotten Diaspora: Jewish Communities in West Africa and the Making of the Atlantic World* (New York, 2011), 66–69, 208.

6. As George Brooks notes, whereas European newcomers to West Africa "lacked knowledge of African languages, trade networks, and political and social institutions," they often "found ready collaborators in Luso-African and African women who, as wives, translators, and business partners, provided access to African commercial networks through relatives"; Brooks, *Eurafricans*, 84, 122–129, 206–221. See also Pernille Ipsen, *Daughters of the Trade: Atlantic Slavers and Interracial Marriage on the Gold Coast* (Philadelphia, 2015); Mariana P. Candido, "Trade Networks in Benguela, 1700–1850," in David Richardson and Filipa Ribeiro da Silva, eds., *Networks and Trans-Cultural Exchange: Slave Trading in the South Atlantic, 1590–1867* (Leiden, 2015), 157–160.

ously less powerful than the Luso-African women who aided and exploited Europeans along the coasts of West Africa in later centuries, free women of color in Spanish Caribbean port cities likewise profited by providing Iberian men with access to local resources including food, drink, housing, and services. As discussed below, many of these women were propertyowners, and it was not at all uncommon for free women of color to marry Iberian men. As nonelite insiders who pursued their own best interests and those of their families and associates, free African and African-descended women participated extensively in Spain's colonization of the Caribbean and in the formations of Spanish Caribbean society.[7]

Morenas Horras *as Propertied, Permanent Residents* (Vecinas)

Free women of color were often recorded with racial classifications, such as "morena," "mulata," and *"negra,"* and categories of legal status, including "libre" and "horra"; these terms make it possible to identify free women of African descent as such. In towns and cities throughout the early Spanish circum-Caribbean, free women of color were also commonly referred to as *vecinas,* which might be translated as "long-term resident," "head of household," or as "propertyowning, permanent resident." The same term was used for residents of Iberian origin. Among the 620 vecinos listed in a rough census of Santo Domingo taken in 1606, 11 heads of household were free men of color; another 27 were free women described as mulatas, morenas, and negras. In this census, free people of color were classified as vecinos based on precisely the same characteristics that made Iberians vecinos: among free African or African-descended vecinas, 22 were said to have a family or children. Two of them owned houses, 1 owned a store, and 2 owned slaves. One was described as a widow, indicating that free women of color who were married do not appear in this census; their spouses are listed as primary heads of household instead. The frequent ascription of "vecina" to free women of color provides a strong indication of their agency and vitality within Spanish Caribbean society.[8]

In 1634, the city's bishop Fray Luis de Córdoba Ronquillo estimated that Cartagena de Indias's inhabitants included "more or less 1,500 veci-

---

7. For a similar comparison between signares and free women of color in the late colonial circum-Caribbean, see Daniel L. Schafer, *Anna Madgigine Jai Kingsley: African Princess, Florida Slave, Plantation Slaveowner* (Gainesville, Fla., 2003), 137n.

8. "Testimonio de quantos lugares ay en esta ysla," Oct. 2, 1606, AGI-SD 83, r.2, s/n, fols. 33–69, transcribed in E[milio] Rodríguez Demorizi, comp., *Relaciones históricas de Santo Domingo* (Ciudad

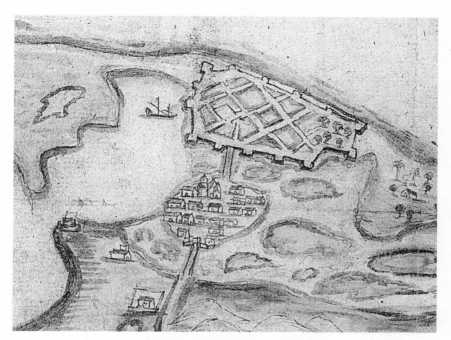

Figure 3 Map of Cartagena de Indias, including the unwalled neighborhood of Gethsemaní. España. Ministerio de Educación, Cultura y Deporte. Archivo General de Indias. Mapas y Planos, Panamá, 45bis, "Plano de la Ciudad de Cartagena de Yndias y sus cercanías." Circa 1628. Detail

nos, including the households of mulatas and freed blacks." In addition to free people of color, Córdoba Ronquillo explicitly recognized the presence of free women of color (mulatas) as heads of household in Cartagena and Gethsemaní. Gethsemaní was an *arrabal,* or outlying neighborhood, just outside Cartagena's city walls, initially separated from the urban center by a swamp. During the early 1620s, bishops, governors, royal officials, and church council members described the neighborhood's residents as "poor" and occasionally as "scandalous." A common thread in their correspondence was that Gethsemaní was believed to be a center of contraband, with many houses in the neighborhood having direct access to the sea. In 1622, a royal official visiting from Bogotá wrote that "in the absence of justice,

Trujillo [Santo Domingo], Dominican Republic, 1945), II, 374–403. For free women of color, see entries 19–21, 87, 94, 101, 198, 220, 247, 257–259, 261, 263–266, 310, 322, 348, 356, 361, 538–540, 542, 617. For free men of color, see entries 213, 221, 262, 267–268, 370, 537, 602, 611–612, 616. The original document includes some marginal notes (such as, "widows") that are not reproduced in Rodríguez Demorizi's otherwise excellent transcription.

[Gethsemaní] is a free population, a receptacle of blacks and contraband merchandise, of delinquents, free people, and lowlife scum."[9]

A number of free women of color owned properties and operated businesses in Gethsemaní in 1620. That year, by order of the crown, royally appointed engineer Cristóbal de Rodas helped Cartagena officials conduct a survey to determine the feasibility of erecting fortifications around the neighborhood. Contemporaneous suggestions by some of the same officials indicate that the construction of a wall around Gethsemaní would serve the two-fold purpose of protecting local residents from seaborne attack while at the same time hindering their access to the sea (and thus, presumably, limiting the extent of contraband). The survey listed more than 150 different houses, along with the owners and/or inhabitants if known. Among the buildings were a number of rental houses *(moradas)*, as well as shops *(pulperías)*, warehouses *(bodegas)*, barbershops, smithies, a tannery, and a hospital. Rather than being inhabited by their owners, several houses were occupied by "negros," *morenos, sclavos* (slaves), or "poor people," some of whom paid rent. Fourteen free morenas and mulatas were propertyowners, including the African woman María Biafara. Another morena libre from Upper Guinea named Beatriz Biafara lived on land owned by a man named Juan de Simancas, though the house itself might have been her own. Several of these free women of color let out houses or rooms to tenants. In addition to her own home and a small store, free morena Mariana Martin owned an adjacent house to rent out to guests. Free morena Catalina Cano owned several palm-thatched houses on her property that "she rents out to some morenos, and she lives there herself as well." A caulker named Luis de Soto cared for three houses bordering the sea and leased them out on behalf of their owner, an unnamed mulata.[10]

9. Obispo fray Diego de Torres Altamirano a S. M., July 23, 1620, AGI-SF 228, n.78, fols. 2v–3r ("el barrio que llaman de Hesemani es donde habita la gente mas escandalosa de esta ciudad"); Obispo fray Luis de Córdoba Ronquillo a S. M., Aug. 10, 1634, AGI-SF 228, n.97; "Relaçion sobre . . . el varrio nuevo de la Çiudad de Cartagena (que llaman la otra vanda y Jejemani)," July 26, 1621, AGI-SF 73, n.66; Contador de cuentas Pedro Guiral a S. M. sobre "cossas que es nesçessario remediar y haçer en Cartagena," July 31, 1622, AGI-SF 73, n.109, fol. 1v–2r ("que por no aver alli Justiçia es una poblaçion libre Reçeptaculo de Negros y mercaderias descaminadas y de Delinquentes y de Jente libre y de mal vivir"); Don García Giron, gobernador de Cartagena a S. M., July 20, 1622, AGI-SF 38, r.6, n.178 ("los mas vezinos y dueños de estas casas son gente pobre"); Cabildo eclesiástico de Cartagena a S. M., Aug. 22, 1623, AGI-SF 232, r.3, n.55.

10. "Relaçion de la distancia del sitio de Jesemani a la çiudad de Cartagena y quantas casas ay de que sirven y cuyas son," July 24, 1620, AGI-SF 39, r.2, n.7, fols. 1r–14r (plots numbered 22, 38, 46, 59, 78, 84–85, 90–92, 95, 105, 109, 127, 135–136, 138, 140–141, 144–146, 148, 154–155, 158). See also Antonino Vidal Ortega, "'Relación del sitio asiento de Getsemaní' en el año 1620," *Historia Caribe*, II, no. 6 (2001), 123–135; Margarita Garrido, "Vida cotidiana en Cartagena de Indias en el siglo XVII," in

During the 1580s, "vecinas of Havana" described as morenas horras provided services for the soldiers stationed in the town's fortress. The women sold food and drink or laundered the men's clothing. Havana's garrison was paid with such notorious infrequency that the soldiers often ended up owing substantial sums of money. In 1586, one soldier owed no less than 52 *ducados* to "Ana Rodríguez morena horra, vecina of Havana," for feeding him in her house over a period of eight months at a rate of 4 ducados per month; she had also washed his white clothing for two and a half years, at the rate of 8 ducados per year. Other soldiers were in debt to Catalina Rezia and Catalina de Avellaneda—both described as morenas horras and vecinas of Havana—for the same services. In some cases, free women of color used the monies due them as credit to pay off their own debts. For example, while morena horra Bárbola Hernández owed two hundred *reales* to a vecino of Havana, a soldier who owed her money formally took on her debt as his own in 1587 and promised to pay it off as soon as he received his wages. In other instances, free women of color borrowed and repaid money, including sums as high as 120 ducados, from soldiers and officers; they also loaned money to soldiers and other Iberian men.[11]

References to free women of color as hardworking, entrepreneurial vecinas in Havana during the 1580s present a notable contrast with legislation issued by Havana's town council two or three decades earlier; extant cabildo records for the 1550s and 1560s provide evidence for prejudice, and perhaps even incipient racism, on the part of Havana's elite. Perhaps the most extreme mid-sixteenth-century act of hostility toward free people of color was the request of Havana's town council for permission to expel them from the city in 1557. The case was not definitively resolved for another two decades. Meanwhile, free women of color who petitioned the

Haroldo Calvo Stevenson and Adolfo Meisel Roca, eds., *Cartagena de Indias en el siglo XVII* (Cartagena, Colombia, 2007), 460–463. For the governor's subsequent recommendation that, for both defensive purposes and to prevent smuggling, some houses in Gethsemaní should be demolished and a twelve-foot-high wall should be constructed around others to limit access to the sea, see Don García Giron, gobernador de Cartagena a S. M., July 20, 1622, AGI-SF 38, r.6, n.178. Later maps of Cartagena show walls around the entire neighborhood; see, for example, "Plano de la ciudad de Cartagena de Yndias y sus cercanías," circa 1628, AGI-MP Panamá 45 (but note that the accompanying map, AGI-MP Panamá 45bis, does not show walls around the arrabal [see Figure 6]); "Planta de la Bahia de Cartagena para lo tocante a los fuertes que a hecho Murga y lo que toca también a la ciudad e Ysla de Xexemani," 1631, AGI-MP Panamá 51.

11. Maria Teresa de Rojas, [ed.], *Índice y extractos del Archivo de Protocolos de la Habana,* 3 vols. (Havana, 1947–1957), I, 272, 380, II, 44, 64–65, 382, 387–388, 390, 406–407. See also Emilio Roig de Leuchsenring, dir., *Actas capitulares del Ayuntamiento de la Habana* (Havana, 1937–), tomo I, vol. II, 75, 286, 294; tomo II, 150; "Obligación contraída por Isabel de Gamboa, morena horra, vecina, a favor de Juan de Talavera, vecino," May 4, 1605, ANC-PN database (Regueyra / JB Guilisasti), mfn 95349534.

town council for land in the late 1550s and early 1560s might have been encouraged to look for plots located at some remove from the town center; some of those whose requests were successful had asked to settle "in front of the hermitage" or to establish an estancia "on the edge of town." When Beatriz Nizarda requested land in 1561, the town council denied her request but noted that if she were to ask for land "near where the other free blacks are" her petition would be granted. Around the same time, town council members attempted to curtail the liberty of free people of color even in rural areas. In 1566, Havana's cabildo ruled that free people of color could no longer hunt (montear) or make hides; if they were to do so it should be as wage laborers working for a patron, rather than on their own behalf. The town council added that Diego de Miranda and his brother Pedro Lopez were not exempt, despite being "vecinos and people who live well." Havana was still small during the 1550s and 1560s; town council members described it as a village of "up to thirty vecinos" in 1553. Evidently, as the settlement grew smaller and poorer, some Havana elites attempted to shore up their own tenuous positions at the expense of local free people of color.[12]

Though town council legislation of this nature was clearly repressive, it also constitutes an official (if grudging) recognition that free people of color in Havana were already beginning to occupy certain social and economic niches: an acknowledgement that some free people of color were vecinos and "live[d] well" as early as the 1560s. Furthermore, much of this legislation never took effect. Some resolutions were rejected by the crown outright; the request to expel free people of color from Havana was not successful, and, upon the case's conclusion in 1577, the governor of Cuba sentenced the town council's spokesman to pay for the costs of the case. Other decrees were evidently forgotten, or simply not enforced, and, in the decades following the 1560s, free people of color gained ground in Havana as vecinos and propertyowners (Table 6). In 1579, just twelve years after Havana's cabildo prohibited free people of color from hunting on their own behalf, negra horra Beatriz Nizarda—the same woman whose initial request for land was denied in 1561—was a "vecina of Havana," owning with her husband (a free man of color) a corral and hunting grounds

12. Roig, dir., *Actas capitulares*, tomo I, vol. II, 201, 229, tomo II, 6, 276; Rojas, [ed.], *Índice y extractos*, II, 378; I. A. Wright, *The Early History of Cuba, 1492–1586* (New York, 1916), 313; Fernando Ortiz, *Cuban Counterpoint: Tobacco and Sugar*, trans. Harriet de Onís (Durham, N.C., 1995), 286; Andrews, *Spanish Caribbean*, 36; de la Fuente, *Havana*, 2–6, 180–181; Ciudad de la Habana de Cuba a S. M., Mar. 20, 1553, AGI-SD 116, r.2, n.54 ("En esta villa ay hasta treynta vezinos y los mas dellos pobres e munchos dellos viejos y enfermos y ynutiles para la guerra").

(*monterías*). They employed an Amerindian man named Diego de Toribio for six months to hunt for them. If some free people of color had been sent to live on the town's outskirts a decade or two earlier, by the 1570s, it was common for free women of color to own, buy, and sell homes and other properties within the town's urban center, often in proximity to Iberian or Spanish American vecinos. For example, in 1575 and 1577, Iberian vecinos Tomás Martin and Pêro Montes requested and were granted plots of land near the old fortress bordering a plot owned by "Bárbola negra horra"; her other neighbors included Francisca Hernandez, Joan de Valle, Francisca de Tamayo, and Francisco de Zamora. In 1587, morena horra Teresa Maldonado, "vecina of Havana," sold her own land and houses to an Iberian vecina on the condition that she could continue to live there. By the final decades of the sixteenth century, much of the pressure free people of color had faced earlier on the part of Havana elites appears to have been alleviated by the port city's rapid demographic growth and bustling service economy, both associated with the consolidation of the Indies fleets.[13]

One of the earliest free women of African descent known to have achieved some degree of prominence in early colonial Havana was the free black woman Catalina Rodríguez, described as a vecina of Havana. In 1565, she was one of four free people of color licensed to sell wine. In her last will, she bequeathed her land and properties, possibly including a tavern, to the Society of Jesus, intending to provide both a school for children and a place for the Jesuits to stay. Though the Jesuits left Cuba in 1579–1580, they continued to use Rodriguez's land afterward for temporary lodging when in town (Havana's Dominicans had also begun to eye the property as a potential annex for their adjacent convent). Another relatively prosperous free woman of color in Havana, Elena de Arteaga, morena horra, in March 1587 noted in her last testament a husband, Nicolás Hernandez, who appears to have been Iberian or Spanish American (he is not ascribed any racial label). In addition to the houses and plot of land (*solar*) where they lived, the couple owned a small fishing boat and two enslaved women named Inés and Isabel Engola. Arteaga left most of her properties to her son from a previous relationship but willed small sums of money to Havana's

13. Rojas, [ed.], *Índice y extractos,* I, 56, II, 381–382; Roig, dir., *Actas capitulares,* tomo III, 34, 50, 108, 172–173; Table 6; de la Fuente, *Havana,* 51–67. A similar sequence of events appears to have taken place in Caracas during the early 1600s: free women of color acquired properties and managed to hold on to them despite discriminatory cabildo legislation, which might not have been enforced. See Mario Briceño Iragorry, comp., *Actas del cabildo de Caracas* (Caracas, 1943-), III, 142, 332, V, 227, 239, VI, 72–73, 76, 168.

Table 6 Free, Propertyowning Women of Color in Havana, circa 1550–1605

Year(s)	Name	Racial and legal descriptors	Property
1550	Catalina	horra	solar
1559	Beatriz García	negra horra	requests solar
1559	Catalina Garay	negra horra	requests solar
1559, 1568	Isabel Velazquez	negra	solar
1561, 1579	Beatriz Nizarda	negra horra, vecina of Havana	requests solar; owns corral, hunting lands
1569	Beatriz Lovera	negra horra	solar
1569	Quiteria Velazquez	negra	solar
1570	Beatriz	negra horra	solar
1570	Juana Garcia	negra horra	houses
1572	Bárbara	negra horra	solar
1572	Catalina	"negra que fue de [was previously owned by] Alonso Velazquez"	solar
1573	Beatriz	morena horra	solar, house
1573	Beatriz de Mesa	negra horra	solar
1573	María de Almeida	negra horra	solar, house
1573, 1587	Isabel Enchica	negra horra, morena horra	solar, estancia
1575, 1577	Bárbola	negra horra	solar
1575	Catalina Yaguarama	negra horra	solar
1577, 1588	Aldonça Luys	morena horra	solar, houses
1579	Catalina Garça	morena horra	houses
1585, 1586	Cecilia Velazquez	morena horra	houses, solar
1585, 1595	Francisca de Miranda	negra horra	two slaves (Catalina de Fonseca criolla, Catalina Biocho)

Year	Name	Status	Property
1585	María Rodriguez Çape	morena horra	solar
1585	Susana Velazquez	morena horra, vecina of Havana	solar
1586	Ana Rodriguez	morena horra, vecina of Havana	house
1587	Elena de Arteaga	morena horra, vecina of Havana	house, solar, small fishing boat, two slaves (Inés and Isabel Engola)
1587	Teresa Maldonado	morena horra, vecina of Havana	houses, solar
1587	Violante Sanchez	morena horra, vecina of Havana	house
1588	Catalina	"morena horra que fue del padre cura" (free black woman who previously belonged to the priest)	houses or solar
1588	Catalina de Figueroa	negra horra, vecina of Havana	solar
1590	Dominga Rodrigues	mulata horra	one slave (María Çape)
1590	Francisca Velazquez	morena horra	Named as heir of houses, solar, one slave (María Angola)
1593	Gostança Çape	morena horra	one slave (Isabel Bañon)
1595	Inés del Comendador	morena horra	one slave (Leonor Bran)
1595	María Sanchez	mulata	one slave (María Angola)
1598	María Batista	morena horra	one slave (María Bran)
1605	Isabel de Gamboa	morena horra	houses, solar

Sources: Emilio Roig de Leuchsenring, dir., *Actas capitulares del Ayuntamiento de La Habana* (Havana, Cuba, 1937–), tomo I, vol. II, 6, 177, 190, 201, 229, tomo II, 73, 105, 113, 204, 205, 258, 262, 276–277, 287–288, 292, tomo III, 34, 50, 108, 143; María Teresa de Rojas, [ed.], *‹ac›Índice y extractos del archivo de protocolos de la Habana*, 3 vols. (Havana, 1947–1957), I, 56, 162, 172, 352–353, 375–376, 379–381, II, 64–65, 123, 283–285, 369, 378, 381–382, III, 123–124, 159, 268–269; "Testamento en el cual el otorgante . . . Nombra por su universal heredera a Francisca Velázquez, morena horra," Jan. 3, 1590, ANC-PN database (Regueyra / J Pérez de Borroto), mfn 55353; "Obligación contraída por Isabel de Gamboa, morena horra, vecina, a favor de Juan de Talavera, vecino," May 4, 1605, ANC-PN database (Regueyra / JB Guilisasti), mfn 9534934; Baptisms of María Çape (Sept. 9, 1590), Ysabel Bañon (Jan. 31, 1593), Madalena Angola (Apr. 30, 1595), Leonor Bran (Nov. 12, 1595), María Bran (Mar. 30, 1598), CH-LB/B, fols. 9v, 24v, 56v, 66r, 121r.

Note: In 1577, Havana's governor and cabildo agreed that each solar should measure sixty *pies* (feet) wide and 100 pies long (Roig, dir., *Actas capitulares*, tomo III, 168).

hospital and two confraternities. As relatively prosperous free women of African descent in Havana, the activities of Rodriguez and Arteaga illustrate that free women of color's roles as Spanish Caribbean vecinas did not differ markedly from those of nonelite Iberian townswomen: they labored as merchants or vendors, married Iberian men, supported religious orders, practiced Catholic rites, and owned land and other properties in Havana that might include enslaved Africans.[14]

During the late sixteenth and early seventeenth centuries, some free people of color did own slaves, though most probably did not. Of the approximately 3,700 enslaved people in Panama City in 1607, 219—almost 6 percent of the city's slave population—were owned by free people of color, who in turn comprised 34 percent of the city's free population. Although the numbers and sexes of free African and African-descended slaveowners are not specified, the average rates of slaveownership among them can be estimated: with a total of 556 adult free people of color in Panama City—assuming that only adults were slaveowners—each free person of color held an average of 0.39 slaves. This figure is quite low in comparison to the 4.1 slaves owned by each of Panama City's 851 European and Spanish American adults, on average, in 1607. There are many examples of individual free women of color owning or directing the labor of enslaved people in other circum-Caribbean locales. In a household census composed the previous year in Santo Domingo, Española, two female heads of household listed as María Hernandez, mulata, and Mariana Suaço, mulata, owned unspecified numbers of slaves; those owned by Suaço possibly labored on her farm in Nigua (see Table 12). In the late 1620s, morena libre María Montera, described as a vecina of Cartagena, owned at least 4 or 5 enslaved West Central African women, whom she employed in her bakery. Like nharas and donas in Atlantic African contexts—and like the *tangomanga* (cross-cultural trader) Luisa Reja, who brought several captives from Buguendo to Española in 1575—free women of color in Spanish Caribbean settlements participated extensively in local economies and Iberian social hierarchies, including those based on slaveholding and slave trafficking, as liaisons and commercial agents.[15]

14. Roig, dir., *Actas capitulares,* tomo I, vol. II, 294; Rojas, "Algunos datos," in *Miscelánea,* II, 1284; Fray Hernando de San Pedro Martir de la orden de Santo Domingo a S. M., July 3, 1587, AGI-SD 153, r.3, n.45, fols. 13r–17v. For a transcription of Arteaga's will, see Rojas, [ed.], *Índice y extractos,* II, 283–285.

15. On slaveownership in Panama City in 1607, see "Descripción de Panamá y su provincia . . .," (1607), in Manuel Serrano y Sanz [ed.], *Relaciones históricas y geográficas de América central* (Madrid, 1908), 168–169. I calculated the number of slaves owned by Spanish, Spanish American, and other

Some sub-Saharan African women in the Spanish Caribbean owned slaves. When a Portuguese merchant's ship was embargoed in Cartagena in 1615, royal officials discovered two West African women onboard and took them into custody. Though both were initially presumed to be the merchant's slaves, María Mandinga was in fact found to be "a free person[,] and Ynes Nalu her slave." Among the eleven free people of color listed in Havana's baptismal records as slaveowners during the 1590s, at least three were sub-Saharan Africans: Gostança Çape, morena horra, owned Isabel Bañon; Antón Bran, moreno horro, owned Pedro Nalu; and Francisco Mandinga, moreno horro, owned Juan Angola. In none of these cases did the ethnonyms ascribed to enslaved Africans and their African owners match. At her marriage in Havana in 1617, a woman named María Angola was described as the "slave of Ana Angola morena horra"—but "Angola" was a toponym referring to captives exported from the Portuguese colony, rather than an ethnic or linguistic group; the catch-all term "Angola" often masked considerable diversity among West Central Africans. Apparently, when freed Africans owned a slave in Spanish Caribbean settlements such as Cartagena or Havana during the late sixteenth and early seventeenth centuries, their possessing an enslaved person of the same ethnolinguistic background was unlikely.[16]

European adults by subtracting 219 enslaved people owned by free people of color and 28 slaves owned by mestiços and Amerindians from the total slave population of 3,721. The resulting figure (3,474) divided by the number of adult Europeans and Spanish Americans (851) yields a ratio of 4.08 slaves per person. See also Appendix 1; Andrews, *Spanish Caribbean*, 35. Santo Domingo slaveowners María Hernández and Mariana Suaço appear in "Testimonio de quantos lugares ay en esta ysla," Oct. 2, 1606, AGI-SD 83, r.2, s/n, fols. 33–69, transcribed in Rodríguez Demorizi, comp., *Relaciones históricas de Santo Domingo*, II, 378. For María Montera in Cartagena, see "Alonso de Peralta . . . con María Montera negra horra sobre la venta de una negra angola," 1629–1630, AGN-FNE, Bolivar 14, hojas 827r–918v. In Cartagena later in the seventeenth century, a free black woman named Marcelina Gelis ran a business housing newly arrived African trade captives until their resale; see Anna María Splendiani and Tulio Aristizábal, eds. and trans., *Proceso de beatificación y canonización de san Pedro Claver, edición de 1696* (Bogotá, 2002), 205, 425–426. For tangomanga Luisa Reja, see Table 5; "Contratadores de Cabo Verde y Guinea con Cristóbal Cayado y otros del reino de Portugal," 1582–1589, AGI-Esc 2A, pieza 2, fols. 54v, 108v, 116r, 496v, 497v, 499v, 540v, 566v–567r.

16. "Testimonio de las quentas que se tomaron . . . de los bienes de Manuel Enriquez Correa," July 9, 1615, AGI-SF 73, n.30d, fol. 2v; Baptisms of Isabel Bañon (Jan. 31, 1593), Pedro Nalu (Nov. 12, 1595), and Juan Angola (July 6, 1597), CH-LB/B, fols. 24v, 66r, 103v; Marriage of Pedro Angola and María Angola (Oct. 9, 1617), CH-LB/M, fol. 172r. For evidence of considerable diversity among diasporic West Central Africans, who were typically described only as "Angolas" in early Spanish Caribbean sources, see "Autos seguidos por Miguel Fernández de Fonseca," 1633, AGI-Esc 4, n.12, pieza 1, fols. 146r–152v. For slaveowners Agustín Enchico and Juan Perez Locumi, see also "Autos sobre la arribada del navío San Pedro," 1628–1631, AGI-SD 119, s/n, pieza 2, fols. 48v, 59v (discussed in Chapter 5, below).

If some free women of color adopted slave ownership as an advantageous business model, other free African and African-descended women experienced slave ownership as a complicated, personal affair. Many had been enslaved themselves and had parents, siblings, partners, or children who were enslaved. In 1585, Francisca de Miranda, negra horra, purchased the manumission of her light-skinned (*de color* mulato) three-year-old son Martín by giving his owner another slave in his stead: a six-year-old black girl named Catalina de Fonseca. Francisca de Miranda was simultaneously paying for her own freedom. Her manumission price was the exceedingly high sum of 500 ducados; as assurance that she would provide the 270 ducados that she still owed, Miranda pledged a second slave, a twenty-year-old woman named Catalina Biocho, as collateral. She also offered monies that she was owed by the crown for food she had been providing to soldiers garrisoned in Havana. Miranda's ability to procure her and her son's freedom largely came from her participation in the service economy, with additional credit derived from her ownership of at least two slaves. Her food provisioning business itself might have been supported by the labor of the enslaved woman Catalina Biocho. As in Upper Guinea, slave trafficking in Havana overlapped with other forms of commercial exchange. Free women of color like Francisca de Miranda—who might have experienced both contexts—integrated slave ownership and slave trading with other economic activities in their own bids for social mobility and security.[17]

Sub-Saharan Africans as Free Women of Color

As free vecinas or townswomen, African women with prior experience of cross-cultural exchange in Luso-African contexts were more likely than their male counterparts to have opportunities to apply that knowledge in Spanish Caribbean settings. By the late sixteenth century, while some free women of color are described in Spanish Caribbean source materials as *criollas* (creoles), others were Luso-Africans or sub-Saharan Africans, including many survivors of the transatlantic slave trade who had managed to free themselves. Unlike Afrocreoles manumitted in late-sixteenth-century Havana, African migrants who obtained their freedom were usually adults by that time, and fully three-fourths of all Africans manumitted were women. References to free women of color who bore an ethnonym indicating African origins or ports of departure are relatively scarce. Yet, in some cases, free

17. Rojas, [ed.], *Índice y extractos*, I, 352–353, 379–381.

women of color did carry a set of markers that identified them with an Iberian surname and an African ethnonym, occasionally adding a racial category and legal status as well. For example, a census of Veragua's residents in early 1576 includes a woman described as Juana Martin, "negra horra, Jolofa," who possessed goods and properties valued at more than one thousand gold pesos. Other women identified by both African ethnonyms and Iberian surnames include "Catalina Diaz Bañol, horra"; "Catalina Lopez Terranova, negra *atezada*"; and "Luis[a] de Torres, negra *de nación Terranova*."[18]

In 1585, María Rodriguez "Çape, morena horra," purchased a plot of land from another morena horra described as a "vecina of Havana" (the land bordered properties owned by two Iberian or Spanish-American men and "Ceçilia Velázquez, morena horra"). Among the seventy to ninety free women of color participating in baptisms in Havana during the 1590s, many are simply described as ex-slaves (horras) with no racial description provided; others are listed by race and legal status (for example, morena horra, mulata libre) (see Appendix 4). Although only seven or eight free women of color were specifically described as criollas, sixteen were associated with African origins. No less than fourteen free women of color bore Upper Guinean ethnonyms, including "Bañon" (Bañun), "Biafara" (Biafada), "Bran" (Brame), "Nalu," "Zape" (or "Çape") and "Linba" (Limba); two more women were ascribed the West Central African ethnonyms "Conga" and "Angola" (Table 7).[19]

Many free women of color identified only by Iberian names and racial designations were probably African-born forced migrants. Changes in the various markers of identity ascribed to one West Central African woman over a period of eight years in Havana's baptismal register illustrate a process in which ethnonyms ascribed to (or professed by) African-born women were gradually replaced by Iberian surnames. Leonor Anchica first appears in 1592 as godmother to a newly baptized woman from Upper Guinea. Though little is known of Leonor Anchica's prior background, she was undoubtedly transported to the Caribbean in captivity; she is identified here as "Leonor Anchica," a "black slave" owned by Francisco de Abalos. She resurfaces the following year, serving as godmother again on two

18. De la Fuente, *Havana,* 173–174; Carol F. Jopling comp., *Indios y negros en Panamá en los siglos XVI y XVII: Selecciones de los documentos del Archivo General de Indias* (Antigua, Guatemala, 1994), 446, 452.

19. Rojas, [ed.], *Índice y extractos,* I, 375–376; for free women described as "criolla," see the baptisms of María (Mar. 4, 1590), Marçela (Oct. 19, 1592), Madalena (Oct. 25, 1592), Ana (Apr. 18, 1594), María Bran (Dec. 26, 1594), María Angola (May 10, 1598), Luis (Feb. 22, 1599), and Sabina (Jan. 13, 1600), CH-LB/B, fols. 3v, 18v, 19r, 42v, 51v, 124r, 141r, 157v.

Table 7 Free Upper Guinean and West Central African Women in Havana's Baptismal Records, 1590–1600

Ethnonym	Name	Racial description and legal status	Baptismal role(s)	Date(s)
UPPER GUINEANS				
"Bañon" (Bañun)	Catalina Bañon	morena horra	mother	Nov. 19, 1597
	Juana Bañon	morena horra	godmother	Jan. 6, 1600
"Biafara" (Biafada)	Marçela Biafara	morena horra negra horra	godmother mother	Oct. 2, 1594 Sept. 28, 1597
	Isabel Biafara	morena horra	godmother	Sept. 1, 1596; Nov. 10, 1596; Sept. 28, 1597
	Catalina Biafara	morena horra	mother	June 15, 1597
	María Biafara	morena horra	godmother	May 10, 1598
"Bran" (Brame)	Vitoria Bran	morena horra	godmother	Sept. 17, 1595; Apr. 5, 1598
	María Bran	morena horra	mother	Nov. 12, 1595
Nalu	Madalena Nalu	morena horra	mother	Sept. 9, 1596
"Zape"	María Çape	morena horra	mother godmother	July 15, 1590 Nov. 17, 1596
	Gostança Çape	morena horra	slaveowner	Jan. 31, 1593
	Felipa Zape	morena horra	godmother	Nov. 12, 1595
	Leonor Çape	morena horra	godmother	Oct. 24, 1599
	María Linba	morena horra	godmother	Nov. 13, 1593
WEST CENTRAL AFRICANS				
"Angola"	Juana Angola	horra	godmother	Jan. 14, 1596
"Congo"	Jeronima Conga	morena horra	godmother	June [?], 1590

Source: Baptisms of Mateo Manicongo (June [10–12], 1590), Isabel Bañon (Jan. 31, 1593), Filipe (Nov. 13, 1593), Pedro Angola (Oct. 2, 1594), Anton Angola (Sept. 17, 1595), Luis (Nov. 12, 1595), Juan Angola (Jan. 14, 1596), Domingo Biafara (Sept. 1, 1596), Juana (Sept. 9, 1596), Francisco Biafara (Nov. 10, 1596), Anton Çape (Nov. 17, 1596), Marçela (June 15, 1597), Dominga (Sept. 28, 1597), Geronima (Nov. 19, 1597), María Bran (Apr. 5, 1598), Ynes Bran (May 10, 1598), Jusepe (Oct. 24, 1599), Bentura Bran (Jan. 6, 1600), CH-LB/B, fols. 6v, 24v, 35v, 45r, 62r, 66r, 71v, 83r, 84r, 87v–88r, 102r, 111r, 115r, 121r, 123v, 150v, 156v.

Note: Although "Maria Linba" is included with other "Zape" women here, she is not specifically identified as "Zape" or "Çape" in Havana's baptismal register or in any other known source.

separate occasions. In both instances, she is described as "Leonor, [a] black woman of [that is, owned by] Francisco de Abalos" (*Leonor negra de Francisco de Abalos*). In 1594, at the baptism of her son Domingo, Leonor Anchica appears a fourth time, this time identified as "Leonor morena," still owned by "captain Francisco de Abalos." Five years later, in 1599, Leonor Anchica served again as godmother at the baptism of a child born to an enslaved Upper Guinean couple. At some point in the preceding five years, Leonor Anchica had gained her freedom; in the 1599 entry, her name is recorded as "Leonor de Abalos morena horra." In this case, Leonor's West Central African ethnonym "Anchica" (Ansiku) was replaced by her former owner's Spanish surname. Over the course of eight years then, the West Central African woman initially identified as Leonor Anchica, a black slave owned by Francisco de Abalos, gradually became known as "Leonor de Abalos morena horra." Although it is impossible to know precisely how she viewed herself, she could have been the author of her own reidentification, choosing to ascribe herself an Iberian surname that associated her with the family or household of her former owner for convenience or security. What is certain is that her Hispanicized identity as "Leonor de Abalos, morena horra" was recognized and duly recorded by the various priests and scribes who made these entries in Havana's sacramental records.[20]

Amancebamiento

Although the topic remains largely unexplored at the ground level, assumptions have been that a dearth of white or European women encouraged extramarital sexual unions between European men and women of African (or Amerindian) origin in the early Spanish Caribbean, thus explaining the rise of mixed-race populations. The suppositions underlying this increasingly dated perspective were that white women were the natural spouses and partners of white men and that formal marriage endorsed by the church was the normal mechanism for family formation and sexual unions between partners of similar status. It is not at all clear that early modern migrants from Iberia and Africa to the Caribbean thought in such terms. In western Europe, especially in Spain and Portugal, informal unions were common and in some cases even legalized by the church. Furthermore, as noted

20. Baptisms of Leonor Bran (Nov. 29, 1592), Ysabella Conga (Jan. 10, 1593), Faustina (Sept. 19, 1593), Domingo (Dec. 18, 1594), and Diego (May 16, 1595), CH-LB/B, fols. 20v, 23v, 30v, 50v, 145r. "Gabriel Rodrigues and Leonor de Abalos, morenos horros" were married in Havana on May 8, 1605; see CH-LB/M, fol. 102r.

above, some African migrants to the Spanish Caribbean came from societies in which common practice provided women for foreign merchants or outsiders during the length of their stay. Large numbers of Portuguese and Luso-Africans in the Caribbean had previously resided in western Africa and were surely familiar with this custom. That informal sexual partnerships between Iberian men and African women were widely viewed as intrinsically abnormal or immoral is unlikely.[21]

Free and enslaved women of color in the early colonial Spanish Caribbean were, indeed, involved in various types of extramarital unions with Iberian men and, given the power relations in question, many such relationships were probably very exploitative of enslaved women in particular. One account extolls the virtues of a vicar who went from door to door in Havana in the 1570s chastising women who "lived in sin" and convincing several of them to marry their partners. Yet, the large number of children of "unknown" paternity born in Havana in the 1590s suggests that this zeal was quite limited within the broader population, or fairly short-lived. During that decade, 270 children baptized in Havana were born to single mothers, with the father either listed as "unknown" *(padre no conocido)* or simply not named. The mothers of these children came from diverse backgrounds; two Iberian or Spanish American mothers were described as *doñas,* signifying higher social standing. But only 35 children of unknown or undeclared paternity were born to Iberian women; the remaining 235 children (about 87 percent) were all born to women of African origin: 128 to sub-Saharan African mothers identified by African ethnonyms, 41 to Afrocreole mothers (criollas), and 66 to women described only as negras, morenas, mulatas, slaves, or free women of color.[22]

Unlike the women in Havana who allegedly "lived in sin" but were not persuaded to marry their partners during the 1570s, most single mothers in Havana in the 1590s would not have had that option: most were enslaved and probably did not live with their childrens' fathers at all. Among the 270 children of unknown paternity, no less than 211 (nearly 80 percent) were born to slaves. Although there is little evidence available to determine the types of sexual unions—ranging anywhere from rape to prostitution to

21. For sixteenth-century Iberian attitudes toward marriage, see, for example, Jutta Sperling, "Marriage at the Time of the Council of Trent (1560–1570): Clandestine Marriages, Kinship Prohibitions, and Dowry Exchange in European Comparison," *JEMH,* VIII (2004), 67–108.

22. "Información hecho en la Habana por parte del bachiller Juan Diaz Aldeano de Mendoça," 1576–1579, AGI-SD 153, r.1, n.24a. For children born to single mothers "doña Agustina de Baldes" and "doña Juana Pimentel" and "unknown" fathers, see the baptisms of Baltasar (Aug. 12, 1595) and Andrea (Oct. 30, 1595), CH-LB/B, fols. 59v, 65r.

long-term partnerships—involved in these cases, in all likelihood, sex was one form of rented slave labor available to travelers temporarily residing in Spanish Caribbean seaports. Among the seventeen women who brought more than one fatherless child to be baptized during the 1590s, only two were Iberian or Spanish American, and only one was a free woman of color. Eight were enslaved sub-Saharan Africans, two were enslaved Afrocreoles, and two were enslaved women of unspecified origin. If repeated appearances at the baptismal font with children of unknown paternity serves as an indication of possible prostitution, then most sex workers in late-sixteenth-century Havana would have been slaves.[23]

By around 1601, at least three hundred enslaved women in Havana labored as *ganadoras,* slaves who hired themselves out for wages that they would later turn over to their owners. During the 1580s, female slaves who worked as cooks for passers-through usually earned a *jornal* (daily wage) of two to four reales; in the early 1590s, black slaves in Havana typically "earn[ed] for their masters four reales each day" and sometimes more, notably when fleets were in port. Some of the enslaved women who gave birth to children of unknown paternity in Havana during that decade might have participated in this service economy as prostitutes or concubines, possibly as the result of pressure or coercion by their owners—most of whom were Iberian or Spanish American men. María Angola, an enslaved woman owned by Rodrigo de Narvaez, had three daughters and two sons baptized in Havana in December 1592, April 1594, October 1595, December 1596, and October 1599. At each of these baptisms, the child's father was either not

23. For children of unknown paternity born to Juana de Blas and María Hernández, see the baptisms of Diego (Sept. 23, 1593), Gonçalo (Oct. 1, 1593), Ana (Nov. 13, 1596), and María (Nov. 28, 1599), CH-LB/B, fols. 31r, 33r, 87v, 153v. For morena horra Agustina de Carreño's children, see the baptisms of Mariana (Dec. 16, 1593) and Diego (Apr. 10, 1596), CH-LB/B, fols. 37r, 78r. For children of unknown paternity born to Catalina Biafara, Vitoria Biafara, María Angola, Juana Bran, Helena Bran, Leonor Conga, Madalena Angola, and Isabel Bran, see the baptisms of María (Sept. 16, 1590), Juana (Dec. 26, 1590), Andrés (Dec. 20, 1592), Isabel (Dec. 20, 1592), Anbrosia (Jan. 3, 1593), Alonso (Feb. 2, 1593), Bartolomé (Feb. 7, 1593), Ana (Apr. 3, 1594), Baltasar and Melchor (Mar. 15, 1595), Ana (Sept. 25, 1595), Luis (Oct. 30, 1595), Luçía (Dec. 29, 1596), Felipa (May 15, 1597), Juan (Aug. 17, 1597), Miguel (Nov. 30, 1597), Leonor (Dec. 27, 1598), Francisca (Oct. 3, 1599), Diego (Oct. 4, 1599), Cristóbal (Oct. 31, 1599), and Ana (Jan. 9, 1600), CH-LB/B, fols. 9v, 12v, 22r–22v, 25r–25v, 42r, 55v, 62v, 65r, 90v, 100r, 108r, 116r, 136r, 148v, 151v, 157r. For children born to Grigoria Criolla, Francisca Criolla, Catalina Criolla, and another Francisca Criolla, see the baptisms of Cristóbal (Mar. 24, 1590), Domingo (Feb. 7, 1593), Luis (Apr. 19, 1593), Francisco (June 19, 1594), Cristóbal (Feb. 6, 1597), Luisa (Sept. 28, 1597), Sebastián (Feb. 22, 1598), and María (Sept. 20, 1599), CH-LB/B, fols. 4r, 25v, 29r, 44r, 94r, 111r, 118v, 148r. See also the baptisms of María (Nov. 21, 1590), Isabel (Nov. 14 or 15, 1591), Juan (Jan. 10, 1593), and Jusepe (Dec. 5, 1593), CH-LB/B, fols. 11v, 16v, 23v, 36v. Slavery does not seem to have been a significant facet of prostitution in contemporary Seville; see Mary Elizabeth Perry, *Gender and Disorder in Early Modern Seville* (Princeton, N.J., 1990).

named or expressly listed as "unknown." Each child was presumably born into slavery, inheriting her or his mother's status; Narvaez would benefit not only from the acquisition of enslaved children but also from their mother's earnings, if she had been engaged in prostitution. At least nineteen children were born in similar circumstances to enslaved women owned by Iberian or Spanish American women identified as widows *(viudas)*. By contrast, not a single free person of color, male or female, was named as the owner of an enslaved mother with one or more children of unknown paternity. Although women who had extramarital sexual relationships came from all social backgrounds, and, although nonelite Iberian women and women of color alike might have supported themselves to varying degrees through prostitution or concubinage, the vast majority of those who might have done so in Havana during the 1590s were slaves owned by Iberians or Spanish Americans—but not by free men or women of African descent.[24]

Penalties for petty crimes could be a better indication of informal sexual relations, including voluntary sexual unions, between women of color and Iberian men in port cities such as Havana and Cartagena. For the years 1598–1602, lists of *penas de cámara,* or fines collected for misdemeanors, indicate that individuals or couples in Havana were occasionally penalized for *amancebamiento* (concubinage, especially referring to the cohabitation of unmarried partners), along with many other infractions such as gambling, smuggling, unlicensed travel, theft, acts of violence, mistreating slaves, selling wine to slaves, tampering with scales, or selling foodstuffs without a license. In February 1600, Antonio del Castillo and María Hernandez were sentenced to pay 22 reales for being *amancebados.* There appear to have been

24. De la Fuente, *Havana,* 154–155; Fray Hernando de San Pedro Martir de la orden de Santo Domingo a S. M., July 3, 1587, AGI-SD 153, r.3, n.45, fols. 14r–15r, 19r; "Diego de Azambuja, vecino de Lisboa, con Juan de Tejeda, governador de La Habana," 1598–1603, AGI-Esc 1011B, fols. 70r, 73v, 80v–81r, 82v, 84v, 86v. For children born to María Angola, owned by Rodrigo de Narvaez, see the baptisms of Ysabel (Dec. 20, 1592), Ana (Apr. 3, 1594), Luis (Oct. 30, 1595), Luçia (Dec. 29, 1596), and Cristóbal (Oct. 31, 1599), CH-LB/B, fols. 22r, 42r, 65r, 90v, 151v. For the children of enslaved single mothers owned by widows, see the baptisms of Bartolome (Aug. 26, 1590), Juana (Sept. 6, 1592), Filipe (Nov. 13, 1593), Juana (Dec. 6, 1593), Hernando (Dec. 11, 1594), Blas (Mar. 22, 1595), Antonia (July 23, 1595), María (Sept. 8, 1595), Catalina (Dec. 3, 1595), Ursula (Aug. 18, 1596), Ypolita (Apr. 15, 1597), Martin (June 22, 1597), Juana (July 6, 1597), Luisa (Sept. 28, 1597), Francisco (Oct. 12, 1597), Ana (Nov. 23, 1597), Luis (early February 1598), Juana (May 24, 1598), and María (Sept. 20, 1599), CH-LB/B, fols. 8r, 17r, 35v, 36v, 47v, 56r, 58v, 61r, 67v, 81r, 98r, 102v, 103v, 111r, 112v, 115v, 118r, 124v, 148r. On widows and other Spanish women as slaveowners and slave merchants, see, especially, Alexandra Parma Cook, "The Women of Early Modern Triana: Life, Death, and Survival Strategies in Seville's Maritime District," in Douglas Catterall and Jodi Campell, eds., *Women in Port: Gendering Communities, Economies, and Social Networks in Atlantic Port Cities, 1500–1800* (Leiden, 2012), 41–68. See also C. R. Boxer, *Women in Iberian Expansion Overseas, 1415–1815: Some Facts, Fancies, and Personalities* (New York, 1975), 59–60; Sally McKee, "Domestic Slavery in Renaissance Italy," *SA,* XXIX (2008), 319–320.

several women who bore the name María Hernandez, or some variation of that name, in Havana at the turn of the seventeenth century, including free women of color described as "Mari Fernandes mulata" and "Marina Hernandez morena libre." Although it is ultimately not clear which, if any, of these individuals were the same person, the woman listed here might have been the same María Hernandez who had children of unknown paternity baptized in Havana in 1593 and again in October 1599, four months before she was fined for amancebamiento. Other lists of penas de cámara for Havana provide names of people who were fined but often did not specify whether the individuals in question were accused of practicing unlicensed prostitution or whether they were involved in extramarital sexual unions viewed as improper by spiritual and civic authorities. Rather, those individuals accused or apprehended were named along with the amounts they were expected to pay, with little or no description of the misdemeanors involved. Several women described as blacks, mulatas, slaves, and ex-slaves appear in Havana's penas de cámara for the years 1569–1575, without their crimes being specified. In one case, two women with names suggesting Portuguese and Upper Guinean origins, Isabel de Almeyda and Isabel Caçanga, were fined jointly. Only "Juana negra" was fined together with a man.[25]

Dozens of fines issued in Cartagena during the 1570s offer slightly greater detail. In some cases, various misdemeanors are specified, with a handful of individuals explicitly accused of amancebamiento. The merchant Diego de Luna, for example, was said to have been *amançebado*—living in a domestic sexual union—"with Ana negra, his slave," and sentenced to pay twenty pesos of common silver in 1575. The mulata innkeeper María de Torres, mentioned at the beginning of this chapter, testified in 1582 that she would never knowingly permit disreputable behavior, namely extramarital sex, in her inn. In her own words, if she had known that a man would spend the night in a room she had rented to a teenaged "maiden" newly arrived

25. Hospital de la Havana a S. M., Mar. 8, 1608, AGI-SD 153, r.4, n.70c, fols. 5v–15r, 17v–25v. Half of the funds generated by penas de cámara levied in Havana had previously been used to support the city's hospital; this list of penas de cámara for the years 1598–1602 was forwarded to the crown in 1608 as part of a request for a continuation of the royal grant. For an earlier request along the same lines, with a list of penas de cámara for the years 1569–1575, see El hospital de la villa de San Cristóbal de la Havana sobre prorrogación de la mitad de penas de cámara, Sept. 2, 1575, AGI-SD 153, r.1, n.16, fols. 6r–12v. For women identified as Maria (or Mari, or Marina) Hernandez (or Fernandes)—including "Mari Fernandez mulata" and "Marina Hernandez morena horra"—see the baptisms of Francisco Bran (Feb. 2, 1593), Gonçalo (Oct. 1, 1593), Francisco (Dec. 23, 1593), Juan (Jan. 10, 1594), Francisco (Dec. 17, 1594), Luis (Dec. 19, 1594), Catalina (Aug. 20, 1596), Mariana (Aug. 10, 1597), Jusepe (Sept. 1, 1597), Luis Nalu (Nov. 23, 1597), María (Nov. 28, 1599), CH-LB/B, fols. 25r, 33r, 37v, 38v, 50r, 82r, 107r, 109r, 115v, 153v.

from Spain, she never would have allowed it (*no lo consintiera esta testigo si tal supiera*). Torres—who had personally reported the couple to Cartagena authorities—was very likely attempting to protect her own reputation and that of her inn. But the innkeeper had further reasons to emphasize her steadfast observation of officially sanctioned policies regarding sexual propriety. Less than a decade earlier, the innkeeper herself was named in Cartagena's list of penas de cámara; "María de Torres mulata" was fined one silver mark in 1575 for being *amançebada* with a shoemaker named Juan de Torres (one silver mark, or 65 reales, was the equivalent of a little more than eight pesos—less than half of the twenty peso fine levied against the merchant Diego de Luna the same year for maintaining a domestic sexual union with his slave). Torres was likely involved in a long-term relationship with Juan, given that they shared the same surname. The shoemaker might have been her former owner, or perhaps she was commonly known as María de Torres through long association with him, despite the fact that they were not formally married.[26]

Although concubinage was clearly penalized to some extent in Cartagena during the 1570s, scattered references indicate that amancebamiento involving Iberian men and women of color in the Spanish Caribbean was often accepted or simply ignored, in spite of occasional complaints. African and African-descended women appear to have maintained long-term sexual unions with soldiers, in particular, without the official recognition of the church. In their last wills and testaments, soldiers stationed in Havana during the late sixteenth century often mentioned having borrowed money from free women of color or entrusting items such as weapons or clothing to their care. During the 1570s, Havana's governor reportedly locked the town's soldiers in the fortress at night, keeping the key under his pillow, to prevent them from spending nights with local vecinas, who would have included women of African descent. In Havana during the 1590s, Iberian soldiers at times appeared at baptisms as *compadres* (co-parents) alongside both free and enslaved women of color, including even newly arrived Africans. Enslaved women also chose soldiers to be their children's godfathers,

26. For fines meted out to Diego de Luna and María de Torres respectively in 1575, see Caja de Cartagena, "Receta de las condenaçiones de penas de camara," 1575–1578, AGI-Ctdra 1382, pliegos 1–2 (the same source notes that María Jolofo—quite possibly the same María Xolofa described as owning a garden or orchard in Cartagena several years later—was sentenced to pay a fine of six pesos of common silver in 1576, for an unspecified offense). María de Torres' 1582 comments signalling her disapproval of her guest's sexual activities appear in "Memorial y testimonio de autos de la ciudad y provincia de Cartagena sobre los abusos y delitos que contra aquellos vecinos cometen los soldados de las galeras y flotas," May 11, 1583, AGI-SF 62, n.28, fols. 19r–20r.

suggesting shared social ties which might have included paternity. In 1603, Havana's governor complained to the Spanish crown that the soldiers under his command were "scandalously dishonoring their uniforms, publicly amançebados with slaves and mulatas, in spite of their owners' wishes." By the turn of the seventeenth century, sexual unions and domestic partnerships between Iberian men and women of color had become common in Havana and in other Spanish Caribbean settlements.[27]

At virtually the same time the governor of Havana was criticizing his soldiers' interactions with free and enslaved women of African descent, Spanish Jamaica's governor Alonso de Miranda lived openly with a mulata concubine named Clara. Several testimonies collected in 1610 relate that he had publicly maintained this intimate relationship throughout the preceding four years. One witness stated that Clara was previously enslaved but that, even then, she had often been seen entering the governor's house at night "to dine with him at the table," then remaining in his house until morning. "And now that this mulata is free," the witness noted, Governor Miranda "keeps her in his house." Far from penalizing concubinage, by the early 1600s some Spanish Caribbean officials were more inclined to follow the example set by Havana's soldiers. Though Clara evidently acquired her freedom, officials' positions of power could have allowed them to develop long- or short-term sexual relationships with women of African descent that might have been much more exploitative or one-sided than those between free women of color and soldiers.[28]

In 1604, Española's governor Antonio Osorio traveled widely throughout the island, visiting several towns that were soon to be depopulated by royal decree. During this tour, he levied fines on a number of unmarried couples found living together. Some of the men involved were already married, thus several of these cases involved adultery on their parts, if not bigamy, as well as concubinage. Most of the women implicated in these cases were free women of African descent, and none were described as married. In the village of San Juan de los Caballeros, free mulata Marsela Segura was

---

27. Rojas, "Algunos datos," in *Miscelánea*, II, 1283–1284; Wright, *Early History of Cuba*, 331; Baptisms of Domingo (Dec. 18, 1594), Antón (July 25, 1595), Leonor (Sept. 17, 1595), Luysa (Sept. 19, 1595), Lucía (Dec. 4, 1595), Simón (Jan. 28, 1596), and Juliana Angola (Dec. 25, 1596), CH-LB/B, fols. 50v, 58v, 61v, 62v, 68r, 73r, 90v; Pedro de Valdes a S. M., Sept. 22, 1603, AGI-SD 100, r.2, n.17, fol. 3r; Macías Domínguez, *Cuba*, 309. For further discussion of Catholic godparentage networks and their social functions for enslaved people in colonial Spanish Caribbean settings, see Jane Landers, *Black Society in Spanish Florida* (Urbana, Ill., 1999), 121–123.

28. "Pleitos y residencias de Jamaica, 1597–1610: Residencia de Alonso de Miranda, gobernador de la isla de Jamaica," [1610], AGI-Esc 158A, piezas 1–3. Quotes from pieza 1, fol. 117r.

accused of being the mistress of a married vecino of Santo Domingo. Several witnesses claimed that the couple had a son and that they were often seen living together in a house and sharing meals. Alternately described as "negra libre" and "morena libre," the free woman of color María Genadora was also believed to have been "amancebada" with a free mulato who was married to another woman. Genadora appealed her case, apparently without success. Two other women in San Juan de los Caballeros, identified only as Madalena, morena libre, and Juana, mulata libre, were each fined twenty ducados for living in a state of concubinage with Iberian or Spanish American men; one of the men implicated was a chief constable (*alguacil mayor*). Another Iberian man was fined for being amancebado with an unnamed "black slave woman." In the town of Azua, a free mulata named María Magdalena was held for questioning along with her presumed lover, an Iberian (probably Portuguese) man named Paulo de Araujo. Later, her friend, another mulata named María Nuñez, spent the night with *oidor* (magistrate) Manso de Contreras, who was investigating the case. In exchange, he allegedly agreed to let the couple leave, without fining them for the misdemeanor of amancebamiento. Free women of color's interactions with Iberian men were at times little more than brief, semicoerced encounters between parties of highly unequal status, with women of color exchanging sex with powerful men in hopes of obtaining their own immediate objectives. Yet, sexual relationships between women of African origin and Iberian men also included voluntary, long-term partnerships. Though officially discouraged outside of the bonds of marriage, in the early Spanish Caribbean such unions were widely tolerated as common practice in much the same way that informal domestic unions were accepted as normal in Iberian and Luso-African settings.[29]

Church-Sanctioned Marriage

In addition to their economic activities and demographic presence, free African and African-descended women's sexual and marital relationships with Iberian men further point to these women's formative roles in the establishment of Spanish Caribbean society. Research on the late colonial

29. Autos de Antonio de Osorio, 1604–1607, AGI-Esc 11A (mf 2705), pieza 1, fol. 8r, pieza 2, fols. 305r–317r, 342r–342v. See also Carlos Esteban Deive, *Tangomangos: Contrabando y piratería en Santo Domingo, 1522–1606* (Santo Domingo, Dominican Republic, 1996), 194; Carlos Rodríguez Souquet, *El concilio provincial dominicano (1622–1623): Un aporte para la historia de las Antillas y Venezuela* (Mexico City, 2003), 38–39, 160.

Spanish Caribbean shows that free women of color married white men upon occasion but that such marriages were often discouraged and increasingly rare after a royal pragmatic in the 1770s made parental approval a prerequisite for marriage. As a result, during the late eighteenth and early nineteenth centuries, concubinage was far more commonly adopted as an option for sexual unions involving African or African-descended women and white men. By contrast, in the sixteenth and early seventeenth centuries the range of sexual relationships between African or African-descended women and Iberian men included church-sanctioned marriages, suggesting possibilities of mutual interest, convenience, advantage, and even love and choice for both partners.[30]

Given the history of interaction between Iberian mariners and sub-Saharan African women in western Africa, Portuguese men might have been especially prominent among Iberians formally married to women of African descent in Spanish colonies. In the late-sixteenth-century Canary Islands, at least one Spanish man and several Portuguese men were married to women of African descent. Other Portuguese men failed to marry their partners but left goods in their last wills to daughters born of sexual unions with black women; one designated his daughter Ana, a mulata, as his universal heir, bequeathing her houses and an enslaved black man. Cartagena's 1630 census of "foreigners" likewise lists Portuguese men married to free women of color. António Diaz, originally from Avero, Portugal, was married to a locally born Cartagenera named María de Rivera, mulata. Domingo Montero of Lamego, Portugal, was married to an unnamed woman from the island of São Tomé, where she apparently continued to reside. The census of Portuguese migrants residing in Havana in 1607 includes no less than five men with wives who were free women of color. The baker Francisco Salgado was married to a mulata and owned both houses and slaves; Duarte de Acuña was married to "a black woman who is also Portuguese"; and Manuel Vaez's wife was a free black woman. Other Portuguese men formally married women of African descent elsewhere in the early colonial Spanish Caribbean. Both Domingo Leyton, a free Portuguese man, and Valentino

30. Patricia Seed, *To Love, Honor, and Obey in Colonial Mexico: Conflicts over Marriage Choice, 1574–1821* (Stanford, Calif., 1988), 205–224; Steinar A. Saether, "Bourbon Absolutism and Marriage Reform in Late Colonial Spanish America," *Americas*, LIX (2003), 475–509. On interracial marriage in Cuba and the Spanish Caribbean during the late eighteenth and nineteenth centuries, see Verena Martinez-Alier, *Marriage, Class, and Colour in Nineteenth-Century Cuba: A Study of Racial Attitudes and Sexual Values in a Slave Society*, 2d ed. (Ann Arbor, Mich., 1989), xiv, 1–2; Landers, *Black Society*, 99, 122–129, 150–155; Matt D. Childs, *The 1812 Aponte Rebellion in Cuba and the Struggle against Atlantic Slavery* (Chapel Hill, N.C., 2006), 71–73.

Acosta, an enslaved mulato originally from Lisbon, married enslaved black women in Havana's *iglesia mayor* (main church) in 1620 and 1621.[31]

Two Portuguese residents in Havana merit further attention for both their prosperity and their marriages to women of color. By 1607, the master mason *(alarife)* Gregório Lopez had lived in Havana for more than twenty years and owned a house, a farm, and livestock. He was also married to a woman described as a mulata. Hernán Rodriguez Tavares, an "ancient" resident in Havana, owned a sugar mill and houses; he, too, was married to an unnamed mulata. As prosperous, long-term residents of one of the most important port cities in the Spanish Caribbean, neither man appears to have suffered any social or economic stigma for his marriage to a woman of African descent. Though Lopez and Tavares might have been unusual among the wealthier residents of late-sixteenth-century Havana, their marriages to women described as mulatas were evidently no less effective in determining Spanish officials' perceptions of stability and loyalty, enabling both men to become vecinos (and avoid deportation), than other Portuguese migrants' marriages to Spanish or Spanish American women. Furthermore, as the wives of prosperous men who owned farms, ranches, a sugar mill, and other properties, these mulata women must have played important roles as elite settlers in the creation of Spanish colonial society in the Caribbean.[32]

Intermarriage between women of African descent and Iberian men was by no means limited to Afro-Portuguese unions. Among the free people of color residing in Panama during the 1570s, many were wives and children of Spanish men. A royal cedula issued in 1574 ordered that free people of color in the Audiencia of Panama were to pay a yearly tribute of one silver mark, or two silver marks for families. After hearing Panama's city council members' argument that the fine would be detrimental for many reasons, the Audiencia of Panama decided to enforce the decree but noted that families would count as one person; upon the city council's insistence, free people of color married to Spaniards would be exempt from paying the annual tribute, as would their children. In a 1575 roster that attempted to list every adult of African descent and their approximate net worth, those married to

---

31. Manuel Lobo Cabrera, *Los libertos en la sociedad canaria del siglo XVI* (Madrid, 1983), 100; "Relaçion y abecedario de los estrangeros que se hallaron en la çiudad de Cartagena, 1630," May 13, 1631, AGI-SF 56B, n.73a, fols. 2v–3r, 6r–6v; Pedro de Valdes a S. M., Aug. 12, 1607, AGI-SD 100, r.2, n.58, fols. 1v–2v; Marriages of Domingo Leyton and Ana Xuares (Mar. 17, 1620) and Valentino Acosta and María de Acosta (Feb. 23, 1621), CH-LB/M, fols. 185r, 190v.

32. Pedro de Valdes a S. M., Aug. 12, 1607, AGI-SD 100, r.2, n.58, fols. 1v–2v. On Gregório Lopez and Hernán Rodriguez Tavares, see also de la Fuente, *Havana*, 93–98.

Spanish spouses, or with children born of a union with a Spanish partner, had ample incentive to convey that information to royal officials.[33]

In Nombre de Dios, Lucía de Rojas "de color mulata" was the "wife of Andres Alonso, Spanish vecino of this city," and mother of a three-month-old son. Another resident of Nombre de Dios named Bárbola de Trejo was a mulata and "the wife of Pedro Gómez de Villanueva, *español*." Trejo was also the mother of a thirteen-year-old "Spanish man's daughter," indicating either the longevity of her marriage or a prior relationship with a different Spanish man. The free black woman Inés Carmonesa negra horra had a fifteen-year-old mulata daughter and was married to a man named Juan Gonzalez del Toro. Other African-descended women residing in Nombre de Dios who were said to be married to Spanish men included mulata Juana Corzo, "wife of Pedro de Campos, español," and Aña Cana, "wife of Francisco Rodriguez, español." Likewise, a formerly enslaved woman in Chepo named "Anana horr[a]" was married to "Juan Martin español." In Panama City, free women of color Lucía Camacha, Lucía de Solis, and Isabel de Torrellas were each "married to a Spanish man"; María Lopez was to marry a Spanish man named Diego Jimenez "tomorrow," that is, the day after the census was taken. In Veragua, the free black woman Inés Ordoñez, an Afro-creole born in Santo Domingo, was married to "Luis Gonzalez, español," originally from the Canary Islands. Together, the couple was described as "poor people" whose earthly belongings were worth less than one hundred pesos. A "dark-skinned black woman" (negra atezada) named Catalina Lopez Terranova was somewhat better off; she and her husband—a Venetian man named Jacome—owned property and goods in Veragua valued at a total of one thousand pesos.[34]

The free women of color in Spanish Caribbean port cities who married or closely associated with Iberian men were at times permitted to ply trades

33. Jopling, comp., *Indios y negros en Panamá*, 440–454. For evidence of royal efforts to levy a similar tribute on free people of color in Cartagena "where it is understood that there are a quantity of negros and negras libres and cambaygos [,] married and single"—though the tribute in Cartagena does not appear to have been enforced—see Carta de los contadores de cuentas del Tribunal de Santa Fe, June 9, 1612, AGI-SF 52, n.87 (quote from fol. 1v); "Serviçio que pagan negros horros mulatos y çanbahigos y yndios ladinos," AGI-Ctdra 1387, Año 1606, pliego 81.

34. Jopling, comp., *Indios y negros en Panamá*, 446, 448, 452. Another resident of Nombre de Dios was Sebastiana de Casal *"de color negra, libre,"* who described herself as single and around forty years old. Casal stated that she had a fourteen-year-old mulata daughter, whose father had been a Spanish man. In Panama City in 1607, at least twenty-seven Iberian men were married to women of African descent; see "Descripción de Panamá y su provincia . . . ," (1607), in Serrano y Sanz, [ed.], *Relaciones históricas y geográficas,* 167–168; Andrews, *Spanish Caribbean,* 35; María del Carmen Mena García, *La sociedad de Panamá en el siglo XVI* (Seville, 1984), 64–67.

reserved only for Iberians and Spanish Americans, including potentially lucrative services to temporary residents associated with Indies fleets. The sale of wine, for example, was heavily regulated in the Spanish Americas. Just as enslaved people were prohibited from purchasing wine, free blacks and mulatos were prohibited from selling it. Exceptions to this rule were made, however, for some free women of color. In the 1560s, Cartagena's town council decreed that "black women who are not married to Spanish men are not to sell wine." During the same decade, fearing that black men would "intoxicate themselves and kill one another," Havana's town council ruled that "no black woman, free or enslaved, shall be permitted to buy or sell wine, except for the negras libres who usually sell it" (de antigua costumbre lo suelen vender). This special allowance was made for Catalina Rodriguez, Juana Garcia, and Angelina Martin, each described as a freed black woman (negra horra), and for one man identified as "Diego negro." In subsequent versions of the same legislation, Havana's town council extended the prohibition to all free people of color, but, again, exceptions were made for some individuals. Despite initial setbacks, "attentive to the fact that she was born free, and has been a woman married to Spanish men," in 1570, the free black woman Juana Garcia successfully petitioned for permission to sell the "two pipas [several hundred liters] of wine she has in her house." Furthermore, it was noted, she mainly "provides food for white men, and pledges to give wine to neither blacks nor Indians."[35]

Legitimate marriages between African or African-descended women and Iberian men regularly occurred in Havana. Between 1586 and 1622, at least 35 marriages between women of color and Iberian or Spanish-American men were contracted in Havana's iglesia mayor (Table 8), representing slightly more than 2 percent of the 1,318 marriages known to have taken place in Havana during this period. A little more than one-third of these marriages are concentrated in the years 1618–1620, yet the chronological distribution of all 35 marriages in the space of thirty-seven years is

---

35. Maria del Carmen Borrego Plá, Cartagena de Indias en el siglo XVI (Seville, 1983), 485, 489–490; Roig, dir., Actas capitulares, tomo I, vol. II, 286, 294, tomo II, 204–205; Rojas, "Algunos datos," in Miscelánea, II, 1284–1285. Though wine was often measured in "pipas," the term was not standardized; two pipas could have been anywhere from three hundred to nine hundred liters. See Carla Rahn Phillips, Six Galleons for the King of Spain: Imperial Defense in the Early Seventeenth Century (Baltimore, 1986), 103; Pablo E. Pérez-Mallaína, Spain's Men of the Sea: Daily Life on the Indies Fleets in the Sixteenth Century, trans. Carla Rahn Phillips (Baltimore, 1998), 66–67; Manuel Lobo Cabrera, El comercio del vino entre Gran Canaria y las Indias en el siglo XVI (Las Palmas, Spain, 1993), 38–43; David E. Vassberg, The Village and the Outside World in Golden Age Castile: Mobility and Migration in Everyday Rural Life (Cambridge, 1996), xv; de la Fuente, Havana, 232n.

Figure 4 Havana, circa 1620. España. Ministerio de Educación, Cultura y Deporte. Biblioteca Nacional de España. MS 2468, "Descripciones geográficas e hidrográficas de muchas tierras." By Nicolás de Cardona. 1632. fol. 49. Detail

significant. Nearly every year, on average, one Iberian or Spanish-American man married an African or African-descended woman in Havana's church. Among the thirty-five brides, twenty were described as morenas, nine as mulatas, and two as negras. Twenty brides are listed by both race and legal status as free women of color, with most identified as horra (freed) as opposed to libre (free). Whereas only five morenas and one mulata were said to be libre, eleven morenas and three mulatas were said to be horra. Several entries suggest that the terms were used in a loose, and perhaps interchangeable, fashion. When a child born to Leonor de Raya and an "unknown" father was baptized in late 1598, she appears as "Leonor de Raia morena horra." At her marriage to a Portuguese man in 1605, she is described as "Leonor de Raya morena hora libre." Likewise, the record of María Gutierrez's marriage to a Spanish or Spanish-American man in 1596 describes her as a mulata horra, but when she served as godmother at the baptism of an Upper Guinean man the previous year, she appears as a mulata libre. For free women of color, the men they married, and the clergy and witnesses in attendance, the distinction between libre and horra was far less important

Table 8 Marriages of African and African-Descended
Women to Iberian Men in Havana, 1586–1622

Bride	Groom	Date of marriage
Catalina Hernandez de Requena (mulata)	Juan Martin (*espaniol* [Spanish])	Sept. 10, 1586
Cecilia Velázquez (morena horra)	Sebastian Brabo	Aug. 5, 1587
Ana de Rojas (morena horra)	Francisco Diaz	Feb. 3, 1592
Madalena Gonzalez (daughter of Francisca, a black woman owned by María Delgada)	Juan Batista [de Rueda] (*mallorquín* [Mallorcan])	Sept. 6, 1593
María Lopez (morena horra)	Pedro, *moço*	Jan. 9, 1594
María Gutierrez (mulata horra)	Cristóbal Crespillo (parents are *vecinos* of Osuna, Castile)	July 25, 1596
Lusía Lopes (morena horra)	Diego Lopes (vecino of this city)	Oct. 27, 1599
Fabiana (morena horra)	Pedro de Escobar (soldier from Portugal)	Oct. 28, 1599
Andrea Criolla (*sclava* owned by Pedro Mendes)	Tomás Martin	May 10, 1603
Ana de Carreño (morena)	Alonso Ramires (parents are *naturales* of Murcia)	Jan. 6, 1604
Isabel Velazquez (morena horra)	Pedro de Lugones (parents are vecinos of this city)	Jan. 11, 1604
Isabel Maldonado (morena owned by don Joan)	Hernando Prieto (son of Juan de la Cruz, vecino of this city)	May 6, 1605
Leonor de Raya (morena horra libre)	Joan Albares (natural of Viana de Camino, Portugal)	May 6, 1605
Ana de Aranda (morena)	Luis Hernandes	Sept. 5, 1605
María Maldonado (daughter of Dominga de los Reyes, morena horra)	Juan de la Insension	Apr. 21, 1608
Juana Velazquez (morena horra)	Sebastián de la Cruz (natural of Puebla de Los Angeles, New Spain)	Nov. 30, 1608
Rufina Andrada (morena)	Martín Argon Vizcaino	Feb. 14, 1613
Mariana Rodriguez (morena libre)	Benito de Tal	Jan. 11, 1614
Ana de Arguello (morena libre)	Andrés de Aguilar	Sept. 20, 1615

Bride	Groom	Date of marriage
Ana de Rojas (morena horra)	Diego Camacho	Oct. 31, 1615
Rufina de Andrada (morena horra)	Jacome Perez	June 12, 1616
Luysa de Pisa (morena libre)	Pedro Hurtado	Sept. 3, 1617
María (negra criolla esclava owned by Bernabé Sanches)	Francisco Lopez (natural of Seville and spañol [Spanish])	Jan. 1, 1618
Luisa Belasquez (mulata libre)	Pedro Antonio Rabasa (*cabo de esquadra* [corporal] of the fort)	Feb. 22, 1618
Melchora de los Reyes (mulata, natural of Sanlúcar)	Alonso Rodriguez (natural of Asturias)	May 14, 1618
Isabel de Contreras (de color mulata)	Cristóbal de Caravajal	Jan. 20, 1619
María Rodrigues (mulata horra)	Antón Montero	Sept. 15, 1619
Francisca de Azuaga (mulata)	Sebastián de Haro	Oct. 9, 1619
Sebastiana (morena horra)	Sebastián Hernandez	Feb. 7, 1620
Inés Sodre (morena libre)	Pedro Hernandez Aleman	Feb. 23, 1620
Ana Xuares (morena esclava owned by Gonsalo Mexia)	Domingo Leyton (Portuguese)	Mar. 17, 1620
Cristina (negra esclava de doña Juana Tamaras)	Juan Peres Portillo (natural)	Sept. 9, 1620
María Guillen Salguera (mulata)	Antonio Hernandes Pimentel (soldier of the fort)	Oct. 22, 1620
Madalena Peres (mulata horra)	Francisco Gonsales	June 7, 1622
Ana de Salamanca (esclava owned by Juan de Salamanca)	Domingo Muños	July 28, 1622

Sources: For the marriages in this table, see CH-LB/M, fols. 9v, 11v, 34v, 40r–40v, 54r, 64v, 78v, 87r–87v, 101v, 105v, 122r, 127r, 129r, 152v, 157r, 162v–163r, 166r, 171r–171v, 174v, 175v, 177r, 179v, 182v–183r, 184v–185r, 187v, 188v, 198v, 199v.

than the facts that the bride was not a slave and that she was in the process of wedding an Iberian or Spanish American groom.[36]

The brides in twenty-nine of these marriages appear to have been free women of color, though at least some of them—if not all—had previously been enslaved. The Afrocreole morena Ana de Carreño married a Spanish man of Murcian origins in 1604, and, since her legal status is unspecified, she was most likely considered free at that time. Yet, while serving as godmother at baptisms in 1593 and 1598, she had been described as "Ana Criolla negra de Rodrigo Careño" and then as "Ana de Carreño morena de Rodrigo Careño." Other free women of color who married Iberian men in Havana might have been born libre, though little direct evidence has been found. The concentration of brides described as libre during the years 1614–1620 indicates that some of these women were likely born free in Havana to an earlier generation of free women of color who had already obtained their own manumissions. Others could have traveled to the Caribbean as passengers or servants on slave ships arriving from Africa or the Atlantic Islands or on merchant vessels arriving from Spain. At her marriage to a man from Asturias in 1618, the Afro-Iberian mulata Melchora de los Reyes is described as a native of Sanlúcar de Barrameda, Seville's port at the mouth of the Guadalquivir; if not born free in Andalusia, she might have arrived in Havana, at least, as a free woman.[37]

Widowhood might have provided considerable autonomy for those who had property or access to resources, yet references to free black women as viudas—such as the morena horra María, widow of a man named San Estevan and head of a household in Santo Domingo in 1606—are fairly scarce. For free women of color in the early Spanish Caribbean, as for nharas and donas in Atlantic African contexts as well as widows in early modern Spain, sequential relationships or marriages with Iberian men could provide a means of accumulating wealth and consolidating their status as free vecinas. Like negra horra Juana Garcia who had been "married to Spanish men" in Havana before 1570, some free women of color might have married Iberian

36. Marriages of Cristóbal Crespillo and María Gutierrez (July 25, 1596) and Joan Albares and Leonor de Raya (May 6, 1605), CH-LB/M, fols. 54r, 101v; Baptisms of Francisco Bran (Oct. 4, 1595) and Baltasar (Dec. 28, 1598), CH-LB/B, fols. 63v, 136v.

37. Marriages of Alonso Ramires and Ana de Carreño (Jan. 6, 1604) and Alonso Rodrigues and Melchora de los Reyes (May 14, 1618), CH-LB/M, fols. 87r, 177r; Baptisms of Juan Bioho (Feb. 28, 1593) and María Bran (Mar. 30, 1598), CH-LB/B, fols. 27v, 121r. See also "Expediente de concesión de licencia para pasar a La Habana a favor de María de Jesús, mulata, natural de Sevilla, hija de Fernando Díaz, blanco español, y de Polonia Hernández, negra, casada con Pedro Arias de Estrada, que reside en La Habana, en compañía de su hijo Cristóbal," 1597, AGI-Indiferente 2069, n.20.

men more than once. Freed morena Ana de Rojas married the carpenter Francisco Diaz in 1592, and their marriage endured throughout most of the decade; she was identified as Diaz's wife four times while serving as godmother for enslaved Africans (twice in 1594 and twice in 1597). It is possible that the morena horra named Ana de Rojas who married Diego Camacho nearly twenty years later in 1615 was the same person, though the Ana de Rojas in question was not listed as a widow. Also, marriage records for 1613 and 1616 both refer to brides named as Rufina Andrada morena and Rufina de Andrada morena horra. Although Andrada is not described as a widow in the 1616 marriage, and these weddings might refer to two different women, this could have been an instance of the same woman marrying in 1613, then remarrying three years later. Perhaps ecclesiastical scribes preferred to identify Rojas and Andrada as morenas horras rather than as widows. For the women themselves, "widow" might have been less useful as a designation of status or as a social reference point than being identified as the wife of an Iberian man.[38]

Free women of color married to Iberian men are often described in Havana sacramental records as "the wife of" their Iberian husband, rather than as a mulata libre or morena horra. At her wedding to a Mallorcan man in 1593, Madalena Gonzalez is identified as the daughter of Francisca morena, an enslaved black woman owned by María Delgada. Though her mother was an enslaved morena, Madalena Gonzalez was not assigned any racial category. Nor was she described by race when she appeared in Havana's baptismal register four years later as "Madalena Gonçalez, the wife of Juan Bautista de Rueda." Likewise, the free morena Ana de Rojas was described only as the "wife of Francisco Diaz" when she served as godmother at the baptisms of two enslaved sub-Saharan African men in 1597. When María Maldonado married an Iberian man named Juan de la Insencion in 1608, she was ascribed neither race nor legal status, though her parents were

---

38. "Testimonio de quantos lugares ay en esta ysla," Oct. 2, 1606, AGI-SD 83, r.2, s/n, fols. 33–69, transcribed in Rodríguez Demorizi, comp., *Relaciones históricas de Santo Domingo*, II, 381; Marriages of Francisco Diaz and Ana de Rojas (Feb. 3, 1592), Martín Argon Viscaíno and Rufina de Andrada (Feb. 14, 1613), Diego Camacho and Ana de Rojas (Oct. 31, 1615), and Jacome Perez and Rufina de Andrada (June 12, 1616), CH-LB/M, fols. 34v, 152v, 163r, 166r; Baptisms of María Angola (Jan. 30, 1594), Graçia Bioho (Jan. 30, 1594), Cristóbal Arará (May 11, 1597), and Francisco Angola (May 11, 1597), CH-LB/B, fols. 39r, 99v. Although remarriage could entail some loss of autonomy and loss of guardianship rights over children from their prior marriage, Spanish (Castilian) law dictated that widows who remarried would still retain rights over their own personal property such as previous dowries, bride gifts, and inheritances; see Stephanie Fink de Backer, *Widowhood in Early Modern Spain: Protectors, Proprietors, and Patrons* (Leiden, 2010), 111–112, 128–129, 148–149.

identified as "Pedro Magallanes and Dominga de los Reyes morena hora." Though Catalina Hernandez de Requena was described as a mulata at her marriage to a "Spanish man" named Juan Martin in 1586, at the baptism of their son Cristóbal four years later, she and her husband appear only as "the swordsmith Juan Martin and his wife Catalina de Requena." Married to Sebastian Brabo in Havana in 1587, morena horra Ceçilia Velazquez appears in Havana's marriage register as a godmother at a slave wedding in 1593. Unlike the other marriage sponsor, described as "Francisco Carlos moreno horro," she is identified only as "Ceçilia Belazques the wife of Sebastian Brabo." In these instances, women of African descent were labeled in the same way as nonelite Iberian women. Although being identified as wives to Iberian men ostensibly signified subordination to their husbands, belonging to an Iberian man indicated not only possession by their spouses but also higher status and greater security than the labels free morena or free mulata could provide.[39]

For free women of color in Spanish Caribbean seaports, marriage to Iberian or Spanish American men might have represented an additional step in their gradual incorporation into Spanish Caribbean society on Iberian terms. Just as African migrants like Leonor de Abalos (formally Leonor Anchica) eventually became known by their owners' surnames rather than an African nation, after their marriages free women of color were sometimes identified as "the wife of" their husbands, rather than as morenas horras; in some cases these processes possibly overlapped. As former slaves, women who had been considered a *negra de* (black woman owned by) an Iberian man or woman might later be known as the *negra que fue de* (black woman who was formerly owned by) that same person. As "the wife of" an Iberian man, free women of color were sometimes still marked as people of African descent, or as free or freed, and often kept their previous Iberian surnames that associated them with a former owner, or the former owner of a parent. Widowhood could represent an additional label which, like these other terms, tended to identify enslaved people in relation to their owners and women in relation to men. Among other heads of household

39. Marriages of Juan Martin and Catallina Hernandez de Requena (Sept. 10, 1586), Sebastián Brabo and Sesilia Belazquez (Aug. 5, 1587), Pascual Hernandez and Francisca Criolla (Feb. 11, 1593), Juan Batista Mallorquin and Madalena Gonçales (Sept. 6, 1593), Juan de la Insencion and María Maldonado (Apr. 21 and Oct. 29, 1608), CH-LB/M, fols. 9v, 11v, 38r, 40r, 122r, 127r; Baptisms of Cristóbal (Aug. 19, 1590), Cristóbal Arará (May 11, 1597), Francisco Angola (May 11, 1597), and Felipe (Aug. 17, 1597), CH-LB/B, fols. 7v, 99v, 107v. On the significance of people of color not being "raced" in sacramental records for French and Spanish New Orleans during the eighteenth century, see Jennifer M. Spear, *Race, Sex, and Social Order in Early New Orleans* (Baltimore, 2009).

in Santo Domingo in 1606, a woman named María was portrayed as "the one of [possessed by] San Estevan, widow, morena horra." She had been the wife of San Estevan and was now the widow of San Estevan. Before her marriage, she could have been known as a slave of a certain slaveowner or a free woman of color formerly owned by a certain slaveowner. In the lives of individual women of African descent, these shifting relational terms also entailed changes in status, with the most significant likely being the transition from association with a particular slaveowner—as a slave or former slave—to association with an Iberian man, as a wife and member of his extended family.[40]

A corollary of these substitutions of terms is that women listed without the ascription of any racial identity were not necessarily white or Spanish. Among African and African-descended women in the early Spanish Caribbean, the transformation of public identity experienced by Leonor de Abalos (from "Leonor Anchica" to "Leonor de Abalos morena horra") was probably far more common than that experienced by Ceçilia Velazquez (from morena horra to "the wife of Sebastian Brabo"). But both processes point to a sixteenth-century Caribbean world in which Africans and people of African descent were not necessarily associated with slave status or systematically excluded from participating in colonial society on the same terms as nonelite Iberians. Rather than an atmosphere of inflexible racial hierarchies, the marriages of these women, and others like them, raise the distinct possibility of more fluid attitudes toward racial identity in the early era of Spanish colonization.[41]

---

40. See, for example, the baptism of María de tierra Bran (Sept. 8, 1591), CH-LB/B, fol. 15r (Beatris Recio negra gora esclaba que fue de Juan Recio). For "María, la de San Estevan, viuda, morena horra" in Santo Domingo, see "Testimonio de quantos lugares ay en esta ysla," Oct. 2, 1606, AGI-SD 83, r.2, s/n, fols. 33–69, transcribed in Rodríguez Demorizi, comp., *Relaciones históricas de Santo Domingo*, II, 381.

41. Stuart B. Schwartz has argued that in the early-sixteenth-century Spanish Caribbean, Iberian colonists married "wom[e]n of the land," probably mestizas, who along with their children were initially able to became "Spanish." He suggests that with the arrival of enslaved Africans and subsequent births of children of mixed Iberian and African ancestry, all forms of miscegenation began to be increasingly associated with inferior status. See Schwartz, "Spaniards, *Pardos*, and the Missing Mestizos: Identities and Racial Categories in the Early Hispanic Caribbean," *NWIG*, LXXI (1997), 9–13. But rather than being intrinsically associated with slavery and servile status, some African and African-descended women in the late sixteenth and early seventeenth centuries appear to have undergone a process similar to that which Schwartz outlines for mestizas one hundred years earlier. For the observation that "from their earliest years in the Caribbean, Spanish settlers crossed ethnic lines in their personal lives and domestic arrangements, blurring the very legal and social categories that they devised," see Ida Altman, "Marriage, Family, and Ethnicity in the Early Spanish Caribbean," *WMQ*, 3d Ser., LXX (2013), 249. See also Lynne A. Guitar, "Cultural Genesis: Relationships among Indians, Africans, and Spaniards in Rural Hispaniola, First Half of the Sixteenth Century" (Ph.D. diss.,

Among the marriages listed in Table 8, six were church-sanctioned unions between enslaved African or African-descended women and free Iberian men. Very little is known of marriages of this sort in early modern Iberia or in the colonial Spanish Americas. A few examples have been turned up in past scholarship, for instance an Iberian or Spanish-American man in Peru who paid for the manumission of his enslaved mulata wife in 1620. The six marriages between Iberian men and enslaved women in Havana appear less unusual in light of sixteen similar marriages between Spanish individuals and spouses of African descent in Santiago de Guatemala. However, these sixteen marriages took place over the course of Guatemala's entire colonial period, while the six marriages listed in Havana's parish records took place over the course of just twenty years (1603–1622).[42]

Though very few in number, these marriages provide evidence that sexual relationships between enslaved women and Iberian men in the early-seventeenth-century Spanish Caribbean were not necessarily limited to either rape or exploitative concubinage, though preexisting power relations possibly manifested themselves within such marriages. For a handful of enslaved women, marriage (rather than concubinage) with Iberian men probably represented an important avenue toward freedom or improved living conditions. The marriage between Francisco Lopez, a Spanish man originally from Seville, and an enslaved Afrocreole woman identified only as "María negra criolla *esclava*" in early 1618 underscores the complexities of legal status and social relations that unions such as theirs could involve. What relationship existed, if any, between Francisco Lopez and María's owner Bernabé Sanches? Would Sanches permit the newly married couple to live together, and, if so, would they live on his properties or elsewhere? If Francisco Lopez and María had children, would they be born as slaves? If María was able to free herself from slavery, how long did it take, and what role did her husband—or her status as an Afrocreole woman married to an

Vanderbilt University, 1998), 418–420; John D. Garrigus, *Before Haiti: Race and Citizenship in French Saint-Domingue* (New York, 2006), 44; Karen B. Graubart, "The Creolization of the New World: Local Forms of Identification in Urban Colonial Peru, 1560–1640," *HAHR*, LXXXIX (2009), 471–499.

42. Frederick P. Bowser, *The African Slave in Colonial Peru, 1524–1650* (Stanford, Calif., 1974), 280; Christopher H. Lutz, *Santiago de Guatemala, 1541–1773: City, Caste, and the Colonial Experience* (Norman, Okla., 1994), 119, 294n. See also Edgar F. Love, "Marriage Patterns of Persons of African Descent in a Colonial Mexico City Parish," *HAHR*, LI (1971), 89–91. Love found that between 1646 and 1746, in one parish of Mexico City, five enslaved mulato men married Spanish women, and one Spanish man married an enslaved mulata. For comparable discussion of six Spanish women married to mulatos and negros in Panama, see Mena García, *La sociedad,* 67; their marriages are referenced in "Descripción de Panamá y su provincia . . . ," (1607), in Serrano y Sanz, [ed.], *Relaciones históricas y geográficas,* 167.

Iberian man—play in this process? When Ana Xuares, "morena esclava," married the Portuguese man Domingo Leyton in 1620, her owner was present at the marriage as a witness. To what extent did their matrimony resemble the sexual unions taking place between Portuguese men and African women in western Africa during the same era?[43]

Perhaps to an even greater degree than the marriages between free women of color and Iberian men, these six marriages offer glimpses of a complex social world, an early modern Spanish Caribbean society that, in some ways, fails to resemble that of the late colonial era. At least one of these six marriages might have resulted from an enslaved woman's interaction with members of her owner's household and extended family: in 1605, Hernando Prieto, son of Havana vecino Juan de la Cruz, married "Ysabel Maldonado morena de don Joan"—an enslaved black woman owned by his father. Tomás Martin's marriage to "Andrea Criolla sclava" in 1603, combined with his sole appearance at a baptism in Havana, illustrates the extent to which the lives of Iberian, African, and Afrocreole people were entwined. In 1598, Tomás Martin appeared as godfather at the baptism of María Bran, an African woman owned by the free morena María Batista. María Bran's godmother was Ana de Carreño, an enslaved Afrocreole woman who would later marry a Spanish man, as noted above. Involved in this single baptism, then, were an Upper Guinean woman owned by a free woman of color (and possible former slave herself), an enslaved Afrocreole woman who soon gained her freedom and married a Spanish man, and an Iberian or Spanish American man, who married another enslaved Afrocreole woman five years later.[44]

During the late sixteenth and early seventeenth centuries, free women of color in the Spanish Caribbean's major population centers were recognized by secular and ecclesiastical authorities alike as vecinas and as legitimate spouses of Iberian men. Realizing the extent of African and African-descended women's socioeconomic mobility in the early colonial Caribbean brings women like María de Torres, Ana Enriquez, and María

43. Marriages of Francisco Lopez and María Criolla (Jan. 1, 1618) and Domingo Leyton and Ana Xuares (Mar. 17, 1620), CH-LB/M, fols. 174v, 185r. For Juan Peres Portillo's marriage to "Cristina negra esclava de doña Juana Tamaras" (Sept. 9, 1620) and Domingo Muñoz's marriage to "Ana de Salamanca esclava de Juan de Salamanca" (July 28, 1622), see ibid., fols. 187v, 199v.

44. Marriages of Tomas Martin and Andrea Criolla (May 10, 1603) and Hernando Prieto and Ysabel Maldonado (May 5, 1605), CH-LB/M, fols. 78v, 101v; Baptism of María Bran (Mar. 30, 1598), CH-LB/B, fol. 121r. For discussion of slaves' social and legal positions within their owners' households in fifteenth- and sixteenth-century Iberia, see Saunders, *Social History*, 113–133; Debra Blumenthal, *Enemies and Familiars: Slavery and Mastery in Fifteenth-Century Valencia* (Ithaca, N.Y., 2009), 122–153.

Xolofa from the margins to the center of Spanish Caribbean society. As African-born survivors of the transatlantic slave trade, as first-generation Afrocreoles, or as migrants from overseas, morenas horras' emergence as key protagonists in the social formations of settlements such as Havana, Santo Domingo, Panama City, and Cartagena epitomizes the transformation and development of the Spanish Caribbean during this period. Historical analysis of these important actors within early colonial Caribbean society can draw parallels with Luso-African nharas, ambitious and independent women who likewise created advantageous socioeconomic positions for themselves in a context of overlapping African and Iberian worlds. Attention to relevant historical precedents found in Atlantic African contexts allows Spain's colonization of the Caribbean to be envisioned in terms of the presence of African women and women of African descent, rather than the absence of white women.

FIVE

Black Peasants

Known as the Hospital of Saint Lazarus, Cartagena's leper asylum was located just outside the city, on the main road leading to and from the province's interior. Alarmed by an outbreak of leprosy in the late 1620s, city council members requested royal funds to pay for the construction of an outer wall to contain the approximately sixty lepers housed there. Various residents, including a royal physician *(protomédico)*, shared the council's concerns about quarantining the disease and maintaining control over the leper population. Since those believed to have contracted leprosy were sent to the asylum regardless of race, sex, or social status, some suggested that separate quarters for men and women be constructed. In the meantime, black lepers snuck into the city at night, and pregnant black women occasionally absented themselves to give birth elsewhere. The asylum's steward had already forced some couples to marry. Although some people appear to have been troubled by what they perceived as the collapse of order within the asylum, most agreed that the principal danger was the possibility of leprosy spreading from Cartagena's urban center to outlying farms. Lepers were frequently seen in the company of enslaved farmworkers or with black women and men who had left the city to gather wood, draw water, or boil seawater to extract salt. According to witnesses, both rural and urban blacks congregated with lepers "in a very friendly manner": they smoked tobacco together, shared food, bartered for produce and livestock, and drank from the same barrels of water. By preventing the disease from spreading, walls around the asylum would protect rural property—including enslaved Africans—from contamination and safeguard the city's food supply. Cartagena's outskirts functioned as a vibrant crossroads featuring extensive interaction among people of African origin. However much Cartagena's cabildo members feared that the presence of lepers in this fluid social environment risked the further spread of disease, they evidently viewed black workers' mobility between urban and rural areas as completely normative.[1]

The cabildo's request for funding is also significant in that it repeatedly mentions "blacks" (*negros*) leaving the city to work on "farms." The vast majority of people residing in Cartagena and its province during the late 1620s were sub-Saharan Africans and people of African descent, most of whom were enslaved and many of whom were agricultural laborers. Yet, Cartagena was not a plantation society. Most of the enslaved workers in the city's hinterland were employed on farms and ranches that served local populations and regional trade. Rural slave labor in the Spanish Caribbean produced hides, ginger, tobacco, and small quantities of sugar for overseas export, but African contributions to pig and cattle farming and to the cultivation of staple crops such as maize, yuca, and plantains were far more important activities during this early colonial period. Farming and animal husbandry were crucial to sustaining Spanish Caribbean settlements, supporting urban populations in port cities, and provisioning fleets. Rural slave labor was also significant for developing commercial links; a variety of agricultural and animal products were exported extensively within the region. Rather than mere satellites of viceroyalties in central Mexico and Peru—or "fringe" areas struggling to remain connected to "trunk lines" that connected highland silver mines to Spain—Spanish Caribbean settlements constituted separate colonies, linked to intercolonial, regional, and transoceanic economies that imperial authorities could only partially control. Enslaved Africans' labor on farms and ranches simultaneously made Spanish colonization possible and facilitated an interregional trade in foodstuffs that often reflected local agendas rather than metropolitan priorities.[2]

1. Expediente de la ciudad de Cartagena, Mar. 29, 1628, AGI-SF 63, n.69; "Imformaçion de los pobres q ay emfermos de St Lazaro y estado del ospital," AGI-SF 63, n.69a, fols. 7r–16r. See also Carta del cabildo de Cartagena sobre la gran cantidad de leprosos que hay en dicha ciudad, July 30, 1627, AGI-SF 63, n.67. This scene contrasts starkly with portrayals of rural slavery in early Spanish America as a stifling social vacuum; see, for example, Frederick P. Bowser, "Africans in Spanish American Colonial Society," in Leslie Bethell, ed., *The Cambridge History of Latin America* (Cambridge, 1984), II, 376–378. For criticism of the notion that "urban slavery" and "rural slavery" constituted separate or drastically different experiences in colonial Spanish American contexts, see María Elena Díaz, *The Virgin, the King, and the Royal Slaves of El Cobre: Negotiating Freedom in Colonial Cuba, 1670–1780* (Stanford, Calif., 2000), 321–322; Herman L. Bennett, *Africans in Colonial Mexico: Absolutism, Christianity, and Afro-Creole Consciousness, 1570–1640* (Bloomington, Ind., 2003), 209n.

2. "Imformaçion de los pobres q ay emfermos de St Lazaro y estado del ospital," AGI-SF 63, n.69a, fols. 7v, 11r, 13v, 16r; Rolando Mellafe, *La esclavitud en Hispanoamérica* (Buenos Aires, Argentina, 1964), 73–75. On Cartagena's population during the late 1620s, see Appendix 1. For the observation that "in sixteenth-century Spanish and Portuguese, the term ["plantation"] did not exist in its present meaning and was never used as such," see Stuart B. Schwartz, "Introduction," in Schwartz, ed., *Tropical Babylons: Sugar and the Making of the Atlantic World, 1450–1680* (Chapel Hill, N.C., 2004), 2. On Havana

In large-scale plantation systems of the eighteenth and nineteenth centuries, some enslaved people acted as "peasants" by cultivating crops on their garden plots in their spare time and reselling the surplus produce; free black farmers were at times able to support themselves by selling provisions to plantations. These developments can be seen as later manifestations of an early Spanish Caribbean subsistence economy that relied on slave·labor to provision port cities and Indies fleets and to respond to local and regional market demands. The daily routines and economic activities of enslaved ranch hands and farmworkers in early Spanish Caribbean settlements closely resembled those of Iberian peasants known in Spain as *trabajadores* or *jornaleros:* agricultural workers and day laborers who did not possess draft animals, land, or tools of their own. Like Iberian *labradores,* or peasant farmers, some free people of color in the Spanish Caribbean did come to own tracts of land, livestock, and farming implements. This rural workforce, mostly composed of people of African descent, was an extension of patterns of agricultural labor in the early modern Iberian world, not a result of the a priori existence of plantations.[3]

Iberian precedents for African migrants laboring as rural workers in the early Spanish Caribbean are abundant. From the late fifteenth through the seventeenth centuries, enslaved Africans and people of African origin worked as gardeners, farmers, herders, and shepherds across the southern Iberian peninsula, from the Algarve to Valencia. Though slavery in early modern Spain is often imagined as an urban phenomenon, it appears to

elites' appropriation of imperial resources for their own purposes, see Alejandro de la Fuente, with César García del Pino and Bernardo Iglesias Delgado, *Havana and the Atlantic in the Sixteenth Century* (Chapel Hill, N.C., 2008), 9–10, 117, 225–227. By contrast, for discussion of central Mexico and Peru as the "central areas of Spanish occupation, with all else constituting a fringe," see James Lockhart, "Trunk Lines and Feeder Lines: The Spanish Reaction to American Resources," in Kenneth J. Andrien and Rolena Adorno, eds., *Transatlantic Encounters: Europeans and Andeans in the Sixteenth Century* (Berkeley, Calif., 1991), 107–110.

3. Ciro Flamarion S. Cardoso, "The Peasant Breach in the Slave System: New Developments in Brazil," *Luso-Brazilian Review,* XXV, no. 1 (Summer 1988), 49–57; John D. Garrigus, *Before Haiti: Race and Citizenship in French Saint-Domingue* (New York, 2006), 74. See also Sidney W. Mintz, "From Plantations to Peasantries in the Caribbean," in Mintz and Sally Price, eds., *Caribbean Contours* (Baltimore, 1985), 127–153; Mintz, "The Question of Caribbean Peasantries: A Comment," *Caribbean Studies,* I, no. 3 (October 1961), 31–34. On class stratification among peasants or agricultural workers and the fuzziness or absence of boundaries separating urban from rural worlds in all but the largest of cities in early modern Spain, see Noël Salomon, *La vida rural castellana en tiempos de Felipe II* (Barcelona, 1964), 259–291; David E. Vassberg, *The Village and the Outside World in Golden Age Castile: Mobility and Migration in Everyday Rural Life* (Cambridge, 1996), xvi, 1–3, 7, 26, 58, 70–72; Teófilo F. Ruiz, "The Peasantries of Iberia, 1400–1800," in Tom Scott, ed., *The Peasantries of Europe from the Fourteenth to the Eighteenth Centuries* (London, 1998), 52–54, 65–70; Allyson M. Poska, *Women and Authority in Early Modern Spain: The Peasants of Galicia* (New York, 2005), esp. 28, 174.

have been slightly more important in some rural areas: in 1565, slaves made up about 8 percent of the residents of Seville but 10 percent of the city's archbishopric, which encompassed pastures, fields, and farmlands adjacent to the city, as well as many smaller towns and villages. Iberian rural populations also included free people of color. Even as late as the eighteenth century, travelers commented on the notable presence of "families of blacks, [and] *mulatos*" in smaller pueblos throughout southern Extremadura. One factor that distinguished rural slavery in the Spanish Caribbean from rural slavery in Iberia was that, by the mid-sixteenth century, nearly all enslaved people in the Spanish Americas were sub-Saharan Africans and Afrocreoles, whereas Iberian slave populations included not only sub-Saharan Africans and their descendants but also North Africans, Ottoman "Turks," Iberians of Muslim heritage known as *moriscos,* and others. Another significant difference was that agricultural production in Iberia relied mainly on free labor, with slave labor playing a supplementary role. Enslaved workers constituted a much larger percentage of Spanish Caribbean populations (see Appendix 1).[4]

The Portuguese colonies of the Cape Verde Islands, São Tomé in the Gulf of Guinea, and Angola in West Central Africa provide additional models of early modern Iberian societies that relied heavily on food produced by enslaved farmworkers. Despite recurrent droughts and the frequent importation of food from Portugal and the Upper Guinea coast, Santiago de Cabo Verde yielded grapes, bananas, coconuts, cassava, millet, and other foodstuffs, in addition to sugarcane and cotton. Livestock, especially goats but also cattle and horses, were raised on Santiago and on the neighboring island of Fogo. Perhaps even more so than Española or Puerto Rico, São Tomé has been characterized as the prototypical Atlantic "sugar island"—and even "a Caribbean island on the wrong side of the Atlantic"—that quickly sank into economic irrelevance after the decline of the sugar industry during the sixteenth century. But, as São Tomé shifted to the production of other exports, such as cotton, ginger, tobacco, and indigo, and even during the years

4. A. C. de C. M. Saunders, *A Social History of Black Slaves and Freedmen in Portugal, 1441–1555* (Cambridge, 1982), 49, 54, 58, 69–71, 86–87, 144, 176; Jorge Fonseca, *Escravos no sul de Portugal, séculos XVI–XVII* (Lisbon, 2002), 77–82; Debra Blumenthal, *Enemies and Familiars: Slavery and Mastery in Fifteenth-Century Valencia* (Ithaca, N.Y., 2009), 80–84, 96–101; Rafael M. Pérez García and Manuel F. Fernández Chaves, "Sevilla y la trata negrera atlántica: Envíos de esclavos desde Cabo Verde a la América española, 1569–1579," in León Carlos Álvarez Santaló, coord., *Estudios de historia moderna en homenaje al profesor Antonio García-Baquero* (Seville, 2009), 601–602; D. Antonio Ponz, *Viage de España* ..., 2d ed. (Madrid, 1784), VIII, 170, 185–186. See also Rocío Periáñez Gómez, *Negros, mulatos y blancos: Los esclavos en Extremadura durante la edad moderna* (Badajoz, Spain, 2010), 72.

when sugar cultivation had been most intense, the islands of São Tomé, Príncipe, and Annobón, with the exception of an occasional drought, were almost entirely self-sustaining. Enslaved workers labored on pig farms and raised cattle, sheep, goats, and chickens; on Annobón, they caught fish. Rice was cultivated for local consumption and regional export, and various accounts mention the production of beans, potatoes, grapes, yams, and maize. Banana groves provided an important part of the local diet, as did citrus fruits. Some of these agricultural products were exported to the Lower Guinea coast, to help sustain the Portuguese outposts Elmina and Axim. In Angola, Luanda benefited doubly from coerced African agricultural labor: *sobas* (local leaders) subjected to Portuguese rule were expected to pay regular tribute in the form of maize, beans, and palm oil, in addition to providing a steady stream of captives. At the same time, extensive properties outside Luanda owned by the city's elites, and presumably operated with slave labor, were primarily dedicated to agricultural production.[5]

African forced migrants in the early Spanish Caribbean lowlands were employed as agricultural workers in ways that directly echoed rural slave occupations in Iberia and in Portuguese colonies in Atlantic Africa. Even more, in addition to diverse tasks previously done by Amerindians, Africans and people of African descent—including many free people of color—performed the various rural labors that Spanish peasants did in Iberia. Although nearly every other sector of the Spanish social order was reproduced in early colonial society, Iberian migrants to the Americas, by and large, did not occupy the agrarian roles they had in Spain. In their stead, Africans raised cattle, swine, and chickens and cultivated food crops, principally maize, yuca, and plantains. They cleared fields for cultivation, processed cassava, tanned hides, cut timber for local shipbuilding and export, and hauled produce to ports and urban markets. By the late sixteenth century, sub-Saharan Africans were the de facto settlers of the rural Spanish Carib-

5. Maria Manuel Torrão, *Dietas alimentares: Transferências e adaptações nas Ilhas de Cabo Verde (1460–1540)* (Lisbon, 1995); António Leão Correia e Silva, "A sociedade agrária; Gentes das águas: Senhores, escravos e forros," in Maria Emília Madeira Santos, coord., *História Geral de Cabo Verde* (Lisbon, 1995), II, 275–357; Malyn Newitt, ed., *The Portuguese in West Africa, 1415–1670: A Documentary History* (Cambridge, 2010), 61; Fernando Castelo Branco, "O comercio externo de S. Tomé no século XVII," *Studia*, no. 24 (August 1968), 73–98; Robert Garfield, *A History of São Tomé Island, 1470–1655: The Key to Guinea* (San Francisco, Calif., 1992), 30–32, 72–73, 80, 84, 148, 182–183, 288; Cristina Maria Seuanes Serafim, *As ilhas de São Tomé no século XVII* (Lisbon, 2000), 76, 108–109, 195–196, 205–210; Catarina Madeira Santos, "Luanda: A Colonial City between Africa and the Atlantic, Seventeenth and Eighteenth Centuries," in Liam Matthew Brockey, ed., *Portuguese Colonial Cities in the Early Modern World* (Burlington, Vt., 2008), 257; Mário José Maestri Filho, *A agricultura africana nos séculos XVI e XVII no litoral angolano* (Porto Alegre, Brazil, 1978), 66–67.

bean: a surrogate peasantry that sustained Spain's major settlements in both the islands and on the Caribbean mainland.[6]

Rural Slave Labor on the "Sugar Islands"

Although Española is widely regarded as the cradle of sugar cultivation in the early colonial Caribbean, farms and ranches had replaced sugar estates as the island's primary economic engines by the late sixteenth century. Most of the enslaved population was employed on farms known as "estancias," a term that has been translated as "farm," "small farm," "truck garden," "plot of ground," "agricultural holdings," and "plantation of food crops" (the synonymous word *chácara* was used more commonly in Peru). An English privateer who visited Española during the early 1590s provided a detailed description: "An *Eastancha* is as it were a Country villadge, where the great men have their servants and Slaves to keepe their Cattle make their *Cassada* [cassava] bread dress their Ginger and their fruites, keepe their Powltry and divers other services." Focusing primarily on the island's exportable commodities, Antonio Vázquez de Espinosa, a Carmelite friar who visited the Americas during the early seventeenth century, wrote of "more than 4,000 slaves owned by the *vecinos* (free, propertied, permanent residents) of Santo Domingo, and many free mulatos." Though some cultivated "sugar on the island's many mills," others labored on farms, orchards, and ranches, producing hides, ginger, tobacco, timber, and resins. Vázquez de Espinosa also briefly mentioned the island's abundance of livestock and "other fruits," probably yuca, also known as cassava or manioc, and maize.[7]

The island's governor, Antonio Osorio, elaborated on slave labor in Española during this period in his 1606 census. According to his report, Española depended on a labor force composed of 9,648 slaves, with more than

6. James Lockhart shows that Spain's peasantry was virtually the only segment of peninsular Spanish society that was not reproduced in the Americas; rural laborers from Spain who managed to reach the Indies quickly found new occupations. In sixteenth-century Peru, "Even those who were skilled gardeners . . . or agriculturalists were more supervisors of blacks and Indians than workers themselves." See Lockhart, *Spanish Peru, 1532–1560: A Social History,* 2d ed. (Madison, Wis., 1994), 258–259.

7. I. A. Wright, *The Early History of Cuba, 1492–1586* (New York, 1916), 307, 375; Lockhart, *Spanish Peru,* 26–27, 142, 145, 219–221; Frederick P. Bowser, *The African Slave in Colonial Peru, 1524–1650* (Stanford, Calif., 1974), 88, 348; James Langton, "A Report of Cumberland's Seventh Voyage," in Kenneth R. Andrews, ed., *English Privateering Voyages to the West Indies, 1588–1595* (Cambridge, 1959), 249; Antonio Vázquez de Espinosa, *Compendio y descripción de las Indias occidentales,* ed. B. Velasco Bayón (Madrid, 1969), 34–35. On the various functions and relative sizes of estancias, *hatos* (cattle or pig farms), and *corrales* (enclosed areas for raising swine and other livestock), see María Cristina Navarrete, *Génesis y desarrollo de la esclavitud en Colombia, siglos XVI y XVII* (Cali, Colombia, 2005), 164–166, 203n; de la Fuente, *Havana,* 119–127. De la Fuente finds that "the average size of the estan-

8,000 engaged in some form of agriculture. Roughly one-sixth of the slave population was employed in domestic service; most of these 1,556 enslaved women and men worked in Santo Domingo, with the exception of 88 domestic slaves employed in the houses of sugar mill owners. Governor Osorio estimated that approximately 800 slaves cultivated sugar, and 550 slaves raised livestock on the island's *hatos* (open-range ranches or cattle or sheep farms). Considered together, Osorio's figures for domestic slaves in Santo Domingo (1,468), domestic slaves in sugar mill owners' houses (88), sugar workers (800), and slave cowboys (550) total only 2,906 enslaved women and men, less than one-third of the total number of slaves working on the island. The remaining two-thirds of Española's enslaved population—approximately 6,742 people—labored on farms, cultivating "ginger, cassava, and maize." If these estimates were to any degree accurate, then enslaved Africans and Afrocreoles were far more likely to work on diversified farms rather than monocrop plantations in early-seventeenth-century Española. Even combining the 800 sugar workers with the 88 domestic slaves employed on sugar haciendas, the resulting sugar workforce would constitute less than 10 percent of the island's total enslaved population.[8]

In addition to reporting the numbers of slaves employed in various occupational categories, Osorio listed each of Española's rural estates individually, making it possible to indirectly gauge the density of slave populations in diverse forms of rural labor. Though Osorio specifically noted that the island contained 170 hatos, he enumerated 189 separate hatos that raised either cows or sheep, as well as four pig farms *(criaderos de ganado cerdo)*. Assuming that the 550 slaves employed on hatos were distributed evenly among these rural properties, then slightly less than 3 enslaved cowboys were employed on each hato. Enslaved rural laborers who raised and cared for livestock on hatos had relatively few coworkers and probably enjoyed a

---

cias during the 1578–1610 period was about 2.5 caballerías (83 acres)," so presumably one *caballería* around Havana measured roughly thirty-three acres (124, 140). See also Roberto Cassá, *História social y económica de la República Dominicana* (Santo Domingo, Dominican Republic, 1983), I, 76–82, 90–92, 98–100; Amadeo Julián, *Bancos, ingenios y esclavos en la época colonial* (Santo Domingo, Dominican Republic, 1997), 186, 190–191.

8. "Testimonio de quantos lugares ay en esta ysla," Oct. 2, 1606, AGI-SD 83, r.2, s/n, fols. 33–69, transcribed in E[milio] Rodríguez Demorizi, comp., *Relaciones históricas de Santo Domingo* (Ciudad Trujillo [Santo Domingo], Dominican Republic, 1945), II, 374–403. Osorio calculates a total of 2,858 slaves employed as domestics, sugar workers, and ranch hands, but his figures add up to 2,906. See also Concepción Hernández Tapia, "Despoblaciones de la isla de Santo Domingo en el siglo XVII," *AEA*, XXVII (1970), 315–320; Kenneth R. Andrews, *The Spanish Caribbean: Trade and Plunder, 1530–1630* (New Haven, Conn., 1978), 213; Juana Gil-Bermejo García, *La Española: Anotaciones históricas (1600–1650)* (Seville, 1983), 87–92; Cassá, *História social,* I, 93–100, 103.

considerable degree of geographical mobility and independence from direct supervision.[9]

The enslaved men and women who operated Española's sugar mills at the beginning of the seventeenth century likely experienced much less flexibility in their daily routines. According to Osorio, in 1606 the island had only twelve sugar mills, yet these *ingenios* employed approximately 800 slaves. On average, then, each sugar mill was maintained by the labor of 67 slaves. If the estimated 88 domestic servants are included as well, then each sugar mill owner employed an additional 6 or 7 domestic servants in their house, on average. The third major form of rural labor—farming—featured neither the extremely low slave population density of hatos nor the densely concentrated slave populations of sugar mills. Osorio tallied 430 estancias on the island in 1606; if the 6,790 slaves employed on estancias were evenly distributed among these farms, each would have been supported by the labor of 16 slaves.[10]

Although many of Osorio's figures appear to be only general estimates, his division of the labor force is significant. Two-thirds of the island's slaves worked on farms, one-sixth were employed in domestic service, and the remaining sixth were spread between sugar cultivation and ranching. Given this distribution of slave labor in 1606, Española's economy was not likely geared toward sugar production during the early seventeenth century. That Española produced no less than 74 percent of all sugar shipped to Seville between 1560 and 1620 clearly indicates sugar's humble position in the Spanish Caribbean's economy during the late sixteenth and early seventeenth centuries.[11]

As early as the 1550s, Española began to shift from sugar cultivation to hides and especially ginger—cash crops for export—as well as maize and yuca, food crops for local consumption and to some extent, perhaps, for export within the Caribbean. Rodríguez Morel and others have suggested that the diversification of enslaved workers' agricultural activities in the second half of the sixteenth century were largely the result of the sharp downturn in the island's sugar industry: as food prices on the island rose, some

9. On Española's hatos, see also Gil-Bermejo García, *La Española*, 52–61; Carlos Esteban Deive, *Tangomangos: Contrabando y piratería en Santo Domingo, 1522–1606* (Santo Domingo, Dominican Republic, 1996), 198; Lorenzo E. López y Sebastián and Justo L. del Río Moreno, "La ganadería vacuna en la isla Española (1508–1587)," *RCHA*, XXV (1999), 11–49.

10. Calculated from "Testimonio de quantos lugares ay en esta ysla," Oct. 2, 1606, AGI-SD 83, r.2, s/n, fols. 33–69, transcribed in Rodríguez Demorizi, comp., *Relaciones históricas de Santo Domingo*, II, 421–443.

11. Alejandro de la Fuente, "Sugar and Slavery in Early Colonial Cuba," in Schwartz, ed., *Tropical Babylons*, 118–119.

Table 9 Food Crops versus Export Crops Cultivated on
Española's Estancias, circa 1606

Main crops	Number of estancias	Percentage of total
Food crops (yuca, maize, vegetables, fruits)	189	43.95
Food crops and tobacco	95	22.09
Food crops and ginger	44	10.23
Ginger	102	23.72
TOTAL	430	100.00

Source: E[milio] Rodríguez Demorizi, comp., *Relaciones históricas de Santo Domingo* (Ciudad Trujillo [Santo Domingo], Dominican Republic, 1945), II, 421–443.

slaveowners who were invested in sugar production might have allowed enslaved workers to spend more time growing foodstuffs for their own subsistence. Yet, this scenario would have applied to relatively few rural slaves after the mid-sixteenth century, since most were no longer employed on large-scale sugar plantations. By the 1570s, even ginger cultivation, which entailed comparatively low startup costs and thus invited the participation of many less prosperous colonists, probably employed a smaller share of the island's enslaved workforce than the cultivation of subsistence crops. Ginger perhaps remained important in 1606 precisely because the root required at most only a few months of labor; yuca, maize, and other foodstuffs could be grown on the same farm for the majority of the year.[12]

Unfortunately, Osorio's figures do not distinguish between enslaved workers primarily engaged in growing food crops as opposed to those raising export crops such as ginger. His division of Española's estancias into various categories based on the types of crops cultivated, however, indicates that slightly less than one-fourth of the island's 430 estancias were devoted to the cultivation of ginger alone. Almost 45 percent—nearly half of all the island's farms—exclusively produced food crops (*casave, maís, y otras legumbres*). Only about 10 percent produced both food crops and ginger, and food crops were cultivated alongside tobacco on the remaining 22 percent of the island's farms (Table 9). Though ginger appears to have been grown exclu-

12. Genaro Rodríguez Morel, "The Sugar Economy of Española in the Sixteenth Century," Schwartz, ed., *Tropical Babylons*, 103, 107–109; Justo L. del Río Moreno and Lorenzo E. López y Sebastián, "El jengibre: Historia de un monocultivo caribeño del siglo XVI," *RCHA*, XVIII (1992), 63–87, esp. 70–72. See also, Andrews, *Spanish Caribbean*, 16, 64; Cassá, *História social*, I, 76–81; Gil-Bermejo García, *La Española*, 65–69.

sively for export, only some of the tobacco grown in Española was shipped back to Spain; tobacco was also consumed locally as well as throughout the Spanish Caribbean. Large quantities of tobacco were probably also exchanged with non-Hispanic merchants in contraband trade known as *rescate*. The division of types of estates reported by Osorio indicates that in 1606 in Española, enslaved rural workers performed diverse types of agricultural labor, devoting most of their time to tasks that provided foodstuffs and regionally traded products rather than export commodities destined for European markets.[13]

Much like Española, if on a smaller scale, Puerto Rico's economy was only oriented toward sugar production until roughly 1570, when hides and ginger became more important export commodities. Only eleven sugar mills were in operation on the island during the entire second half of the sixteenth century; by 1610, this number was reduced to eight. These mills employed 60 slaves on average (though if one outlier with 170 slaves were removed, the average would be closer to 50). In contrast, forty-one estancias and haciendas were producing yuca, maize, ginger, rice, and citrus fruits. Several also maintained livestock, and, in five cases, sugar cane was cultivated alongside food crops. Thirty-five hatos raised pigs, horses, mules, and, above all, cattle.[14]

Although the precise numbers of slaves employed on these rural estates are unknown, Africans and people of color appear to have formed the backbone of Puerto Rico's agricultural workforce. Mentioning export commodities (hides, ginger, sugar), food crops (maize, yuca), and livestock (cattle, horses, and pigs), Vázquez de Espinosa noted that in Puerto Rico, "blacks and free mulatos" were "quite important for ranching and other agricultural labor." San Juan's three hundred vecinos employed two thousand "blacks and free mulatos" on the island's "sugar mills, cattle ranches, and farms." Among these estancias, one relied on the labor of twelve

13. "Testimonio de quantos lugares ay en esta ysla," Oct. 2, 1606, AGI-SD 83, r.2, s/n, fols. 33–69, transcribed in Rodríguez Demorizi, comp., *Relaciones históricas de Santo Domingo*, II, 428–442; Gil-Bermejo García, *La Española*, 69–73; Michiel Baud, "A Colonial Counter Economy: Tobacco Production on Española, 1500–1870," *NWIG*, LXV (1991), 27–49. See also Lorenzo E. López y Sebastián and Justo L. del Río Moreno, "La crisis del siglo XVII en la industria azucarera antillana y los cambios producidos en su estructura," *RCHA*, no. 23 (1997), 137–166.

14. Assumptions derived from scholarship on later sugar economies have also influenced historians' interpretations of early colonial Puerto Rico. For depiction of the island's seventeenth-century sugar exports as "scarce" and "far below [the island's] potential," see Enriqueta Vila Vilar, *Historia de Puerto Rico, 1600–1650* (Seville, 1974), 10. See also Elsa Gelpí Baíz, *Siglo en blanco: Estudio de la economía azucarera en el Puerto Rico del siglo XVI (1540–1612)* (San Juan, Puerto Rico, 2000), 4–5, 29, 40–68, 84–93, 235–240.

enslaved "negros y negras," including Africans bearing the ethnonyms "Berbesí," "[M]andinga," "Bañol," and "[M]anicongo" and the toponym "[M]alagueta."[15]

Portraying Spanish Jamaica in very similar terms, Vázquez de Espinosa wrote that the village of La Vega—later dubbed "Spanish Town"—was the island's principal urban center. Though he provided no estimate of La Vega's urban population of slaves or free people of color, he noted that the town was inhabited by five hundred Spanish vecinos. These individuals employed "more than 1,000 black slaves and mulatos who labor in the countryside," raising livestock, including cattle, horses, pigs, and goats, and cultivating food crops, such as maize, rice, and yuca. According to Vázquez de Espinosa, rural black workers also grew tobacco and produced honey using *trapiches,* or mills. These mills were usually associated with sugar production, but sugar itself is not mentioned in this early-seventeenth-century portrait of Jamaican agriculture. Tellingly, when the "English" captured La Vega in the late 1590s, the town's residents paid a ransom in the form of cassava bread, not sugar.[16]

A more detailed glimpse of Spanish Jamaica's population provided by the island's abbot in 1611 is roughly consistent with the figures reported by Vázquez de Espinosa. Whereas the Carmelite friar estimated that "1,000 black slaves and mulatos" performed rural labor on the island, Jamaica's abbot noted the presence of 558 slaves and 107 free people of color. Though he did not specifically link them to agricultural labor, he mentioned that the islands' residents relied on free-range livestock (mainly cattle) for their hides and tallow; he also referred to wild pigs, fruit, and yuca ("the bread that is eaten here is made from a root they call *caçabe* [cassava], and it keeps for many months"). Like Vázquez de Espinosa, the abbot made no mention of sugar cultivation, instead pointing to the island's forests as a potential source of economic development.[17]

On the neighboring island of Cuba, the bustling seaport of Havana was

15. Vázquez de Espinosa, *Compendio,* ed. Velasco Bayón, 37–38; Gelpí Baíz, *Siglo en blanco,* 41–42, 47. See also Vila Vilar, *Historia de Puerto Rico,* 16–24, 37–38, 122. On the continued economic importance of ranching and related activities in the seventeenth- and eighteenth-century Spanish Caribbean, see David M. Stark, *Slave Families and the Hato Economy in Puerto Rico* (Gainesville, Fla., 2015).

16. Vázquez de Espinosa, *Compendio,* ed. Velasco Bayón, 81–84; "Fernando Varela, juez . . . contra Pedro López, Francisco Bejerano y otros vecinos," 1597, AGI-Esc 158A. See also Francisco Morales Padrón, *Jamaica Española* (Seville, 1952), 267–287. Morales Padrón incorrectly supposed that Spanish Jamaica's enslaved population consisted mainly of *"coromantis* from the Gold Coast" (273) and that sugar was "the island's sole industry" (287).

17. Carta del Abad de Jamaica a S. M., July 14, 1611, AGI-SD 177, r.5, n.78, fols. 1v–2r.

also sustained by an agricultural economy that was diversified rather than driven by sugar and in which enslaved workers of African origin played important roles. During the 1560s and 1570s, descriptions of the countryside around Havana often mention the presence of a rural black labor force. As early as the 1550s, Havana's cabildo sometimes associated "blacks," rather than Amerindians, with the cultivation and sale of maize and yuca, crops intended to sustain the urban population and Indies fleets. In 1561, the same town council noted that "many blacks of this village have swords and lances and other weapons in their houses and estancias" and ordered officials to collect the weapons. Yet, thirteen years later, in 1574, the cabildo hesitated to apply this rule to enslaved cowboys and other rural workers who used a variety of sharp tools in their daily work. In the same year, Havana's town council ruled that itinerant merchants were to be prohibited from selling wine, cloth, or any other goods on outlying farms and ranches; they worried that "blacks and overseers" had been paying for these types of merchandise with hides and produce at the expense of absentee landowners. Although this legislation may be interpreted as an attempt to curtail agricultural workers' participation in illicit markets, it also sought to safeguard rural landowners' control over the distribution and sale of goods produced on their properties. This dilemma was common in the early Spanish Caribbean, since most farms and ranches were owned by colonists who resided in ports and other urban settlements, rather than on their rural properties.[18]

Havana's notarial records for the 1570s further indicate that slaves carried out agricultural labor on estancias, though sometimes enslaved people were only referred to indirectly. In 1579, Havana vecino Juan Aceituno and a man named Pedro Flores agreed to pool their resources to operate Aceituno's farm in Guanabacoa, splitting the profits equally. Aceituno provided the estancia itself, including fields of plantains, livestock, tools, and two black slaves named Miguel and Antón. For his part, Flores provided two more slaves (unnamed), as well as his own labor "administering and commanding the slaves," and pledged to "make them work and cultivate the *conucos* [small garden plots or perhaps raised mounds, in the style of Taíno agriculturalists] and *hortaliza* [vegetables]." Other contracts refer only indirectly to slaves, making it impossible to gauge the actual composition of the estancia

18. Emilio Roig de Leuchsenring, dir., *Actas capitulares del Ayuntamiento de La Habana* (Havana, 1937–), tomo I, vol. II, 97–98, 110, 189, 192, 223, 286; Petición de Gaspar de Çarate, Jan. 14, 1574, AGI-SD 116, r.2, n.63, fols. 9v–10v. See also de la Fuente, *Havana*, 179–180. For similar concerns regarding black workers on coastal estancias near Cartagena that provisioned Spanish galleys during the 1590s, see El obispo Fr. Juan de Ladrada a S. M., June 28, 1599, AGI-SF 228, n.24, fol. 1v.

workforce. In the same year, when Tomás Martin was hired to serve on an estancia and corrals in Matanzas for a period of four years, his tasks were specified as "visiting [the farms and corrals] and commanding the people, blacks and *mozos* [boys or servants]," who worked there; as payment, he would receive "one sixth of all the produce: hides, beef, tallow, butter, maize, cassava, pork, cattle, poultry, and honey." The wide variety of these goods and foodstuffs suggest that the labor force employed on these rural properties in Matanzas was highly versatile.[19]

In Havana, as elsewhere in the Spanish Caribbean, landowners with large or multiple estates relied on mobile and adaptable slave workers to perform diverse tasks at different locations in and outside of town, depending on seasonal work cycles such as the arrival of fleets, the growing and harvest periods for diverse crops, and the transportation of livestock to market. In addition to rural properties, Nicolás de Acosta, described as a prosperous *hombre del campo* (man of the countryside), in 1582 owned a home in Havana and a ship that made voyages to Spain and the southern Caribbean mainland. He rented out enslaved women and, at one point, hired an Amerindian servant. He and his wife, a Portuguese woman named Maria de los Reyes, bought and sold enslaved Africans identified as Esperanza Biafara, Domingo Bañol, Catalina Anchica, Juan Congo, Pedro Angola, and Catalina Angola, some of whom might have worked or resided on Acosta's rural property or properties. Some Africans might have resided in his Havana home, performing rural labor only periodically or seasonally. If Acosta owned multiple estancias, enslaved farmworkers could have been transferred from one property to another. In 1608, Cuba's bishop Juan de las Cabezas Altamirano wrote that "in the distances from one pueblo to another, there are ranches and corrals where there are always a number of blacks, and a few Spanish workers depending on the owner's resources." He also observed that in addition to Iberian vecinos, each of Cuba's towns contained "negros and negras, and mulatos and mulatas, [and] *mestiços* and *mestiças*," particularly in the towns of Havana, Puerto Príncipe, and Bayamo, and that "throughout the entire island there are many male and female slaves." During the late sixteenth and early seventeenth centuries, these enslaved Africans and

---

19. María Teresa de Rojas, [ed.], *Índice y extractos del Archivo de Protocolos de la Habana,* 3 vols. (Havana, 1947–1957), I, 200–201, 208–209. On conucos, yuca mounds, and Africans' adoption of Amerindian agricultural practices in the early-sixteenth-century Caribbean, see Lynne A. Guitar, "Cultural Genesis: Relationships among Indians, Africans, and Spaniards in Rural Hispaniola, First Half of the Sixteenth Century" (Ph.D. diss., Vanderbilt University, 1998), 67–73; de la Fuente, *Havana,* 121; Carl Ortwin Sauer, *The Early Spanish Main* (Berkeley, Calif., 1966), 212.

people of African descent figured prominently within an agricultural labor force that produced food and livestock for a diversified economy.[20]

Based on the evidence for rural slave labor in settlements elsewhere in the Spanish Caribbean, enslaved Africans likely performed most rural labors associated with farming and perhaps ranching around the city of Havana by the early seventeenth century, if not sooner. There were at least forty hatos, seventy-three corrals, and 148 estancias in the rural and semirural lands around Havana between 1578 and 1610. By the mid-1620s, "more than 350 estancias around Havana" kept the city "very well supplied with vegetables[,] yuca and cassava." During precisely the same period, members of Havana's city council noted that "all the haciendas are operated with slaves[,] and there is no one else to make use of[,] particularly on this island[,] since native-born Indians are lacking." As many as 20 to 25 sugar mills, all presumably relying on the labor of enslaved people of African origin, could also be found in rural lands around Havana by 1610. Yet, unlike those in Española at the time, most of these mills produced small quantities of sugar in artisanal fashion; some sugarcane fields were located on estancias that also produced tobacco, corn, bananas, cassava, pumpkins, rice, legumes, and other types of vegetables. In these cases, like the foodstuffs and tobacco grown on the same properties, sugar was mainly destined for local consumption.[21]

For the twelve sugar mills known to have been in operation outside Havana during the years 1601 to 1615, notarial records indicate an average of

20. Rojas, [ed.], *Índice y extractos,* I, 111, 341, 381–382, II, 38, 90–94, 149, 309, 407–408, III, 238–239; Baptism of Catalina Angola, Aug. 24, 1597, CH-LB/B, fol. 109r; Levi Marrero, *Cuba: Economía y sociedad: Siglo XVI: La economía* (Madrid, 1974), II, 96–102, 332–334; Marrero, *Cuba: Economía y sociedad: El siglo XVII (I)* (Madrid, 1975), III, 53, 229–242; Peter E. Carr, *Censos, padrones y matrículas de la población de Cuba, siglos 16, 17 y 18* (San Luis Obispo, Calif., 1993), 16–19; Obispo de Cuba a S. M., Sept. 22, 1608, AGI-SD 150, r.2, n.48, fol. 3r. See also Isabelo Macías Domínguez, *Cuba en la primera mitad del siglo XVII* (Seville, 1978), 15–20. By contrast, an extensive analysis of Havana's notarial records between 1578 and 1610—including nearly sixty labor contracts—unearthed relatively little evidence of the use of slave labor on ranches or estancias; see de la Fuente, *Havana,* 124–125, 157–158. Although I suspect that labor contracts underrepresent the presence of enslaved workers (since landowners who employed their own slaves had little cause to draw up formalized contracts), it is possible that Havana's position in relation to the Indies fleets resulted in the availability of former soldiers, sailors, passengers, and other nonelite European laborers who would have been less numerous in Española or Panama and less attractive to rural landowners in Cartagena who had far greater access to enslaved Africans.

21. De la Fuente, *Havana,* 119–127, 141, 158; Expediente y autos promovido por Mathias Rodriguez de Acosta, visto en Madrid, Jan. 22, 1628, and July 9, 1629, AGI-SD 117, s/n; Oficina del Historiador y Museo de la Ciudad de La Habana, Actas Capitulares del Ayuntamiento de La Habana (Trasuntadas), v. 1624–1630, fol. 264v, cited in Alejandro de la Fuente, "Introducción al estudio de la trata en Cuba, siglos XVI y XVII," *Santiago,* LXI (March 1986), 165; de la Fuente, "Sugar and Slavery," in Schwartz, ed., *Tropical Babylons,* 116.

only 14 or 15 slaves employed on each mill, with numbers ranging from 3 to 31 slaves at most. Alejandro de la Fuente has estimated that among Havana's overall slave population of roughly 4,000 to 6,000 people, only 350 to 400 enslaved workers were employed in sugar cultivation around Havana by approximately 1610. The fact that some mills and cane fields were located on diversified farms rather than large-scale sugar estates helps to explain why there were so few slaves employed in sugar cultivation around Havana (by comparison, 800 sugar workers labored on twelve sugar estates in Española in 1606, as noted above). Many of Havana's enslaved sugar workers were also farmworkers, and, indeed, an average of 15 slaves per rural unit is much closer to the average number of workers on modest-sized estancias elsewhere in the Spanish Caribbean at the same time. If the hatos, corrals, and estancias around Havana between 1578 and 1610 employed the same numbers of slaves as their counterparts in Española during roughly the same period—in other words, if Havana's 113 hatos and corrals employed 2.9 slaves on average and the 148 estancias outside Havana employed 16 slaves on average—then one could estimate a slave population of 3,071 people (375 sugar workers, 328 ranch hands, and 2,368 farmworkers) laboring in the countryside and rural estates around Havana at the start of the seventeenth century. Just as in Española, the cultivation of subsistence crops for local consumption must have been far more representative of the rural labors performed by Havana's slave population than tasks associated with export-oriented sugar production.[22]

During the early 1600s, Havana and its hinterlands probably held the largest concentration of enslaved Africans on the entire island, given the city's relative wealth and position vis-à-vis the Indies fleets. Though very little is known about slave populations on the rest of the island during this period, sufficient evidence suggests that the inhabitants of Santiago de Cuba, too, relied on Africans and people of African descent to perform rural labor. In a general report to the crown penned in 1606, Cuba's bishop Juan de las Cabezas Altamirano enclosed a rough census of the city of Santiago de Cuba and its surroundings taken the previous year, detailing not only the residents of seventy-four households in urban Santiago but also the occupants and owners of six hatos in nearby Guantánamo. An enslaved black man identified only as "Juan" was the only employee working on a ranch owned by Manuel Francisco Bastiqueri, who does not appear in the

22. See de la Fuente, *Havana*, 107, 137, 141, 144–145, 158; de la Fuente, "Sugar and Slavery," in Schwartz, ed., *Tropical Babylons*, 116, 123–124, 142–143.

census himself. An Iberian man named Andrés de Estrada maintained a large household in Santiago, including his wife, their five children, and twelve slaves, three of whom—Francisco mulato, Vicente negro, and Bartolomé negro—were also listed as the sole occupants of Estrada's ranch, "Baratagua," in Guantánamo. Although they likely returned to Estrada's home in Santiago periodically, these cowboys or ranch hands worked on their own, rather than under the direct supervision of their owner or an overseer.[23]

On some of these rural ranches near Santiago de Cuba, enslaved men worked alongside their Iberian owners, the proprietors' family members, and hired employees, who might include Iberians, free people of color, and occasionally Amerindians. Only one hato appears to have employed no slaves. Hato owner Blas Dias lived on his ranch, accompanied by his son and two slaves, Antón Guayacan and Antón Enchico. Santiago's mayor Andrés de Chinchilla also owned a ranch in Guantánamo, operated by enslaved men named Juan Borrego, Francisco negro, and Francisco *yndio;* all three are also listed as residents of the mayor's urban household. Other employees on Chinchilla's ranch included Juan Guzman mulato and two "Spanish" men. The average ratio of two to three ranch hands per hato—with at least one or two likely to have been enslaved Africans or Afrocreoles—corresponds well with the numbers of slaves laboring on ranches in Española in 1606.[24]

In an area not far from Santiago, royal slaves constituted a "peasant subordinate communit[y]" or "rural settler . . . society" in the town of El Cobre during the seventeenth and eighteenth centuries. Although royal slaves were initially sent to El Cobre to mine for copper and continued to perform various labors for the crown when directed to do so, within the space of just one or two generations their main economic activities consisted of cultivating yuca and tobacco; they also raised cattle, grew some sugarcane, and mined copper on an informal basis. In her study of El Cobre's royal

23. "Minuta y Padrón de la gente y casas de la çiudad de Santiago de Cuba," Oct. 6, 1605, AGI-SD 150, r.2, n.33, fol. 4v. For the bishop's report in which this census was initially enclosed, see "Carta del obispo de Cuba, Fr. Ju[an] de las Cavezas, para su magd. en su real consejo," June 24, 1606, AGI-SD 150, r.2, n.34. For a similar example of enslaved but unsupervised black cowboys employed on the hato Guaniguanico, near Cabo San Antón in western Cuba—their owner, Pedro Suárez de Gamboa, was a vecino of Havana—see Oficiales reales de la Habana a S. M. sobre "onze pieças de esclavos boçales," Jan. 31–Mar. 24, 1590, AGI-SD 118, r.5, n.215, fols. 4r–5v.

24. "Minuta y Padrón de la gente y casas de la çiudad de Santiago de Cuba," Oct. 6, 1605, AGI-SD 150, r.2, n.33, fols. 1r–1v. Although the 1605 census fails to mention sugar mills at all, see de la Fuente, *Havana,* 123–124, for evidence that sugar was produced in Santiago and Bayamo for export to Cartagena de Indias from the late 1610s until the 1660s.

slaves, María Elena Díaz shows that they possessed a remarkable degree of voice and agency and that they experienced "a particularly ambiguous form of slavery" far more flexible than the conditions of slave labor associated with "the ubiquitous sugar plantation complex in the island's western region." By the late eighteenth century, when her study ends, El Cobre might well have been an "unusual kind of rural community." But the town as described also fits well within an older tradition of rural slavery established in Cuba during the sixteenth and early seventeenth centuries.[25]

African Hinterlands of the Spanish Main

The existence of early sugar industries in Española, Puerto Rico, and, arguably, Cuba have obscured the importance of other forms of rural slave labor in the islands, but sugar cultivation was never an important sector of the colonial economy in rural areas along the Caribbean's southwestern littoral. Though officially synonymous with the Audiencia of Panama, headquartered in Panama City, by the late sixteenth century, the term *Tierra Firme* ("the Spanish Main" in English) was commonly used in broader fashion to designate the entire coastline from Venezuela to Panama, especially the port complex of Cartagena de Indias, Nombre de Dios, and Portobelo, with the latter sites linked by land and water routes to Panama City on the Pacific coast. By around 1600, the major Spanish settlements in this region probably featured denser concentrations of Africans and people of African descent—as much as 75 percent of the total population—than anywhere else in the Spanish Americas at that time (see Appendix 1). Enslaved Africans labored on estancias, ranches, and corrals in the hinterlands of both Panama and Cartagena.[26]

As early as the mid-1570s, rural areas in this southwestern corner of the Spanish Caribbean were settled by populations predominantly made up of sub-Saharan Africans and Afrocreoles. In his "Sumaria descripción del reino de Tierra Firme" dated 1575, government official Alonso Criado de Castilla reported that Panama City and its district contained a total population of 3,900 inhabitants, of whom an estimated 3,100 were "blacks." These

25. Díaz, *Virgin*, 112, 148, 166, 224–228, 233, 314–315, 352n.

26. Alfredo Castillero Calvo, "El comercio regional Caribe: El complejo portuario Cartagena-Portobelo, siglos XVI–XIX," in *Primer Congreso Internacional de Historia Económica y Social de la Cuenca del Caribe, 1763–1898* (San Juan, Puerto Rico, 1992), 293–373; Alberto Abello Vives and Ernesto Bassi Arévalo, "Un Caribe por fuera de la ruta de la plantación," in Alberto Abello Vives, comp., *Un Caribe sin plantación* (San Andrés, Colombia, 2006), 11–43.

included 300 freed black men and women and 1,600 domestic slaves (*negros de servicio*) employed in Panama City. The remaining 1,209 "blacks" were employed in a variety of rural and semirural labors: 401 "blacks," presumably enslaved men, operated *récuas*, or mule trains, connecting the city to Cruces and Nombre de Dios. Three-hundred-sixty-three enslaved "blacks," some of whom were based on the Pearl Islands, cleared fields, planted, and harvested crops; 150 labored on cattle ranches; 193 operated sawmills; and 102 worked in Panama City's orchards.[27]

According to Criado de Castilla, within the entire Audiencia of Panama, roughly 1,250 enslaved people were engaged in gold mining, primarily near Concepción. But, despite their numbers, these miners represented only one-fifth of the region's total slave population. In Panama City, Nombre de Dios, and Concepción combined, 2,400 people of African origin were urban or domestic slaves. Throughout the region, at least another 2,000 slaves were employed in agricultural labor, ranching, forestry, and transportation services, including both boats and récuas. Slightly more than half worked in rural areas around Panama City (Table 10). Three decades after Criado de Castilla's survey, an official report and description of Panama confirmed that in 1607, enslaved Africans and people of African descent continued to perform most of the rural tasks supporting Spanish colonization: "only black slaves serve on these estancias and hatos."[28]

Cartagena de Indias was probably the largest seaport in the Caribbean by the start of the seventeenth century because of its position as both a major port of call for the Indies fleets and the Spanish Americas' main hub for the transatlantic slave trade. Although many of the enslaved Africans disembarked in Cartagena would be reexported elsewhere, several thousand captives were employed in agricultural labor on farms outside the city. The beginnings of this rural African labor force can be traced to the 1560s, when Cartagena's population was still relatively small. During the early 1570s, traveler Juan López de Velasco described Cartagena as "a town of 300 Spanish vecinos," primarily "vendors and merchants." Directed by sixteen

27. See Carol F. Jopling, comp., *Indios y negros en Panamá en los siglos XVI y XVII: Selecciones de los documentos del Archivo General de Indias* (Antigua, Guatemala, 1994), 10–15. Also reproduced in Manuel M. de Peralta, *Costa-Rica, Nicaragua y Panamá en el siglo XVI: Su historia y sus límites segun los documentos del Archivo de Indias de Sevilla, del de Simancas, etc.* (Madrid, 1883), 527–540. On hatos in the district of Panama City circa 1609, see María del Carmen Mena García, *La sociedad de Panamá en el siglo XVI* (Seville, 1984), 33–34, 65, 90–91, 126–132.

28. "Descripción de Panamá y su provincia," (1607), in Manuel Serrano y Sanz, [ed.], *Relaciones históricas y geográficas de América central* (Madrid, 1908), 171 ("Siruen en estas estancias y hatos solamente negros esclauos").

Table 10 Enslaved Laborers in the Audiencia of Panama by Types of Labor Performed, 1575

Type of labor	Panama City	Isla de Perlas	Nombre de Dios	Natá	Los Santos	Concepción	Santa Fe	Meriato	Total	Percentage
Domestic service	1,600	0	500	0	0	300	0	0	2,400	41.10
Gold mining	0	0	0	0	0	1,200	0	50	1,250	21.41
Agriculture	102	363	0	0	300	0	0	0	765	13.10
Boats	0	0	500	0	0	0	0	0	500	8.56
Mule trains	401	0	0	0	0	0	0	0	401	6.87
Sawyers	193	0	0	0	0	0	0	0	193	3.31
Ranching	150	0	0	0	0	0	30	0	180	3.08
Unspecified	0	0	0	150	0	0	0	0	150	2.57
TOTAL	2,446	363	1,000	150	300	1,500	30	50	5,839	100.00

Source: Alonso Criado de Castilla, "Sumaria descripción del reino de Tierra Firme," May 7, 1575, AGI-Panamá 11, reproduced in Manuel M. de Peralta, Costa-Rica, Nicaragua, y Panamá en el siglo XVI: Su historia y sus límites segun los documentos del Archivo de Indias de Sevilla, del de Simancas, etc. (Madrid, 1883), 527–540; Carol F. Jopling, comp., Indios y negros en Panamá en los siglos XVI y XVII: Selecciones de los documentos del Archivo General de Indias (Antigua, Guatemala, 1994), 10–15. See also María del Carmen Mena García, La sociedad de Panamá en el siglo XVI (Seville, 1984), 33–34, 65, 90–91.

Spanish men, roughly two thousand tributary Amerindians labored for the benefit of the Spanish crown on adjacent encomiendas. Fifty Spanish vecinos resided in Cartagena's province outside the town, along with five or six thousand Amerindians nominally subject to Spanish authority. Though López de Velasco makes no mention of black slaves, five hundred Upper Guineans had been distributed among Cartagena's residents in 1568. This sudden influx of enslaved Africans—considerably large compared to Cartagena's Spanish population at the time—was authorized by metropolitan authorities on the condition that they were to remain within the province, working on outlying farms and ranches.[29]

Both Amerindian and African labor contributed to Cartagena's growth. However, while African populations in Cartagena and its province grew rapidly over the following decades, the area's Amerindian populations declined by as much as 90 percent. In 1588, Cartagena's governor Pedro de Lodeña noted: "In this land, . . . Spaniards provide no service whatsoever, especially the lower occupations which no household can do without. Those who are employed here are all blacks." The following year, Cartagena's bishop stated that the province was "running out of Indians." Shortly after his arrival in Cartagena, Jesuit missionary Alonso de Sandoval estimated in 1606 that five thousand "blacks and Indians" were employed on the provinces's estancias alone. Despite Sandoval's mention of Amerindians, other contemporary references suggest that most of these agricultural laborers would have been Africans. At least 117 slave ships had arrived in Cartagena during the previous decade. By 1607, Cartagena's entire province was said to contain "very few Indians," all of whom spoke Spanish well. By the start of the seventeenth century, Cartagena church officials' concern over the spiritual welfare of African farmworkers rarely extended to Amerindians, who were understood to have been few in number and already assimilated into Spanish colonial society.[30]

A large rural labor force comprised of enslaved Africans and their descendants also worked in Mompox (also spelled Mompós) and Tolú, the

29. Juan López de Velasco, *Geografía y descripción universal de las Indias,* eds. Marcos Jiménez de la Espada and María del Carmen González Muñoz (Madrid, 1971), 194–198; María del Carmen Borrego Plá, *Cartagena de Indias en el siglo XVI* (Seville, 1983), 47, 55, 427, 473–478; Linda A. Newson and Susie Minchin, *From Capture to Sale: The Portuguese Slave Trade to Spanish South America in the Early Seventeenth Century* (Leiden, 2007), 137–140.

30. Carta de Don Pedro de Lodeña, Feb. 13, 1588, AGI-SF 37, r.6, n.76, fols. 5v–6r; Obispo Fray Antonio de Herbias a S. M., Aug. 2, 1589, AGI-SF 228, n.18; Juan Manuel Pacheco, *Los Jesuitas en Colombia* (Bogotá, 1959), I, 249; Nicolás del Castillo Mathieu, *La llave de las Indias* (Bogotá, 1981), 239; David Wheat, "The First Great Waves: African Provenance Zones for the Transatlantic Slave Trade to Cartagena de Indias, 1570–1640," *JAH,* LII (2011), 4, 16–18, 22; Obispo Fray Juan de Ladrada

Figure 5 Fields Outside Cartagena de Indias. Ministerio de Educación,
Cultura y Deporte. Archivo General de Indias. Mapas y Planos, Panamá, 76,
"Mapa de Cartagena de Yndias y de sus inmediaciones." Circa 1665. Detail

two most important villages in Cartagena's province. Each was linked to
Cartagena by water routes. Deep in the province's interior, up the Magdalena River, the village of Mompox was a center for capturing manatee and
the processing of manatee lard. It was also the headquarters of a system of
canoe transportation connecting Cartagena to Santa Fé de Bogotá, capital
of the Audiencia of the New Kingdom of Granada. In addition to the movement of passengers in both directions, imported goods such as wine and
clothing were transported upriver toward Bogotá, while valuables intended
for export to Seville, such as gold and emeralds, were sent downriver to
Cartagena along with food products. The *boga*—the onerous task of paddling canoes and rafts laden with goods or passengers up and down the
Magdalena River, the water route linking Cartagena to the New Kingdom

a S. M., June 24, 1607, AGI-SF 228, n.41. See also Alonso de Sandoval, *Un tratado sobre la esclavitud,*
introduction and transcription by Enriqueta Vila Vilar (Madrid, 1987), 237; Navarrete, *Génesis y desa-*
rrollo, 162–174, 202n. On the Amerindian population's decline, see Adolfo Meisel Roca, "Esclavitud,
mestizaje y haciendas en la provincia de Cartagena, 1533–1851," *Desarollo y Sociedad,* IV (1980), 227–277;
Borrego Plá, *Cartagena de Indias,* 48–54, 105–247, 348–372, 417–423, 457–472; Julián Ruiz Rivera, *Los*
indios de Cartagena bajo la administración española en el siglo XVII (Bogotá, 1996), 24–41.

of Granada—had traditionally been associated with Amerindian tribute labor, but, by the late sixteenth century, Spanish authorities increasingly relied on enslaved Africans and Afrocreoles. In 1597, one friar in Bogotá estimated that more than seven hundred "blacks" were employed on canoes on the Magdalena River. A decade later, Mompox's residents asked to be excused from militia duties in Cartagena in approximately 1606, fearing possible slave revolts during their absence. They described the town as "a village of more than 1,500 blacks, and a few Indians."[31]

The village of Tolú, located on the Caribbean coast south of Cartagena, was an important source of maize, yuca, and pork for Cartagena throughout the sixteenth and early seventeenth centuries. As one traveler noted, Cartagena was provisioned by "frigates from the village of Tolú, loaded with fattened pigs, turtles, chickens, plantains, lumber, and other things." These "fruits of the land" were often then exported from Cartagena to other nearby regions; Cartagena's principal commercial exports seem to have been pork and maize for most of the sixteenth century. Some of this produce might have been supplied as tribute by Amerindians. Tolú had been home to more than two thousand Amerindians in the 1560s, and perhaps as many as eight hundred remained during the 1590s. As early as 1576, however, enslaved Africans began replacing Indian laborers, planting and harvesting maize and yuca. In 1609, Cartagena's bishop described the city's province as "very poor, with only two villages of eighty or ninety vecinos each, named Tolú and Mompox." In Tolú, there were two *doctrinas* (missionary posts) of Indians and another for the "blacks and a few Indians" who worked on nearby cattle ranches. Sources generated in the following decades regularly mention enslaved "blacks" working in the hills around Tolú, felling trees, clearing fields, and burning off plots of land to plant maize and plaintains.[32]

31. Fray Alberto Pedrero a S. M., May 7, 1597, AGI-SF 238, r.3, n.26, fols. 1v–2r; Expediente de la villa de Mompox, s/f [est. 1606], AGI-SF 62, n.106. See also Expedientes del capitán Martin Camacho del Hoyo, Nov. 19, 1596, AGI-SF 93, n.25, May 15, 1598, AGI-SF 96, n.5; Antonio Ybot León, *La arteria histórica del Nuevo Reino de Granada, Cartagena–Santa Fe, 1538–1798: Los trabajadores del Río Magdalena y el Canal del Dique, según documentos del Archivo General de Indias de Sevilla* (Bogotá, 1952), 35–157, 250–253, 263, 279, 299–319; Castillo Mathieu, *La llave de las Indias*, 103–131; Borrego Plá, *Cartagena de Indias*, 42–43, 63, 117, 225–247, 323, 330, 378.

32. Vázquez de Espinosa, *Compendio*, ed. Velasco Bayón, 219–222; Borrego Plá, *Cartagena de Indias*, 42, 53, 63, 66, 221, 231–239, 257, 330, 362–363, 477–478; Obispo Fray Juan de Ladrada a S. M., Apr. 6, 1609, AGI-SF 228, n.47; Inquisición de Cartagena al Rey, July 1, 1611, AGI-SF 242, s/n; Don García Giron a S. M., July 15, 1621, AGI-SF 38, r.6, n.173; Francisco de Rebolledo y Juan de la Huerta a S. M., Aug. 1, 1621, AGI-SF 73, n.74; Carta del cabildo secular de Cartagena, Dec. 14, 1623, AGI-SF 63, n.50, fol. 1r; Expediente de la ciudad de Cartagena por su procurador Nicolás Eras Pantoja, Dec. 20, 1642, AGI-SF 63, n.105c.

Though probably larger than estancias elsewhere in the circum-Caribbean, the workforce operating Juan de Arze's farm on the Sinú River (which flows into the Caribbean just south of Tolú) appears to have been typical within Cartagena's province during the early 1620s. Arze employed twenty-seven black slaves, of whom only two were Afrocreoles (*criollos*). Another enslaved man described as "Portuguese" might have been Luso-African, and two individuals were simply identified as a "black woman" and a "black girl." The remaining workers were all sub-Saharan Africans, including twelve Upper Guineans, eight West Central Africans, and two men from Lower Guinea. Two black girls (*muchachas*) performed house-work, and three women served in the house's kitchen, while eighteen slaves "planted maize and cut wood" with the aid of two mules and five oxen. All but two were men. Another four African men were listed as old, crippled, blind, or otherwise incapacitated and no longer capable of working (Table 11).[33]

Arze's estancia provides a useful illustration of Cartagena's extensive reliance on African farmworkers during the late 1610s and 1620s, when a renewed surge in the transatlantic slave trade delivered at least twenty-five thousand sub-Saharan Africans to the Caribbean port. As landowners like Arze incorporated new arrivals into the existing rural labor force, local religious authorities consistently sought to ensure that enslaved workers would have access to sacraments and Catholic teachings. During the 1620s, Cartagena's bishops reported that "many people have estancias and rural properties with a great number of blacks who . . . go all year without hearing mass" and that "more than one thousand five hundred *negros de estancias*" in Cartagena's hinterland were "as needy of indoctrination as if they were in Guinea." Following a pastoral visit of Cartagena's province in 1632, Bishop Luis de Córdoba Ronquillo likewise found that "on the estancias within Cartagena's district, which are many, a great quantity of black slaves are employed in sowing [the land], raising livestock, and performing other labors." Perhaps inspired by his predecessors, or by his Jesuit contemporaries Alonso de Sandoval and Pedro Claver, Córdoba Ronquillo mounted a campaign to establish doctrinas for the enslaved people working on Cartagena's

33. Pedro Guiral con Joan de Arce y Juan de Acosta, 1622, AGI-Esc 632B, pieza 2, fols. 196r, 591r–593v, 738r–738v. In 1602, the builder Simón Gonçales employed at least six slaves on his estancia and hato: Luis Biafara, Manuel Angola, Anton Nalu, Agustin Congo *porquero* (swineherd), Mandinga *vaquero* (cowboy), and Francisca negra; El obispo y cabildo de la cathedral de Cartagena de Tierra Firme a S. M., July 11–August 15, 1602, AGI-SF 232, r.2, n.28, fols. 36r–36v. See also Navarrete, *Génesis y desarrollo*, 162–174.

Table 11 Enslaved Workers on Juan de Arze's Estancia
on the Sinú River, Tolú, Cartagena province, 1622

Type of Labor	Upper Guineans	West Central Africans	Others
Kitchen	María Bañol	Catalina Angola	Vitoria
Housework			Simona Lucía Criolla
Estancia labor	Antón Bañol capitán Salvador Bañol Nicolás Baño Sebastián Bioho Juan Biafara Blas Biafara Luis Mandinga Santiago "de los Rios"	Domingo Angola Lorenço Angola Francisco Angola Lucrecia Angola Isabel Angola Mateo Anchico	Miguel Carabalí Salbador Carabalí Antón Portugues Juan Criollo
Old, lame, "useless"	Juan Bran Pedro Bran Baltassar Biafara	Alonso Angola	

Source: Pedro Guiral con Joan de Arce y Juan de Acosta, 1622, AGI-Esc 632B, pieza 2, fols. 196r, 591r–591v, 738r–738v.

outlying farms and ranches. Though he acknowledged that some "free blacks and white people," on account of their poverty, lived in the same rural areas rather than in Cartagena, where nearly all of the Spanish population was concentrated, the bishop emphasized that this rural population largely consisted of enslaved people of African origin. His "conscience was heavily burdened" by the knowledge of "more than three thousand blacks" working without respite on estancias where, he claimed, they were unable to hear mass, confess, or receive religious instruction.[34]

Bishop Córdoba Ronquillo proposed a number of sites for new doctrinas, meeting places that priests could visit on a weekly or monthly basis, and *agregaciones* (aggregations) in which existing doctrinas would incorporate additional populations. In practice, this meant that a priest currently serving a small Amerindian community would spend more time in the area, also seeing to the spiritual needs of neighboring African and Afrocreole

34. Wheat, "First Great Waves," *JAH,* LII (2011), 18; Obispo fray Diego de Torres Altamirano a S. M., July 23, 1620, AGI-SF 228, n.78, fol. 3r; Obispo doctor Diego Ramirez de Cepeda al presidente del Consejo Real de Yndias, Aug. 4, 1627, AGI-SF 228, n.86, fol. 1r; Obispo fray Luis de Córdoba Ronquillo a S. M., Aug. 10, 1634, AGI-SF 228, n.100; "Agregacion de estancias a dotrinas," May 2, 1634, AGI-SF 228, n.100a, fols. 1r, 9r.

populations. According to the bishop's proposal, priests would conduct a census of "farms, houses, and ranches, and all their inhabitants" in these rural areas to determine the continual cost of upkeep for churches and doctrinas, including their own salaries. Priests would receive a minimum payment of four pesos per year from each small farm, house, or ranch. Larger rural properties that employed "more than four male and female slaves of an age appropriate for indoctrination and for receiving the sacraments" would each provide priests with a salary of "one peso per slave per year, and no more." "Thus, when there are more than four slaves," he reasoned, "they will be paid by the head, and, where there are less than four slaves, they will be paid four pesos" per year.[35]

Córdoba Ronquillo's proposal offers the clearest indication of the influence and financial resources that Cartagena's ecclesiastical authorities stood to gain during the 1620s or 1630s by taking on the responsibility of indoctrinating rural slave populations. City council members actively opposed the creation of a network of doctrinas on farms and ranches in Cartagena's province, arguing that Córdoba Ronquillo's plan would merely generate revenues and a broader base of power for the church at the expense of rural landowners. Although Córdoba Ronquillo was not permitted to compose a detailed census of Cartagena's rural black population, he managed to produce a list of more than seventy landowners, accompanied by approximate numbers of slaves and free people of color laboring on their properties. Those who owned rural lands in Cartagena's province included the convent of Santo Domingo, a priest, a surgeon, a scribe, two free Lower Guinean men named Agustín Arará and Bartolomé Arará, and ten women, two of whom were described as widows. Unsurprisingly, several city council members—Alonso de Quadrado Cid, Diego de Rebolledo, Andrés de Banquezel, and Francisco de Simancas—owned extensive rural properties themselves. Although Córdoba Ronquillo's figures were rough and incomplete, his proposal provides an invaluable glimpse of the density of slave populations on fifty-five rural estates. Resembling estancias on the island of Española in 1606, one group of thirteen estates in Cartagena's hinterland employed "more than 200 slaves and other people," averaging slightly more than 15 slaves per rural property. Likewise, "300 blacks" labored on another group of sixteen farms and ranches, indicating the presence of nearly 19 black workers per estate, on average. Grouped together in similar fashion, other rural properties employed considerably higher averages of 27.5 and

35. "Agregacion de estancias a dotrinas," May 2, 1634, AGI-SF 228, n.100a, fols. 3r–3v.

30 enslaved agricultural workers (see Appendix 2). The latter figures are consistent with the number of slaves on Juan de Arze's estancia in the same region a decade earlier.[36]

Representing Cartagena's city council, Baltasar de Escobar Maldonado—captain of a local police force and maroon patrol known as the *Santa Hermandad*—argued that raising funds for new doctrinas would mean extra, unnecessary expenses for estancia owners. "For the past one hundred years," he noted, Cartagena residents who owned farms and ranches outside the city had never provided funds for the indoctrination of their rural workers. Instead, overseers and slaves who lived within three leagues of Cartagena normally traveled to the city on Saturdays to confess and hear mass and to purchase supplies. Those who lived on estancias more than three leagues away from Cartagena, he argued, already went to confess and hear mass in the Indian villages of Turbaco, Mohates, Timiruaco, and Turbana, where priests resided. According to Escobar Maldonado, when slaves became sick, their owners took them to Cartagena for medical treatment, and, if necessary, last rites. When black women were seven or eight months pregnant, they were taken to Cartagena so they could give birth with the aid of a midwife and the newborn children could be baptized.[37]

In addition to the expense of new priests' salaries, Escobar cited security as a major concern. If enslaved blacks left their farms and ranches every weekend to go to hear mass, the deserted properties would be easy targets for maroons. Furthermore, bringing "more than three hundred blacks" from various estancias together in *el monte* (the hills, or woods) could be dangerous; even if they were supposedly learning Catholic doctrine, they might start drinking alcohol and decide to revolt. For this very reason, recent laws had been passed prohibiting large dances. Besides, he reasoned, if Spain's rural workers and shepherds were not obliged to attend mass, "Why should these blacks—many of whom live quite close to the city, or to an Indian pueblo—be forced to attend mass on their one day off, weary from having worked all week long?"[38]

Although Escobar Maldonado and Córdoba Ronquillo each represented secular and ecclesiastical interests that might have viewed enslaved Africans as pawns for their own respective agendas, their writings also reveal key social dynamics of the African populations living and working in Cartagena's hinterland. Perceiving a serious threat to their own finances, secular

36. Ibid., fols. 1v–3r.
37. Ibid., fols. 4v–6v.
38. Ibid., fols. 5r–6v.

authorities stressed the social and spiritual resources already available to Cartagena's rural black population; Escobar Maldonado's objections on behalf of the city council and rural propertyowners suggest considerable mobility between ranches and farmlands, Amerindian doctrinas, and the urban port of Cartagena. In his telling, rural slaves frequently visited Cartagena to purchase provisions. On the other hand, Bishop Córdoba Ronquillo and others argued that extending the reach of the church in Cartagena's hinterland would ensure the spiritual well-being of slaves on isolated farms and ranches, while helping to maintain social order in the process. In so doing, these church leaders documented substantial numbers of enslaved farmworkers and ranch hands in Cartagena's province. Córdoba Ronquillo's list also provides a means of identifying specific landowners and the approximate locations of their rural properties. Some were distant from Cartagena, and in these cases enslaved workers likely resided in Tolú or Mompox, or on rural estates. On sites closer to the city, slaves probably resided in Cartagena, traveling to and from nearby farmlands on a daily basis in the same manner as Iberian peasants.

Free Black Peasants

Following his visits to Cuba at the beginning of the nineteenth century, Alexander von Humboldt argued that "phrases such as *black peasants of the Antilles, black vassalage,* and *patriarchal protection*" were nothing more than "linguistic fictions" invented to veil the "institutionalized barbarity" of slavery. Yet, in the early Spanish Caribbean, Iberian agricultural workers were generally scarce, and black slaves engaged in a wide range of rural labors that would be performed by free or indentured workers in other European colonies. Furthermore, the Spanish Caribbean's agricultural workforce included significant numbers of free people of African origin who earned wages as workers or overseers on estates owned by Spanish colonists or who possessed and operated their own farms and ranches.[39]

Humboldt would likely not have been surprised to learn that free people of color in early-seventeenth-century Cuba were at times forced to perform corvée labor and subjected to the attempts of other Havana residents to appropriate their land. Havana's maroon patrols harassed free blacks in order to loot their properties under the pretext of searching for runaway

39. Alexander von Humboldt, *Political Essay on the Island of Cuba: A Critical Edition,* eds. Vera M. Kutzinski, Ottmar Ette, trans. J. Bradford Anderson, Kutzinski, Anja Becker (Chicago, Ill., 2011), 142–143.

slaves. However, the free people of color in question worked their own land outside Havana, undermining any easy equation of rural black life with slavery. In the early 1620s, Havana's free black community addressed the Spanish crown and officials of the Audiencia of Santo Domingo, protesting discriminatory practices by describing themselves as hardworking farmers and loyal vassals:

> The free blacks of the city of Havana say that in that land, they are like the laborers in these realms of Castile, working and cultivating the land with all types of crops. They are well-established with their estancias, with which they sustain not only the city and its inhabitants, but also others who arrive and leave with Your Majesty's fleets and armadas.

If early seventeenth-century Havana was a site of competing agricultural agendas, with various sectors advocating either farming, grazing, or sugar cultivation, then free people of color were among those who held a strong stake in farming. In 1636, authorities in Madrid received an anonymous letter complaining that sugar mills' waste—"purging honeys, bagasse from the crushed cane, bleach, ashes[,] urine and excrements of fifty horses and mules per mill, *lavaduras* [dirty wash water] from cauldrons and molds"— flowed into the channel that brought fresh water from the Chorrera River to Havana, "from which everyone drinks, having no other water to drink from." Although the letter ostensibly took issue with sugar mills' threat to public health, the underlying conflict was one of competition over agricultural resources and the threat of disenfranchisement for some farmers, ranchers, and other rural propertyowners. Free people of color were probably among those who were most vulnerable.[40]

But free people of color's presence in the rural Spanish Caribbean and their participation in local economies as rural propertyowners, farmers, and ranchers long predated serious efforts to establish a sugar industry in Cuba. Already by the late sixteenth century, free people of color—including African-born freedmen—owned rural and semirural properties outside the Spanish Caribbean's major port cities. Wealthy Iberians who owned farms or ranches generally lived in the urban seaports, leaving an overseer in charge of their agricultural enterprises. Most of the actual labor in such circumstances was performed by enslaved Africans either belonging to the

---

40. "Papers Bearing on the Negroes of Cuba in the Seventeenth Century," *JNH*, XII (1927), 55–67; "Expediente de la Ciudad de la Habana, prohibiendo a sus vecinos las talar y rocar en el monte que esta sobre la presa de la Chorrera," visto en Madrid, Oct. 25, 1636, AGI-SD 117, s/n. See also Marrero, *Cuba Economía y sociedad: El siglo XVII (III)* (Madrid, 1976), V, 25–26; de la Fuente, *Havana*, 118–185.

estancia owner or an overseer or rented from a different slaveowner. As little as is known about rural slavery on farms and ranches in the early colonial Americas, even less is known about free black wage laborers employed in rural occupations or the numerous free blacks who owned estancias themselves.[41]

As in early modern Iberia, free people of color and former slaves in the sixteenth- and seventeenth-century Spanish Caribbean worked as wage laborers on farms, ranches, and corrals. Unlike the more respectable *mayordomos* (chief stewards), estancia overseers known as *estancieros* were usually Iberian men of humble means in sixteenth-century Peru. In Spain's circum-Caribbean colonies, overseers also included free people of color and even slaves. The captain in charge of commanding other African workers on Juan de Meneses' estancia outside Cartagena in 1608 was an enslaved Upper Guinean named Luis Bran; the estancia's mayordomo was a sixty-year-old free man of color named Francisco de Puerta. In some cases, free people of color seem to have been able to alternate between rural and urban labors, performing agricultural labor seasonally or temporarily, when profitable labor in town was harder to find. In 1585, a freed black man named Hernando found work as a swineherd near Havana for a salary of fifty-seven *ducados* per year. The contract stipulated, however, that "during the time which the fleet is in this village's port, the aforementioned Hernando will be free from this agreement in order that he may earn what he might on his own account."[42]

Other free people of color operated rural properties of their own. During the 1560s and 1570s, Havana's town council granted land to a number of *negros horros* and *morenos horros* (freed blacks) who proposed to raise livestock and cultivate food crops. Hernando de Salazar, moreno horro, received authorization to cultivate up to ten thousand mounds of yuca and half a *fanega* of maize near the Chorrera River. The council also approved the request of moreno horro Diego de Rojas for a site to raise *ganado menor* (sheep, pigs, or goats), as well as negro horro Hernando de Rojas's petition

41. For the observation that "notarial registers give the impression that [free] black sharecroppers were more common . . . than Indian ones" in late-sixteenth-century Peru's coastal lowlands, see Robert G. Keith, *Conquest and Agrarian Change: The Emergence of the Hacienda System on the Peruvian Coast* (Cambridge, Mass., 1976), 97.

42. Lockhart, *Spanish Peru*, 27; "Pleito entre Juan de Meneses y Francisco Camargo sobre un negro esclavo y sus jornales," 1608, AGN-FNE, Bolívar 6, hojas 10r, 36r–37r, 68r–69r; Rojas, [ed.], *Índice y extractos*, I, 309 ("Y es condiçión quel tienpo que estuviere la flota en el puerto desta dicha villa, el dicho Hernando sea libre deste conçierto para que pueda ganar para sí lo que pudiere"). See also de la Fuente, *Havana*, 175–176.

for land to raise swine. The same council records recognize "the estancia of Francisco, the freed black swineherd." Each of these formerly enslaved men are described as vecinos of Havana, propertyowning, tax-paying, permanent residents. Several freed people of color in both Havana and Cartagena owned large tracts of land known as *caballerías*. This unit of measurement varied considerably from place to place in early modern Spain and its colonies. Although royal ordinances defined a "caballería" as big enough for a house measuring one hundred feet wide by two hundred feet long, with land for fields, orchards, and pastures, the size of a caballería differed depending on location. Records of land allotments in Cartagena for the 1590s show that negro horro Gaspar de Mendoza owned a caballería outside the city near the hill known as "La Popa de la Galera" (the same records also show that negro horro Lucas de Soto owned a small island "in the swamp of Cenapote"). In Havana, Juan Gallego, negro horro, requested and received a caballería of land in 1569 to cultivate yuca, "since he is a vecino, and it is for the good of this village." In the same year, freed black Julián de la Torre, "sheriff of the blacks," was granted a caballería of land outside Havana to cultivate yuca and maize. In Havana and Cartagena alike, cabildo members recognized these free people of African origin as vecinos and rural propertyowners whose agricultural activities helped to sustain both settlements.[43]

Some freed black farmers and ranchers bore African ethnonyms, indicating that African-born forced migrants managed not only to free themselves from slavery but also to support themselves through agricultural labor. As early as 1569, Havana's cabildo mentioned rural land owned by "Diego Brame, negro horro." In 1577, Francisco de Rojas, moreno horro, received authorization to plant up to six thousand mounds of yuca and half a fanega of maize for "the sustenance of this village" on land two leagues outside of Havana, next to land owned by a freed black man named Pedro Ibo. The following year, Havana's town council authorized Francisco Engola, "moreno horro and vecino of this village," to ranch cattle near a lake known as "Graçia a Dios" (Thanks be to God). In 1602, freed moreno Antón Bran sold a farm located outside Havana along the road to Guanabacoa for the price of 270 ducados. The property consisted of three thousand *montones*

43. Roig, dir., *Actas capitulares,* tomo II, 166–167, 240, tomo III, 160–161, 166, 218; María Teresa de Rojas, "Algunos datos sobre los negros esclavos y horros en la Habana del siglo XVI," in *Miscelánea de estudios dedicados a Fernando Ortiz* (Havana, 1956), II, 1283–1284; Eduardo Gutiérrez de Piñeres, *Documentos para la História del Departamento de Bolívar* (Cartagena, Colombia, 1924), 138–145, cited in Borrego Plá, *Cartagena de Indias,* 313–318. Borrego Plá posits that in Cartagena, the caballería was a plot of land intended "for the sustenance of the higher-ranking vecinos" (318).

(mounds) of yuca, a grove of plantains, several *bohios* (huts or humble buildings), several rows of maize already sown, five fanegas' worth of maize already harvested, various tools, five chickens, and a rooster. In the 1580s, free African-born women also owned rural properties and agricultural holdings, such as María Xolofa's garden or corral in the poor neighborhood of Gethsemaní just outside Cartagena's city walls. In Havana, Isabel Enchica, *morena horra*, sold half of an estancia to a man named Antón Perez.[44]

By the dawn of the seventeenth century, free people of color also owned and operated estancias in Española. Governor Osorio enumerated nineteen free people of color, including eight women and eleven men, as estancia owners in 1606 (Table 12). Several of these individuals also had households in Santo Domingo or in one of the island's smaller towns. As in Havana and Cartagena, Española's free black propertyowners included a number of African-born farmers. Although the exact dates of their arrivals are unknown, Catalina Bran, Juan Bran, Juan Biafara, and Gaspar Çape almost certainly first came to the Caribbean as captives on one or more slave ships. Regardless of their African origins or any association with their past as former slaves, by 1606 the island's governor recognized this Upper Guinean woman and three Upper Guinean men as free estancia owners (Juan Biafara is also described as a vecino of La Vega). With only two exceptions—a man named Juan de Castañeda, who cultivated ginger, and another identified as Domingo de Rivas, who grew tobacco in addition to food crops—nearly all of these free black farmers owned estancias producing maize, yuca, and other fruits and vegetables.[45]

When Bishop Córdoba Ronquillo proposed sites for new agregaciones in Cartagena's province in 1634, he, too, listed several dozen rural propertyowners (see Appendix 2). Agustin Arará appears on this list as the owner of a ranch or estancia on the coast north of Cartagena, near the Punta de la Canoa, where the construction of a new church was proposed for the religious instruction of approximately "230 blacks." The bishop also noted the presence of "more than 400 freed blacks and slaves" who lived in houses

44. Roig, dir., *Actas capitulares*, tomo II, 162, tomo III, 172, 194–195; Venta de estancia otorgada por Antón Bran, moreno horro, a favor de Juan de la Cruz, Dec. 19, 1602, ANC-PN database (Regueyra / J. B. Guilisasti) mfn 75847584; "Memorial y testimonio de autos de la ciudad y provincia de Cartagena sobre los abusos y delitos que contra aquellos vecinos cometen los soldados de las galeras y flotas," May 11, 1583, AGI-SF 62, n.28, fols. 36r–36v; Rojas, [ed.], *Índice y extractos*, II, 378. For María Xolofa and her garden or corral in Gethsemaní, see Chapter 4, above.

45. "Testimonio de quantos lugares ay en esta ysla," Oct. 2, 1606, AGI-SD 83, r.2, s/n, fols. 33–69, transcribed in Rodríguez Demorizi, comp., *Relaciones históricas de Santo Domingo*, II, 390, 406, 428–432, 435–437, 442.

Table 12 Free Black Farmers in Española, circa 1606

Estancia owner	*Vecino* of	Estancia location	Crops
Juan de Castañeda, negro horro	—	Buena Ventura	Ginger
Bernaldina Solana, morena libre	Santo Domingo	*La otra banda*	Cassava, maize, vegetables
Juana de la Puebla, negra libre	—	Savana de la Venta, Esperilla y Canoa	—
Simón, negro horro	Santo Domingo	Isabela	Cassava, maize
Catalina Bran	—	Isabela	Cassava, maize
Pedro Cid, negro horro	—	Isabela	Cassava, maize
Gaspar Çape, negro horro	—	Isabela	Cassava, maize
Sebastián Chaves, negro horro	—	Isabela	Cassava, maize
Juan Lopez, negro horro	—	Isabela	Cassava, maize
Alejandro Martel, negro horro	Santo Domingo	Isabela (La Yaguasa)	Cassava, maize
Juan Bran, negro horro	—	Isabela	Cassava, maize
Elvira, negra horra	—	Nigua	Yuca, maize, vegetables
Mariana Suasso, mulata	Santo Domingo	Nigua	Yuca, maize, vegetables
Domingo de Rivas, de color moreno, horro	Santiago	—	Cassava, maize, tobacco
Leonor, negra libre	—	La Vega	Cassava, maize, vegetables
Tomás Franco, negro libre, shoemaker	La Vega	La Vega	Cassava, maize, vegetables
Juan Biafara, negro libre	La Vega	La Vega	Cassava, maize, vegetables
Ana de Alarcon, negra libre	—	La Vega	Cassava, maize, vegetables
Marta, negra libre	—	Azua	Cassava, maize, vegetables

Source: E[milio] Rodríguez Demorizi, comp., *Relaciones históricas de Santo Domingo* (Ciudad Trujillo [Santo Domingo], Dominican Republic, 1945), II, 376–443.

and on farms "in the Swamp of Tesca and Cascaxal," working "on pig farms and fields." Many of these individuals were already accustomed to "gathering to hear mass in the church which Bartolomé Arará has constructed on his ranch." The ethnonym "Arará" ascribed to each of these men links them to Arda (Allada) in Lower Guinea, a region later known to Europeans as the "Slave Coast."[46]

In addition to owning farms and ranches, some free black estancia owners possessed African slaves. Sailing from Angola toward Mexico in 1628, the slave ship *San Pedro* stopped in Havana, selling its cargo of 230 enslaved women, men, and children without authorization; subsequent criminal investigations two years later generated more than five hundred pages of testimony and legal proceedings. On November 9, 1630, a royal inspector publicly announced in Havana that every individual who had purchased slaves from the *San Pedro* was legally obliged to come forth to testify within eight days. Regardless of whether their slave purchases had followed legal protocols, no one would be prosecuted (though the governor of Cuba was in fact imprisoned for having allowed the sale to take place). Over the following weeks, 149 people acknowledged their purchase of one or more West Central African captives. Those who had purchased slaves from the *San Pedro* included widows, carpenters, caulkers, pilots, sheriffs, scribes, military officers, a shoemaker, a tailor, a blacksmith, a priest, a barber, a doctor, and a midwife. Fourteen free people of color also admitted that they or their spouse had purchased slaves from the *San Pedro*. Two free black slaveowners were sub-Saharan Africans who identified themselves as Agustín Enchico and Juan Perez Lucumí. On November 15, 1630, "Agustín Enchico *moreno libre*" testified to having purchased "a negra named Madalena" from among the captives disembarked. "Juan Perez Locumi moreno libre" appeared slightly late, having been absent from Havana for the past two months, but, on November 29, he testified that he had purchased "a negra named Agueda" from one of the passengers traveling on the same slave ship.[47]

Several of the free black slaveowners were unable to appear in person or testified after the eight-day deadline had passed because they were "absent" in rural areas outside of the city. A free black woman named Juana de Morta presented a bill of sale on behalf of her husband, free moreno Cristóbal

46. "Agregacion de estancias a dotrinas," May 2, 1634, AGI-SF 228, n.100a, fols. 1r, 2v–3r.

47. "Autos sobre la arribada del navío San Pedro," 1628–1631, AGI-SD 119, s/n, pieza 2, fols. 37v, 39r, 41r, 42r, 47r–47v, 48v, 50r, 55r–55v, 58r–60r. For Agustín Enchico and Juan Perez Locumí, see fols. 48v, 59v.

Velazquez, who had purchased a "black woman named Graçia" from the *San Pedro*. Morta stated that her husband could not be present, since he was "out in the countryside." Moreno libre Francisco de Noriega, who had purchased "a little black boy named Lucas," appeared before royal officials to testify three days after the deadline had passed, explaining that, for the past month, he had been "absent from the city on his estancia," on the island's southern coast, "with his wife." Testifying the following day, free mulato Martín Garcia blamed his tardiness on having been "absent in the countryside" and noted that he had bought "a black woman named María." The very last person to testify was free moreno Antón Mendes, who presented himself before royal officials in Havana on December 10 to acknowledge his purchase of "a black woman named Ysabel." He, too, had been "absent on his estancia." For these rural workers and estancia owners, newly arrived Africans likely represented a means of replacing or supplementing their own agricultural labor or that of a family member. The acquisition of enslaved African workers must have allowed some free black farmers to maintain or increase their production of subsistence crops for local markets, in turn enabling them to participate more fully in urban economies linked to regional and transatlantic commercial circuits.[48]

DURING THE LATE SIXTEENTH and early seventeenth centuries, Spain's Caribbean colonies were sustained by local and regional economies largely geared toward the production and processing of subsistence foods and livestock. The rise of a rural black workforce—a surrogate Iberian peasantry—was central to this development. People of African origin appear to have performed the bulk of all forms of agricultural labor throughout the Spanish Caribbean, and most of this labor was associated with the cultivation of food crops and animal husbandry, rather than with export crops such as sugar. Although hides, ginger, sugar, tobacco, resins, timber, and other valuable commodities were exported to Iberia, the main purposes of agricultural labor in and around the region's major settlements were to provision local populations and Indies fleets and to produce foodstuffs and animal products for regional exchange. In this environment, rural slavery typically entailed laboring on diversified farms that were primarily devoted to raising subsistence crops. On some estates, export commodities were grown alongside foodstuffs; on others, sugar and tobacco were cultivated for local consumption. Rather than toiling in isolation, enslaved agricultural

48. Ibid., fols. 42r, 58r–58v, 59v–60r.

workers often moved regularly between the urban areas or towns where they resided and adjacent farmlands or nearby corrals. Most rural workers were slaves, but it was not uncommon for free people of color to earn wages by supervising or laboring alongside enslaved workers, and some owned farms or ranches themselves. Unlike plantations, these sites of agricultural production sustained port cities and imperial fleets and promoted local and regional commerce. These Caribbean hinterlands, operated and peopled almost entirely by sub-Saharan Africans and people of African descent, were vital extensions of Spanish colonial society.

SIX

Becoming "Latin"

Like other non-Iberians in early modern Iberian societies, African migrants to the Spanish Caribbean were commonly classified according to their degree of familiarity with Spanish or Portuguese languages and cultures. At the bottom of a widely employed scale of perceived acculturation, sub-Saharan Africans were often described as *bozal,* an adjective and noun signifying "muzzle" in present-day Spanish. To some extent, the term is comparable to *chapetón,* a Spanish-American word that referred to rosy-cheeked Iberians newly arrived in the Americas. But Africans labeled as "bozales" were not merely inexperienced greenhorns; they were viewed as newcomers to the Iberian world in general, unacquainted with its social and cultural practices. The commonly agreed-upon translation of the early modern term "bozal" is "unacculturated" or "un-Hispanicized," though the word probably carried more negative or derogatory connotations as well. Beyond their African birth and a general lack of exposure to the Iberian world, two main factors determined whether an African person would be characterized as bozal. First, they could not speak or understand Spanish or Portuguese, at least not at the time they were thus described. Secondly, they were judged to be unfamiliar with Iberian systems of meaning espoused in Catholic practices. Thus, Africans who were unbaptized or only recently baptized and individuals with little or no experience of Catholic indoctrination were likewise considered bozales. By all accounts, these two sets of knowledge—Iberian language skills and visible Catholicity—were the fundamental standards by which acculturation to Iberian society was measured.[1]

On the opposite end of this Ibero-centric scale of adaptation, sub-Saharan Africans and other non-Iberians who learned to master key elements of Iberian culture were described as *ladinos.* African ladinos and

---

1. For a list of studies that define the term "bozal"—and its counterpart, "ladino"—as described here, see David Wheat, "The Afro-Portuguese Maritime World and the Foundations of Spanish Caribbean Society, 1570–1640" (Ph.D. diss., Vanderbilt University, 2009), 191–193.

ladinas are customarily referred to as "Latinized Africans," "acculturated Africans," and "Hispanicized Africans." Language acquisition was perhaps the most commonly cited qualification for being considered "Latin." In addition to their high levels of proficiency in Portuguese or Spanish, active participation in Iberian religious traditions—or, at least, Iberian perceptions of devotion to the Catholic Church—was a second major characteristic of African ladinos. In some cases, the amount of time spent in Iberian society was a third important factor. In 1572, royal officials wrote from Havana to inform the crown that thirteen recently arrived African captives had died of a contagious illness, along with fourteen Africans "who were already ladinos here." Cartagena's governor employed the term in similar fashion in 1617, referring to a group of Africans who, "having arrived bozales, made themselves ladinos, both in the language and in their familiarity with the land." In these examples, the condition of being Latin was associated with the amount of time African forced migrants had resided in the Spanish circum-Caribbean, gaining familiarity with the ostensibly new physical, linguistic, and spiritual environments of the Iberian world.[2]

"Latinness," or mastery of Iberian mores, was widely understood as an acquired trait; Jesuits' instruction of children in early-seventeenth-century Panama City was equated with "teach[ing] latinness to the children." But only foreigners or outsiders were described as "Latinized." The term "ladino" probably originated in medieval Iberian society; today, "Ladino" most commonly signifies a distinct form of Spanish spoken by Jewish communities in medieval Spain, maintained afterward by Sephardic Jews. Throughout the early modern era, Iberians designated a variety of other peoples as ladinos; all were non-Iberians or non-Catholic Iberians who possessed a high degree of acculturation to the Spanish- and Portuguese-speaking Catholic world. Unlike "bozal," which in the Caribbean was usually applied only to enslaved sub-Saharan Africans, "ladino" was used to refer to both slaves and foreigners of diverse backgrounds, including Amerindians. An Iberian inspector visiting Cartagena in the late 1560s wrote that "the Indians are already so ladino that they will not work without being paid." Following his pastoral visit throughout Cartagena's province, one bishop noted in 1634 that "all the Indians of the Province are ladino in the Spanish language, both in understanding and speaking it." There is even an example of a "Latinized" Englishman, captured by galleys on patrol not

2. Diego Lopez Duran y Juan Bautista de Rojas a S. M., Nov. 29, 1572, AGI-SD 118, r.2, n.101, fol. 1r; Diego de Acuña, gobernador de Cartagena, a S. M., Aug. 2, 1617, AGI-SF 38, r.5, n.144.

far from Cartagena in the first decade of the seventeenth century. Spanish authorities described Captain Simon Bourman as both ladino and "intelligent" (his mother, apparently, was Spanish). Furthermore, he was "a Christian," that is, a Catholic, "and has given signs that he desires to remain one, in the service of your Majesty." Upon recommendation of Spain's Council of the Indies, Philip III freed Bourman and awarded him a post serving on Spain's galleys.[3]

As sub-Saharan Africans gradually attained various levels of Iberian cultural fluency, Iberians measured their transformations on a scale of acculturation ranging from "bozal" to "ladino," with intermediate levels such as "half bozal," "not very ladino," and "between bozal and ladino." For example, following the wreck of the slave ship *Nuestra Señora de la Concepción* near Santa Marta in 1593, one surviving captive identified himself as "Gaspar ladino of the Cassanga land." Royal officials also mentioned "another ladino black named Sebastian Nalu" and described Estaçia "of the Mandinga nation," who arrived on the same voyage, as "between bozal and ladina." The ship's pilot further noted that one of the captives he had brought on his own behalf was "a half ladino black slave named Domingo of the Bañul land."[4]

Such distinctions often appear in notarial records documenting slave sales, indicating that acculturation sometimes influenced slave prices. In 1569, one English merchant, recently returned from a voyage to Mexico and the Spanish Main in the company of John Hawkins, observed:

> If a negro be a Bossale that is to say ignorant of the spanishe or Portugale tonge then he or she is commonlye soulde for 400 and 450 pesos. But if the Negro can speake anye of the foresaide languages any thinge indifferentlye (whiche is called Ladinos) then the same negro is commonlye soulde for 500 and 600 pesos.

3. "Descripción de Panamá y su provincia . . . ," (1607), in Manuel Serrano y Sanz, [ed.], *Relaciones históricas y geográficas de América central* (Madrid, 1908), 165 ("la compañia de Jesus . . . enseña latinidad a los muchachos"); "Testimonio de la visita y cuenta," 1568, AGI-Ctdra 1384, n.1, fol. 12r; Obispo fray Luis de Córdoba Ronquillo a S. M., Aug. 10, 1634, AGI-SF 228, n.98; "Testimonio de como el capitan Simon Bourman yngles se a reduzido a nuestra santa fe catolica," Feb. 16, 1603, AGI-SF 38, r.2, n.52a; Consulta del consejo "sobre lo que toca al Capitan Simon Borman yngles," Nov. 9, 1604, AGI-SF 1, n.309; K. R. Andrews, "English Voyages to the Caribbean, 1596 to 1604: An Annotated List," *WMQ*, 3d Ser., XXXI (1974), 250–251. For an unusual reference to Amerindian "bozales" in Spanish Florida, see Jane Landers, *Black Society in Spanish Florida* (Urbana, Ill., 1999), 48.

4. "El fiscal de su magestad contra el capitán Valentin Velo," 1593, AGN-FNE, Magdalena 4, hojas 19v–21r. For additional references to intermediate stages between "bozal" and "ladino," see, for example, James Lockhart, *Spanish Peru, 1532–1560: A Social History,* 2d ed. (Madison, Wis., 1994), 198–199; Colin A. Palmer, *Slaves of the White God: Blacks in Mexico, 1570–1650* (Cambridge, Mass., 1976), 39.

The relative values Iberians ascribed to enslaved ladinos and bozales during the sixteenth and seventeenth centuries varied over time and from region to region. Linguistic ability increased slave prices in the New Kingdom of Granada, but, evidently in Peru, during the same years, ladinos were generally considered less malleable and potentially disruptive. Meanwhile, in Mexico, the main determinants of slave prices appear to have included sex, age, fitness, and previously acquired skills rather than perceived acculturation.[5]

But widespread differentiation between enslaved Africans described as "bozales," as opposed to those recognized as "ladinos," had far greater ramifications for Spanish colonization of the Caribbean—and for enslaved sub-Saharan Africans themselves—than slaveowner preferences or price differentials. Despite their inherent cultural bias, these terms signal the presence or absence of various opportunities for interaction and social mobility within Spanish Caribbean society; they afford a deeper understanding of African forced migrants' experiences during their own lifetimes, providing indications of change over time that are seldom reflected, for example, in racial labels. Terms such as "bozal" and "ladino" take on additional significance in light of the Spanish empire's reliance on first-generation African captives to sustain its key Caribbean port cities. Throughout the late sixteenth and early seventeenth centuries, as Africans and people of African descent became de facto settlers on Spain's behalf, the Latinization of enslaved Africans played a structural role in sustaining Spanish colonization of the Caribbean.[6]

Since the publication of Fernando Ortiz's *Cuban Counterpoint,* scholars of the colonial Spanish Caribbean have been reluctant to examine African acculturation to Iberian cultural practices as a one-way transmission of culture. Ortiz coined the term "transculturation" to portray cross-cultural exchange more accurately as a multidirectional process. By his definition,

5. "Deposition of William Fowler of Ratcliffe, Merchant," Apr. 30, 1569, in Elizabeth Donnan, *Documents Illustrative of the History of the Slave Trade to America* (Washington, D.C., 1930–1935), I, 72; María Cristina Navarrete, *Génesis y desarrollo de la esclavitud en Colombia, siglos XVI y XVII* (Cali, Colombia, 2005), 132; Frederick P. Bowser, *The African Slave in Colonial Peru, 1524–1650* (Stanford, Calif., 1974), 77–80, 342–345; Palmer, *Slaves of the White God,* 34.

6. Earlier works tended to dismiss African acculturation to colonial Spanish American norms as merely a superficial gloss masking deeply rooted (if vaguely defined) African identities; see, for example, Bowser, *African Slave in Colonial Peru,* 78–79, 222–223. For scholarship that engages more seriously with this topic, see Herman L. Bennett, *Colonial Blackness: A History of Afro-Mexico* (Bloomington, Ind., 2009), 66–76. Although Bennett equates African conversion to Christianity with "cultural loss," "cultural suppression," and "potential cultural conflict between . . . African and Christian identities," he also suggests that Africans in colonial Mexico never became "exclusively Christian" and that "selected African beliefs coexisted alongside aspects of Christianity."

however, such exchanges in colonial Cuba were processes "of disadjustment and readjustment, of deculturation and acculturation." As Paul E. Lovejoy points out, Ortiz's "transculturation" is one of several "creolization" models that effectively "skips over African history." "Compressing the African past into some generalized shape," this framework largely "divorce[s] slaves from their origins." Processes of cultural exchange often referred to as "creolization" began in Africa half a century before the earliest Iberian attempts to colonize the Americas, and it was not uncommon for African forced migrants to be recognized as "ladinos" even when first setting foot on Caribbean shores. Taking into consideration historical events and precedents in sub-Saharan Africa revises creolization models by accounting for many African migrants' prior familiarity with multiple cultures and languages.[7]

If Inquisition records are an index of practices that Spanish officials viewed as unorthodox, sub-Saharan Africans in the Caribbean appear to have seldom violated Inquisitors' cultural norms. Africans comprised only 10 percent of all individuals tried by the Inquisition in seventeenth-century Cartagena; even combining Africans with all other people described as having any degree of African ancestry, this figure rises to only 30 percent. Given Cartagena's demographic structure at the time, Africans and people of African descent were vastly underrepresented in the city's Inquisition tribunals, which were mainly intended to root out crypto-Judaic practices anyway. Unlike crypto-Jews or Protestants, sub-Saharan Africans had little need to conceal non-Iberian identities. The relative scarcity of Africans in Cartagena's Inquisition records suggests that, rather than being culturally silenced or isolated, the speech and customs of various sub-Saharan peoples were probably accepted as ordinary in a seaport in which people of African origin constituted the overwhelming majority of the population. In 1607, a description of nearby Panama City reported: "There are no Indians; the Spanish speak the Castilian language; [as for] the blacks[,] among themselves, those from each land speak their own [language]; they also speak Castilian, but very poorly, if they are not . . . creoles." Yet, all the while, in

---

7. Fernando Ortiz, *Cuban Counterpoint: Tobacco and Sugar,* trans. Harriet de Onís (Durham, N.C., 1995), 97–103; Paul E. Lovejoy, "Identifying Enslaved Africans in the African Diaspora," in Lovejoy, ed., *Identity in the Shadow of Slavery,* 2d ed. (New York, 2009), 1–29. For attention to African precursors for creolization in the colonial Americas, see Linda M. Heywood and John K. Thornton, *Central Africans, Atlantic Creoles, and the Foundation of the Americas, 1585–1660* (Cambridge, 2007); José Lingna Nafafe, "Lançados, Culture, and Identity: Prelude to Creole Societies on the Rivers of Guinea and Cape Verde," in Philip J. Havik and Malyn Newitt, eds., *Creole Societies in the Portuguese Colonial Empire* (Bristol, England, 2007), 65–91; Toby Green, *The Rise of the Trans-Atlantic Slave Trade in Western Africa, 1300–1589* (New York, 2012).

these sites and in other Spanish Caribbean settlements, thousands of Africans participated in the rituals of the Catholic Church on a daily basis, often using sacramental rites and Catholic institutions in the same ways that Iberian laymen and other non-Iberians did: as spaces to formalize social ties and for diverse economic, political, and social activities.[8]

African acculturation to Spanish Caribbean society extended, rather than obliterated, ongoing social and cultural changes taking place in sub-Saharan Africa and the Atlantic islands. The acquisition of Iberian languages and the appropriation of Iberian religious practices did not necessarily signify the loss of African identities, loyalties, beliefs, or memories. For some Africans, active participation in Catholic rites and the rapid acquisition of the Spanish language was a fluid continuation of previous experiences in western Africa. Even those with little prior exposure to Iberian and Luso-African worlds had ample incentive to master Iberian language and religious practices as tools providing access to resources, social networks, and other opportunities to improve their immediate material conditions. On an even more basic level, Caribbean Spanish and Iberian Catholicism served as a lingua franca and a public set of cultural reference points respectively, enabling Africans to communicate with other peoples—including other Africans—with whom they did not share mutually intelligible languages or similar belief systems. In short, most African migrants actively participated in their own acclimation to Iberian customs as a means of addressing practical matters or advancing their immediate interests. Many would serve as intermediaries for subsequent generations of forced migrants, especially those with backgrounds similar to their own. During the late sixteenth and early seventeenth centuries, as successive waves of captives flooded into Cartagena and other ports, this cyclical process of African acculturation fueled the expansion of Spanish Caribbean society, facilitating the growth of stable populations in key ports and reinforcing Spanish colonization of the region.[9]

8. Pablo Fernando Gómez Zuluaga, "Bodies of Encounter: Health, Illness, and Death in the Early Modern African-Spanish Caribbean" (Ph.D. diss., Vanderbilt University, 2010), 31, 47–48, 191, 291; Kathryn Joy McKnight, "'En su tierra lo aprendió': An African *Curandero*'s Defense before the Cartagena Inquisition," *CLAR,* XII (2003), 65; Luz Adriana Maya Restrepo, *Brujería y reconstrucción de identidades entre los Africanos y sus descendientes en la Nueva Granada, siglo XVII* (Bogotá, 2005), 506n; "Descripción de Panamá y su provincia . . .," (1607), in Serrano y Sanz, [ed.], *Relaciones históricas y geográficas,* 162 ("En la ciudad no ay indios; los españoles hablan la lengua castellana; los negros entre sí, los de cada tierra la suya; tambien hablan castellano, pero muy mal, si no son los que dellos son criollos"). See also María Cristina Navarrete, *Historia social del negro en la colonia: Cartagena, siglo XVII* (Cali, Colombia, 1995), 110–111.

9. See Juan C. Godenzzi, "Spanish as a Lingua Franca," *Annual Review of Applied Linguistics,* XXVI

Ladinos *in Iberian Atlantic Context*

Spain's heavy reliance on the labor of African forced migrants to sustain its Caribbean colonies often mirrored aspects of Portuguese colonization of the Atlantic islands and western Africa. Ecclesiastical authorities on both sides of the Iberian Atlantic during the late sixteenth and early seventeenth centuries wrote of the necessity of incorporating sub-Saharan Africans into the Catholic Church. They often debated the most effective means of indoctrination and the validity of baptisms administered to captives at various stages of their involuntary journeys to the Caribbean. African acculturation to Iberian spiritual practices was frequently viewed as a form of social control, but Iberian clergy appear to have disagreed over whether this was the primary goal of indoctrination, or, simply, in their view, a fortunate side effect. A comparison of Africans' adoption of Iberian Catholicism in both western Africa and the Caribbean reveals a number of parallels, and, for many captives, adopting, or appropriating, Catholic practices represented a continuation of cross-cultural exchanges that preceded their enslavement and coerced migration. African ladinos' activities in the Spanish Caribbean indicate that, among the many Africans who adapted quickly to their new environment, some were plainly familiar with Portuguese religious culture before disembarking in the Americas.[10]

Although fluency in Spanish or Portuguese was the single most important factor in determining whether an African would be described by Iberians as "ladino," the term was also closely associated with Africans' perceived familiarity with and practice of Iberian Catholicism. Yet, the two forms of acculturation did not necessarily go hand in hand; nor did African migrants' proficiency in Spanish or Portuguese automatically constitute proof of their religious indoctrination. In Cartagena, Jesuit missionary Alonso de Sandoval cautioned that priests should be "especially careful in examining those who are more ladino," since African ladinos were generally assumed to have already been baptized and indoctrinated. In the Cape Verde Islands and São Tomé, catechization and the administration of sacraments, rather than language acquisition, were viewed as fundamental first steps in the so-

---

(January 2006), 100–122. For a fascinating study that traces the existence of "earlier contact situations that may have involved broad(er) creole multilingualism," see also Armin Schwegler, "Portuguese Remnants in the Afro-Hispanic Diaspora," in Patrícia Amaral and Ana Maria Carvalho, eds., *Portuguese-Spanish Interfaces: Diachrony, Synchrony, and Contact* (Amsterdam, 2014), 403–441.

10. John Thornton, "The Development of an African Catholic Church in the Kingdom of Kongo, 1491–1750," *JAH*, XXV (1984), 147–167.

cial incorporation of enslaved Africans and other foreign immigrants. Early modern ecclesiastical authorities perceived Latinization as more than just the spread of Iberian Catholic values among an ethnically diverse populace. In the Caribbean, as elsewhere in the Iberian world, professions of loyalty to the church often carried political implications, denoting obedience to the Spanish crown and its representatives. Official policies regarding the evangelization and incorporation of Africans into the church were often treated as mechanisms for ensuring stability by deterring resistance or revolt.[11]

In the late seventeenth century, authorities in the Cape Verde Islands feared that unacculturated Africans would rebel against their enslavement and perpetrate coordinated acts of theft and violence. Likewise in Cartagena de Indias, the city's bishops regularly portrayed indoctrination as a means of controlling a potentially dangerous rural black population. In the words of Cartagena's governor Jerónimo de Zuazo, one group of "veteran" *(baquiano)* and "ancient" Africans had recently revolted because they "were not being treated well by their masters." Specifically, the Africans' owners, who lived in Cartagena proper, had neglected to leave anyone to "administer our sacred Religion to them, nor white people to control them." He portrayed this situation as fairly typical, lamenting that on any given "estancia of forty blacks[,] there would be at most one measly Spanish overseer[,] who in his ways would be similar to them." In his view, even Africans who had lived in Cartagena's province for many years and were well accustomed to life in the Spanish Caribbean were liable to become a threat to the social order unless they received thorough indoctrination and regular access to Catholic sacraments. Such complaints fit well within the context of contemporaneous Jesuit efforts to consolidate and standardize religious cultures in rural Spain and Portugal during the decades after the Council of Trent. Zuazo's depiction of a hypothetical Spanish overseer in Cartagena who "in his ways would be similar" to Africans also mirrors the 1607 comment of a Portuguese Jesuit who, passing through the port town of Biguba on the Rio Grande estuary in Upper Guinea, observed "little difference" in the cultural mores of Portuguese inhabitants, their African slaves, and former slaves

11. Alonso de Sandoval, *Un tratado sobre la esclavitud,* introduction and transcription by Enriqueta Vila Vilar (Madrid, 1987), 442–443, 600, 604–607; António Carreira, *Cabo Verde: Formação e extinção de uma sociedade escravocrata, 1460–1878,* 2d ed. (Lisbon, 1983), 277, 294; António Ambrósio, "Alguns problemas da evangelização em África no século XVI: D. Frei Gaspar Cão, OSA, Bispo de São Tomé (1554–1574)," in *Congresso internacional de história missionação portuguesa e econtro de culturas: Actas* (Braga, Portugal, 1993), I, 501–564; Enriqueta Vila Vilar, "La evangelización del esclavo negro y su integración en el mundo americano," in Berta Ares Queija and Alessandro Stella, coords., *Negros, mulatos, zambaigos: Derroteros africanos en los mundos ibéricos* (Seville, 2000), 189–206.

identified as *christãos* (Christians). In early-seventeenth-century Cartagena, concerns regarding the adequacy with which enslaved farmworkers outside the city were evangelized or the cultural influence that sub-Saharan Africans might have exerted on lower-status Spanish migrants reflected Iberian officials' broader unease over the degree to which they could control rural laborers—or distant colonists—of any ethnic origin.[12]

Metropolitan efforts to promote or enforce African migrants' incorporation into the Catholic Church often began before their departure for the Spanish Americas. The modern perception that captives held in coastal barracoons received either bogus baptisms or none at all originated with Sandoval. In his well-known *De instauranda Aethiopum salute,* published in Seville in 1627, he copied three letters describing the inadequacy of efforts to indoctrinate captives baptized in African ports. The first two letters, penned in 1614 and 1616 by the rector of a Jesuit college in the Cape Verde Islands, described the superficial nature of baptisms administered to "brute blacks" *(negros brutos)* on slave ships departing Cacheu and the difficulty of catechizing newly arrived Africans before their departure from Cape Verde. According to a Jesuit in Tucumán—the source of Sandoval's third letter, dated 1622—the day before slave ships departed Luanda, priests lined captives up for mass baptism with no explanation whatsoever; they were merely given a copy of their new Christian name in writing, perhaps on a small slip of paper, so they would not forget. Sandoval followed these letters with further examples of inadequate religious instruction given to African captives, including a series of sworn testimonies collected from slave ship captains in Cartagena in 1610 and 1613. Several of these men indeed participated in slave trade voyages to Cartagena during the years 1598, 1601, and 1616.[13]

---

12. Carreira, *Cabo Verde,* 286–290; Don Jerónimo de Zuazo a S. M., Nov. 1, 1605, AGI-SF 38, r.2, n.73, fols. 3r–3v ("quando mucho en una estançia de 40 negros avia un miserable mayordomo español que en las costumbres devia ser semejante a ellos"); "Carta do Padre Baltasar Barreira a el-rei D. Filipe II," May 13, 1607, in Brásio, *MMA* (2), IV, 260–264. On Jesuit evangelization of the Iberian countryside, see Federico Palomo [del Barrio], *Fazer dos campos escolas excelentes; Os jesuítas de Évora e as missões do interior em Portugal (1551–1630)* (Lisbon, 2003); Francisco Luis Rico Callado, *Misiones populares en España entre el Barroco y la Ilustración* (Valencia, Spain, 2006). The Iberian philosophy equating slaves' docility with their incorporation into the Catholic Church contrasted starkly with policies in British slave societies, where conversion was believed to foster slave rebellions, and slave baptisms and church attendance—even among ostensibly inclusive congregations—were extremely limited. See Katharine Gerbner, "The Ultimate Sin: Christianising Slaves in Barbados in the Seventeenth Century," *SA,* XXXI (2010), 57–73; Nicholas M. Beasley, *Christian Ritual and the Creation of British Slave Societies, 1650–1780* (Athens, Ga., 2009), 52, 76–78, 149n; Kristen Block, *Ordinary Lives in the Early Caribbean: Religion, Colonial Competition, and the Politics of Profit* (Athens, Ga., 2012), 151–152, 173, 192–195.

13. Sandoval, *Un tratado sobre la esclavitud,* transcription Vila Vilar, 382–388; *Voyages,* accessed May 19, 2014, voyages 28153, 29049, 29115, 29559. However, Sandoval also notes that, "normally," cap-

A separate letter written in 1607 also confirmed that unbaptized captives in the Cape Verde islands were often given Christian names, making it difficult for priests in Santiago to determine whether those on slave ships bound for "Quartajena" (Cartagena) had been baptized. By 1630, the arguments presented by Sandoval and his colleagues reached Spain's Council of the Indies. Informing the crown that "every year more than eight or nine thousand blacks arrive at the Port of Cartagena, and attempting to catechize them, it has been found that it is first necessary to re-baptize almost all of them," the council recommended the appointment of priests who would demonstrate greater zeal in catechizing Africans before they embarked on slave ships.[14]

Yet, Sandoval's oft-cited criticism of deficient baptisms administered in African ports during the early seventeenth century reflected long-running debate and official concern over the indoctrination of Africans and their incorporation into the Catholic Iberian world. Sandoval's sources, mostly collected during the 1610s, represent only part of this much longer story. One major question that remained unresolved for most of the sixteenth and early seventeenth centuries was the length of time that Africans who had been disembarked in the Americas should be instructed in Catholic doctrine before receiving baptism. Although some ecclesiastical authorities including Sandoval argued for immediate baptism, others favored a period of indoctrination lasting twenty to thirty days. Writing from Española in 1576, fifty years before Sandoval's treatise was published, Santo Domingo's archbishop asked the Spanish crown whether it would be preferable to baptize *boçales* immediately upon arrival (given their risk of dying) or whether their baptism should be postponed "until they know the Christian doctrine." In response, the archbishop was informed of a previously established policy by which "a negro boçal must be kept thirty days continuously learning the doctrine and then baptized[,] however much or little he may know." Later, one month was viewed as insufficient time. In 1623, Portugal's overseas

---

tives brought to Cartagena from Luanda and São Tomé "arrive truly baptized" and that those arriving from Luanda, in particular, were nearly always able to "give an account of [the baptism] they had received" (382, 605). According to Sandoval, the slave ship captain Pasqual Carvalho claimed in 1614 to have been "twenty times in San Paulo de Loanda, in Angola, during the last twenty years" (387). Carvalho was also *maestre* (shipmaster) of the vessel that brought "Luis Congo" from Angola to Cartagena in 1601 (See Chapter 3, above).

14. "Carta do Padre Manuel de Almeida ao Provincial da Companhia de Jesus," June 11, 1607, in Brásio, *MMA* (2), IV, 278–282; Carreira, *Cabo Verde*, 278; Consulta del consejo sobre . . . "el gran daño que ay en los baptismos que hazen los curas de los negros de Guinea," Dec. 30, 1630, AGI-SF 3, r.1, n.16. See also Vila Vilar, "La evangelización," in Ares Queija and Stella, coords., *Negros, mulatos, zambaigos*, 192–196.

council recommended the appointment of two priests in the Cape Verde islands to catechize and baptize captives for a period of two months before "the monsoon," when slave ships had to depart. A royal order issued the same year suggests that efforts to "Christianize" enslaved Africans before and after their transatlantic passage were supplemented by indoctrination on slave ships themselves. The decree, issued on August 4, 1623, instructed that "when possible, clergy must travel onboard all the ships that carry slaves, occupying themselves with the indoctrination and improvement of their souls, and those of the other passengers."[15]

Despite a litany of ecclesiastical correspondence and royal decrees aimed at improving the indoctrination of African captives, early modern Iberians often regarded African baptisms as valid and viewed African converts as legitimately Christianized. When questioned by Inquisition officials in Cartagena de Indias in 1650, Sebastián Bran related that he was captured as a boy in Upper Guinea and initially taken to the Cape Verde Islands where he distinctly remembered the name of the church in which he was baptized. On the Upper Guinean mainland, Catholicism—often in syncretic form—was a major component of Portuguese identity; conversion was closely associated with economic, political, and military alliances with Iberians or Luso-Africans. Around 1600, Portuguese Jesuit Lopo Soares de Albergaria described the "nations of blacks" living along the São Domingos River, noting: "The Banhuns, Casangas, and Buramos, who continually communicate with us Portuguese, are very ladino. Many speak the Portuguese language, and are baptized of their own free will, traveling to the Island of Santiago to become Christians." The missionary also mentioned a Christian "Zape" village ruled by a literate king in which newborn children were raised as Christians and Christian teachings were read aloud in the village every night. There, identification with Iberian Catholicism was likely cemented earlier in the sixteenth century; residents of the village were probably refugees from the Mane invasions of Sierra Leone, resettled near Cacheu with Iberian aid. Another report written in approximately 1621

15. Carta real al arzobispo de Santo Domingo, May 8, 1577, AGI-SD 868, libro 3, fols. 61r–61v; "Consulta da junta sobre o baptismo dos negros adultos da Guiné," June 27, 1623, in Brásio, *MMA* (2), V, 3–7, "Carta régia sobre a missão da Guiné," Aug. 4, 1623, V, 10; Maria João Soares, "A Igreja em tempo de mudança política, social e cultural," in Maria Emília Madeira Santos, coord., *História Geral de Cabo Verde* (Lisbon, 2002), III, 354; Vila Vilar, "La evangelización," in Ares Queija and Stella, coords., *Negros, mulatos, zambaigos,* 200; Johannes Meier, "The Beginnings of the Catholic Church in the Caribbean," in Armando Lampe, ed., *Christianity in the Caribbean: Essays on Church History* (Barbados, 2001), 45–49. For related earlier debates, see "Alvará para os oficiais de S. Tomé," Mar. 22, 1556, in Brásio, *MMA* (1), II, 383, "Carta de Fernão Roiz a el-Rei," Dec. 10, 1558, II, 428–429; Walter Rodney, *A History of the Upper Guinea Coast, 1545–1800* (New York, 1970), 119–120.

straightforwardly described many of the African inhabitants of Cacheu, Bichangor, and Porto da Cruz as "Christians." Even in Sierra Leone to the south, according to this report, the kings Dom Felipe and Dom Pedro de Caricuri, along with most of their vassals, were genuine "Christians."[16]

Though Portuguese missionary activity in Upper Guinea is far better documented for the years before the mid-seventeenth century, Africans in Lower Guinea also appear to have appropriated Iberian Catholicism. Among the Portuguese garrison at São Jorge da Mina, a small number of priests exercised various duties that included proselytizing residents of the adjacent town of Elmina. By the 1630s, some four hundred people, approximately half of Elmina's African population, had become converts. A decade earlier in Cartagena, Sandoval mentioned having received "certified" information that the king of Warri and the inhabitants of his kingdom (southeast of the kingdom of Benin), were "Catholic, committing no error against our holy Faith." Although little is known of Iberian evangelization efforts in Arda (Allada) during the years of Portuguese influence, from roughly 1570 to 1630, Portuguese continued to be spoken as a lingua franca in the region well after the 1630s. The accounts of Spanish and French expeditions to the same area in 1660 and 1670 further suggest that many of the region's inhabitants must have already been exposed to Catholic practices long before their arrival.[17]

When Bishop Fray Luis de Córdoba Ronquillo proposed sites for the religious instruction of rural black congregations in Cartagena's province in 1634, he reported that "more than four hundred freed blacks and slaves" lived in houses and on farms "in the Swamp of Tesca and Cascaxal," working "on pig farms and sown fields." Many of these individuals were already accustomed to "gather to hear mass in the church that Bartolomé Arará has constructed on his ranch." Bartolomé Arará might have been considered

16. Navarrete, *Génesis y desarrollo,* 102; Peter Mark, "The Evolution of 'Portuguese' Identity: Luso-Africans on the Upper Guinea Coast from the Sixteenth to the Early Nineteenth Century," *JAH,* XL (1999), 173–191; José da Silva Horta, "Evidence for a Luso-African Identity in 'Portuguese' Accounts on 'Guinea of Cape Verde' (Sixteenth–Seventeenth Centuries)," *HA,* XXVII (2000), 99–130; "Relação de Lopo Soares de Albergaria sobre a Guiné do Cabo Verde," circa 1600, in Brásio, *MMA* (2), IV, 3–5, "Relaçao da cristandade da Guiné e do Cabo Verde," circa 1621, IV, 662–665.

17. John Vogt, *Portuguese Rule on the Cold Coast, 1469–1682* (Athens, Ga., 1979), 41, 184; Sandoval, *Un tratado sobre la esclavitud,* transcription Vila Vilar, 65; Robin Law, "Religion, Trade, and Politics on the 'Slave Coast': Roman Catholic Missions in Allada and Whydah in the Seventeenth Century," *Journal of Religion in Africa,* XXI (1991), 44; Law, "Problems of Plagiarism, Harmonization, and Mis-understanding in Contemporary European Sources: Early (pre-1680s) Sources for the 'Slave Coast' of West Africa," *Paideuma,* XXXIII (1987), 356n. For the argument that historians have too hastily assumed that Kongolese Catholicism was not "real" Catholicism, see John K. Thornton, *The Kingdom of Kongo: Civil War and Transition, 1641–1718* (Madison, Wis., 1983), 63–68.

"bozal" when he first arrived in Cartagena, afterwards growing increasingly familiar with Iberian spiritual practices over a period of many years. However, his remarkable role as a free, propertyowning African man who sponsored the indoctrination and religious participation of rural black workers was more likely a reflection of the intensity of Catholic evangelization and Portuguese cultural influences in Lower Guinea.[18]

Regardless of elite Iberian motives for proselytizing and indoctrinating Africans, sub-Saharan African communities and individuals probably viewed the adoption of Catholic religious practices as a means of gaining entry into the Iberian world—a world that in many cases offered tangible benefits such as access to trade goods and an international market, military support and protection, and international networks of communication and transportation. Although Africans' adoption of Iberian languages and religious culture provided Iberians with opportunities to extend their own economic reach, it simultaneously gave Africans greater access to useful connections and Iberian-controlled resources. Rather than neatly complementing one another, however, African motives for acquiring and maintaining Iberian religious identities sometimes came into direct conflict with Iberian motives for incorporating Africans. In the midst of one early-seventeenth-century famine, Cape Verde's governor Nicolau de Castilho wrote that "many Christian women" *(muitas molheres cristãs)* left the islands to reside on the Upper Guinean mainland. In his view, their relocation was disadvantageous not only because they would be left to live "in evil" and "at their own will" among "gentiles" but also because their departure was detrimental to the operation of the slave trade. As skilled weavers, these women were responsible for the production of *panos* and *besafulos,* Cape-verdean textiles highly valued by Africans on the mainland.[19]

From Upper Guinea to Angola, sub-Saharan African peoples traded and communicated with Iberians and Luso-Africans in highly diverse circumstances, often adopting selected aspects of Iberian culture for utilitarian purposes. Although this process was probably scattered and uneven, even within societies that maintained extensive contact with the Iberian world,

18. "Agregacion de estancias a dotrinas," May 2, 1634, AGI-SF 228, n.100a, fol. 3r. For further discussion of Córdoba Ronquillo's proposal, see Chapter 5, above.

19. Mark, "Evolution of 'Portuguese' Identity," *JAH,* XL (1999), 178; Carta do gobernador de Cabo Verde, Nicolau de Castilho, Ribeira Grande, Dec. 19, 1614, AHU-Guiné, cx.1, n.1, fol. 2v. See also António Carreira, *Panaria Cabo-Verdiano-Guineense: Aspectos históricos e sócio-económicos* (Lisbon, 1969); K. David Patterson, "Epidemics, Famines, and Population in the Cape Verde Islands, 1580–1900," *IJAHS,* XXI (1988), 303–306; George E. Brooks, *Landlords and Strangers: Ecology, Society, and Trade in Western Africa, 1000–1630* (Boulder, Col., 1993), 147, 157, 165–166, 259.

it constituted an important prelude to Africans' subsequent roles as surrogate colonists in the Spanish Caribbean, providing many forced migrants with foundational knowledge of Iberian language and religious practices. Sustained exposure to Portuguese culture transformed some coastal African communities, producing multilingual and knowledgeable individuals such as those identified by Ira Berlin as "Atlantic creoles," who would have been known in African and Luso-African contexts as ladinos, christãos, or simply Portuguese. Even African migrants who were not immediately recognized in the Spanish Caribbean as ladinos might have possessed prior knowledge of Iberian customs. In Española in 1633, when the slave ship *San Cristóbal* arrived from Angola without authorization, royal officials questioned several of the captives disembarked and found that one was "ladino," "understood what was being said," and "says that [he] is baptized." Other surviving captives evidently did not speak or understand Portuguese and were interviewed with the aid of a translator. Among them, however, one "answered through the interpreter that [he] is Christian[,] and that [he] is named Antonio[,] and that [he] is of the Angola land." As this example illustrates, some forced migrants arriving in ports such as Santo Domingo and Cartagena were already familiar with Iberian culture, though not all of them would be described right away as ladinos. Soon after their own arrival in the Spanish Caribbean, many such individuals would participate in the Latinization of other enslaved Africans on a much larger scale.[20]

Negros Chalanes: *African Interpreters*

Command of Iberian language was a valuable asset for African ladinos, whose skills often enabled them to play important roles as cultural intermediaries. Some of the earliest Portuguese mariners traveling to Africa purchased or captured Upper Guineans who would be taken back to Portugal for training as interpreters; during the mid-fifteenth century, each Portuguese slave ship allegedly carried one of these multilingual Africans on board. Latinized Africans also aided Portuguese clergy in their endeavors to

20. Ira Berlin, "From Creole to African: Atlantic Creoles and the Origins of African-American Society in Mainland North America," *WMQ*, LIII (1996), 251–288; Heywood and Thornton, *Central Africans*, 2, 17–42, 60–67, 79–82, 98–105, 169–170, 267; "Autos seguidos por Miguel Fernández de Fonseca," 1633, AGI-Esc 4, n.12, pieza 1, fols. 134r–138r. For fascinating examples of Kongolese Christians in Cartagena and Spanish Florida during the late seventeenth and eighteenth centuries, see also Navarrete, *Génesis y desarrollo*, 106; Landers, *Black Society*, 48. On ladinos' roles in the Latinization of captives in São Tomé and other African slaving ports, see Maya Restrepo, *Brujería y reconstrucción*, 376–380, 390–393.

convert African communities to Catholicism and to indoctrinate enslaved Africans newly brought into the Portuguese world. For example, during the late fifteenth and early sixteenth centuries, priests relied on Africans who spoke Portuguese to help them indoctrinate other Africans living in the vicinity of Elmina. Likewise, a royal order issued in 1556 set aside twenty thousand *réis* per year to pay for African translators to assist priests in their efforts to catechize slaves. In Lisbon itself in 1568, the city's archbishop acknowledged the need for African interpreters to aid priests who administered Catholic sacraments. In the first decade of the seventeenth century, Jesuits in Santiago, in the Cape Verde Islands, "asked slaveowners to send us those [slaves] who were spread about the Island so that we could catechize them, since interpreters here are readily available, and baptize them." In West Central Africa, Catholic priests were similarly dependent on translators provided by the Kingdom of Kongo's heads of state, until some Capuchins began to learn Kikongo in the 1640s. By the late sixteenth and early seventeenth centuries, directly mirroring their counterparts in western Africa and Portugal, sub-Saharan African ladinos in the Spanish Caribbean commonly interpreted for Africans with little or no prior knowledge of Spanish or Portuguese.[21]

In Cartagena de Indias, a host of Latinized African interpreters worked for the Jesuit missionaries Sandoval (1577–1652) and Pedro Claver (1580–1654). Sandoval depended on a multitude of volunteer interpreters, African women and men alike, often requisitioned from their owners on short notice. Acutely conscious of the need for Spanish-speaking Africans who could translate Iberian Catholic concepts into more than seventy different languages, he kept a notebook with an alphabetized list of African "castes" and languages, accompanied by the names, addresses, owners, and language abilities of available interpreters. Although Sandoval's notebook has not been found, he refers to several occasions in which he enlisted the short-term assistance of Africans described by ethnonyms associated with both Lower Guinea ("Arda," "Carabalí"), and Upper Guinea ("Bran," "Bañon," "Falupo," "Zape"). Even when boarding slave ships just arrived in Carta-

---

21. Carreira, *Cabo Verde,* 279–280; António Leão Correia e Silva, "A sociedade agrária; Gentes das águas: Senhores, escravos e forros," in Maria Emília Madeira Santos, coord., *História Geral de Cabo Verde* (Lisbon, 1995), II, 310–311, 320; Ivana Elbl, "Cross-Cultural Trade and Diplomacy: Portuguese Relations with West Africa, 1441–1521," *JWH,* III (1992), 165–204; Vogt, *Portuguese Rule,* 54; "Alvará para o almoxarife de S. Tomé," Mar. 22, 1556, in Brásio, *MMA* (1), II, 384; A. C. de C. M. Saunders, *A Social History of Black Slaves and Freedmen in Portugal, 1441–1555* (Cambridge, 1982), 99; "Carta do Padre Manuel de Almeida," June 11, 1607, in Brásio, *MMA* (2), IV, 278–282; Anne Hilton, *The Kingdom of Kongo* (Oxford, 1985), 67, 81, 101, 134, 185, 193.

gena's port, Sandoval tells his readers that he would find Latinized Africans among the captives who aided him in proselytizing the others. Aboard one ship newly arrived from Cacheu, Sandoval recorded, "I called for the most ladino black among them—who is never lacking, at least serving as *grumete* [apprentice mariner]—and told him to talk to those people, asking them if they wanted to be like whites." On one such occasion, after having examined some two hundred captives arriving on a slave ship, Sandoval estimated that very few had received adequate baptism. The only exceptions, he noted, were twelve or fourteen "ladinos, who came guarding the rest."[22]

When Sandoval wrote of having commanded ladino captives or grumetes to "talk" to other newly arrived African migrants (*dixele que chalonasse a aquella gente*), he used the verb *chalonar*—to translate or interpret—rather than *hablar* (to talk) or *decir* (to say or to tell). He employed closely related vocabulary at least twice more in *De instauranda Aethiopum salute*. Among the Serer in Upper Guinea, according to Sandoval, protocol dictated that those who desired to speak with "the king of the Berbesies," even if he understood the language being spoken, were only allowed to communicate through "interpreters and *chalonas*." Although the Spanish word *intérprete* and the Upper Guinean or Luso-African word *chalona* meant the same thing (interpreter) and might refer to the same individual, they evoked very different perspectives; Sandoval's pairing of these synonymous terms perhaps reflected his own experience and that of other go-betweens who facilitated cross-cultural exchanges in coastal western African contexts and in the Spanish Caribbean. Near the end of his treatise, the word "chalona" appears again as Sandoval recounted his prolonged effort to baptize two men "of the Zape caste" with whom he was unable to communicate. After "more than a month of work searching for anyone who could understand them," Sandoval finally learned of "a certain ladina black woman" (*morena ladina*) who understood their language (Boloncho) and quickly "went in search of the Chalona and interpreter."[23]

Although the etymologies of "chalona" and "chalonar" are not clear, the terms undoubtedly share roots with the Spanish words *chalán* (trader or dealer) and *chalanear* (to bargain or haggle), which was in fact one of the primary services African interpreters provided to Iberians in coastal

---

22. Sandoval, *Un tratado sobre la esclavitud*, transcription Vila Vilar, 373–375, 389, 600–606; Juan Manuel Pacheco, *Los Jesuitas en Colombia* (Bogotá, 1959), I, 253. In Luso-African contexts, grumetes performed a wide range of tasks, serving as pilots, guides, interpreters, guards, and stevedores, among other activities; for further discussion, see Chapter 3, above.

23. Sandoval, *Un tratado sobre la esclavitud*, transcription Vila Vilar, 112, 389, 600–601.

western Africa. The same word—"chalona" (also *xalona* or *tcholona*)—meant "interpreter" along the Gambia River by the 1580s, if not earlier. Eventually Sandoval, and later, his colleague Claver, came to rely on a team of professional interpreters purchased by the Jesuit college. In 1657, among the numerous residents of Cartagena who gave testimonies as evidence of Claver's saintliness, one deponent recalled: Claver "relied especially on many negros *'Chalones,'* which is how those who know many languages are called. He arranged for them to arrive from Guinea and elsewhere, collecting [as] alms from his followers the sum necessary to purchase them." The deponent also mentioned that pilot Bartolomé de Flores, who had "made many trips to Guinea," brought Claver "two or three of these negros 'Chalones.'" Some of these skilled interpreters spoke up to six or eight different languages; the Jesuits' slave Capelino is believed to have known eleven. The role of enslaved African "chalonas" in Cartagena constitutes a direct extension and modification of an older model for cross-cultural exchange between Iberians and sub-Saharan Africans: in the Spanish Caribbean, the same multilingual individuals who had facilitated slave trafficking in western Africa would help familiarize newly arrived captives with Iberian mores and Catholic rites.[24]

During the years he served Cartagena's African population, Claver relied on more than twenty enslaved African-language interpreters. Although those owned by the Jesuits in Cartagena were all men, Claver also used the language skills of conscripted females like María de Mendoza, a free black woman "of the Biaf[a]ra nation." Among the professional interpreters owned by the Jesuits, Francisco Yolofo, a former Muslim who spoke Wolof, Mandinka, Serer, and Portuguese, surely would have been considered a negro chalona. José Monzolo spoke both Kikongo and "Monzolo" (an Ansiku or Teke language), and Andrés Sacabuche "of the Angola nation" probably spoke multiple languages as well. By his own estimate, Sacabuche served as one of Claver's interpreters for more than thirty years (that is, from roughly 1624, or perhaps earlier, to 1654). In 1634, for the interrogation of a captured maroon identified as Domingo Anchico, Cartagena's

24. Anna María Splendiani and Tulio Aristizábal, eds. and trans., *Proceso de beatificación y canonización de San Pedro Claver, edición de 1696* (Bogotá, 2002), 121; Angel Valtierra, *El santo que libertó una raza: San Pedro Claver S. J., esclavo de los esclavos negros: Su vida y su época, 1580–1654* (Bogotá, 1954), 217; Pacheco, *Jesuitas,* I, 254; Navarrete, *Historia social,* 110; Philip J. Havik, *Silences and Soundbites: The Gendered Dynamics of Trade and Brokerage in the Pre-Colonial Guinea Bissau Region* (Münster, Germany, 2004), 123, 361. See also Nicolas Ngou-Mve, "Traite négrière et évangélisation en Afrique Centrale aux XVIe et XVIIe siecles," *Kilombo: Revue Annuelle du Centre d'Etudes et de Recherches Afro-Ibéro-Américains,* no. 3 (June 2006), 5–35.

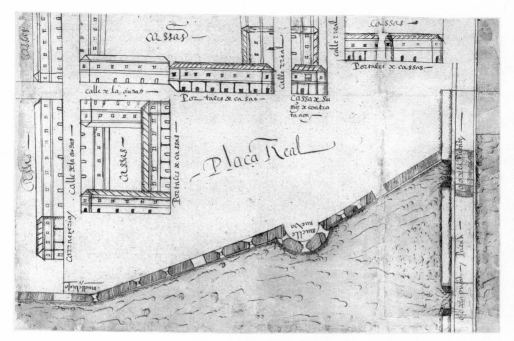

Figure 6 Docks and Customs House of Cartagena de Indias. Ministerio de Educación, Cultura y Deporte. Archivo General de Indias. Mapas y Planos, Panamá, 2, "Modelo de como quedará el muelle de Cartagena después de hecho como agora el Señor Governador lo quiere hacer." 1571

secular authorities called on the services of "Andrés Angola"—possibly Andrés Sacabuche—"a black ladino slave owned by the fathers of the Society of Jesus . . . because he is an interpreter of the Anchico language." Sacabuche was one of at least six West Central African interpreters owned by the Jesuits and employed by Claver and one of four who were described as "Angolas." Since Claver himself was said to have learned to speak "the Angola language," it seems probable that each of these "Angola" interpreters spoke multiple West Central African languages.[25]

25. Pacheco, *Jesuitas*, I, 276–278; Valtierra, *El santo*, 211–224; Nicolás del Castillo Mathieu, *La llave de las Indias* (Bogotá, 1981), 220–224; Splendiani and Aristizábal, eds. and trans., *Proceso de beatificación*, 86–95, 101–118, 132–144, 162, 171–185, 193–196, 207–230, 254–264, 271–273, 293, 305–312, 320, 329–331, 407; "Testimonio de los autos . . . contra los negros cimarrones," 1634, AGI-Patronato 234, r.7, bloque 2, fols. 161v–162v. Claver's interpreters included Francisco Yolofo, José Monzolo, Andres Sacabuche (Angola), Ignacio Angola, Alfonso Angola, Pedro Angola, Antonio Congo, Simón Biafara, Manuel Biafara, Francisco Biafara, Ignacio Soso, Lorenzo Zape (Cocolí), Ventura Cocolí, Domingo Folupo, Diego Folupo, Francisco Folupo, Joaquín Nalu, Bartolomé Nalu, Domingo Bran, Francisco Bran, Manuel Bran, Antonio Balanta, and Cosme Bioho.

Becoming "Latin"   233

The language(s) known to Iberians as *la lengua de Angola* (the language of Angola) was evidently widely spoken by West Central African migrants throughout the Spanish Americas during the first half of the seventeenth century. For example, although a small group of "Angolas" arriving in Havana in 1590 drew geographical distinctions among themselves, they nonetheless claimed they could "all understand one another." Little is known of the so-called "language of Angola," which seems more likely to have referred to various dialects of seventeenth-century Kimbundu than to some type of Bantu pidgin. But the possibility that West Central Africans could communicate with one another in a common language or mutually intelligible languages would represent a notable contrast to the experiences of captives arriving from Upper and Lower Guinea. Sandoval wrote that "castes" arriving in Cartagena from Luanda included "Angolas, Congos or Monicongos which are the same, Angicos, Monxiolos, and Malembas" and that, "although all of these castes, and others which arrive in smaller numbers, are diverse from one another, each is generally coherent unto itself, especially the Angolas, who are understood by almost all of these other nations." Despite Sandoval's observation that many West Central Africans could easily comprehend one another, the Jesuits' acquisition of at least six enslaved interpreters specialized in diverse West Central African languages undermines his assertion and indicates that the individuals described in numerous Spanish Caribbean sources as "Angolas" were perhaps considerably less homogenous than they appeared.[26]

Based on his reading of Sandoval, Nicolás del Castillo Mathieu suggests that "the 'language of Angola' (surely Kimbundu) served as the predominant language" among Africans in Cartagena throughout the first half of the seventeenth century. Little evidence exists for making this claim, other

26. Oficiales reales de la Habana a S. M. sobre "onze pieças de esclavos boçales," Jan. 31–Mar. 24, 1590, AGI-SD 118, r.5, n.215, fol. 3r; Sandoval, *Un tratado sobre la esclavitud,* transcription Vila Vilar, 141. Descriptions of captives arriving in Española on the ship *San Cristóbal* in 1633 reveal a large number of additional West Central African ethnolinguistic designations that rarely appear in Spanish-language sources for this era; see "Autos seguidos por Miguel Fernández de Fonseca," 1633, AGI-Esc 4, n.12, pieza 1, fols. 146r–152v. For references to the "language of Angola" or "the Angola language" as spoken in various Spanish American colonies during the first half of the seventeenth century, see, for example, Splendiani and Aristizábal, eds. and trans., *Proceso de beatificación,* 210; Pablo Pastells, *Historia de la Compañía de Jesús en la provincia del Paraguay (Argentina, Paraguay, Uruguay, Perú, Bolivia y Brasil) según los documentos originales del Archivo General de Indias* (Madrid, 1912), tomo I, 298n; Luis Querol y Roso, "Negros y mulatos de Nueva España (Historia de su alzamiento en Méjico en 1612)," in *Separado de los anales de la Universidad de Valencia, año XII, cuad. 90* (Valencia, Spain, 1935), 15. See also Jan Vansina, "Portuguese vs Kimbundu: Language Use in the Colony of Angola (1575–c.1845)," *Bulletin des seances: Academie Royale des Sciences d'Outre-Mer,* XLVII (2001), 267–281.

than the intensity of slave traffic from Luanda to Cartagena during the 1620s and 1630s. That Claver studied "the language of Angola" is certainly significant. Other Jesuits in Lima and Upper Peru also attempted to indoctrinate Africans using "the language of Angola" during the early seventeenth century, and nearly fifteen hundred copies of an "Angola" grammar book were printed in Lima in 1629 and 1630. Peru's Jesuits even considered using a catechism written in "the language of Angola" (perhaps like the Kikongo text produced in 1624 by Jesuits working in the Kingdom of Kongo), but the idea was ultimately rejected as unnecessary, since enslaved Africans tended to learn Spanish quickly anyway.[27]

Although the catechization of unacculturated Africans was often facilitated by ladino slaves who spoke the same primary language, the process was also sped along by African interpreters and newly arrived captives alike who spoke mutually intelligible or multiple languages. For example, despite living in different states, Biafadas spoke a common language. Unsurprisingly then, when a Biafada woman named Isabel testified before the Inquisition, a Biafada man named Bartolomé served as her interpreter; in similar fashion, Claver employed a "Folupa" (Floup) woman to indoctrinate a newly arrived "Folupa." In many other instances, communication was made possible when ladino interpreters and Africans with no previous knowledge of Spanish or Portuguese spoke mutually intelligible languages or different dialects of the same language. Attempting to indoctrinate a "black man of the Caravalí caste," Sandoval relied on an African ladina to translate for him, noting that, though she was "of a more remote caste," the Caravalí man "understood her well." Sandoval also noted that while "Bran" (Brame) peoples were divided into numerous subgroups, each of which spoke a different language, they were all each understandable to the others, and, moreover, "Brans commonly speak and understand many other languages" spoken by their neighbors on the Upper Guinea coast. However, although Brames and Bañuns could often communicate with one another, Sandoval also provided an example in which a newly arrived, unacculturated "Bran" was not able to understand a "Bañon" (Bañun) woman interpreting on Sandoval's behalf.[28]

27. Castillo Mathieu, *La llave de las Indias*, 184, 216–224, 290–291, 332n; Bowser, *African Slave in Colonial Peru*, 234–235, 245; Jean-Pierre Tardieu, "Los Jesuitas y la 'lengua de Angola' en Peru, (siglo XVII)," *Revista de Indias*, LIII, no. 198 (May–August 1993), 627–637. For the Kikongo catechism, see François Bontinck and D. Ndembe Nsasi, *Le catéchisme Kikongo de 1624: Réédition critique* (Brussels, Belgium, 1978).

28. Carreira, *Cabo Verde*, 289; Sandoval, *Un tratado sobre la esclavitud*, transcription Vila Vilar, 137–138, 373–374, 389, 600, 606; Navarrete, *Historia social*, 110–111; Splendiani and Aristizábal, eds. and trans., *Proceso de beatificación*, 110–111.

Africans of the same ethnic background sometimes spoke different languages and, in some cases, could not readily comprehend one another. According to Sandoval, while Balantas communicated easily with Brames and "Mandingas," they often had difficulty understanding other Balantas. "Zapes" provide a more complex example of this phenomenon. Newly arrived Africans of "the Zape caste" actually included "a great diversity of languages and nations" who "do not always understand one another," since they spoke a number of distinct languages including "Cocolí, Limba, Baca, Lindagoza, Zozo, Peli Coya, Baga, Boloncho," and others. Among Lower Guineans, Sandoval portrayed the "Caravali" in a similar fashion, listing no less than nineteen subgroups who frequently "do not understand each other." Sandoval mainly distinguished between "pure Caravalies" and distinct subgroups he referred to as *"Caravalies particulares."* Subgroups in the latter category, he observed, were "innumerable" and included "Ambo . . . , Abalomo, Bila, Cubai, Coco, Cola, Dembe, Done, Evo, Ibo, Ido, Mana, Moco, Oquema, Ormapri, Quereca, Tebo, Teguo" (this alphabetical arrangement supports Sandoval's claim that he kept an alphabetized list of African nations, languages, and interpreters).[29]

The spread of coastal pidgins and creole languages also aided Latinized African interpreters, as well as Iberians, in their attempts to communicate with recently arrived African forced migrants who spoke little or no Spanish or Portuguese. During the fifteenth and sixteenth centuries in Portugal, Africans were often said to speak an adaptation of Portuguese that was typically referred to as *fala de Guiné* or *fala dos negros.* Meanwhile, creole languages developed in both the Cape Verde Islands and in São Tomé. Describing "the language of S. Thome" as a "very corrupt and backwards form of Portuguese," Sandoval interestingly compared the language and its usage to "the way that we now understand and speak with all types of blacks and [African] nations, with our Spanish language corrupted, as it is commonly spoken by all the blacks." Sandoval's observation suggests the possible existence of an African-Spanish creole, or pidgin, in the early colonial Spanish Caribbean. If this were the case, then this African-Spanish form of communication would have been primarily derived from a preexisting Afro-Portuguese creole rather than a direct mix of Spanish with sub-Saharan African languages. Varying conditions in and around early Spanish Caribbean settlements, including the relative presence or absence of different African languages—some of which had already incorporated

29. Sandoval, *Un tratado sobre la esclavitud,* transcription Vila Vilar, 138–140, 389, 601.

Portuguese vocabulary into their lexicon—gave rise to diverse dialects of this Afro-Spanish creole and possibly even multiple Afro-Spanish creoles. In short, many first-generation African migrants to the Spanish Caribbean became familiar with Iberian language and religious practices quickly; for some, this transformation was enabled by prior exposure to Portuguese and to Afro-Portuguese creoles spoken in São Tomé, the Cape Verde Islands, or the Upper Guinea coast.[30]

African Godparents in Havana

Many sub-Saharan Africans in the early Spanish Caribbean possessed considerable knowledge of Iberian religious culture, and most participated in Catholic rites and associations that allowed them to assert and formalize various types of social ties. Association with Africans of similar ethnolinguistic background was a common pattern; a royal decree of 1612 refers to a Biafada *cofradía* (Catholic brotherhood) in Santo Domingo devoted to the dark-skinned Virgin of Candelaria, patron saint of the Canary Islands. Large-scale African participation in the basic Catholic sacrament of baptism in late-sixteenth-century Havana provides further insight into this process of acculturation or appropriation as it functioned at the ground level. Between January 1590 and January 1600, more than one thousand baptisms were performed in the city's *iglesia mayor* (church). Among the 1,223 individuals baptized, 481 appear to have been sub-Saharan Africans and at least 276 were children born to African or African-descended parents. Together, African and Afrocreole baptisms comprise more than 60 percent of all baptisms (see Appendix 3). Of equal importance, the baptismal records also list many more Havana residents as godparents, parents, spouses, and slaveowners. Africans and people of African descent appear in all of these capacities, revealing gradations in their levels of familiarity with Iberian

---

30. Saunders, *Social History*, 99–102; Sandoval, *Un tratado sobre la esclavitud*, transcription Vila Vilar, 140; John M. Lipski, "The *Negros Congos* of Panama: Afro-Hispanic Creole Language and Culture," *Journal of Black Studies*, XVI (1986), 409–428; Armin Schwegler, "Rasgos (afro-) portugueses en el criollo del Palenque de San Basilio (Colombia)," in Carmen Díaz Alayón, ed., *Homenaje a José Pérez Vidal* (La Laguna, Tenerife, 1993), 667–696; John H. McWhorter, *The Missing Spanish Creoles: Recovering the Birth of Plantation Contact Languages* (Berkeley, Calif., 2000), 17–20; John Ladhams, "The Formation of the Portuguese Plantation Creoles" (Ph.D. diss., University of Westminster, 2003); Bart Jacobs, "Upper Guinea Creole: Evidence in Favor of a Santiago Birth," *Journal of Pidgin and Creole Languages*, XXV (2010), 289–343. See also Carreira, *Cabo Verde*, 274–275; Castillo Mathieu, *La llave de las Indias*, 290, 339n; John K. Thornton, *Africa and Africans in the Making of the Atlantic World, 1400–1800*, 2d ed. (Cambridge, 1998), 213–218; Navarrete, *Génesis y desarrollo*, 102, 104.

values and religious practices. Throughout the 1590s, Latinized African intermediaries in Havana commonly served as godparents for newly arrived captives, particularly for those with backgrounds similar to their own.[31]

Although they are not explicitly labeled as ladinos in the baptismal register, individual Africans' appearance as godparents strongly indicates that they were perceived by Iberians as acculturated. Godparents were expected to act as spiritual parents, entrusted with their godchild's religious education. For sub-Saharan Africans, as for non-elite Iberians, these obligations might have been overshadowed by the social relationships they formalized or by the ceremony's significance as a public acknowledgement of those social or familial bonds. Regardless of the extent to which godparents fulfilled their spiritual duties, familiarity with Spanish religious culture must have been a fundamental prerequisite for their selection as godparents in the first place. In ports like Havana, African godparents' social and cultural functions very much resembled those of African-language interpreters. Writing circa 1620, and drawing on his own extensive experience indoctrinating Africans in Cartagena, Sandoval in fact suggested that priests' interpreters serve as godparents for newly baptized Africans. When he boarded slave ships, organizing captives in groups of ten for baptism, Sandoval often instructed his interpreters to fill the role of godfather or godmother for newly arrived captives in their group, presumably matching captives with interpreters who spoke the same language or a mutually intelligible language. If this arrangement was not possible, then the godparent should ideally be either "some other Moreno or Morena ladina of the same caste" or "someone chosen by them." (If the godparent were selected by soon-to-be-baptized captives themselves, the options available to them must have been extremely limited, particularly if they had yet to disembark from the slave ship.) Much like African interpreters, African godparents' role was to bridge dissimilar languages and systems of meaning. As godparents, African ladinos were to transmit Iberian world views embodied in Catholic doctrine—concepts with which they were already familiar—to newly arrived African captives perceived as bozales. Unlike interpreters, however, African

---

31. Real cédula sobre cofradías de negros, Sept. 9, 1612, AGI-SD 869, libro 6, fol. 154v (many thanks to Jane Landers for bringing this source to my attention). For futher discussion of Havana's earliest extant baptismal records (CH-LB/B) recorded in the "Libro de Barajas" or "Miscellaneous Book" during the 1590s and currently housed in the Sagrada Catedral de San Cristóbal de La Habana, see Appendix 3. The records may also be viewed online at "Ecclesiastical and Secular Sources for Slave Societies," accessed May 1, 2013, http://www.vanderbilt.edu/esss/. Differing markedly from other sources generated in the early Spanish Caribbean that characterized enslaved Africans as either "bozal" or "ladino," Havana's parish records do not employ either term.

godparents were intended to facilitate the transmission of unfamiliar ideas and practices in one direction only.[32]

Three decades before Sandoval published his treatise on slavery, the matching of newly arrived Africans with ladino godparents of similar background was already common practice in Havana. Some African migrants—notably those from Upper Guinea—were identified, and identified themselves, by ethnonyms such as "Bran," "Biafara," "Bañon," "Caçanga," "Folupo," "Nalu," and others that directly reflected their ethnolinguistic and geographical origins. In other cases, the nations claimed by Africans, or ascribed to Africans by Iberians, seem likely to have collapsed specific African identities into broader categories easier for Iberians to comprehend (that is, "Angola," "Arará," "Mandinga"). Even in the former case, Africans who served as godparents for newly baptized Africans bearing the same ethnonym did not necessarily share identical backgrounds or even common languages. For example, when Francisco Bañon was baptized in January 1599, his godparents were Pedro Bañon and Guiomar Bañon; all three were enslaved and owned by three different men. Yet, the Bañun could be divided into smaller polities, with languages often unintelligible to other Bañuns. Perhaps this explains why godparents of Bañuns were frequently Biafada, Brame, or "Zape." There is no reason to believe that these three individuals necessarily shared a common language. The same might be said, to some extent, of "Zapes": when Antón Zape was baptized in November 1596, his godfather was an enslaved man named Simón Zape; his godmother was a free woman identified as María Zape morena horra. Did these three individuals speak a common language before arriving in Havana? And, if so, was it Kokoli, Susu, Baga, or one of many other languages spoken by the diverse peoples identified in early modern Iberian sources as "Zape"?[33]

Although Havana's parish records provide no indication as to who selected Africans' godparents, the consistency with which newly baptized Africans were matched with godparents ascribed the same ethnonym reveals that ethnolinguistic commonalities—the ability for godparents and godchildren to communicate effectively—were a major criterion. As Sandoval noted, "Brans" were composed of a number of different groups but could all generally understand one another without difficulty. In several instances,

32. Sandoval, *Un tratado sobre la esclavitud,* transcription Vila Vilar, 434. See also Valtierra, *El santo,* 225; Splendiani and Aristizábal, eds. and trans., *Proceso de beatificación,* 84.

33. Baptisms of Antón Çape (Nov. 17, 1596) and Francisco Bañon (Jan. 17, 1599), CH-LB/B, fols. 88r, 138r. See also the baptisms of Juan Cape (Jan. 17, 1593), Francisca and Ysabel, hijas de María Çape (Sept. 26, 1593), Simón Bañon (Jan. 31, 1599), fols. 24r, 32v, 139v.

Brame godchildren are paired with a Brame godmother and a Brame god-father. In April 1598, an enslaved woman named María Bran was baptized in Havana's church; her godparents were Baltasar Bran—also enslaved, but with a different owner—and a free black woman named Vitoria Bran. Even more striking examples have African adults serving as godparents for children born to parents of the same "nation." A black girl named Juana was baptized in Havana on the first day of January 1595. Her mother was an enslaved woman named Bernaldina Biafara; her father is identified only as "Juan negro Biafara." The newly baptized girl was probably named after her godmother, if not both her godparents, who were enslaved Biafadas named Juana and Juan. Though her mother and both godparents were slaves, none shared an owner. According to Sandoval, Biafadas lived in communities spaced well apart from one another in Upper Guinea, but all spoke the same "elegant" language. In this case, more than a sign that these forced migrants continued to communicate with one another in their own language, the ceremony shows how Biafada parents in the Spanish Caribbean employed Catholic rites to consolidate social ties with other migrants of similar background. Even as these Biafada adults formalized their relationship within the officially approved framework of the church, they might have expected that the first-generation Afrocreole girl, Juana, would perpetuate their common language and traditions.[34]

At the same time acculturated Upper Guineans frequently served as god-parents for newly baptized Upper Guineans bearing different ethnonyms. Relationships among diverse peoples in Upper Guinea during the same era provide a context for interpreting these baptisms as diasporic extensions of cross-cultural exchanges in Upper Guinea. As a client state of Kaabu, Casa exerted pressure on its coastal neighbors during the sixteenth century, seeking tribute and acquiring captives from Bañun in particular. Despite a recent history of mutual hostility, the Cassangas were closely related to the Bañuns, and Casa itself was a former Bañun state. Although Sandoval acknowledged the uneven power relations and political tension between the

34. Ibid., baptisms of Juana (Jan. 1, 1595) and María Bran (Apr. 5, 1598), fols. 52v, 121r; Sandoval, *Un tratado sobre la esclavitud,* transcription Vila Vilar, 138. For similar examples, see the baptisms of Gaspar Bran (Feb. 18, 1590), Juan Bran (Jan. 31, 1593), Antón Bran (Apr. 11, 1593), Gaspar Bran (Oct. 31, 1593), Filipe Biafara (May 30, 1594), María Bran (Sept. 17, 1595), María Biafara (Sept. 25, 1595), Juan Biafara (Oct. 15, 1595), Domingo Biafara (Sept. 1, 1596), Francisco Biafara (Nov. 10, 1596), Cristóbal Bia[fa]ra (Feb. 16, 1597), Dominga, hija de Marçela Biafara (Sept. 28, 1597), Antón Angola (Sept. 28, 1597), María Bran (May 3, 1598), Antón Angola (May 3, 1598), Manuel Angola (May 3, 1598), María Engola (May 3, 1598), Leonor, hija de Ysabel Bran (Dec. 27, 1598), María Bran (May 23, 1599), Catalina, hija de Clemensia Bran (June 27, 1599), Gregoria, hija de María Bran (Nov. 7, 1599), CH-LB/B, fols. 2v, 24v, 28v, 34v, 43v, 62r–62v, 64r, 83r, 87v, 95r, 111r, 123v, 136r, 145r, 146r, 152v.

two Upper Guinea peoples—"the Casangas are Kings over the Banunes"—he also observed that "pure" Bañuns and Cassangas could usually understand one another. Rather than simply filling a ceremonial role, the enslaved woman named Madalena Caçanga who served as godmother for Juan Bañon at his baptism in Havana in 1598 would have been fully capable of explaining Catholic practices and Iberian values to him on African terms in a language that he would understand (assuming that he was, in Sandoval's rendering, a "pure" Bañun). Likewise, Ana Biafara's presence as godmother at the baptism of María Nalu's daughter in 1594 might be viewed in light of long-standing trade relations between the two groups in Upper Guinea and the fact that these groups, according to Sandoval, were generally able to communicate with one another. Thus, at the same time that Biafada middlemen facilitated commercial exchange between Nalu and Portuguese traders in Upper Guinea, Ana Biafara served as an intermediary enabling cross-cultural exchange between Nalus and Iberians in the Spanish Caribbean.[35]

Instances of godparentage relationships also link peoples who had little if any contact with one another before arriving in the Spanish Caribbean. At Constantino Angola's baptism in 1598, his godfather was also described as "Angola," but his godmother was Juana Jolofa. Both godson and godmother were owned by Cuba's governor, Juan Maldonado Barrionuevo, suggesting that shared ownership—and perhaps shared living quarters or shared occupations—might have been the most important factors in pairing an acculturated Wolof godmother with a newly baptized, West Central African man. In other cases, godparents and godchildren shared neither origins nor owners; perhaps geographical proximity (residence on the same street or on neighboring farms), close relationships between their owners, or decisions made by clergy played a part in determining who would serve as godparents. The extent to which slaveowners or ecclesiastical officials arranged these baptisms or assigned godparents is unclear, particularly when those involved were enslaved. In general, however, language acquisition and occupational training very likely figured (at least implicitly) among the responsibilities of Latinized African godparents officially entrusted with the spiritual and social welfare of their newly baptized godchildren.[36]

---

35. Sandoval, *Un tratado sobre la esclavitud,* transcription Vila Vilar, 137–138, 373–374; Baptisms of Francisca, hija de María Nalu (Apr. 17, 1594) and Juan Bañon (Apr. 5, 1598), CH-LB/B, fols. 42v, 121v.

36. Baptism of Costantino Angola (May 3, 1598), CH-LB/B, fol. 123r. See also, for example, the baptisms of Bartolomé Çape (Mar. 31, 1596), Sebastián Nalu (Mar. 23, 1597), Antón Angola (Mar. 28, 1598), María Angola (May 10, 1598), Bernabel Bran (Aug. 16, 1598), Francisco Mandinga (Feb. 14, 1599), María Enchica (Feb. 21, 1599), Francisco (Oct. 17, 1599), fols. 77r, 97r, 120v, 123v, 129v, 140v, 149v.

Shifts in the direction of the transatlantic slave trade also help to explain instances in which ladino Africans served as godparents for captives of dissimilar background. Most African migrants to the circum-Caribbean during the late sixteenth century were Upper Guineans, but captives from Angola began to arrive in substantial numbers during the 1590s. Baptisms for this decade included a large number of West Central Africans; "Angola" was by far the most common ethnonym ascribed to newly baptized Africans over the entire decade (see Appendix 4). Meanwhile, Upper Guineans played important roles as godparents not only for Upper Guineans and their Afrocreole children but also for West Central Africans. Fifty-four Brame men in the 1590s were *padrinos* (godfathers), and an African ethnonym is ascribed to the godchild in all but four cases. Among these fifty baptisms, more than half of all newly baptized Africans sponsored by Brame godfathers were either described as "Bran" or as the child of at least one "Bran" parent. In another six cases, Brame padrinos' godchildren were Bañun, Wolof, Cassanga, and Nalu. The remaining fifteen godchildren sponsored by Brame godfathers were nearly all either West Central Africans or children born to West Central Africans.[37]

"Angolas" baptized in Havana during the 1590s—especially during the second half of the decade, when ladino West Central African godparents were more readily available—also show a general tendency for newly baptized Africans to be matched with godparents of similar ethnolinguistic background. From 1590 to 1594, just under 10 percent of all newly baptized "Angolas" had godparents ascribed the same ethnonym. Over the course of the decade, as West Central Africans already present in Havana became increasingly Latinized (or were increasingly perceived as such), it became much more common for "Angolas" to serve as godparents for newly arrived West Central Africans. By the years 1597 and 1598, a full 50 percent of all baptized "Angolas" had godparents also described as "Angolas."[38]

"Angola" women in particular were much more likely than anyone else

---

37. For Brames serving as godfathers for newly baptized Brames, see ibid., fols. 2v, 4v, 24v, 25r, 26v, 28v, 34v, 44r, 60r, 62r, 64r, 83r, 86r, 93r, 121r, 123v, 130r, 145r, 156v. For the Brame godfathers of children born to at least one Brame parent, see fols. 13v, 34v, 44r, 74v, 79r, 136r, 146r, 152v. For other Upper Guinean godchildren sponsored by Brame padrinos, see fols. 23v ("Caçanga"), 109r ("Jolofa"), 109v ("Nalu"), 121v ("Bañon"), 129r ("Bañon"), 139v ("Bañon"). Sandoval reminds us that Brames often spoke the languages of other Upper Guinean groups, including the Bañun; see Sandoval, *Un tratado sobre la esclavitud,* transcription Vila Vilar, 137. For other baptisms in which Brames served as godparents, see CH-LB/B, fols. 3r, 5v–6r, 22v, 62r, 63v, 93v, 96r, 100v, 115v–116r, 127r, 140v, 144r, 145r.

38. Of the 41 "Angolas" baptized between 1590 and 1594, only 4 had "Angola" godfathers and only 4 had "Angola" godmothers; see the baptisms of Cristóbal Angola (May 31, 1590), Manuel Angola

to serve as godmothers for newly arrived captives bearing the same ethnonym. Viewed as a group, godmothers for newly baptized "Angolas" were fairly diverse, including thirty-five Upper Guinean women (Biafadas, Brames, "Zapes"); twenty-four Afrocreole women *(negras criollas);* and five presumably Iberian women who were ascribed neither ethnonyms or racial descriptions. But the great majority of those who served as *madrinas* (godmothers) at the baptisms of newly arrived "Angolas" were West Central Africans themselves, including an "Anchica" (Ansiku) woman, five "Congas," and no less than sixty-two women described as "Angolas." Significantly, and perhaps of necessity given the sudden influx of West Central African captives in the mid-1590s, "Angola" godmothers often had two or three "Angola" godchildren and sometimes more. Between them, the sixty-two "Angola" godmothers in question sponsored ninety-nine newly baptized "Angola" godchildren, accounting for nearly half of all newly baptized "Angolas" entering Havana during the decade. Between 1597 and 1599, for example, Isabel Angola, owned by the priest Nicolás Geronimo, served as godmother for four newly arrived "Angola" captives and for the daughter of Lucía Angola. During the same years, one enslaved woman identified as Madalena Angola served as godmother to five newly baptized "Angolas."[39]

Although West Central African women identified as "Angolas" primarily served as godmothers for other "Angolas," they also performed the same role at the baptisms of other sub-Saharan Africans and Afrocreoles. Approximately ninety "Angola" women appear as godmothers in 142 baptisms. In more than 90 of those baptisms, "Angola" women served as godmothers for newly baptized "Angolas." In another 24 baptisms, "Angolas" acted as godmothers for West Central Africans described as "Congo," or "Moçongo," and for children born to "Angola" mothers. They also served as godmothers for smaller numbers of newly baptized Upper Guineans, for children born to Upper Guineans and to one "Lucume" woman, and for others listed simply as "blacks" or "slaves." Though here, too, "Angolas" acted as godparents for captives from dissimilar backgrounds, shared owners, shared occupations, and geographical proximity were again likely important factors in such cases. Nonetheless, when "Angola" women served as godparents

<hr />

(June 3, 1590), Juliana Angola (Nov. 15, 1592), Bartolomé Angola (Apr. 20, 1593), Ana Angola (Dec. 11, 1594), Ysabel Angola (Dec. 28, 1594), CH-LB/B, fols. 6r, 20v, 29r, 47v, 51v. During the years 1597 and 1598 alone, in which a total of 101 "Angolas" were baptized, 47 had an "Angola" godfather, and 51 had an "Angola" godmother.

39. Ibid., fols. 100r, 109r, 126v, 145r (Ysabel Angola); 99r, 117v, 125v, 140v (Madalena Angola). Like two of her godchildren, Madalena Angola was owned by Jorge Fernandes.

in Havana, their godchildren were either other West Central Africans or the children of West Central Africans in 82 percent of all cases.[40]

Whether Havana's church officials and slaveowners selected godparents for newly arrived Africans or whether the latter were able to choose their own godparents is not known. Either way, ecclesiastical authorities and slaveowners in Havana clearly viewed hundreds of African women and men as sufficiently acculturated to transmit Iberian religious precepts and world views to recently arrived "bozales." Despite occasional consternation in early modern Iberia, Africa, and the Americas regarding the validity of baptisms performed by clergy in Africa, the Havana baptismal register suggests that, during the late sixteenth century, many African migrants were indoctrinated at the hands of acculturated godparents of similar background. Furthermore, the presence of significant numbers of African godparents indicates that Latinized sub-Saharan Africans were available to serve as cultural intermediaries for more recent arrivals regardless of any formally recognized social or religious ties.

Speed of Acculturation

Aided by ladino African intermediaries, and perhaps by their own prior experiences of Iberian and Luso-African practices in western Africa, many sub-Saharan African migrants to the Spanish Caribbean quickly became accustomed to their new environments. A parallel can be found in early colonial Peru, where newly arrived Africans rapidly adapted to Spanish culture. Africans who had been characterized as bozales upon their arrival in Lima were said to have learned basic Catholic rites within the space of six months. Likewise in the Cape Verde Islands toward the close of the seventeenth century, enslaved Upper Guineans learned Crioulo and became eligible for baptism in less than one year's time, often within the space of four to six months. In the Spanish Caribbean, African-born migrants initially viewed as bozales lost little time in becoming familiar with Catholicism, the

40. Some entries provide limited information; for example, it is not clear whether "Francisca Angola negra" and "Francisco Angola negra de Antonio Hernandes" were the same person. Thus, a total of somewhere from 85 to 98 "Angola" women served as godmothers in 142 baptisms (likewise, 54 to 74 "Angola" men were godfathers for 112 individuals, including 88 "Angolas"). The 142 godchildren of Angola women included 93 newly baptized "Angolas," 8 other West Central Africans, 16 children born to one or more "Angola" parents, and 25 others. For "Angolas" serving as godmothers for children born to "Angola" mothers, see ibid., fols. 10v, 20v, 58r, 68r, 98v, 103r, 111v, 113r, 130v, 131v, 133r, 134r, 135r, 139r, 145r, 151v. For "Angolas" as godmothers for "Congos," see fols. 84r, 96r, 108r, 120v, 136v, 155v, 157r. For enslaved "Angola" godmothers who shared the same owners as their non–West Central African godchildren, see fols. 62v, 89v, 129r, 145r.

Spanish language, and other key aspects of Iberian society, often becoming known as ladino—or serving as godparents for other newly arrived Africans—within six years or less.[41]

For non-Catholic outsiders brought into the Iberian world, forcibly or otherwise, baptism ostensibly symbolized incorporation into this world and a display of shifted loyalties and values. In the case of enslaved sub-Saharan Africans disembarked in the Spanish Caribbean, to envision baptism itself as straightforward conversion to Catholicism seems unrealistic. As noted above, church policy in the Caribbean during the mid-sixteenth century was to indoctrinate newly arrived Africans for "thirty days continuously" and then baptize them, "however much or little [they] may know." On at least one occasion, Sandoval attempted to convince Africans onboard a slave ship to accept baptism by simply "asking them if they wanted to be like whites." Yet, for African "bozales"—as for the vast majority of their Iberian and Spanish American contemporaries—baptism was surely far more important for its tangible social functions than for any arcane theological implications. At the very least, the baptism of an enslaved African in the early colonial Spanish Caribbean might be viewed as the public recognition of an outsider's initiation into the Iberian world. That an African was baptized indicates that she or he had previously been perceived as non-Catholic and not yet accustomed to the values and practices upheld as central to early modern Spanish society. The opposite could be said of Africans who served as godparents for the newly baptized; these women and men were judged to have been cognizant of Iberian religious perspectives and fully capable of communicating them to new arrivals. If newly baptized Africans were viewed as bozales, then African godparents were presumably perceived by Iberians as acculturated ladinos. If these assumptions are accurate, then Havana's sixteenth-century baptismal register indicates the speed of acculturation for nearly thirty African women and men who appear both as newly baptized "bozales" and, subsequently, as godparents for other new arrivals (Table 13).

41. Lockhart, *Spanish Peru*, 198; Tardieu, "Los Jesuitas," *Revista de Indias*, LIII, no. 198 (May–August 1993), 635; Bowser, *African Slave in Colonial Peru*, 234; Carreira, *Cabo Verde*, 286–291. Berlin's emphasis on some Africans' "cosmopolitan ability to transcend the confines of particular nations and cultures" represents a complete reversal of historical interpretations that categorically discredited the extent of African acculturation to Iberian systems of meaning; see Berlin, "From Creole to African," *WMQ*, LIII (1996), 262. By contrast, notable studies trace distinctly sub-Saharan African influences in the making of colonial Latin American societies, foregrounding the experiences of individuals who refused to adopt western European mores or had no need to do so. See, especially, James H. Sweet, *Domingos Álvares, African Healing, and the Intellectual History of the Atlantic World* (Chapel Hill, N.C., 2011), 4–6, 230–233; Pablo F. Gómez, "The Circulation of Bodily Knowledge in the Seventeenth-Century Black Spanish Caribbean," *Social History of Medicine*, XXVI, no. 3 (2013), 386.

Table 13 Baptized Africans Who Reappear as Godparents in Havana's Baptismal Records by Time Elapsed, 1590–1600

Name	Owner	Date baptized	First appears as godparent	Approximate time elapsed	Folios
Pedro Angola	Gomes de Rojas	Aug. 17, 1597	Apr. 26, 1598	8 months	107v, 123r
Francisco Angola	Juan Mordaz	Nov. 17, 1596	Aug. 24, 1597	9 months	88r, 109r
Madalena Angola	Hernando Soluzio	Aug. 17, 1597	June 28, 1598	10 months	108r, 127r
Sebastian Angola	Jorge Fernandes	May 11, 1597	Apr. 26, 1598	11 months	99r, 123r
María Angola	María Sanchez mulata, wife of pilot Juan Sanches	Jan. 30, 1594	Apr. 30, 1595	1 year, 3 months	39r, 56v
Manuel Angola	Sebastian Garcia	May 3, 1598	Nov. 12, 1599	1 year, 6 months	123v, 153r
Domingo Biafara	Francisco Vazquez de Carrion, priest	Sept. 1, 1596	Apr. 5, 1598	1 year, 7 months	83r, 121v
María Angola	Jorge Fernandes	Jan. 7, 1596	Sept. 28, 1597	1 year, 9 months	71r, 111r
Ysabel Angola	Nicolás Gerónimo, vicar	Aug. 15, 1595	May 18, 1597	1 year, 9 months	60r, 100r
Luisa Angola	Baltasar Gonçales	July 30, 1595	June 1, 1597	1 year, 10 months	59r, 101r
Madalena Angola	Jorge Fernandes	Apr. 30, 1595	May 11, 1597	2 years	56v, 99r
Pedro Angola	Convent of San Francisco	Jan. 14, 1596	May 3, 1598	2 years, 4 months	71v, 123r
María Bran	Julian Hernandez	Sept. 17, 1595	Apr. 6, 1598	2 years, 7 months	62r, 121v
Lucrecia Angola	Antonio de Salazar	Dec. 25, 1595	Aug. 16, 1598	2 years, 8 months	69r, 129v
María Angola	Hernando Dias	July 30, 1595	Apr. 26, 1598	2 years, 9 months	59r, 123r
Bartolomé Angola	Manuel Dias, treasurer	Apr. 20, 1593	Sept. 8, 1596	3 years, 5 months	29r, 84r
Gaspar Bran	Diego de Herrera	Oct. 31, 1593	May 18, 1597	3 years, 7 months	34v, 100v
Gaspar Biafara	*El rey* (the King)	Feb. 21, 1593	Jan. 19, 1597	3 years, 11 months	26v, 91v
Pedro Angola	Diego de Herrera	Jan. 10, 1593	Jan. 19, 1597	4 years	23v, 92r

Name	Owner	Date baptized	First appears as godparent	Approximate time elapsed	Folios
Sebastian Bañon	Hernando Rodrígues Tavares	Dec. 28, 1593	Mar. 29, 1598	4 years, 3 months	38r, 121r
Francisco Angola	Alfonso Lorenço	Apr. 12, 1594	Sept. 6, 1598	4 years, 5 months	42r, 130r
Domingo Biafara	Juan Rezio	Feb. 6, 1594	Sept. 6, 1598	4 years, 7 months	40r, 130v
Ysabel Bran	Alfonso Lorenço	Sept. 29, 1593	Dec. 27, 1598	5 years, 3 months	32v, 136r
Juliana Angola	Juan Mordaz	Nov. 15, 1592	July 27, 1597	5 years, 8 months	20v, 105v
María Angola	Melchor Rodrigues, pilot of the galleys	Sept. 8, 1590	Sept. 8, 1596	6 years	9r, 84r
Juan Bran	Pedro de Portierra, *alférez* (ensign)	Jan. 31, 1593	May 23, 1599	6 years, 4 months	24v, 145r
Jeronimo Nalu	Pedro de Rubio	June 10, 1590	Dec. 29, 1596	6 years, 7 months	6r, 90v
María Angola	Sebastian Fernandez	May 20, 1590	July 6, 1597	7 years, 2 months	5r, 103v

Source: CH-LB/B: Sagrada Catedral de San Cristóbal de La Habana, "Libro de Barajas," Bautismos, 1590–1600.
   Note: Alfonso Lorenço might have owned two women named Ysabel Bran (fol. 136r).

Though neither godparents nor the newly baptized are explicitly identified as bozales or ladinos in the baptismal entries, the process of gaining familiarity with Iberian religious practices must have paralleled the acquisition of Iberian language skills; indeed the latter might have served as evidence of the former. Though the exact or even approximate ages of most godchildren or their padrinos remains unknown, age might have also been a factor in the process of Latinization. In addition to different degrees of capability—and, presumably, varying degrees of desire to emulate Iberian practices—diverse experiences of enslavement and captivity possibly also account for a difference in intervals of acculturation (or perceived acculturation). Laboring in urban environments, for instance, might have contributed to more rapid acculturation. Perhaps Madalena Angola, an enslaved black woman owned by Hernando Soluzio, had been previously indoctrinated in Africa; though she was baptized in August 1597, she appears as godmother just ten months later at the baptism of another enslaved West Central African named María Angola in June 1598.[42]

For the twenty-eight individuals listed in Table 13 (thirteen women and fifteen men), the time elapsed between their initial baptisms and their first appearances as godparents varies widely, from as little as eight months to as long as seven years and two months. On average, however, approximately three years and three months elapsed from the time of their own baptism to the time when they were initially perceived as adequately acculturated to serve as godparents for newly arrived captives. The median time elapsed— two years and eight and one-half months—is perhaps even more revealing. Of the fourteen persons who were baptized and then reappeared as godparents within the space of two years and eight months or less, all but two were described as "Angolas"; all but one were baptized in 1595 or later (María Angola, owned by María Sanchez, was baptized in 1594). Among the fourteen Africans who were baptized and then reappeared as godparents two years and nine months later or longer, only half (seven) were listed as "Angolas." All but one were baptized in 1594 or earlier, with one exception: María Angola, owned by Hernando Dias, was baptized in 1595, then served as godmother just two years and nine months later. Although ladino "Angolas" were scarce in comparison to their Upper Guinean counterparts

---

42. Baptisms of Madalena Angola (Aug. 17, 1597) and María Angola (June 28, 1598), CH-LB/B, fols. 108r, 127r; Bowser, *African Slave in Colonial Peru*, 80. Although Bowser emphasizes slaveowner preferences, his data also suggests that labor in urban environments tended to produce acculturated slaves. For the observation that enslaved people older than thirty were more likely to experience difficulty learning Crioulo in the Cape Verde Islands, see Carreira, *Cabo Verde*, 289.

throughout the sixteenth century, a burgeoning slave trade from Luanda began to reshape the Spanish Caribbean's African populations during the 1590s, rapidly increasing West Central Africans' presence in settlements throughout the region. By the second half of the 1590s, larger numbers of West Central Africans—including the "Angola" godmothers discussed above—were available to facilitate the indoctrination of new arrivals from their own homelands. During the late 1590s, the speed with which some enslaved "Angolas" acquired knowledge of Spanish religious culture perhaps owed more to West Central Africans' increasing presence in Havana than to the earlier diffusion of Iberian culture in Angola.

Although Sandoval's treatise indicates that some captives were baptized soon after their arrival in Cartagena, other forced migrants' baptisms took place months after their disembarkation. For example, the ten "Angola" castaways brought before Havana's royal officials in January 1590 were baptized four and five months later, in May and June. For twenty-two Africans sold in Havana in 1596, their baptism took place one year and four months after their sale, on average. At a Dominican provincial council held in Santo Domingo in 1622–1623, high-ranking clergy based in Española, Cuba, Puerto Rico, Jamaica, and Venezuela agreed that newly arrived "adult Ethiopians" should be baptized after "a period of two or three months," during which time they "should be instructed in the Christian doctrine." For each of the women and men listed in Table 13, then, a full accounting of their transition from "bozal" to "ladino" should include first, any prior exposure to Iberian or Luso-African languages and cultural practices in western Africa, or during the transatlantic crossing; second, the time elapsed between their arrival in Havana and their baptism; and third, the time elapsed between their baptism and their first appearance as a godparent. For new arrivals who possessed little prior experience of Iberian customs, a fourth significant factor was the timing of their arrival in the Caribbean in relation to that of other forced migrants of similar ethnolinguistic background. The presence of ladino Africans who spoke their own languages significantly accelerated the acculturative process.[43]

---

43. Oficiales reales de la Habana a S. M. sobre "onze pieças de esclavos boçales," Jan. 31–Mar. 24, 1590, AGI-SD 118, r.5, n.215; Baptisms of royal slaves Sebastián Angola, Francisco Angola, Pedro Angola, Francisco Angola, Marco Angola, Mateo Angola, Antón Angola, Cristóbal Angola, Manuel negro Angola, Gaspar Angola, May 6–June 10, 1590, CH-LB/B, fols. 5r–6r; Alejandro de la Fuente, with César García del Pino and Bernardo Iglesias Delgado, *Havana and the Atlantic in the Sixteenth Century* (Chapel Hill, N.C., 2008), 162; Carlos Rodríguez Souquet, *El concilio provincial dominicano (1622–1623): Un aporte para la historia de las Antillas y Venezuela* (Mexico City, 2003), 133–134.

Several African migrants to the Spanish Caribbean described themselves in terms of this scale of acculturation, with attention to change over time, in a legal suit initiated in Cartagena in 1607. This *pleito* aimed to determine the African background of a man from Wandu known as Luis Congo. Luis was one of more than two hundred West Central Africans who sailed from Luanda on the *San Francisco,* a slave ship captained by Pasqual Carvalho, arriving in Cartagena on February 15, 1601. Luis and four other captives had been purchased by the scribe Juan de Meneses and were immediately sent to work on his estancia outside the city. According to Meneses, all five arrived as "bozales." The farm's overseer or "captain"—an Upper Guinean man described as "Christian"—also noted that Luis "was bozal" when he first arrived in Cartagena. Shortly after fleeing from Meneses's estancia, Luis found himself in Mompox, working for a different owner. When Cartagena officials later asked whether the new owner ever tried to ascertain whether he had run away, Luis answered simply that at the time he met his new owner, he "was bozal and did not know how to understand or respond to the questions he was asked."[44]

Yet, in December 1606, five years and ten months after his arrival in Cartagena, Luis testified primarily in Spanish (no interpreter is mentioned at any point in the investigation). He was permitted to give sworn testimony on his own behalf "because he said that he was Christian"; he stated that he had been baptized by a priest in Honda on the Magdalena River, some time after fleeing from his first owner's estancia outside Cartagena. Two of his shipmates, also initially purchased by Meneses, gave testimonies regarding Luis's background, identifying themselves as "Christians" or as "ladino." Another enslaved man owned by Meneses identified as Francisco Congo testified twice, in February and April 1607. Like Luis, he was ceremonially sworn in "since he said that he was ladino and Christian." According to Francisco, "About six years ago[,] more or less[,] this deponent came from the kingdoms of Angola to this city in the company of four others[:] two males and two females[,] brought by a Portuguese man." "This deponent," he noted, "was called Francisco." The others were Luis, María Antona, Isabel Angola, and Antón Angola. After arriving in Cartagena, Francisco

---

44. "Pleito entre Juan de Meneses y Francisco Camargo sobre un negro esclavo y sus jornales," 1608, AGN-FNE, Bolívar 6, hojas 11v, 65v, 69r (for further discussion of this case, see Chapter 3, above). See also Sandoval, *Un tratado sobre la esclavitud,* transcription Vila Vilar, 383. On the slave ship *San Francisco,* see "Copia de la Relasion de Cartagena de los negros q Alli han entrado desde primero de Mayo de 1600," July 27, 1601, AGI-SF 72, n.105, fol. 24v; Enriqueta Vila Vilar, *Hispanoamérica y el comercio de esclavos: Los asientos portugueses* (Seville, 1977), 250–251; *Voyages,* accessed May 19, 2014, voyage 29115.

Congo "saw that . . . his master Juan de Meneses bought all of them, and sent them to his estancia."[45]

María Antona, an enslaved woman now owned by Meneses's mother-in-law, also testified in February and April 1607. In the legal suit, she is described as "a black woman who said that she was named María Antona[,] of the Angola land[,] and [that she] was Christian and a slave of the widow Leonor de Carmona." In María Antona's words, she

> came to this city with another black woman and three black slave men. . . . All were owned by Pasqual Caravallo [the] Portuguese man who brought them[.] And in this land the scribe Juan de Meneses bought all five [of them,] and the black man Luis[,] of the Congo land[,] was among the three males [Meneses] purchased[.] And only a few days after [Meneses] bought him[,] Luis fled and never appeared again until now[,] when they brought him from Mompox.

Thus, almost exactly six years after arriving in Cartagena, three enslaved West Central Africans identified not only the slave ship captain who brought them from Angola but also several fellow captives transported to Cartagena on the same vessel. Significantly, they used Iberian referents in identifying themselves for a Spanish American audience as Christian or Latinized Africans. Whereas six years earlier they were "bozales," unable to speak Spanish or Portuguese and probably with little if any prior exposure to Iberian religious practices, by late 1606 or early 1607 they were not only viewed by Iberians as Christian or ladino but were also sufficiently familiar with Iberian categories of acculturation to describe themselves using such terms.[46]

MANY AFRICAN MIGRANTS to the late-sixteenth and early-seventeenth-century Spanish Caribbean rapidly became familiar with Iberian languages and religious practices, blurring some of the boundaries that separate the conceptual categories of Africans and Spaniards. As interpreters and as godparents, Latinized Africans facilitated the acculturation of newly arrived "bozales," particularly (though not exclusively) those of similar

45. "Pleito entre Juan de Meneses y Francisco Camargo sobre un negro esclavo y sus jornales," 1608, AGN-FNE, Bolívar 6, hojas 9r–9v, 37r–38r, 50r–51r, 70r–71r.

46. Ibid., hojas 35r–36r, 63v, 69r–70r. For similar examples of West Central African women in Cartagena described as *ladina y entendida* (Latinized and well understood) and *christiana bautizada* (baptized Christian), see "Alonso de Peralta . . . con María Montera negra horra sobre la venta de una negra angola," 1629–1630, AGN-FNE, Bolívar 14, hojas 882r–884v.

background. Regardless of the extent or duration of ceremonial relationships established by church authorities, the African godparents listed in Havana's baptismal records alone signal the presence of hundreds of African women and men capable of serving as cultural brokers and guides for newly arrived forced migrants with little previous experience of Iberian or Luso-African languages and world views. Sub-Saharan Africans' social integration into early colonial Spanish Caribbean society was in this respect a cyclical process, with African ladinos serving as intermediaries for new arrivals who in time might became Latinized themselves and would in turn serve as intermediaries for those who arrived later. Alonso de Sandoval and Pedro Claver's efforts to evangelize Africans in Cartagena during the early seventeenth century might be seen as episodes of a much broader process in which African migrants, rather than Jesuit missionaries, were the most significant agents of change. The stories of these overlapping waves of diasporic Africans, many of whom acquired Iberian cultural fluency, demonstrate a widespread cultural transformation among generations of enslaved Africans—a cultural transformation in which they themselves extensively participated.

Conclusion

In April 1635, Spanish shipmaster Francisco Fernandez set out from Nicaragua on a routine business trip to Portobelo. Upon reaching the Caribbean coast, he was surprised to discover a "white man" trudging along the shoreline. The stranger immediately surrendered, walking toward Fernandez with his hands behind his head, then sinking to his knees. Though he spoke no Spanish, the stranger repeated one word—*"negro, negro"*—and pointed toward the San Juan River, which emptied into the Caribbean roughly one league away. That night over dinner, the stranger, who Fernandez judged to be English or Dutch, spoke freely in his own language, but the only words intelligible to Fernandez were "Catalina" and "negros." As he spoke, the man continued to gesture in the same direction. Uncertain what he would find, Fernandez set forth the next day in two canoes with seven men: two armed with harquebuses and five Amerindians wielding bows. At the San Juan's mouth, the expedition came across four "Latinized" black men (*negros ladinos*) and another young "Englishman," who was actually Flemish. When Fernandez's group arrived, the four black men quickly came forward, saying: *"Señor,* we are peaceful and slaves owned by the widow of Amador Perez[,] a *veçina* [permanent resident] of Cartagena[!] We are the ones who were stolen by a Dutchman eight or nine months ago [from] our mistress's frigate which was laden with wine[,] bound for the River Magdalena[!]"[1]

Fernandez delivered all six castaways to Spanish officials in Portobelo, where they were promptly interrogated. The four ladino black men were sub-Saharan Africans who identified themselves as Francisco Biafara, Juan Biafara, Damián Carabalí, and Gerónimo Angola. They repeated that they were owned by a wealthy widow in Cartagena. As part of a larger crew of

---

1. "Ynformaçion fecha çerca de la poblaçion que . . . el enemigo Yngles en la Ysla Santa Catalina," May 9, 1635, AGI-SF 223, n.34 (quotes from fols. 2r–3v). A partial transcription and translation of this document can be found in David Wheat, "A Spanish Caribbean Captivity Narrative: Africans Sailors and Puritan Slavers, 1635," in Kathryn Joy McKnight and Leo J. Garofalo, eds., *Afro-Latino Voices: Narratives from the Early Modern Ibero-Atlantic World, 1550–1812* (Indianapolis, Ind., 2009), 195–213.

eleven enslaved Africans and one Spanish pilot, they had worked on her ship, transporting merchandise throughout Cartagena's province. Captured by a Dutch pirate the previous year, the four men—along with their co-workers Pedro Folupo, Baltasar Folupo, Martín Balanta, Andrés Jolofo, Francisco Angola, Juan Angola, and Cristóbal Arará—had been sold as slaves to English colonists on Santa Catalina Island, off the coast of Nicaragua (the pilot was left ashore near Santa Marta). After roughly seven months on the island, the four African sailors had managed to escape. Accompanied by Pedro Folupo, five English deserters, and the young Flemish man, they snuck away in a small launch with a sail.[2]

After two days at sea, they reached the Central American coast, where the Africans' leader Pedro Folupo grew ill and died. They continued along the coast, however, and when the sea destroyed their boat, they left it behind, proceeding on foot. Tensions among the group led to violence, and here their stories diverge. According to the main African deponents Francisco Biafara and Juan Biafara—described as "ladino" and *"muy* ladino," (Latinized and very Latinized) respectively—the Englishmen planned to attack them. They were forced to kill one Englishman in self-defense; three others escaped and had not been seen since. This story was confirmed by the Flemish man, but the remaining English deserter—a soldier named Herbatons, whom Fernandez had first discovered walking along the beach—claimed that the Africans had killed all four of his countrymen. Spanish officials were more interested in the island's population and fortifications than in the possible deaths of four English interlopers or the various heresies the Africans had witnessed, including Bible readings, sermons delivered by a married priest, and the confiscation of their rosaries. As Juan Biafara noted, they had no choice but to attend the sermons, but "neither understood nor wanted to know[,] because [he] and his companions are Christians." The information provided by this small group might have triggered the first of three Spanish assaults on Santa Catalina Island—better known as the short-lived Puritan colony of Providence Island—two months later.[3]

Following their escape from the Puritans and standing before Spanish officials in Portobelo, Juan Biafara and Francisco Biafara had ample incentive to portray themselves as good Catholics and loyal vassals of the Spanish

2. "Ynformaçion," May 9, 1635, AGI-SF 223, n.34. See also Alison Games, "'The Sanctuarye of Our Rebell Negroes': The Atlantic Context of Local Resistance on Providence Island, 1630–1641," *SA,* XIX (1998), 1–21.

3. "Ynformaçion," May 9, 1635, AGI-SF 223, n.34. See also Karen Ordahl Kupperman, *Providence Island, 1630–1641: The Other Puritan Colony* (New York, 1993).

crown; their fluent Spanish and familiarity with Iberian religious culture gave them the means to do so. By identifying themselves as slaves owned by a prominent woman in nearby Cartagena, perhaps they hoped to establish their standing and to obtain her protection. Perhaps they sought assurance that Portobelo officials would return them to Cartagena, where they might have had families and friends. Or, perhaps the nature of their labor as boatmen was simply preferable to other alternatives.[4]

Although the details they provided (and withheld) were likely calculated to ensure the best possible outcome for themselves, the performative aspect of their testimonies, nevertheless, reveals the pivotal roles African forced migrants played within the Spanish Caribbean. Africans quickly adapted to Iberian customs and cultural mores and were more than capable of undertaking the sundry skilled and unskilled labors necessary to ensure the basic functioning of colonial society. Their presence as both an all-purpose workforce and a stable population of ostensibly loyal vassals took on additional importance, as both Iberians and Africans recognized, during an era of growing geopolitical rivalry. Clearly, the Spanish empire was no less complicit in its reliance on slavery and the transatlantic slave trade than any other western European power, and enslaved Africans in the early Spanish Caribbean engaged in many of the same forms of resistance documented by historians of other American colonies. But, the African sailors who testified in Portobelo in 1635 had returned to a Spanish Caribbean world they already knew: a network of port cities and hinterlands in which African migrants like themselves labored, not as chattel, but as surrogate colonists—in effect, a world that often bore more than a passing resemblance to Luso-African societies they might have known beforehand.

The four African sailors who escaped from Providence Island in 1635 point to the existence of an early modern Iberian and African world in which slavery was a means of reinforcing Spanish expansion and strengthening territorial claims overseas. The sailors' testimonies provide an exemplary illustration of the historical problem at the heart of this book: the seemingly paradoxical appearance of black majorities in Caribbean colonies that no longer had important mining or sugar industries or that never had them to begin with. By the late sixteenth century, Spanish Caribbean settlements featured demographic profiles resembling "slave societies" more than

---

4. See Walter Hawthorne, "Gorge: An African Seaman and His Flights from 'Freedom' Back to 'Slavery' in the Early Nineteenth Century," *SA*, XXXI (2010), 411–428; Mariana P. Candido, "Different Slave Journeys: Enslaved African Seamen on Board of Portuguese Ships, c.1760–1820s," *SA*, XXXI (2010), 395–409.

"societies with slaves." Yet, slave labor and large slaveholdings were central in these colonies that clearly were not designed to efficiently exploit local resources or produce export commodities in the most profitable manner.[5]

If the Spanish Caribbean colonies were "slave societies," then they were oriented toward settlement. Though there were certainly attempts to resuscitate industries such as sugar cultivation and pearl fishing, these were for the most part unsuccessful and rarely constituted concerted efforts. Beginning in the final third of the sixteenth century, port cities like Cartagena and Havana thrived as maritime hubs and commercial centers, defending and maintaining the Spanish Atlantic's primary sea roads. Along with the much smaller ports Nombre de Dios and Portobelo, Panama City played an equally vital role as a commercial hub and transit point linking the Pacific world and Peru to the Spanish Caribbean. Though no longer the region's most important urban center, Santo Domingo remained the administrative capital for much of the Caribbean long after the demise of the island's sugar industry. These were the very Spanish Caribbean sites that featured the largest and most dense concentrations of African forced migrants and free people of color by the dawn of the seventeenth century.[6]

Africans' prominence in these seaports was one outcome of their function as surrogate colonists, to some extent echoing previous and contemporary developments in Portuguese colonies off the coast of western Africa. Even before 1570, Africans had not only replaced the Spanish Caribbean's dwindling Amerindian workforce but had also increasingly become the region's de facto townspeople and rural laborers. As was the case in Iberian and Luso-African societies in the Cape Verde Islands, São Tomé, and Luanda, African forced migrants and their descendants took the place of nonelite Iberian workers who either never materialized in significant numbers or almost categorically avoided any form of labor associated with lower socioeconomic status—even if they had performed such labors in Portugal and Spain.

Luso-African ports provide highly useful models for understanding the

5. Franklin W. Knight, "Slavery and the Transformation of Society in Cuba, 1511–1760," in Brian L. Moore et al., eds., *Slavery, Freedom, and Gender: The Dynamics of Caribbean Society* (Kingston, Jamaica, 2001), 76–80; Ira Berlin, *Many Thousands Gone: The First Two Centuries of Slavery in North America* (Cambridge, Mass., 1998), 8–9.

6. I do not believe the term "slave societies" is entirely accurate for the early Spanish Caribbean, given the relatively fluid nature of social relations between slaves and slaveowners. My argument here is essentially a corollary of Knight's point that both colonies oriented toward settlement and colonies oriented toward extraction could be "societies with slaves." See Knight, "Slavery," in Moore et al., eds., *Slavery, Freedom, and Gender*, 72, 78–79.

formations and ground-level structure of Spanish Caribbean societies during the late sixteenth and early seventeenth centuries. Indeed, direct connections between the two regions were precisely what made Africans' roles as colonists possible. In addition to the establishment of Indies fleet trajectories and the reallocation of imperial resources toward major seaports such as Cartagena and Havana during the 1570s, the growth of these port cities was facilitated—and in the case of Cartagena, considerably magnified—by the concomitant growth of the transatlantic slave trade. During the decades after 1570, especially during the era of the Iberian Union (1580–1640), Spain's Caribbean settlements were directly connected to the Cape Verde Islands, São Tomé, Luanda, and smaller ports on the Upper Guinea coast. The sub-Saharan Africans who survived the journey from these various points—and the merchants, mariners, and passengers who transported them—brought precedents for cross-cultural exchange that would soon be replicated or adapted in the context of Spanish Caribbean society.[7]

More than a century of interaction in western Africa, particularly in Upper Guinea and the Cape Verde Islands, had set the stage for social relations between Africans and Iberians in the early Spanish Caribbean. The widespread recognition of specific ethnolinguistic identities in extant Spanish Caribbean sources is easily one of the most visible manifestations of Upper Guinean influence. In taking down Juan Biafara and Francisco Biafara's testimonies, an Iberian scribe *(escribano)* described all eleven African sailors sold to Puritan colonists on Providence Island by Iberian first names and African ethnonyms or toponyms. All six Upper Guinean mariners listed bore ethnonyms ("Folupo," "Balanta," "Jolofo," "Biafara") that can be directly matched with specific Upper Guinean peoples (Floup, Balanta, Wolof, Biafada). The same cannot be said for their coworkers ascribed the West Central African ethnonym "Angola" or the Lower Guinean ethnonyms "Arará" and "Carabalí." Iberians' and Upper Guineans' greater familiarity with one another might help explain the frequency with which the latter are depicted in various Spanish Caribbean sources as leaders encharged with supervising other Africans. Like the enslaved sailors of diverse backgrounds supervised by Pedro Folupo, others worked on estancias under the command of Upper Guinean overseers like Antón Bañol (see Table 11).

West Central Africans brought experiences utterly different from

---

7. On Havana's growth in relation to the Indies fleets, and the various imperial resources diverted toward the city to protect and sustain the fleets, see Alejandro de la Fuente, with César García del Pino and Bernardo Iglesias Delgado, *Havana and the Atlantic in the Sixteenth Century* (Chapel Hill, N.C., 2008).

those of Upper Guinean migrants to the Spanish Caribbean. Portuguese expansion in Angola was relatively recent but it was intense, with Iberian colonists and their allies essentially waging a war of conquest against the region's inhabitants; there was no comparable conflict (or Iberian colonization project) of this magnitude at that time in Upper Guinea. Within just a decade of Luanda's founding in 1575—the same year Cartagena de Indias was officially declared a city—Angola began to export large numbers of enslaved West Central Africans captured in battles between massed armies or enslaved as a form of tribute. Slaving voyages from Angola to the Caribbean were frequent and numerous after the early 1590s; Luanda elites' regular presence on these voyages provides a strong indication of the extent to which Iberian colonialism in Angola and the Caribbean, no less than Angola and Brazil, mutually reinforced one another. A great many of the captives transported on these ships appear to have been children, which might help to explain the speed with which some West Central Africans adapted to Spanish Caribbean society. Of all the newly baptized Africans who reappeared as godparents in Havana's baptismal register later in the 1590s, two-thirds were "Angolas" (see Table 13).

Luanda colonists who came to the Spanish Caribbean as slave ship captains or passengers were heavily implicated in both the forced migration of West Central African captives and the events that led to their enslavement in the first place. During the sixteenth and early seventeenth centuries, many of the Spanish Caribbean's Iberian residents were considered Portuguese, and many had reached the Caribbean as crew members or passengers on slave ships. Although most were involved in slave trafficking in one way or another, and some might have been crypto-Jews fleeing Inquisitorial persecution, their most significant characteristic from the vantage point of early Spanish Caribbean history is that many had previously lived in Luso-African colonies like the Cape Verde Islands and São Tomé: islands that were creolized half a century or more before. Some of these migrants were in fact Luso-Africans, people of African or European ancestry (or both) born or raised in one of Portugal's overseas colonies. Others were free or enslaved sub-Saharan African mariners. Iberian and Luso-African passengers on these voyages were also accompanied by domestic slaves, personal servants, and family members, all of whom were very likely to be either Luso-Africans or sub-Saharan Africans, too. In seaports throughout the early Spanish Caribbean, these migrants constituted part of the region's social fabric and an extension of cross-ethnic contacts that had taken place earlier in western Africa.

Though many examples of African settlers and Luso-African intermediaries are men, free women of African origin played crucial roles in forging early colonial Spanish Caribbean societies. These free women of color rarely wielded a degree of economic or social power comparable to that of *nharas,* the Euroafrican merchants who partnered with European men in various African ports. In the story above, the widow *doña* Mariana de Armas Clavijo—who was probably not a free woman of color—held a social status that more closely approximates that of nharas or donas in coastal western African contexts. She owned eleven slave sailors, the boat they worked on, and presumably the merchandise it carried, in addition to an estancia in Cartagena's interior (see Appendix 2). Yet, in Spanish Caribbean settlements, some free women of color—including sub-Saharan Africans—did own estancias. The free *mulata* Mariana Suaço, described as a slave-owning *vecina* (permanent resident or townswoman, and, in this case, head of household) of Santo Domingo, also owned an estancia southwest of the city, in Nigua (Table 12). In addition to owning rural properties on the outskirts of Santo Domingo, Cartagena, Havana, and elsewhere, free women of color were urban propertyowners, slaveholders, businesswomen, and heads of households. They interacted extensively with Iberian men—frequently less prosperous men, such as impoverished soldiers—providing services as innkeepers, shopkeepers, cooks, and laundresses, and borrowing and loaning money; in one case, a woman described as "mulata" employed an Iberian or Spanish American man to rent out her properties to guests. Iberian men and free women of color often formed families, or joint households, through informal sexual unions and formal marriage. Marriage to an Iberian man gave many advantages to free women of color, and, much like nharas, those who were most successful economically tended to have had one or more Iberian husbands.

Despite their backgrounds as former slaves and forced migrants, many free women of color in early Spanish Caribbean settlements appear to have undergone a rapid transformation in public identity that reflected their increased socioeconomic mobility and status. Examples of free or freed sub-Saharan African women identified as such do exist, but free colored vecinas were usually described by categories of racial and legal status such as "mulata libre" or "morena horra," with no overt mention of their African origins. The modification of one West Central African woman's name from Leonor Anchica to Leonor de Abalos in a series of parish records suggests a path by which African migrants gradually became known by their former owners' Iberian surnames instead of African ethnonyms. This substitution of Iberian surnames partially masks the degree to which African women participated in Spanish Caribbean society as free persons. However, the frequency with which free women of color were ascribed Iberian surnames and markers of race and status, rather than African nations, raises the possibility that this transformation in public identity—from African-born slave to black or free colored vecina—was very common.

The free sub-Saharan Africans who owned farms, orchards, or ranches are perhaps the most straightforward examples of African migrants acting as surrogate settlers in the early colonial Spanish Caribbean (see Table 12). But enslaved workers, too, performed tasks that in Spain would have been done by Iberian agricultural workers. As enslaved sailors, men like Juan Biafara and Francisco Biafara were likely accustomed to a form of maritime slavery that entailed a considerable degree of autonomy and geographical mobility. Yet, if the nature of their labor aboard Mariana de Armas Clavijo's ship was different, some of the conditions of their servitude would not have been entirely foreign to the enslaved farmworkers employed on her estancia in Cartagena's hinterland. Before their capture by a Dutch sea rover and their sale to Puritans, Juan Biafara and Francisco Biafara had been part of a crew of eleven men, all sub-Saharan Africans, accompanied by one Spanish pilot. Other than the pilot, the only authority figure mentioned was their leader, Pedro Folupo. Enslaved farmworkers on Cartagena's estancias during the 1620s and 1630s labored in groups of similar size or larger, perhaps supervised by "at most one measly Spanish overseer." Others worked alongside free black wage laborers or on properties owned by free people of color.[8]

The extensive participation of sub-Saharan Africans in Spain's colonization of the circum-Caribbean created an economically and socially diversified population that does not resemble models of later monoculture slave systems. At the same time, that most of these de facto colonists arrived as involuntary migrants on slave ships makes their participatory roles far more ambiguous than those of voluntary migrants performing similar labors in other settings. It would be inaccurate, or at most only partially accurate, to suggest that enslaved Africans consciously collaborated in the Spanish colonization of the Caribbean. Yet, most of the women, men, and children who survived the transatlantic slave trade to some extent became invested in their settlements' stability and security. Like most Iberian colonists, the Africans and people of African descent who were willing to voluntarily risk

8. Don Jerónimo de Zuazo a S. M., Nov. 1, 1605, AGI-SF 38, r.2, n.73, fol. 3v.

their lives serving the crown—defending Nombre de Dios from English invasion, for example, as Pedro Yalonga did in 1595—were probably relatively few, and those who did so might have had some expectation of reward. Most sub-Saharan Africans and Afrocreoles reinforced Spanish colonization through everyday interactions and activities that seem mundane by comparison, but their cumulative impact on Spanish Caribbean society was of much greater significance.[9]

No less than the free black farmer Bartolomé Arará, who constructed a church on his ranch (see Appendix 2), sub-Saharan Africans identified as ladinos are superb examples of diasporic Africans who created niches for themselves in their new environments, adapting to Spanish rule rather than resisting it. Africans' frequent appearance as godparents at baptisms and weddings (usually as sponsors for other Africans or their children) reveals their widespread participation in Spanish Caribbean society; hundreds of Africans acted as godparents in Havana during the 1590s alone. Regardless of their status as slaves and foreigners, many African forced migrants learned to maneuver, and to pursue their own best interests, within the colonial social order. At the very least, they mastered basic early modern Iberian religious precepts and acquired a rudimentary knowledge of Spanish as it was spoken in the Caribbean.[10]

Latinized Africans like Juan Biafara and Francisco Biafara were adept at negotiating between African and Iberian worlds. Although those multilingual individuals purchased by Cartagena's Jesuit college to serve as professional translators were probably exceptional, African interpreters were regularly employed in criminal cases, investigations, and other judicial proceedings that required testimony from African migrants who had not yet learned Spanish or Portuguese. The extensive presence of Africans well-versed in Iberian customs and language and their vital roles as go-betweens in settlements throughout the Spanish Caribbean do not prove that all en-

9. Henry Kamen, *Empire: How Spain Became a World Power, 1492–1763* (New York, 2003), 488; Regina Grafe and Alejandra Irigoin, "A Stakeholder Empire: The Political Economy of Spanish Imperial Rule in America," *Economic History Review,* LXV (2012), 609–651.

10. In nearly one-third (373) of the 1,223 baptisms recorded in Havana's Libro de Barajas between January 1590 and January 1600, one or both godparents were ascribed ethnonyms indicating sub-Saharan African origin. See also Carla Rahn Phillips, "Twenty Million People United by an Ocean: Spain and the Atlantic World Beyond the Renaissance," in Gauvin Alexander Bailey, Phillips, and Lisa Voigt, "Spain and Spanish America in the Early Modern Atlantic World: Current Trends in Scholarship," *Renaissance Quarterly,* LXII (2009), 38; Jane G. Landers, *Atlantic Creoles in the Age of Revolutions* (Cambridge, Mass., 2010), 5–8, 233–235; Pablo F. Gómez, "The Circulation of Bodily Knowledge in the Seventeenth-Century Black Spanish Caribbean" *Social History of Medicine,* XXVI (2013), 386.

slaved Africans became ladinos—but they do indicate that mechanisms for incorporating newly arrived sub-Saharan Africans into Spanish Caribbean societies existed alongside mechanisms for exploiting their labor. On the ground level—for instance, on ships and estancias in Cartagena's province— acculturated Africans might have been responsible for overseeing either, or both, of these processes. However, in their interactions with new arrivals, African intermediaries could have selectively filtered aspects of Iberian language or culture, translating concepts in ways that were most intelligible or most practical in the context of their own social relationships—contexts that might have had very little to do with their formal roles as godparents or interpreters.

THE EXTENSIVE TRANSATLANTIC slaving networks that flourished during the era of the Iberian Union, connecting Spanish Caribbean settlements to Portuguese outposts and Luso-African societies along the coasts and rivers of western Africa, virtually vanished or were directed elsewhere altogether after Portugal's renewed independence in 1640. The Spanish Caribbean's direct links to sub-Saharan Africa were severed; beginning in the second half of the seventeenth century, slave traffic to the entire region dropped to a fraction of its previous volume, with English, French, and Dutch merchants thenceforth supplying captives to the Spanish Americas via their own slave trade entrepôts. First-generation African migrants soon became minorities in the Spanish Caribbean and, in some areas, free people of color began to outnumber the enslaved. In Cuba, only in the very late eighteenth or early nineteenth century would Africans and people of African descent once again form a demographic majority. But, as Cuba was "Africanized" for a second time, the island's slave labor regime would be modeled after those of non-Hispanic plantation colonies such as Barbados, Jamaica, and Saint-Domingue, rather than vice versa. The African and Luso-African world that had once heavily influenced Spanish Caribbean social formations had not entirely disappeared, but there had been very little direct exchange between the two regions for 150 years. Most enslaved Africans arriving in nineteenth-century Cuba would find themselves laboring on vast sugar and coffee estates that bore very little resemblance to the farms and ranches of the earlier colonial era.[11]

11. On Cuba's rapid demographic growth during the late eighteenth and nineteenth centuries, see Franklin W. Knight, *Slave Society in Cuba during the Nineteenth Century* (Madison, Wis., 1970), 5, 22; Gordon Douglas Inglis, "Historical Demography of Colonial Cuba, 1492–1780" (Ph.D. diss.,

But the African migrants who helped establish permanent Spanish settlements in the Caribbean remained influential long after 1640; their descendants would provide the demographic core—large shares or majorities of the population—of Puerto Rico, Española, Panama, and Cartagena during the late 1600s and the 1700s. Free and enslaved people of color together composed slightly more than half of the inhabitants of urban San Juan, Puerto Rico, in 1673, and, by the 1680s, free people of color alone outnumbered both the white and enslaved populations combined in much of Española. Along with small numbers of people of mixed European and Amerindian descent, free and enslaved people of African origin made up an estimated 80 percent of Panama City's population at the time it was sacked by British privateer Henry Morgan in the early 1670s; the city's African-descended population became even more prominent during the eighteenth century. A similar pattern appears to have unfolded in Cartagena, where, by the 1770s, free people of color constituted more than 60 percent of the province's inhabitants and almost half of the city's urban population. Despite occasional efforts to resuscitate the slave trade after 1640, the demographic legacy of earlier waves of forced migration was of much greater significance as a factor shaping these Spanish Caribbean populations until the late eighteenth century.[12]

Africans' roles as surrogate settlers from the 1500s to the mid-1600s also helps to explain why Spanish Caribbean societies differed so drastically from other European colonies in the region throughout the eighteenth century. By 1750, while neighboring non-Hispanic colonies were beginning to receive the majority of their own enslaved African populations—most of whom would labor on plantations—the Spanish Caribbean contained more

Texas Christian University, 1979), 146–167, 186–190; Pablo Tornero Tinajero, *Crecimiento económico y transformaciones sociales: Esclavos, hacendados y comerciantes en la Cuba colonial (1760–1840)* (Madrid, 1996), 109–140; Matt D. Childs, *The 1812 Aponte Rebellion in Cuba and the Struggle against Atlantic Slavery* (Chapel Hill, N.C., 2006), 54–56; Sherry Johnson, *Climate and Catastrophe in Cuba and the Atlantic World in the Age of Revolution* (Chapel Hill, N.C., 2011), 9; William C. Van Norman Jr., *Shade-Grown Slavery: The Lives of Slaves on Coffee Plantations in Cuba* (Nashville, Tenn., 2013), 147–148.

12. David M. Stark, "'There Is No City Here, But a Desert': The Contours of City Life in 1673 San Juan," *Journal of Caribbean History*, XLII, no.2 (2008), 262; "Relación de las ciudades, villas y lugares de la isla de Sancto Domingo y Española," Apr. 30, 1681, transcribed in Emilio Rodríguez Demorizi, comp., *Relaciones Históricas de Santo Domingo* (Santo Domingo, Dominican Republic, 1957), III, 10–19; Alfredo Castillero Calvo, *Sociedad, economía y cultura material: Historia urbana de Panamá la Vieja* (Panama, 2006), 305–306; María Aguilera Díaz and Adolfo Meisel Roca, *Tres siglos de historia demográfica de Cartagena de Indias* (Cartagena, Colombia, 2009), 16–23. On Spanish American cycles of "Africanization" followed by periods of *mestizaje*—widespread biological and cultural exchanges between peoples of African, European, and Amerindian origin—see Alex Borucki, David Eltis, and David Wheat, "Atlantic History and the Slave Trade to Spanish America," *AHR*, CXX (2015), 437–438, 457–459.

whites (especially in Cuba), who were relative newcomers, and far more free people of color, descended from earlier African and Iberian populations. These white and free colored populations, aided by comparatively small numbers of enslaved workers, continued to perform the same diverse economic activities that had formerly been carried out by sub-Saharan Africans, from farming and homesteading to participation in urban service economies. The earlier influx of Africans established the *hato* (ranching) economy that would thrive during the eighteenth century; free black militias, a key component of late colonial Spanish Caribbean defenses, likewise represented an expansion and codification of sixteenth- and seventeenth-century authorities' reliance upon people of African descent to help protect settlements in the event of an assault. In major ports such as Havana, royal slaves further contributed to eighteenth-century defenses through their toil on massive fortification projects—extensions of the smaller-scale fortifications built by enslaved Africans owned by the Spanish crown, and supervised by royal officials, in the same port cities two centuries earlier. Free black political mobilization and perhaps even slave resistance during the eighteenth and early nineteenth centuries might be viewed not only as a response to immediate oppression but also as a reaction against the sudden reversal of patterns established during this earlier era.[13]

This is not to say that multiple forms of brutality did not exist in the early modern Iberian world or that enslavement and forced migration were any less painful or destructive for sub-Saharan Africans in the sixteenth century than they would be 200 or 250 years later. Some of the most brutish elements of this early Spanish and African world—notably reliance on the transatlantic slave trade—were adopted and extended by other European powers during the seventeenth century. Indeed, plantation colonies scattered around the eighteenth-century Caribbean, and even the harsh slave societies of nineteenth-century Cuba and the antebellum United States,

13. Stanley L. Engerman, "A Population History of the Caribbean," in Michael R. Haines and Richard H. Steckel, eds., *A Population History of North America* (Cambridge, 2000), 494–495; Sherry Johnson, *The Social Transformation of Eighteenth-Century Cuba* (Gainesville, Fla., 2001), 24, 39–70. On ranching, see David M. Stark, *Slave Families and the Hato Economy in Puerto Rico* (Gainesville, Fla., 2015); Andrew Sluyter, *Black Ranching Frontiers: African Cattle Herders of the Atlantic World, 1500–1900* (New Haven, Conn., 2012). On royal slavery, see Evelyn Powell Jennings, "War as the 'Forcing House of Change': State Slavery in Late-Eighteenth-Century Cuba," *WMQ*, 3d Ser., LXII (2005), 411–440; María Elena Díaz, *The Virgin, the King, and the Royal Slaves of El Cobre: Negotiating Freedom in Colonial Cuba, 1670–1780* (Stanford, Calif., 2000). For seminal studies of free people of color in the eighteenth-century Spanish circum-Caribbean, see Kimberly S. Hanger, *Bounded Lives, Bounded Places: Free Black Society in Colonial New Orleans, 1769–1803* (Durham, N.C., 1997); Jane Landers, *Black Society in Spanish Florida* (Urbana, Ill., 1999).

were arguably iterations, if not the direct descendants, of slavery and slave trafficking in the early Iberian Atlantic world.

Yet, although early Spanish Caribbean society was forged by slavery and coerced migration, it was also shaped by the extensive participation of free and enslaved Africans. As cooks, mariners, artisans, herdsmen, agricultural workers, and military effectives, they colonized the Caribbean in lieu of nonelite Iberians who could not or would not travel to Spanish America to perform labors associated with lower socioeconomic status. Iberians commonly recognized African migrants who displayed familiarity with Catholic rites and fluency in Spanish or Portuguese as "Latinized." As permanent residents, propertyowners, and heads of household, with social and commercial networks that might include Iberian partners and spouses, many Africans and people of African descent were also recognized as *vecinos*. The widespread usage of African and Luso-African terms describing economic activities, ages, units of value, occupations, and ethnolinguistic identities—and in some cases, references to African polities and political leaders—reveals that Spanish Caribbean settlements did not just absorb African labor; they were influenced by precedents and contemporary events in Atlantic Africa just as much as by attitudes and customs that originated in western Europe and the Mediterranean world. Attending to this complex Iberian and African past makes the early Spanish Caribbean comprehensible—and, in so doing, illuminates large swaths of a burgeoning, early modern Atlantic world. Without this understanding, we remain much like Herbatons, the English deserter stranded on the coast of Nicaragua in 1635, who could only point vaguely southward, saying, "Negro! Negro!"

APPENDIX 1

Population Estimates, circa 1600

Scholarly works on Spanish colonies in the Greater Antilles and along the southern Caribbean littoral have often observed that Africans and people of African origin outnumbered Iberian residents at various moments during the sixteenth and early seventeenth centuries. To provide an overview of Africans' demographic presence in the region toward the beginning of the seventeenth century, I have compiled known sources and estimates for various settlements during the 1590s, 1600s, 1610s, and sometimes the 1620s, with emphasis on those that provide some means of gauging the size of African and African-descended populations relative to population as a whole.[1]

Excellent original source materials exist for the Greater Antilles, including household census records and relatively detailed population counts for the island of Española in 1606, Jamaica in 1611, and the town of Santiago de Cuba in 1605. For the southern Caribbean mainland, a population count for Panama City in 1607 is equally rich in detail. These sources are well known to historians of each of these respective regions. Since no similar records for Havana or Cartagena de Indias have been discovered, my estimates for these sites are based on a broader range of published and archival sources and necessarily involve a greater degree of speculation. I include Puerto Rico for the purposes of comparison, though early-seventeenth-century sources for the island thus far permit only crude estimates.

First, a note about terminology. Commonly translated as "European colonist," "white settler," "permanent resident," or "head of household," the term *vecino* is a loaded one for anyone attempting to derive population estimates from Spanish- and Portuguese-language sources written during an era for which reliable statistics are basically nonexistent. Historians of Iberian colonies overseas have long employed the practice of multiplying known numbers of vecinos by various coefficients to estimate the total size of white or European populations. One major difficulty with

1. Kenneth R. Andrews, *The Spanish Caribbean: Trade and Plunder, 1530–1630* (New Haven, Conn., 1978), 15, 17, 22, 31–37, 222; María del Carmen Mena García, *La sociedad de Panamá en el siglo XVI* (Seville, 1984), 3–34, 59–61, 89–92, 389; Enriqueta Vila Vilar, with Wim Klooster, "Forced African Settlement: The Basis of Forced Settlement: Africa and Its Trading Conditions," in Pieter C. Emmer and German Carrera Damas, eds., *General History of the Caribbean,* II, *New Societies: The Caribbean in the Long Sixteenth Century* (London, 1999), 166–170; Linda A. Newson and Susie Minchin, *From Capture to Sale: The Portuguese Slave Trade to Spanish South America in the Early Seventeenth Century* (Leiden, 2007), 137–140; Alejandro de la Fuente, with César García del Pino and Bernardo Iglesias Delgado, *Havana and the Atlantic in the Sixteenth Century* (Chapel Hill, N.C., 2008), 107, 172; Isabelo Macías Domínguez, *Cuba en la primera mitad del siglo XVII* (Seville, 1978), 21–22; Juana Gil-Bermejo García, *La Española: Anotaciones históricas (1600–1650)* (Seville, 1983), 40–42, 81–97.

this practice is determining which multiplier to use. In colonial Spanish American contexts, historians have traditionally calculated Spanish or white populations by multiplying known numbers of vecinos by 5. This methodology has proven inaccurate in several cases. Scholars of Puerto Rico prefer multipliers of 6 or 7; studies of Panama City and Venezuela propose coefficients of 3 or 4. In other cases, primary sources clearly use "vecino" to refer to just 1 individual inhabitant. Relying on multipliers to generate estimates thus risks distorting population sizes and misrepresenting the numerical importance of specific segments within broader populations.[2]

A second problem with multiplying the stated number of vecinos by 5 (or any other number) to estimate white or Spanish population figures for a given settlement is that vecinos were not necessarily white or Spanish. Portuguese and free people of color were both very prominent in the early Spanish Caribbean, and, as this study argues in Chapters 3 and 4, members of both groups were absorbed into free Spanish populations through intermarriage and participation in diverse economic activities. Officials often described Portuguese migrants and free people of color by their names, local family connections, and as vecinos and *vecinas,* rather than exclusively employing national or racial descriptions that would distinguish them as intrinsically foreign or racially inferior. Furthermore, even if all heads of household were peninsular Spaniards or Spanish Americans, it does not necessarily follow that every member of their household was also white. It was not uncommon for Iberian men to marry or cohabit with women of African origin, and many households included a mix of free and enslaved people of various backgrounds. The very categories of "vecino" and "Spanish" were fluid, and colonial Spanish Caribbean sources often make it easier to draw distinctions between free and enslaved inhabitants than to distinguish white residents from black residents.[3]

Early colonial Spanish American sources frequently describe Africans and people of African descent in vague terms rendering straightforward interpretation difficult if not impossible. It is often hard to know whether the word "blacks" *(negros),* as used by colonial-era observers, referred only to enslaved people or to enslaved people and free people of color. *Negros de servicio,* which might roughly translate as "servant blacks" or "domestic slaves," presents a similar problem. Does

2. For the observation that simply employing the category "vecino" is likely more accurate than applying some universal multiplier that might further conceal "important racial and social differences," see Alejandro de la Fuente, "Población y crecimiento en Cuba (siglos XVI y XVII): Un estudio regional," *European Review of Latin American and Caribbean Studies,* no. 55 (December 1993), 62–63. For examples of multipliers used to estimate the colonial populations of Puerto Rico, Panama City, and Venezuela, see Elsa Gelpí Baíz, *Siglo en blanco: Estudio de la economía azucarera en Puerto Rico del siglo XVI (1540–1612)* (San Juan, Puerto Rico, 2000), 25; David M. Stark, "'There Is No City Here, But a Desert': The Contours of City Life in 1673 San Juan," *Journal of Caribbean History,* XLII, no. 2 (2008), 278; Mena García, *La sociedad,* 32–34, 65–66; Eduardo Arcila Farias, dir., *Hacienda y comercio de Venezuela en el siglo XVII: 1601–1650* (Caracas, 1986), 49.

3. Stark, "'There Is No City Here,'" *Journal of Caribbean History,* XLII, no. 2 (2008), 262. As Gordon Douglas Inglis observes, historical population counts for colonial Cuba almost always "break down the inhabitants into two major categories: the free and the non-free," rather than racial categories; see Inglis, "Historical Demography of Colonial Cuba, 1492–1780" (Ph.D. diss., Texas Christian University, 1979), 74.

the phrase include free people of color? Does it refer only to urban slaves or to enslaved people in both urban and rural areas? Such questions are further compounded by the fact that the early modern Iberians, Africans, and other peoples who inhabited these places largely did not view their world through these modern classifications of race and legal status. It is often not clear how much urban slave labor blended into rural slave labor, and the deeper one looks the more tenuous the boundaries between slaves and free people of color, or between the latter and Iberians, often appear to have been.

I provide two charts below. The first one (Table 14) summarizes demographic information available for selected circum-Caribbean sites. The data is by no means uniform, consisting primarily of contemporary estimates recorded by Spanish colonial administrators, travelers, and church officials. Although the figures presented in Table 14 are often somewhat vague, they nonetheless indicate that free and enslaved people of African origin comprised numerical majorities in every site listed except Santiago de Cuba and perhaps Jamaica, where they appear to have at least formed significant minority populations. The second chart (Table 15) multiplies stated numbers of vecinos by 5 to estimate Spanish and free colored populations, substituting more specific information whenever possible. Although Table 15 is more speculative, it allows us to imagine—if we keep in mind that the Spanish populations as listed here included many individuals who were only nominally Spanish or would not have been identified as Spanish at all—what these places might have looked like by approximately 1600.

The sites I focus on here are relatively few. The figures presented in these tables completely overlook important towns in Cuba, including Bayamo, Trinidad, Puerto Príncipe, Baracoa, and Sancti Spiritus. Nor are Spanish Florida's Iberian, African, and more significant Amerindian populations included. Venezuela is perhaps an even more glaring omission: Maracaibo, Caracas, Coro, and the island of La Margarita, among others, were important Caribbean settlements linked to Cartagena, Santo Domingo, Veracruz, and elsewhere. Like Florida, Venezuela included significant Amerindian populations; though, by the late sixteenth century, some had been devastated by disease and others were considerably diminished. The same could be said of the province of Santa Marta, which is only briefly alluded to as the site of the wreck of a slave ship, and its towns Riohacha and Tenerife. My figures for Panama City focus on the city and its surrounding district, neglecting Portobelo, Nombre de Dios, the resettled maroon villages of Santiago del Príncipe and Santa Cruz la Real, and other settlements in the provinces of Panama and Veragua (see, for example, Table 10). Other important areas neglected include all of Central America north of Panama—Costa Rica, Honduras, and Guatemala—as well as Yucatán and the entire Gulf of Mexico, including Veracruz and the surrounding lowlands.[4]

4. De la Fuente, "Población," *European Review of Latin American and Caribbean Studies*, no. 55 (December 1993), 59–93; Juan Ignacio Arnaud Rabinal, Alberto Bernárdez Álvarez, Pedro Miguel Martín Escudero, and Felipe del Pozo Redondo, "Estructura de la población de una sociedad de frontera: La Florida española, 1600–1763," *RCHA*, no. 17 (1991), 93–120; Robert J. Ferry, "Encomienda, African Slavery, and Agriculture in Seventeenth-Century Caracas," *HAHR*, LXI (1981), 609–635; Rafael A. Strauss, "Aproximación a una demografía de la esclavitud negra en Venezuela, siglos XVI y XVII,"

In short, it should be very clear that the tables presented here are not representative of the entire population of the early Spanish Caribbean; in fact, they are particularly weak for areas that maintained significant Amerindian populations. However, these figures do provide a good idea of the magnitude of Africans' demographic presence in the core Spanish Caribbean settlements and several smaller towns at the dawn of the seventeenth century.

ESPAÑOLA

1606   Española's governor Antonio Osorio provided a list of 1,117 vecinos, including 49 free people of color and 1 "Indian," residing in Santo Domingo and in several other settlements throughout the island. In this case, "vecino" clearly referred to free heads of household; for many of the people listed, he specifically noted whether they had a spouse, a family, or slaves. However, 12 free people of color described as estancia owners are not listed as vecinos of any urban center; it seems likely that they resided on their rural properties. Osorio also mentioned 40 clergy and calculated a total of 9,648 slaves employed in various forms of labor throughout the island (See Chapter 5).[5]

1611   Supporting recent requests made by Santo Domingo's city council to send as many as 1,000 families of rural workers *(labradores)* from Spain to help populate the interior, the Audiencia of Santo Domingo informed the crown in 1611 that there were no more than 600 Spanish families on the entire island.[6]

circa 1615   According to the traveler and Carmelite friar António Vázquez de Espinosa, the city of Santo Domingo contained 600 "Spanish vecinos," 200 soldiers, "many free *mulatos,"* and "a great quantity of negros y mulatos de servicio" (presumably black and mulato urban slaves). He also mentioned "more than 4,000 slaves owned by the vecinos of Santo Domingo, and many free mulatos" raising livestock and performing agricultural labor on the island. At one point Vázquez de Espinosa

Tierra Firme, XXII, no. 85 (2004), 75–105; Rina Cáceres Gómez, *Negros, mulatos, esclavos y libertos en la Costa Rica del siglo XVII* (Mexico City, 2000); Kent Russell Lohse, "Africans and Their Descendants in Colonial Costa Rica, 1600–1750" (Ph.D. diss., University of Texas at Austin, 2005); Paul Lokken, "From the 'Kingdoms of Angola' to Santiago de Guatemala: The Portuguese Asientos and Spanish Central America, 1595–1640," *HAHR,* XCIII (2013), 171–203; Georges Baudot, "La population des villes du Mexique en 1595 selon une enquête de l'Inquisition," *Cahiers du Monde Hispanique et Luso-Brésilien,* XXXVII (1981), 9–10.

5. "Testimonio de quantos lugares ay en esta ysla," Oct. 2, 1606, AGI-SD 83, r.2, s/n, fols. 33r–69v, transcribed in E[milio] Rodríguez Demorizi, comp., *Relaciones históricas de Santo Domingo* (Ciudad Trujillo [Santo Domingo], Dominican Republic, 1945), II, 374–421. See also Concepción Hernández Tapia, "Despoblaciones de la isla de Santo Domingo en el siglo XVII," *AEA,* XXVII (1970), 315–320; Roberto Cassá, *História social y económica de la República Dominicana* (Santo Domingo, Dominican Republic, 1983), I, 93–100, 103; Cassá, "Cuantificaciones sociodemográficas de la ciudad de Santo Domingo en el siglo XVI," *Revista de Indias,* LVI, n.208 (1996), 637–657.

6. Audiencia de Santo Domingo a S. M., July 17, 1611, AGI-SD 54, r.2, n.71, fol. 1r ("no se hallaran en toda ella de presente mas de hasta seysçientas casas de españoles"). See also Juana Gil-Bermejo García, *La Española: Anotaciones históricas (1600–1650)* (Seville, 1983), 83.

Table 14 Population Estimates for Selected Settlements in the Early-Seventeenth-Century Spanish Caribbean (I)

	Free *vecinos*		Slaves				
	Spanish (?) residents	Free people of color (FPC)	Urban slaves	Rural slaves	Amer-indians	Others	Total
ESPAÑOLA							
1606 (entire island)	1,117 vecinos, including at least 49 FPC, 1 "Indio"		1,468	8,180		40 clergy; 12 FPC estancia owners	
1611 (entire island)	No more than 600 Spanish families						
circa 1615 (Santo Domingo)	600 "Spanish vecinos"	"many free mulatos"	"a great quantity"	more than 4,000		200 soldiers	
PUERTO RICO							
circa 1615	300 "Spanish vecinos"	"very important" for ranch-ing and agriculture		2,000, including some "free mulatos"		300 soldiers	
HAVANA							
circa 1600				3,071 (est.)			
1608	less than 500 veci-nos, not includ-ing FPC or soldiers				Guanabacoa		
1609–1611	600–800 vecinos		4,000–5,000 slaves, including maroons				
circa 1615	more than 1,200 "Spanish vecinos"		"a great quantity"			450 sol-diers, not including officers	
circa 1628				5,600 (est.)			

Table 14 (continued)

	Free *vecinos*		Slaves				
	Spanish (?) residents	Free people of color (FPC)	Urban slaves	Rural slaves	Amer-indians	Others	Total
SANTIAGO DE CUBA							
1605	369 people of unspecified race				76		675
	230 people listed as black, mulato, slave						
JAMAICA							
1611	523	107	558		74	163 children, 75 *forasteros*, 8 (or 10?) clergy	1,510
circa 1615	600	"more than 1,000 black slaves and mulatos"					
PANAMA CITY							
1607	1,173	742	3,721		27	85 mestizos; 149 clergy and monastics	5,897
1610	1,301		3,500				4,801
CARTAGENA DE INDIAS							
1594–1595	800 military effectives		4,000 "blacks"			"many *gente forastera*," soldiers, sailors	
1604–1605	3,000		7,000 *negros de servicio*				
1606			5,000 "blacks and Indians"				
1607					"very few Indians"		
1610					1,569 tribute-paying Indians in the entire province of Cartagena		

| | Free vecinos | | Slaves | | | | |
	Spanish (?) residents	Free people of color (FPC)	Urban slaves	Rural slaves	Amer-indians	Others	Total
1611	500 vecinos		8,000 negros de servicio				
circa 1615	more than 1,500					400 soldiers	
circa 1619–1620			12,000–14,000 negros de servicio				
1622			more than 20,000 "blacks" in city and province				
MOMPOX circa 1606			1,500 "blacks"				
1609	80–90 vecinos						

Sources: "Testimonio de quantos lugares ay en esta ysla," Santo Domingo, Oct. 2, 1606, AGI-SD 83, r.2, s/n, fols. 33r–69v, transcribed in E[milio] Rodríguez Demorizi, comp., *Relaciones históricas de Santo Domingo* (Ciudad Trujillo [Santo Domingo], Dominican Republic, 1945), II, 374–421; Audiencia de Santo Domingo a S. M., July 17, 1611, AGI-SD 54, r.2, n.71, fol. 1r; Antonio Vázquez de Espinosa, *Compendio y descripción de las Indias occidentales,* ed. Balbino Velásco Bayón (Madrid, 1969), 15–18, 34–35, 37–38, 81–84, 219–222; El obispo de Cuba a S. M., Sept. 22, 1608, AGI-SD 150, r.2, n.48, transcribed in Isabelo Macías Domínguez, *Cuba en la primera mitad del siglo XVII* (Seville, 1978), 18–21; Expediente y autos promovido por Mathias Rodriguez de Acosta, visto en Madrid, Jan. 22, 1628, July 9, 1629, AGI-SD 117, s/n; Alejandro de la Fuente, "Sugar and Slavery in Early Colonial Cuba," in Stuart B. Schwartz, ed., *Tropical Babylons: Sugar and the Making of the Atlantic World, 1450–1680* (Chapel Hill, N.C., 2004), 123–124, 142–143; de la Fuente, with César García del Pino and Bernardo Iglesias Delgado, *Havana and the Atlantic in the Sixteenth Century* (Chapel Hill, N.C., 2008), 144–145, 158; de la Fuente, "Introducción al estudio de la trata en Cuba, siglos XVI y XVII," *Santiago,* LXI (March 1986), 165; "Minuta y padrón de la gente y casas de la çiudad de Santiago de Cuba," Oct. 6, 1605, AGI-SD 150, r.2, n.33; Carta del Abad de Jamaica a S. M., July 14, 1611, AGI-SD 177, r.5, n.78, fol. 1v; "Descripción de Panamá y su provincia . . .," (1607), in Manuel Serrano y Sanz, [ed.], *Relaciones históricas y geográficas de América central* (Madrid, 1908), 166–170; María del Carmen Mena García, *La sociedad de Panamá en el siglo XVI* (Seville, 1984), 31, 35–36; Alfredo Castillero Calvo, *Sociedad, economía y cultura material: Historia urbana de Panamá La Vieja* (Panama, 2006), 1033; Alonso de Tapia y Joan de Yturrieta Alcevia a S. M., June 25, 1594, AGI-SF 72, n.91, fol. 2r; Carta de D. Pedro de Acuña, Dec. 11, 1595, AGI-SF 37, r.7, n.145, fol. 1r; Obispo Fray Juan de Ladrada a S. M., June 24, 1607, AGI-SF 228, n.41; Royal cedula addressed to the governor of Cartagena, Sept. 10, 1611, in Richard Konetzke, [ed.], *Colección de documentos para la historia de la formación social de Hispanoamérica, 1493–1810* (Madrid, 1958), vol. II, tomo 1, 179–180; Carta del cabildo secular de Cartagena, Oct. 26, 1619, AGI-SF 63, n.22; Obispo fray Diego de Torres Altamirano a S. M., July 23, 1620, AGI-SF 228, n.78; Don García Giron a S. M., Mar. 28, 1622, AGI-SF 38, r.6, n.176; J[osé] T[oribio] Medina, *Historia del Tribunal del Santo Oficio de la Inquisición de Cartagena de Indias* (Santiago de Chile, 1899), 139; Juan Manuel Pacheco, *Los Jesuitas en Colombia* (Bogotá, Colombia, 1959), I, 249; Julián B. Ruiz Rivera, *Encomienda y mita en Nueva Granada en el siglo XVII* (Seville, 1975), 66–67; Nicolás del Castillo Mathieu, *La llave de las Indias* (Bogotá, Colombia, 1981), 238; Enriqueta Vila Vilar, "Introducción," in Alonso de Sandoval, *Un tratado sobre la esclavitud,* transcription and introduction by Vila Vilar (Madrid, 1987), 20; Antonino Vidal Ortega, *Cartagena de Indias y la región histórica del Caribe, 1580–1640* (Seville, 2002), 266–267; Expediente de la villa de Mompox, 1606, AGI-SF 62, n.106; Obispo Fray Juan de Ladrada a S. M., Apr. 6, 1609, AGI-SF 228, n.47.

included free people of color and slaves in the figure of "more than 4,000"—in another instance, he used this number with reference to slaves alone.[7]

PUERTO RICO

1581–1582   At the beginning of the 1580s, Puerto Rico's governor wrote that there were only 210 vecinos on the entire island. At the same time, according to the island's bishop, San Juan's church served no less than 1,325 *almas de confesión* (that is, parishioners), including 925 "mulatos, mestizos, and free blacks."[8]

circa 1615   Vázquez de Espinosa noted that Puerto Rico's inhabitants included 300 soldiers and 300 "Spanish vecinos," describing "blacks and free mulatos" as "very important" to the operation of cattle ranches and other agricultural activities. He reiterated that San Juan's residents employed approximately 2,000 "blacks and free mulatos" on sugar mills and cattle ranches and in other rural labors.[9]

1644   Bishop Damián López de Haro noted the presence of less than 300 soldiers and less than 200 vecinos (it is not clear whether he was referring to San Juan or to the entire island). In his words, "some say that women alone, including *negras* and *mulatas*," numbered more than 4,000. He also commented that "in the countryside there are many estancias and seven sugar mills, where many vecinos with their families and slaves spend most of the year."[10]

HAVANA, CUBA

1590s   Havana's population doubled in the space of just four years, which one official attributed to the establishment of a channel to bring water from the Chorrera River directly to the city.[11]

circa 1600   Alejandro de la Fuente estimates 350 to 400 slaves employed on sugar mills around Havana and finds evidence of 113 *hatos* (large livestock farms or ranches) and corrals as well as 148 estancias outside Havana between 1578 and 1610. Multiplying the number of hatos and *corrals* (113) by 2.9 (the average number of ranch hands working on hatos in Española and in Santiago in 1605–1606) yields an estimated total

7. Antonio Vázquez de Espinosa, *Compendio y descripción de las Indias occidentales,* ed. B. Velásco Bayón (Madrid, 1969), 34–35. See also Genaro Rodríguez Morel, *Orígenes de la economía de plantación de La Española* (Santo Domingo, Dominican Republic, 2012), 130–136.

8. Gelpí Baíz, *Siglo en blanco,* 21–22, 26–28.

9. Vázquez de Espinosa, *Compendio,* ed. Velasco Bayón, 37–38.

10. Damián López de Haro, *Carta-relación a Juan Díez de la Calle,* ed. Pío Medrano Herrero (San Juan, Puerto Rico, 2005), 94, 124, 176. See also Luis M. Díaz Soler, *Historia de la esclavitud negra en Puerto Rico,* 3d ed. (San Juan, Puerto Rico, 1981), 82.

11. "La çiudad de San Christoval de la Havana, isla de Cuba, sobre que se hagan merced de ocho mill ducados prestados," July 24, 1596, AGI-SD 116, r.3, n.117, fols. 4v–5r. See also de la Fuente, *Havana,* 107; de la Fuente, "Población," *European Review of Latin American and Caribbean Studies,* no. 55 (December 1993), 64–67, 90.

of 328 slaves. Multiplying the number of estancias (148) by 16 (the average number of estancia workers in Española in 1606) yields an estimated total of 2,368 slaves employed on estancias. Assuming 375 slaves were working on sugar mills, these figures suggest an estimated 3,071 rural slaves working near Havana around 1600.[12]

1608   In 1608, Cuba's bishop Juan de las Cavezas estimated that Havana contained less than 500 vecinos, not including soldiers, passers-through, or "blacks and mulatos." This also did not include rural areas or Guanabacoa, "a little town of Indians who keep watch . . . most of whom are already half Hispanicized."[13]

1609–1611   Vecinos testified that Havana was home to "more than 600" or "more than 800" vecinos and "more than 4,000" or "more than 5,000" slaves, with the latter figure including maroons.[14]

circa 1615   According to Vázquez de Espinosa, Havana's population consisted of "more than 1,200 Spanish vecinos," not including "a great quantity of *gente de servicio de negros y mulatos*" (black and mulato urban slaves?) and "passers-through arriving on fleets and galleons." He also mentioned 450 soldiers, not including officers.[15]

circa 1628   Havana residents estimated that, before 1628, there were "more than 350 estancias around Havana" growing "vegetables, yuca and cassava." According to cabildo members, "all the haciendas are operated with slaves, and there is no one else to make use of, particularly on this island, since native-born Indians are lacking." If there were 350 estancias employing 16 slaves each (the average number of enslaved farmworkers employed on Española's estancias in 1606), then approximately 5,600 rural slaves labored on farmland outside Havana during the late 1620s (though some would have probably resided in the city).[16]

12. Alejandro de la Fuente, "Sugar and Slavery in Early Colonial Cuba," in Stuart B. Schwartz, ed., *Tropical Babylons: Sugar and the Making of the Atlantic World, 1450–1680* (Chapel Hill, N.C., 2004), 123–124, 142–143; de la Fuente, *Havana*, 144–145, 158. Although my estimate assumes that people working on hatos and corrals in western Cuba were enslaved Africans or people of African descent—like the black ranch hands who found eleven lost and starving West Central Africans on the hato Guaniguanico, near Cabo San Antón, in January 1590 (see Chapter 2, above)—some might have been Iberians, Amerindians, mestizos, or free people of color, as the 1605 household census of Santiago de Cuba indicates for eastern Cuba. Yet, even halving the estimated 328 enslaved ranch workers would not greatly affect my overall estimate of approximately 3,000 slaves employed in agricultural labor and animal husbandry.

13. El obispo de Cuba a S. M., Sept. 22, 1608, AGI-SD 150, r.2, n.48, transcribed in Macías Domínguez, *Cuba*, 18–21. See also Levi Marrero, *Cuba: Economía y sociedad: El siglo XVII (I)* (Madrid, 1975), III, 53.

14. "Petición de la çiudad de Havana," Mar. 9, 1609 (seen in Madrid on Nov. 14, 1611), AGI-SD 116, r.3, n.124. See also "Papers Bearing on the Negroes of Cuba in the Seventeenth Century," *JNH*, XII (1927), 74–95.

15. Vázquez de Espinosa, *Compendio*, ed. Velasco Bayón, 73–76; Macías Domínguez, *Cuba*, 15–18.

16. Expediente y autos promovido por Mathias Rodriguez de Acosta, visto en Madrid, Jan. 22, 1628, July 9, 1629, AGI-SD 117, s/n; Alejandro de la Fuente, "Introducción al estudio de la trata en Cuba, siglos XVI y XVII," *Santiago*, LXI (March 1986), 165.

1605   According to a detailed census of Santiago de Cuba, the town contained 74 households and 6 hatos in Guantánamo in 1604–1605. The inhabitants of each household are listed individually. Among a total of 675 persons, neither race nor status is specified for 369 residents; another 230 are described as black, mulato, or enslaved; and 76 are listed as Amerindians (2) or *naturales* (74). Notations at the bottom of the document read that it was composed in 1604 and transcribed with corrections in 1605, but "now there are more people in 1606."[17]

JAMAICA

1611   According to the abbot of Jamaica, the island's population in 1611 consisted of 1,510 people: 523 Spanish men and women, 107 free people of color, 558 slaves, 74 Amerindians native to the island, 75 *forasteros* (outsiders or foreigners), 163 children of unspecified race or status, and 8 clergy (presumably the remaining 2 inhabitants were additional clergy, including himself).[18]

circa 1615   Vázquez de Espinosa wrote that the village of La Vega was home to 500 "Spanish vecinos" and that "more than 1,000 *esclavos negros y mulatos*"—which could be translated as either "black and mulato slaves" or as "black slaves and mulatos"—were employed on ranches and farms on the island.[19]

PANAMA CITY

1607   According to the "Descripción de Panamá y su provincia" (1607), Panama City's population was composed of 5,897 inhabitants, including 2,176 free people of all racial descriptions (37 percent) and 3,721 enslaved inhabitants (63 percent), with nearly all members of the latter group described as "black," except for a few "mulatos" (10 men and 15 women). The free "Spanish" population of 1,173 individuals included 495 ostensibly Spanish men, 31 Portuguese men, 18 Italian men, 2 Flemish men, 2 French men, 156 boys (aged 16 or under), 303 Spanish women (of whom 78 were "creoles" born in the Americas), and 166 girls (aged 14 or younger). There were 742 free people of color, including 79 *quarterones* (quadroons)—this term does not appear to have been in common usage at the time, and its appearance here is something of an anomaly—(11 men, 17 women, 20 boys, 31 girls); 286 mulatas and mulatos described as *horros,* or freed (69 men, 146 women, 31 boys, 40 girls); 361 negras horras and negros horros (148 men,

---

17. "Minuta y padrón de la gente y casas de la çiudad de Santiago de Cuba," Oct. 6, 1605, AGI-SD 150, r.2, n.33; Marrero, *Cuba,* III, 58–60.

18. Carta del Abad de Jamaica a S. M., July 14, 1611, AGI-SD 177, r.5, n.78, fol. 1v; Andrews, *Spanish Caribbean,* 222n.

19. Vázquez de Espinosa, *Compendio,* ed. Velásco Bayón, 81–84.

165 women, 22 boys, 26 girls); and 16 *zambahigos* or individuals of mixed African and Amerindian ancestry (11 males and 5 females). Other inhabitants of Panama City included 85 "mestizos" (38 men, 26 women, 13 boys, and 8 girls), 27 Amerindians "out of their pueblos" (14 men, 13 women), and 149 clergy and monastics.[20]

1610 The "Descripción de la ciudad de Panamá" (1610) notes that Panama City's population consisted of 4,801 inhabitants, of whom 3,500 were "black slaves" (73 percent).[21]

circa 1615 According to Vázquez de Espinosa, Panama City had 500 "Spanish vecinos," not including passers-through, servants, "blacks," or free people of color *(los entrantes y salientes y demás chusma de servicio, negros y mulatos libres).* In Portobelo, he noted "150 houses of Spaniards, free blacks, and mulatos."[22]

CARTAGENA DE INDIAS

1579–1586 Various sources mention "4,000 *españoles"* (Spanish residents) in Cartagena between 1579 and 1586.[23]

1594–1595 In 1594, Cartagena's royal officials mentioned "many *gente forastera* [that is, foreigners or temporary residents], soldiers and mariners, in addition to 4,000 blacks that are ordinarily in this city." Around the same time (late 1595), Cartagena's population included approximately 800 military effectives, including soldiers. Among the approximately 800 men judged capable of bearing arms, an unknown number—probably less than half—were, in fact, soldiers.[24]

1599 In 1599, Cartagena was described as "the most important and most visited port in all the Indies," with the potential to become "another Venice or Mexico [City]." "Other towns in the area are cities in name only." Santa Marta consisted of "forty or fifty straw shacks." Panama, despite its status as the seat of the Audiencia of Panama is described as "an *aldea* [small village] compared to Cartagena."[25]

20. "Descripción de Panamá y su provincia . . . ," (1607), in Manuel Serrano y Sanz, [ed.], *Relaciones históricas y geográficas de América central* (Madrid, 1908), 137–218, esp. 166–170. See also Andrews, *Spanish Caribbean,* 20, 35; Mena García, *La sociedad,* 25, 30–36, 53–67, 72, 81–82, 90–100; Alfredo Castillero Calvo, *Sociedad, economía y cultura material: Historia urbana de Panamá La Vieja* (Panama, 2006), 860, 870, 1033.

21. Mena García, *La sociedad,* 31, 35–36; Castillero Calvo, *Sociedad, economía y cultura material,* 1033.

22. Vázquez de Espinosa, *Compendio,* ed. Velásco Bayón, 211–215.

23. Carta de don Pedro Fernández de Busto, gobernador de Cartagena, Jan. 27, 1579, AGI-SF 37, r.5, n.26; Irene A. Wright, ed. and trans., *Further English Voyages to Spanish America, 1583–1594: Documents from the Archive of the Indies at Seville Illustrating English Voyages to the Caribbean, the Spanish Main, Florida, and Virginia* (London, 1951), 144. See also María del Carmen Borrego Plá, *Cartagena de Indias en el siglo XVI* (Seville, 1983), 47–48, 473–478.

24. Alonso de Tapia y Joan de Yturrieta Alcevia a S. M., June 25, 1594, AGI-SF 72, n.91, fol. 2r; Carta de D. Pedro de Acuña, Dec. 11, 1595, AGI-SF 37, r.7, n.145, fol. 1r. For a similar estimate of "quatro mill negros y mulatos" in Cartagena, see Carta de don Alonso de Sotomayor, Jan. 23, 1596, AGI-SF 37, n.153a, fol. 1v.

25. Fernández de Medina a S. M., July 1, 1599, AGI-SF 94, n.26, fols. 1r–2r.

1600	In 1600, Cartagena's city council requested authorization to found a Jesuit convent in the city, noting that "there are a great number of blacks who will be indoctrinated and taught with their diligence and help, *con mucho aprovechamiento* [to great benefit]."[26]
1603	Three companies raised in Cartagena were sent out to search for maroons in early 1603; the total number of men in all three companies was "more than 250." One of the companies was composed of free men of color and was led by "Agustin Martin captain of the free blacks."[27]
1604–1605	According to Enriqueta Vila Vilar, one of Cartagena's newly arrived Jesuits estimated in 1604 or 1605 that Cartagena's population included 3,000 "white" inhabitants and 7,000 "negros de servicio."[28]
1606	In 1606, Alonso de Sandoval wrote that there were 5,000 "blacks and Indians" employed on estancias in Cartagena's province.[29]
1606	Mompox vecinos described their village, located up the Magdalena River as home to "more than 1,500 blacks." A royal cedula dated 1606 described Mompox the same way, noting "more than 1,500 blacks and a few Indians."[30]
1607	In Cartagena's province, "there are very few Indians," according to bishop Fray Juan de Ladrada.[31]
1609	Cartagena's bishop Fray Juan de Ladrada wrote that Tolú (on the Caribbean coast, south of Cartagena) and Mompox had a total of approximately 80 or 90 vecinos each. In Tolú, there were "two *doctrinas* [missionary posts] of *yndios* [Indians] and another one of some cattle ranches worked by blacks, and a few yndios."[32]
1610	According to a survey of the indigenous population conducted in 1610, the entire province of Cartagena contained 1,569 tribute-paying Amerindian inhabitants. The total indigenous population, including those who did not pay tribute, was 5,397 individuals.[33]
1611	Cartagena Inquisitors noted the presence of 500 vecinos in the city. The same year, a royal cedula described Cartagena as containing "8,000 *negros del servicio de los vecinos*," plus another "two to four

---

26. Carta de la ciudad de Cartagena a S. M., July 22, 1600, AGI-SF 62, n.84, fol. 7r.

27. Carta de Don Jerónimo de Zuazo, gobernador de Cartagena, a S. M., Feb. 16, 1603, AGI-SF 38, r.2, n.48.

28. Enriqueta Vila Vilar, "Introducción," in Alonso de Sandoval, *Un tratado sobre la esclavitud,* introduction and transcription by Vila Vilar (Madrid, 1987), 20.

29. Juan Manuel Pacheco, *Los Jesuitas en Colombia* (Bogotá, 1959), I, 249; see also Nicolás del Castillo Mathieu, *La llave de las Indias* (Bogotá, 1981), 238–239.

30. Expediente de la villa de Mompox, s/f [est. 1606], AGI-SF 62, n.106.

31. Obispo Fray Juan de Ladrada a S. M., June 24, 1607, AGI-SF 228, n.41.

32. Obispo Fray Juan de Ladrada a S. M., Apr. 6, 1609, AGI-SF 228, n. 47.

33. Julian B. Ruiz Rivera, *Encomienda y mita en Nueva Granada en el siglo XVII* (Seville, 1975), 66–67. See also Ruiz Rivera, *Los indios de Cartagena bajo la administración española en el siglo XVII* (Bogotá, 1995); Adolfo Meisel Roca, "Esclavitud, mestizaje y haciendas en la provincia de Cartagena, 1533–1581," *Desarollo y Sociedad,* IV (1980), 227–277.

thousand" captives arriving in the city every year from "Angola and the Rivers of Cabo Verde and Guinea."[34]

circa 1615   According to Vázquez de Espinosa, Cartagena had "more than 1,500 Spanish vecinos," not including "mestizos, mulatos, free blacks," and "other nations." He noted that the city was growing and that there were also 400 soldiers garrisoned there.[35]

1619–1620   Epidemics of *viruela* (smallpox) and *sarampión* (measles) are said to have killed more than 2,000 slaves. At the same time, Cartagena was judged to have had 12,000 to 14,000 "negros de servicio in this city and its district." Bishop Diego de Torres estimated that Cartagena really depended on only 50 or 60 vecinos; everyone else was either poor or just passing through, only in town to do business while fleets were present.[36]

1622   Governor García de Giron notified the crown that "the blacks of this province and city . . . number more than 20,000."[37]

1634   Bishop Luis de Córdoba Ronquillo estimated "1,500 *veçinos*," including "the homes *[viviendas]* of mulatas and free blacks," in Cartagena and Gethsemani. Because of continuous commerce and royal armadas, there were actually much larger numbers of people who were difficult to count. He estimated there were "more than 3,000 blacks" working on estancias outside Cartagena. The same year, another vecino estimated that there were "12,000 blacks in the city and in its province" capable of bearing arms.[38]

1638   Augustinian friars in Bogotá asked to requisition slaves from ships arriving in Cartagena, noting that "the city and province of Cartagena" already contained "more than 25,000," with most employed in "works of little utility for the common good."[39]

---

34. Castillo Mathieu, *La llave de las Indias*, 238; Royal cedula addressed to the governor of Cartagena, Sept. 10, 1611, in Richard Konetzke, [ed.], *Colección de documentos para la historia de la formación social de Hispanoamérica, 1493–1810* (Madrid, 1958), vol. II, tomo 1, 179–180.

35. Vázquez de Espinosa, *Compendio*, ed. Velásco Bayón, 219–222.

36. Carta del cabildo secular de Cartagena, Oct. 26, 1619, AGI-SF 63, n.22; J[osé] T[oribio] Medina, *Historia del tribunal del santo oficio de la Inquisición de Cartagena de las Indias* (Santiago de Chile, 1899), 139; Obispo fray Diego de Torres Altamirano a S. M., July 23, 1620, AGI-SF 228, n.78. See also Antonino Vidal Ortega, *Cartagena de Indias y la región histórica del Caribe, 1580–1640* (Seville, 2002), 266–267.

37. Don García Giron a S. M., Mar. 28, 1622, AGI-SF 38, r.6, n.176 ("todos los negros de esta provinçia y çiudad que pasan de veinte mill").

38. Obispo fray Luis de Córdoba Ronquillo a S. M., Aug. 10, 1634, AGI-SF 228, n.97, 100; "Testimonio de los autos que formó el gobernador de Cartagena Francisco de Murga," 1634, AGI-Patronato 234, r.7, bloque 2, fol. 361v ("los muchos que ay en esta ciudad y su provinzia que jusga seran mas de doze mill negros que pueden tomar armas").

39. Descalzos de San Agustin, Mar. 4, 1638, AGI-SF 246, s/n ("la mucha copia de negros que ay en la çiudad y provinçia de Cartagena que seran mas de veynte y cinco mill que los mas de estos Esclavos estan ocupados en obras poco utiles al comun y la multitud abunda de manera que se puede esperar algun suçeso de rebelion o alçamiento como lo an hecho muchas veçes quando avia menos").

Table 15 Population Estimates for Selected Settlements in the
Early-Seventeenth-Century Spanish Caribbean (II)

	Spanish	Free people of color (FPC)	Slaves	Amerindians	Others	Total	(FPC + Slaves) as % of Total
[A] Santiago de Cuba, 1605	369	—	230	76	—	675	34.07
[B] Jamaica, 1611	583	135	623	84	85	1,510	50.20
[C] Puerto Rico, circa 1615	1,250	350	1,900	—	300	3,800	59.21
[D] Havana, circa 1610	2,500	875	4,000	40	525	7,940	61.40
[E] Española, 1606	3,535	1,375	9,648	370	405	15,333	71.89
[F] Cartagena province, circa 1605–1611	2,700	800	12,800	1,569	700	18,569	73.24
[G] Panama City, 1607	1,173	742	3,721	27	234	5,897	75.68
TOTAL	12,110	4,277	32,922	2,166	2,249	53,724	69.24
% OF TOTAL	22.54	7.96	61.28	4.03	4.19	100.00	

Sources: See Table 14, and notes [A] through [G] below.

Notes: [A] I assumed that all 369 people who were ascribed no racial classification were "Spanish" and that all 230 people described as "black," "mulato," and "slave" were enslaved. A weakness to this methodology is that it discounts the likelihood that there were FPC in Santiago de Cuba in 1605.

[B] I arbitrarily grouped the 163 children listed in Table 14 as follows: 60 "Spanish," 28 FPC, 65 slaves, 10 Amerindians. If all 163 children were considered "Spanish," then the numbers of FPC and enslaved people combined would have comprised only 44.04 percent of the total population of Spanish Jamaica in 1611. It seems likely that this assessment of the island's enslaved population is low; in any case the numbers of African migrants grew rapidly in the 1610s. Circa 1615, Fray Antonio Vázquez de Espinosa estimated there were "more than 1,000 esclavos negros y mulatos" working on farms and ranches in Jamaica. Moreover, at least twenty-five slave ships disembarked more than 1,000 enslaved Africans in Jamaica between 1610 and 1621. See Antonio Vázquez de Espinosa, *Compendio y descripción de las Indias occidentales*, ed. Balbino Velásco Bayón (Madrid, 1969), 81–84; Enriqueta Vila Vilar, *Hispanoamérica y el comercio de esclavos: Los asientos portugueses* (Seville, 1977), 170n, 256–265.

[C] Vázquez de Espinosa associated "blacks and free mulatos" with rural labor but provided no number for slaves or FPC residing in San Juan. I assume that 50 of the 300 "Spanish vecinos" were FPC. Multiplying by 5 yields estimated "Spanish" and FPC populations of 1,250 and 250, respectively. I also assume that the 2,000 rural workers included 100 FPC, raising the total number of FPC to 350. Given that FPC and mestizos were said to have comprised nearly 70 percent of San Juan's parishioners three decades earlier, this very rough estimate likely undercounts the numbers of FPC in the city. Nor do these figures account for urban slaves, though many who performed rural labor might have actually lived in San Juan or in smaller towns.

[D] Comparing the 1608 estimate of "less than 500 vecinos"—which specifically excluded FPC and soldiers—with estimates of 600–800 vecinos (and 4,000–5,000 slaves, including maroons) in 1609–1611, I assume that by approximately 1610 Havana's population included 500 "Spanish" vecinos, 175 free colored vecinos, and approximately 25 foreign-born vecinos. Multiplying each of these figures by 5 yields an estimated 2,500 "Spanish" residents, 875 FPC, and 125 foreigners; an additional 400 soldiers would bring Havana's free population to 3,900 people. For Havana's enslaved population, I used the lower figure of 4,000 (if my estimate of 3,071 enslaved rural workers in circa 1600 is correct, this would leave almost 1,000 urban slaves). I included an estimate of 40 Amerindians to account for a handful of individuals described as "Indians from Florida" and other sites who appear in Havana's baptismal register and for a small number of people in Guanabacoa who might have still been considered Indians rather than Spanish, mestizos, or mulatos. A total estimated population of nearly 8,000 fits well within the range of 7,000 to 10,000 people residing in Havana and its hinterland at this time, as proposed in Alejandro de la Fuente, with César García del Pino and Bernardo

Iglesias Delgado, *Havana and the Atlantic in the Sixteenth Century* (Chapel Hill, N.C., 2008), 107, 121. However, my estimates suggest that free and enslaved people of African origin together comprised a little more than 60 percent (rather than slightly less than half) of Havana's total population.

[E] Osorio's 1606 report provides relatively detailed numbers of slaves and clergymen but lists everyone else—1,067 ostensibly "Spanish" residents, 49 FPC, and 1 Amerindian—only to the extent that they appear as heads of household (vecinos). But just five years later, the Audiencia of Santo Domingo noted that the entire island contained only 600 "Spanish households." Taken together, these sources indicate that approximately 467 "Spanish" vecinos were either single or cohabited with family members who were not considered "Spanish." Multiplying these 467 mixed households by 5 provides a total of 2,335 individuals; I assume that this number included 535 "Spanish" and twice as many (1,070) FPC and divide the remaining 730 evenly between "Amerindians" (365) and "Others" (365). Multiplying the 600 "Spanish" households by 5 and then adding the 535 "Spanish" individuals who lived in mixed households yields a total estimated "Spanish" population of 3,535. In addition to 49 FPC described as vecinos, Osorio's report lists 12 free black estancia owners. I multiplied these 61 FPC heads of household and propertyowners by 5 (= 305) and added the 1,070 FPC to obtain an estimated total FPC population of 1,375. For slaves, I used Osorio's figures. I added 40 clergy to the hypothetical 365 "others"—presumably foreigners—who resided in mixed households, for an estimated "Other" population of 405. I multiplied the single Amerindian vecino by 5 then added the estimated 365 living in mixed households to obtain a total of 370 Amerindians (this figure is plausible; some might have been brought from the southern Caribbean). Although they might not have been identified as such, mestizos and perhaps Amerindians might have figured within the "Spanish" population as well.

[F] For the province of Cartagena de Indias, we have estimates for the numbers of vecinos in the city of Cartagena itself in 1611, and for the towns of Mompox and Tolú in 1609. I assume that Cartagena's 500 vecinos included roughly 400 "Spanish" and 100 free colored heads of household and that the 160–180 vecinos in Tolú and Mompox combined consisted of 140 "Spanish vecinos" and 20 FPC. These add up to totals of 540 Spanish vecinos (x 5 = 2,700 "Spanish" residents) and 120 free colored vecinos (x 5 = 600 FPC). Estimated numbers of "negros de servicio"—enslaved people based primarily in the city of Cartagena—are fairly consistent for the years 1604–1605 (7,000) and 1611 (8,000); I assume there were 8,000. To this figure, I add most of the 5,000 slaves who Sandoval (1606) estimated were employed on farms within the province, but I subtract 200 to account for FPC working in rural areas. This yields an estimated FPC population of 800 and an estimated total slave population of 12,800 for the whole province. I assume the latter figure included the approximately 1,500 slaves said to have been in Mompox around the same time. To account for soldiers, foreigners, clergy, and monastics, I estimated that an additional 700 "Others" resided in the province, primarily in the city of Cartagena. As with Havana, this population would have been considerably larger while fleets were in port. The Amerindian population of 1,569 includes only those who paid tribute; these estimates do not account for non-tributary Amerindian populations or maroon communities.

[G] Although it refers to Panama City and its hinterland only, the 1607 "Descripción of Panamá" provides the most detailed population count of any Spanish settlement in the circum-Caribbean for the early 1600s; see "Descripción de Panamá y su provincia . . . ," (1607), in Manuel Serrano y Sanz, [ed.], *Relaciones históricas y geográficas de América central* (Madrid, 1908), 166–170. The population glossed here as "Spanish" included 31 Portuguese men, 18 Italian men, and 78 Spanish American "creole" women born in the Americas. The 742 FPC included 79 "quarterones" (this term was evidently used very infrequently; it does not appear in any other source consulted for this study), 286 mulatos horros, 361 negros horros, and 16 "zambahigos" or individuals of mixed African and Amerindian ancestry. The source provides information on the ages, sexes, and marital status of people within each group (among free mulatos and negros, women predominated). "Others" listed here included 85 "mestiços."

APPENDIX 2

Table 16 Bishop Córdoba Ronquillo's Proposed Sites for Agregaciones in Cartagena's Province, 1634

Proposed agregación (aggregation)	Location	Rural propertyowners	Estimated number of slaves	Average slaves per rural property
Mohates	Estancia in Arjona, owned by Doña Mariana de Armas Clavijo	1. Doña Mariana de Armas Clavijo 2. Cristóbal de Castro 3. Andrés de Herrera 4. Martín Sanchez 5–7. Three estancias owned by Juan de Simancas 8. Captain Alonso Quadrado [Cid]* 9. Julián de Molinedo 10. Estancia owned by the convent of Santo Domingo 11. Don Martín Polo 12. Don Juan de Atiença 13. Francisco Dias	"More than 200 slaves and other people"	15.4
Doctrinas (missionary posts) of Bahayre and Turvana	Bahayre, Turvana	1. Francisco de Simancas regidor (cabildo member)* 2. Diego de Mesa 3. Joana Gutierres 4. Don Juan de Espinosa 5. Magdalena de la Cruz, widow	150 slaves	30
Población (settlement) of Indians of Timiruaco	Timiruaco	1. Captain Diego Matute 2. Sipacóa, estancia of Don Sebastián Polo 3. Don Nicolás de los Eras 4. Juan Baptista de Segovia 5. Houses and ranches of the palm grove 6. Captain Diego de Rebolledo* 7. Father Joan Diez, presbyter 8. Don Pedro de Mendoça 9. Diego Caro 10. Simón Marquez 11. Martín Gonçales 12. Houses and ranches of the [S]avaneta 13. Camino de la Barranca	—	—

Table 16 (continued)

Proposed *agregación* (aggregation)	Location	Rural propertyowners	Estimated number of slaves	Average slaves per rural property
		14. Antón del Rio 15. Juan Martin 16. Diego Moran		
Pueblo of Indians of Turbaco	Turbaco	1. Estancia and slaves of Captain Andrés de Banquezel*	—	—
Road to Turbaco	Estancia owned by Diego Gonzalez	1. Diego Gonzalez 2. Captain Diego de Rebolledo* 3. Ambrosio Arias de Aguilera 4. Juan de León del Castillo 5. *Torrezilla* (small tower) owned by Don Francisco Sarmiento 6. *Puerta* (door or entrance) owned by Captain Diego de Matute 7. Doña Agustina de Barros 8. Diego Dias 9. Alférez Mateo de Baldes 10. Don Juan Bonifaz, captain of *la gente de la tierra adentro* (people residing in the interior) 11. Gaspar Martin 12. Houses and ranches adjacent to Gaspar Martin's properties 13. Houses and ranches of the Bijagual 14. Antonio de Prado 15. Don Cristóbal Bermudes de Luna, regidor 16. Doña María de Herrera, widow of Gregorio Ortiz de la Maça	"300 blacks"	18.8
Doctrina on the *camino bajo de Timiruaco y la Barranca*	Estancia owned by Captain Juan Ruiz de la Vega	1. Captain Juan Ruiz de la Vega 2. Juan de Ayala 3. Baltasar Ponce 4. Don Vicente de Villalobos, *alguacil mayor* (chief constable) 5. Juan Baptista de Segovia 6. Don Pedro de Mendoça 7. Diego Bernal de Heredia 8. Juan Dias del Alamo	"220 blacks"	27.5

Proposed _agregación_ (aggregation)	Location	Rural propertyowners	Estimated number of slaves	Average slaves per rural property
Doctrina on the coast between Canoa and Punta Blanca	Estancia owned by Diego Gonzalez	1. Diego Gonzalez 2. Ignacio de Losoya 3. Sergeant Miguel Garçia, surgeon 4. Pedro Ballestas, alférez 5. Captain Antonio Sabariego 6. Juan Peres de Abedillo 7. Doña María de Mesa 8. Doña Lorençana de Acereto 9. Antonio de Barros 10. Alférez Rodrigo de Çarate 11. Filipe de Garmendia 12. Mariana Enriquez 13. Agustín Arará	"230 blacks"	17.7
Doctrina in Cascaxal and Tesca swamp	"The church that Bartolomé Arará has built on his ranch"	1. Estancia owned by Don Juan Maldonado 2. Doña María de Viloria 3. Doña Catalina de Castro 4. Blas de Paz Pinto 5. Juan Camacho	"400 freed blacks and slaves"	—

Source: "Agregacion de estancias a dotrinas," May 2, 1634, AGI-SF 228, n.100a, fols. 1r–3r.

Note: Individuals marked with an asterisk (*) are known to have served on Cartagena's city council.

Africans, Afrocreoles, Iberians, and Others
Baptized in Havana's Iglesia Mayor, 1590–1600

Spanning the decade from January 1590 to January 1600, Havana's earliest extant baptismal register consists of 156 double-sided folios containing 1,223 baptisms. Historians of colonial Cuba have long been aware of the baptismal register's existence, though it has never been analyzed systematically as a source for Havana's early social history. Whereas similar ecclesiastical records for the eighteenth and nineteenth centuries are usually racially segregated, this tome includes both black and white baptisms. There are many months for which no baptisms are recorded, particularly in 1591 and 1592. Given Havana's occasional reliance on itinerant priests to provide basic sacraments, additional baptisms administered in Havana's main church (*iglesia mayor*) during this period might yet be found elsewhere. Surges in the number of baptisms could be explained by the arrival of a priest, an increase in the number of births, or the docking of a ship carrying enslaved Africans who had not been previously baptized. For each individual baptized, the baptismal register lists parents if known (sub-Saharan African migrants were evidently not asked to provide this information); owner, if the person being baptized was enslaved; godfather and godmother; the name of the clergyman officiating at the baptism; and the date the ceremony was performed. Many individuals are described by race, place or nation of origin, occupation, rank, legal status, and marital status. If married, a spouse's name was often provided; other family relationships are frequently mentioned, too.[1]

The chart below lists the number of individuals baptized in Havana between January 1590 and January 1600, by month and year. To highlight the demographic presence of Africans and people of African origin, I have organized the baptisms into four categories: "Africans," "Afrocreoles," "Iberians," and "Others." Although useful for the purposes of this study, it is important to note that these are modern—

---

1. Sagrada Catedral de San Cristóbal de La Habana, "Libro de Barajas: Bautismos, 1590–1600" (abbreviated as CH-LB/B). Digital images of this source are available online at "Ecclesiastical and Secular Sources for Slave Societies," accessed May 1, 2013, http://www.vanderbilt.edu/esss/. See also Ferdinand Stibi, *El Libro de barajas de la Catedral de La Habana* (Madrid, 1974), a genealogical guide that contains limited information on people of African origin. Previous studies that have cited this source include María Teresa de Rojas, "Algunos datos sobre los negros esclavos y horros en la Habana del siglo XVI," in *Miscelánea de estudios dedicados a Fernando Ortiz* (Havana, 1956), II, 1275–1287; Alejandro de la Fuente García, "El mercado esclavista habanero, 1580–1699: Las armazones de esclavos," *Revista de Indias*, L (1990), 371–395; de la Fuente García, "Esclavos africanos en La Habana: Zonas de procedencia y denominaciones étnicas, 1570–1699," *Revista española de antropología americana*, XX (1990), 135–160; Alejandro de la Fuente, with César García del Pino and Bernardo Iglesias Delgado, *Havana and the Atlantic in the Sixteenth Century* (Chapel Hill, N.C., 2008), 8.

not early modern—conceptual categories. It is unlikely that people I refer to here as "Africans" thought of themselves in such a broad fashion in the late sixteenth century. Terms such as "Afrocreole" and "Spanish American" did not exist; the word "creole" *(criollo, criolla)* was used for both people of Iberian origin born in the Americas and for people of sub-Saharan African origin born in the Americas or in Portuguese colonies in Africa. However, while other sources for this era refer to both Spanish American creoles of Iberian origin and Luso-African creoles born or raised in the Cape Verde Islands, São Tomé, and elsewhere, the word "creole" in Havana's baptismal register for the 1590s appears to have only been ascribed to people of African origin born in the Spanish Americas. Individuals of African ancestry born in Iberia were identified as "Spanish" or "Portuguese." My criteria for grouping individuals into each of these four categories—based on their geographical origins, ethnic backgrounds, and racial designations as portrayed by religious officials and scribes in late-sixteenth-century Havana—are outlined below.[2]

AFRICANS

The category "Africans" lists 481 people whom I believe to have been sub-Saharan African forced migrants. This includes 415 individuals who are ascribed African ethnonyms or toponyms, referred to in the baptismal register as "lands" or "castes" (see Appendix 3). It also includes 66 people described at their baptisms as "slaves," or as *negro* (black) or *moreno* (brown)—and, in one case, *mulato*—but for whom no parents are mentioned. The total number of 481 sub-Saharan Africans may be viewed as conservative. This figure is somewhat lower than the only other assessment of the number of enslaved Africans baptized in Havana during the 1590s. Furthermore, relatively few slave ships legally disembarked African captives in Havana during the 1590s. If captives were typically baptized before embarkation (for example, in Luanda), or in their first major port of disembarkation (such as Cartagena), then Havana's baptismal records reflect only a small percentage of the African migrants arriving in Havana during this decade.[3]

2. For "Antona de San Tomé," "Francisca de Cabo Berde," and "Maria de San Tomé"—none of whom, in this case, were described as "creoles"—see the baptisms of Francisca Bioho (Jan. 24, 1593), Domingo negro (Dec. 11, 1593), and Lucresia Angola (Jan. 24, 1599), CH-LB/B, fols. 24v, 36v, 139r. For "Juan Portugues moreno horro" and "Mateo moreno español," see the baptisms of María Angola (Jan. 30, 1594), Mariana esclava (Dec. 28, 1595), and Graçia Bioho (Dec. 28, 1595), ibid. fols. 39r, 70r.

3. For the argument that "between 1590 and 1600, 546 adult African slaves were baptized in Havana," see de la Fuente, *Havana,* 38. One individual who I have included in the "Africans" category was identified only as "Sebastian *mulato esclabo de* Gaspar Peres de Borroto"; see the baptism of Sebastián mulato (Feb. 28, 1593), CH-LB/B, fol. 28r. Alonso de Sandoval noted that, "although it is true that we commonly refer to all of these nations as blacks, they are not all dark-skinned." See Sandoval, *Un tratado sobre la esclavitud,* introduction and transcription by Enriqueta Vila Vilar (Madrid, 1987), 136. For a Balanta man and a Brame woman described as *loro* and *lora* (a term that designated light-skinned persons of color) in Española in 1575, see "Contratadores de Cabo Verde y Guinea con Cristóbal Cayado y otros del reino de Portugal," 1582–1589, AGI-Esc 2A, pieza 2, fol. 495r. For references to royal slaves in Havana during the 1620s and 1630s identified as "Manuel Angola mulato," "Pedro loro Arará," and "Anton Angola loro," see "Lista de esclavos y forzados de su magestad," AGI-Ctdra 1117, section 2, pliego 1, and section 3; "Lista por abecedario de los esclavos y forzados, 1636–1638," Dec. 20, 1638, AGI-Ctdra 1118, n.2A, pliegos 1, 4.

The category "Afrocreoles" refers to children born in Havana—or, perhaps, born in some other location in the Americas but baptized in Havana soon afterward—to parents who were ascribed an African nation or were described as negros, morenos, or mulatos. This category also includes 72 children who were not described by race at their baptism but who were born to mothers described only as "slaves" (I assume that most, if not all, enslaved women in Havana during the 1590s were either African-born or of African descent). Of the 276 individuals identified here as "Afrocreole," approximately 150 had at least 1 sub-Saharan African parent, and 51 had at least 1 Afrocreole parent. At least 3 children were born to 1 sub-Saharan African parent and 1 Afrocreole parent. In the great majority of these cases, the father's name is not provided (*padre no conocido*). In the twenty-two entries in which fathers' identities are specified, nineteen were sub-Saharan Africans and three were Afrocreoles.[4]

In several of these cases, Afrocreole children were born to married couples such as "Anton Bañon and María Bañon his wife," with both parents ascribed the same African ethnonym. Children like Diego and Luis, the sons of Diego Biafara and María Bran, were also born to sub-Saharan African parents of similar background. Meanwhile, the parents of some Afrocreole children were of widely different African backgrounds. In such cases, both parents were usually owned by the same person, though some of these cross-cultural marriages and sexual unions appear to have been voluntary: three individuals baptized in Havana during the 1590s were the children of moreno horro Francisco Mandinga and his enslaved wife, Beatriz Angola. At least three children described as *mulatas* were born to African women, indicating that their fathers were Iberian, or Spanish American, or, relatively light-skinned persons of African origin. Several Afrocreole children were born to free African women, who were especially likely to find partners of similar African background.[5]

4. Sandoval, *Un tratado sobre la esclavitud,* transcription Vila Vilar, 139. Sandoval noted that Africans who would be considered *ladinos* (Latinized) in Spanish America were known as "creoles" in the Cape Verde Islands if they were raised there from the time they were children. People of African origin born in the Cape Verde Islands and known locally as *naturales* were considered "creoles" in Spanish America.

5. For children born to Antón Bañon and María Bañon, see the baptisms of Francisca negra (Nov. 25, 1596) and Diego negro (May 16, 1599), CH-LB/B, fols. 88v, 145r. See also the baptisms of Francisca, daughter of Pedro Bran and Catalina Bran (Oct. 18, 1592), ibid., fol. 18v, María, daughter of María Bran and Domingo Bran (Oct. 10, 1593), fol. 33v, Juana, daughter of Bernaldina Biafara and Juan Biafara (Jan. 1, 1595), fol. 52v, Juana, daughter of Madalena Nalu and Juan Nalu (Sept. 9, 1596), fol. 84r, and Ana, daughter of María Angola and Francisco Angola (Mar. 21, 1599), fol. 142r. For children born to sub-Saharan African parents of similar background, see the baptisms of Diego (Oct. 31, 1593) and Luis (Nov. 12, 1595), sons of Diego Biafara and María Bran, ibid., fols. 34v, 66r, María (Nov. 8, 1592), Baltasar (Feb. 5, 1595), and Felipe (Aug. 17, 1597), children of Juan Caçanga and Ana Çape, fols. 19v, 54r, 107v, Juan (Nov. 26, 1595) and Pedro (May 2, 1599), sons of Pedro Arará and María Terranova, fols. 67r, 144v, Francisco (Oct. 17, 1593) and Ana (Oct. 13, 1595), children of Diego Congo and Madalena Angola, fols. 34r, 85v. For children born to Francisco Mandinga and Beatriz Angola see the baptisms of Luis (Nov. 21, 1592), Baltasar (Aug. 6, 1595), and Marta (Nov. 28, 1599), ibid., fols. 20v, 59v, 153v. For children born to parents of different backgrounds, see the baptisms of Andrés (May 18, 1597), son of

The category "Iberians" refers to Spanish Americans, ostensibly people of Iberian origin, born in the Americas. This category consists of individuals born to parents who are ascribed no racial background or legal status; here, I tentatively presume that these individuals were Iberian or Spanish American and free. I have also included newly baptized children who are not identified by race at their baptism and whose parents are not listed at all. Three completely illegible baptisms performed in December 1592 and January 1596 are also arbitrarily included here as Iberian. These criteria yield a total of 455 children of Iberian or Spanish American origin baptized in Havana during the 1590s.[6]

It should be noted from the outset that this entire category remains problematic for two reasons. First, the formation of "Spanish" families in the early-sixteenth-century Caribbean, just a generation or two before the period under study, involved a considerable degree of racial and ethnic mixture. Second, historians have often assumed that, if people were not ascribed any racial designation in early colonial Spanish Caribbean sources, they must have been of primarily Iberian origin. This assumption is not always accurate. In the context of the early colonial Spanish Caribbean, it masks the presence of free people of color like "Ana de Rojas, wife of Francisco Diaz." Likewise, at her son's baptism in 1593, Francisca Delgada was not listed as a person of African descent, even though her son's godmother was a *morena horra* (free woman of color). However, when Delgada herself served as godmother at baptisms in 1594 and 1597, and when her daughter was baptized in 1599, she was described as "Francisca Delgada morena horra" or "morena." A growing number of such cases indicates that for the late-sixteenth-century Caribbean, "Iberian" (or "white") may be no more useful an analytical category than "black."[7]

OTHERS

Consisting of only eleven individuals, this final category includes the baptisms of several Amerindians—identified in the baptismal register as "Sebastian *yndio* de la Florida," "Alonso yndio de la Florida," "Felipa *yndia*," and "Lucia Yndia de

---

Catalina Angola and Lazaro Caçanga her husband, both owned by doña Madelena de Rojas, ibid., fol. 100r, Juan (July 13, 1597) and Catalina (Nov. 1, 1599), children of Marcos Criollo and Guiomar Angola his wife, both owned by Juan Rezio, fols. 104r, 151v, Isabel (Dec. 8, 1598), daughter of Isabel Nalu and an unnamed "Angola," fol. 135r, and Juan (Sept. 28, 1598), son of María Engola and Francisco Criollo, fol. 131v. Daughters born to María Bran, Beatris Biafara, and Juana Angola were each described as mulatas; see the baptisms of María (Oct. 10, 1593), María (Oct. 1, 1595), and María (Dec. 28, 1599), fols. 34r, 63r, 155v. For children born to morenas horras María Çape, María Bran, Madalena Nalu, Catalina Biafara, Catalina Bañon, and Marçela Biafara (negra horra), see the baptisms of Isabel (July 15, 1590), Luis (Nov. 12, 1595), Juana (Sept. 9, 1596), Marçela (June 15, 1597), Dominga (Sept. 28, 1597), Gerónima (Nov. 19, 1597), fols. 6v, 66r, 84r, 102r, 111r, 115r.

6. Illegible baptisms are on ibid., fols. 21r–21v, 72v.

7. Ida Altman, "Marriage, Family, and Ethnicity in the Early Spanish Caribbean," *WMQ*, 3d Ser., LXX (2013), 225–250. For "Ana de Rojas, wife of Francisco Dias," see the baptism of Cristóbal Arará (May 11, 1597), CH-LB/B, fol. 99v. For Francisca Delgada, see the baptism of her son Pedro (Oct. 28, 1593), her godsons Juan Angola (Dec. 13, 1594) and Francisco (Nov. 6, 1597), and her daughter Catalina (Mar. 4, 1599), ibid. fols. 34v, 48v, 114r, 141v. See also, Chapter 4, above.

Santa Marta"—and three children born to Amerindian parents. It also includes four "newly converted" men who were evidently Protestants or Muslims before their conversion in Havana. One is listed as "Francisco Yngles" (that is, "English," though the term was used rather loosely within the Spanish Caribbean at this time). Another named Juan de la Cruz claimed to have been born in North Africa. No information is given for the other two converts, who took the full names of their godfathers.[8]

8. For Amerindians, see the baptisms of Juana (Nov. 27, 1590), Sebastián yndio de la Florida (Apr. 17, 1594), Lorenço (Aug. 24, 1594), Felipe (July 11, 1595), Alonso yndio de la Florida (July 23, 1595), Felipa yndia (Aug. 1, 1595), and Lucía yndia de Santa Marta (Jan. 20, 1597), CH-LB/B, fols. 11v, 42v, 44v, 57r, 58r, 59r, 92r. For individuals who were presumably Protestant and Muslim converts, see the baptisms of Francisco Yngles (Feb. 12, 1593); Juan de la Cruz, "nuevamente convertido N[atura]l que dixo ser de las partes de Africa en Verberia" (Nov. 1, 1593); Andrés Sanchez de Torquemada "nuevamente convertido" (July 1, 1599); and Antonio Maldonado "nuevamente convertido" (July 8, 1599), ibid., fols. 26v, 35r, 146v. For more information on enslaved North Africans in Havana during the 1590s, see David Wheat, "Mediterranean Slavery, New World Transformations: Galley Slaves in the Spanish Caribbean, 1578–1635," SA, XXXI (2010), 327–344.

Table 17 Africans, Afrocreoles, Iberians, and Others Baptized in Havana, 1590–1600

Year and Month Baptized		Africans	Afrocreoles	Iberians	Others	Total	CH-LB/B folios
1590	Jan	1	2	3		6	1r–1v
	Feb	6	1	3		10	2r–3r
	Mar	2	3	2		7	3v–4r
	Apr	1	1	3		5	4r–4v
	May	13		1		14	4v–6r
	June	7		1		8	6r–6v
	July		1			1	6v
	Aug	4	3	7		14	6v–8v
	Sept	4	4	6		14	8v–10v
	Oct		1	1		2	10v
	Nov		3	4	1	8	11r–12r
	Dec	1	2	3		6	12r–12v
1591	Jan		3	6		9	12v–13v
	Aug	4		4		8	14r–14v
	Sept	5	4	1		10	14v–15v
	Oct		2	3		5	15v–16r
	Nov		3	2		5	16r–16v
1592	Aug			1		1	17r
	Sept		1	3		4	17r–17v
	Oct	1	5	6		12	17v–19r
	Nov	3	5	3		11	19v–20v
	Dec		3	9		12	21r–22v
1593	Jan	13	2	2		17	22v–24v
	Feb	12	7	6	1	26	25r–28r
	Mar	1	1	3		5	28r–28v
	Apr	2	2	1		5	28v–29r
	May		2	1		3	29v
	July	2				2	29v–30r
	Sept	4	5	6		15	30r–33r
	Oct	3	8	7		18	33r–34v
	Nov	2	4	4	1	11	35r–36r
	Dec	4	5	6		15	36r–38r
1594	Jan	2	2	6		10	38r–39v
	Feb	5	2	4		11	39v–40v
	Mar	2	1	4		7	41r–41v
	Apr	2	4	2	1	9	42r–42v
	May	1	1	2		4	43r–43v
	June		1	2		3	43v–44r
	July	1				1	44r
	Aug		2		1	3	44r–44v
	Sept		2	1		3	44v–45r
	Oct	2	1	2		5	45r–45v

Year and Month Baptized		Africans	Afrocreoles	Iberians	Others	Total	CH-LB/B folios
	Nov		1			1	46r
	Dec	10	7	23		40	46r–52r
1595	Jan	4	3	5		12	52–54r
	Feb		3	3		6	54r–55r
	Mar	2	4	5 .		11	55r–56v
	Apr	1				1	56v
	June		1	1		2	56v–57r
	July	4	6	5	2	17	57r–59r
	Aug	9	1	3	1	14	59r–60v
	Sept	11	6	6		23	61r–63r
	Oct	9	3	4		16	63r–65r
	Nov	9	3	7		19	65r–67v
	Dec	9	4	5		18	67v–70r
1596	Jan	23	1	8		32	70r–73v
	Feb	4	3	6		13	73v–75r
	Mar	2	1	12		15	75r–77r
	Apr	6	1	2		9	77v–78v
	May	2				2	78v
	June		1			1	79r
	July	3	2	4		9	79r–80r
	Aug	1	8	10		19	80r–82v
	Sept	13	1	5		19	82v–85r
	Oct	13	3	4		20	85r–97r
	Nov	7	2	7		16	87v–89r
	Dec	5	2	4		11	89v–90v
1597	Jan	9	2	3	1	15	91r–92v
	Feb	10	4	7		21	92v–96v
	Mar	13		4		17	94v–98r
	Apr	2	1			3	98r
	May	10	6	4		20	98v–100v
	June	9	6	3		18	101r–103r
	July	13	3	4		20	103v–106r
	Aug	11	7	7		25	106r–109r
	Sept	4	5	8		17	109r–111v
	Oct	6	6	5		17	111v–113v
	Nov	9	4	10		23	113v–116r
	Dec	9	2	5		16	116r–117v
1598 .	Feb		2	5		7	118r–118v
	Mar	16	2	4		22	119r–121r
	Apr	10	1	5		16	121r–123r
	May	15	3	4		22	123r–125r
	June	9		8		17	125v–127v

Table 17 (continued)

Year and Month Baptized		Africans	Afrocreoles	Iberians	Others	Total	CH-LB/B folios
	July	5		4		9	127v–129r
	Aug	4		3		7	129r–130r
	Sept	5	3	5		13	130r–131v
	Oct	1	1	7		9	131v–133r
	Nov		3	9		12	133r–134r
	Dec	4	8	9		21	134v–137r
1599	Jan	13	4	7		24	137r–139v
	Feb	6	4	5		15	139v–141r
	Mar		5	7		12	141v–142v
	Apr	1	1	10		12	143r–144v
	May	1	3	1		5	144v–145r
	June	1	4	2		7	145r–146r
	July	1	1	1	2	5	146v–147r
	Sept	1	3	4		8	147v–148v
	Oct	6	8	10		24	148v–151v
	Nov	5	3	9		17	151v–153v
	Dec	6	1	11		18	153v–156r
1600	Jan	9	4	5		18	156r–158r
TOTAL		481	276	455	11	1,223	
PERCENT OF TOTAL		39.33	22.57	37.20	0.90	100.00	

Source: CH-LB/B.

Notes: One of the March 1590 baptisms was recorded in CH-LB/M, fol. 26r. Two entries for December 1592 are illegible as a result of a tear in fol. 21r/v; they are arbitrarily counted as "Iberian" here. One of the February 1594 baptisms is located on fol. 41v. One entry on fol. 72v for January 1596 is too faded to be legible; it is arbitrarily listed here as "Iberian." Baptisms for February and March 1597 are not listed chronologically. February 1597 baptisms appear on fols. 92v–94r, 96v, 95r, 94v. The last entry for February 1597 appears to be incorrectly labeled as "28 diciembre 1597." March 1597 baptisms appear on fols. 94v, 96r, 95v, 97r–98r.

APPENDIX 4

Table 18 Sub-Saharan Africans Baptized in Havana by
Ethnonym and Year, 1590–1600

Ethnonym	1590	1591	1592	1593	1594	1595	1596	1597	1598	1599	1600	Total
UPPER GUINEA												
"Bañon" (Bañun)	0	0	0	5	0	2	4	1	7	5	0	24
"Biafara" (Biafada)	1	1	1	2	3	4	3	3	1	3	0	22
"Bioho" (Bijago)	1	0	0	3	2	1	3	0	0	2	0	12
"Bran" (Brame)	9	4	2	12	4	7	6	10	10	4	2	70
"Caçanga" (Cassanga)	0	0	0	1	0	0	0	0	0	0	0	1
"Jolofo" (Wolof)	1	0	0	0	0	0	0	2	1	0	0	4
"Mandinga"	0	0	0	1	1	1	1	1	1	1	0	7
Nalu	1	0	0	0	0	1	0	5	1	0	0	8
"Zape"	2	0	0	3	0	0	3	1	0	0	0	9
LOWER GUINEA												
"Arará"	0	0	0	0	0	0	1	1	0	0	0	2
"Terranova"	0	1	0	2	0	1	0	0	0	0	0	4
WEST CENTRAL AFRICA												
"Anchico" (Ansiku)	1	0	0	0	0	0	1	1	2	1	0	6
"Angola"	19	2	1	8	11	18	32	62	39	23	6	221
"Congo"	1	0	0	1	0	1	3	9	6	2	1	24
"Moçongo"	0	0	0	0	0	0	0	1	0	0	0	1
UNSPECIFIED	3	1	0	5	4	22	22	8	1	0	0	66
TOTAL	39	9	4	43	25	58	79	105	69	41	9	481

Sources: CH-LB/B. For Bañuns, see the baptisms of Ysabel Bañon (Jan. 20, 1593), Ysabel Bañon
(Jan. 31, 1593), Juana Bañon (Feb. 21, 1593), Pedro Bañon (Dec. 28, 1593), Sebastian Bañon (Dec. 28,
1593), Juan Bañol (Sept. 17, 1595), [María?] Bañon (Nov. 9, 1595), Juan Bañon (Feb. 11, 1596), Catalina
Bañon (Sept. 8, 1596), Ysabel Vañon (Dec. 9, 1596), María Banoñon (Dec. 29, 1596), Vitoria Bañon
(Nov. 23, 1597), Francisco Bañon (Mar. 24, 1598), Juan Bañon (Apr. 5, 1598), Francisco Bañon (June 7,
1598), Gaspar Bañon (June 21, 1598), Bartolome Bañon (July 26, 1598), Leonor Bañon (Dec. 28, 1598),
Salvador Baño (Dec. 28, 1598), Francisco Bañon (Jan. 17, 1599), Simon Bañon (Jan. 31, 1599), Pedro
Bañon (Jan. 31, 1599), Pedro Bañon (July 11, 1599), Leonor Bañon (Nov. 7, 1599), fols. 24r–24v, 27r,
38r, 62r, 65v, 74r, 84r, 89v, 90v, 115v, 120r, 121v, 125v, 126v, 129r, 136v, 138r, 139v, 147r, 152v.

For Biafadas, see the baptisms of Xpobal Biafara (Aug. 26, 1590), Barbola de tierra Biafara (Sept. 8,
1591), Mateo Biafara (Oct. 25, 1592), Gaspar Biafara (Feb. 21, 1593), Andres Biafara (Feb. 28, 1593),
Bartolome Biafara (Feb. 6, 1594), Domingo Biafara (Feb. 6, 1594), Filipe Biafara (May 30, 1594),
Hernando Biafara (Sept. 17, 1595), Xpoval Biafara (Sept. 17, 1595), María Biafara (Sept. 25, 1595), Juan
Biafara (Oct. 15, 1595), Domingo Biafara (Sept. 1, 1596), Cathalina Biafara (Oct. 27, 1596), Francisco
Biafara (Nov. 10, 1596), Antonio Biafara (Jan. 5, 1597), Çeçilia Biafara (Jan. 12, 1597), Xpobal Bia[fa]ra
(Feb. 16, 1597), Nicolas Biafara (June 29, 1598), Pedro Biafara (June 29, 1599), Domingo Biafara

(Oct. 17, 1599), María Biafara (Nov. 7, 1599), fols. 8r, 15r, 19r, 26v, 27v, 39v–40r, 43v, 62r–62v, 64r, 83r, 87r–87v, 91r, 95r, 127v, 146r, 150r, 152v.

For Bijagos, see Antonia Bioho (Sept. 9, 1590), Francisca Bioho (Jan. 24, 1593), Juan Bioho (Feb. 28, 1593), Ysabel Bihoo (Dec. 8, 1593), Graçia Bioho (Jan. 30, 1594), Ysabel Bioho (Dec. 11, 1594), Francisco Bihojo (Nov. 12, 1595), Luisa Bioho (Jan. 28, 1596), Diego Bioho (Sept. 1, 1596), Miguel Bioho (Sept. 1, 1596), Antonia Bioho (Sept. 12, 1599), Felipe Bioho (Nov. 28, 1599), fols. 9v, 24v, 27v, 36v, 39r, 47v, 66r, 73r, 82v–83r, 147v, 153v.

For Brames, see Helena Bran (Feb. 4, 1590), Gaspar Bran (Feb. 18, 1590), Catalina Bran (Feb. 25, 1590), Luisa Bran (Mar. 5, 1590), Juan Bran (Apr. 25, 1590), María Bran (May 6, 1590), Francisca Bran (Aug. 19, 1590), Juan Bran (Aug. 22, 1590), Diego Bran (Dec. 18, 1590), Juan de tierra Bran (Aug. 11, 1591), Graçia de tierra Bran (Aug. 25, 1591), Madalena de tierra Bran (Sept. 8, 1591), María de tierra Bran (Sept. 8, 1591), Francisco Bran (Nov. 8, 1592), Leonor Bran (Nov. 29, 1592), Juan Bran (Jan. 6, 1593), Juan Bran (Jan. 31, 1593), Francisco Bran (Feb. 2, 1593), Ysabel Bran (Feb. 14, 1593), Francisco Bran (Feb. 21, 1593), Beatriz Bran (Feb. 28, 1593), Francisca Bran (Feb. 28, 1593), Anton Bran (Apr. 11, 1593), Martin Bran (July 25, 1593), Ysabel Bran (Sept. 29, 1593), Gaspar Bran (Oct. 31, 1593), Catalina Bran (Nov. 21, 1593), Domingo Bran (Feb. 27, 1594), Catalina Bran (Mar. 8, 1594), Anton Bran (July 24, 1594), María Bran (Dec. 26, 1594), Juan Bran (Aug. 20, 1595), Juan Bran (Aug. 20, 1595), María Bran (Sept. 17, 1595), Sebastian Bran (Sept. 17, 1595), Francisco Bran (Oct. 4, 1595), Beatriz Bran (Oct. 15, 1595), Leonor Bran (Nov. 12, 1595), Juan Bran (Jan. 7, 1596), Ysabel Bran (Sept. 1, 1596), Diego Bran (Oct. 6, 1596), Pedro Bran (Oct. 9, 1596), Catalina Bran (Nov. 17, 1596), María Bran (Dec. 9, 1596), Ana Bran (Jan. 19, 1597), María Bran (Feb. 2, 1597), Agustin Bran (Feb. 9, 1597), Juan Bran (Feb. 13, 1597), Malgarita Bran (Aug. 17, 1597), Catalina Bran (Dec. 8, 1597), Catalina Bran (Dec. 15, 1597), Juan Bran (Dec. 27, 1597), Pedro Bran (Dec. 27, 1597), Felipe Bran (Mar. 1, 1598), María Bran (Mar. 23, 1598), María Bran (Mar. 30, 1598), Francisco Bran (Mar. 29, 1598), María Bran (Apr. 5, 1598), María Bran (May 3, 1598), Ynes Bran (May 10, 1598), Bernabel Bran (Aug. 16, 1598), María Bran (Sept. 6, 1598), Antonio Bran (Sept. 6, 1598), Juan Bran (Jan. 3, 1599), Ana Bran (Jan. 10, 1599), María Bran (Jan. 10, 1599), María Bran (May 23, 1599), Bentura Bran (Jan. 6, 1600), Xpobal Bran (Jan. 16, 1600), fols. 2r–3v, 4v, 7v, 12r, 14r–15r, 19v, 20v, 23r, 24v–25r, 26v–27v, 28v, 29v, 32v, 34v, 36r, 40v–41r, 44r, 51v, 60r, 62r, 63v–64r, 66r, 70v, 83r, 85r, 86r, 88r, 89v, 92r, 93r, 94r, 96v, 108r, 116v, 117v, 119r, 120r, 121r, 123v, 129v–130v, 137r, 138r, 145r, 156v, 158r.

For one newly baptized Cassanga, see Antonio Caçanga (Jan. 10, 1593), fol. 23v.

For Wolofs, see the baptisms of Sebastian Jorofo (Sept. 26, 1590), Ysabel Jolofa (Aug. 24, 1597), Anton Julufu (Dec. 28, 1597), Pedro Jolofo (Dec. 30, 1598), fols. 10v, 109r, 117v, 137r.

For "Mandinga[s]," see the baptisms of Francisco Mandinga (Nov. 1, 1593), Francisco Mandinga (Feb. 22, 1594), Blas Mandinga (Mar. 5, 1595), Juan Mandinga (Oct. 20, 1596), Juana negra Mandinga (June 1, 1597), Martin Mandinga (Mar. 8, 1598), Francisco Mandinga (Feb. 14, 1599), fols. 35r, 40v, 55r, 86r, 101r, 119v, 140v.

For Nalus, see the baptisms of Jeronimo Nalu (June 10, 1590), Pedro Nalu (Nov. 12, 1595), Sebastian Nalu (Mar. 23, 1597), Domingo Nalu (Sept. 8, 1597), Martin Nalu (Sept. 8, 1597), Luis Nalu (Nov. 23, 1597), Marta Nalo (Dec. 27, 1597), María Nalu (Aug. 9, 1598), fols. 6r, 66r, 97r, 109v, 110r, 115v, 117r, 129r.

For "Zape[s]," see the baptisms of Diego Çape (June 10, 1590), María Çape (Sept. 9, 1590), Juan Cepe (Jan. 17, 1593), Juana Çape (Mar. 28, 1593), Anton Çape (Oct. 10, 1593), Bartolome Çape (Mar. 31, 1596), Guiomar Çape (Sept. 8, 1596), Anton Çape (Nov. 17, 1596), Guiomar Çape (Mar. 9, 1597), fols. 6r, 9v, 24r, 28v, 33v, 77r, 84r, 88r, 96r.

For newly baptized Lower Guineans described as "Terranoba" and "Arará," see the baptisms of Graçia de tierra Terranoba (Aug. 25, 1591), Manuel Terranoba (Jan. 3, 1593), Susana Teranoba (July 25, 1593), Ysabel Terranoba (Oct. 15, 1595), María Arara (Apr. 21, 1596), and Xpobal Arara (May 11, 1597), fols. 14v, 22v, 30r, 64v, 78r, 99v.

For Ansikus, see the baptisms of Anton Anchico (Aug. 5, 1590), Juan negro Enchico (Apr. 21, 1596), Bitoria Anchica (Jan. 12, 1597), Agustin Anchico (Mar. 15, 1598), Anton Enchico (Apr. 12, 1598), and María Enchica (Feb. 21, 1599), fols. 6v, 78r, 91r, 119v, 122r, 140v.

For West Central Africans described as "Angola[s]," see the baptisms of Ysabel Angola (Jan. 20, 1590), Antonio Angola (Feb. 4, 1590), Ysabel Angola (Feb. 18, 1590), Catalina Angola (Feb. 25, 1590), Lucas Angola (May 6, 1590), Sebastian Angola (May 6, 1590); María Angola (May 20, 1590), Francisco Angola (May 20, 1590), Pedro Angola (May 27, 1590), Francisco Angola (May 27, 1590), Marco Angola (May 31, 1590), Juan Angola (May 31, 1590), Mateo Angola (May 31, 1590), Anton Angola

(May 31, 1590), Xpobal Angola (May 31, 1590), Manuel negro Angola (June 3, 1590), Gaspar Angola (June 10, 1590), Antonio Angola (June 12, 1590), María Angola (Sept. 8, 1590), María de tierra Angola (Aug. 18, 1591), Ysabel de tierra Engola (Sept. 3, 1591), Juliana Angola (Nov. 15, 1592), María Angola (Jan. 6, 1593), Antonio Angola (Jan. 6, 1593), Pedro Angola (Jan. 10, 1593), Agustin Angola (Jan. 31, 1593), Catalina Angola (Feb. 7, 1593), Antonio Angola (Feb. 21, 1593), Bartolome Angola (Apr. 20, 1593), Madalena Angola (Dec. 19, 1593), María Angola (Jan. 30, 1594), Catalina Angola (Feb. 13, 1594), Gonçalo Angola (Mar. 27, 1594), Francisco Angola (Apr. 12, 1594), Antonio Angola (Apr. 12, 1594), Pedro Angola (Oct. 2, 1594), María Angola (Oct. 23, 1594), Francisco Angola (Dec. 11, 1594), Ana Angola (Dec. 11, 1594), Juan Angola (Dec. 13, 1594), Ysabel Angola (Dec. 28, 1594), Manuel Angola (Jan. 6, 1595), Sabina Angola (Jan. 8, 1595), Anton Angola (Jan. 8, 1595), Madalena Angola (Apr. 30, 1595), Luisa Angola (July 30, 1595), María Angola (July 30, 1595), Pedro Engola (Aug. 27, 1595), Lusia [A]ngola (Aug. 27, 1595), Anton Angola (Sept. 15, 1595), Ysabel Engola (Sept. 15, 1595), Francisco Angola (Oct. 1, 1595), Anton Angola (Oct. 1, 1595), Juana Angola (Oct. 15, 1595), María Angola (Oct. 15, 1595), María Angola (Oct. 18, 1595), Antonio Angola (Nov. 9, 1595), Anton Angola (Nov. 12, 1595), Francisco Angola (Nov. 12, 1595), Juan Angola (Jan. 7, 1596), Francisco Angola (Jan. 7, 1596), Juana Angola (Jan. 7, 1596), María Angola (Jan. 7, 1596), Juan Angola (Jan. 14, 1596), Juana Angola (Jan. 22, 1596), Melchor Angola (Jan. 28, 1596), Pedro Angola (Jan. 28, 1596), Felipa Angola (Feb. 18, 1596), Anton Angola (Mar. 3, 1596), Juana Angola (Apr. 7, 1596), Catalina Angola (Apr. 7, 1596), María Angola (Apr. 7, 1596), Juana Angola (May 6, 1596), Francisco Angola (July 28, 1596), Anton Angola (Aug. 11, 1596), Pedro Angola (Sept. 1, 1596), Juana Angola (Sept. 8, 1596), Pedro Angola (Sept. 22, 1596), Pedro Angola (Sept. 29, 1596), María Angola (Oct. 6, 1596), María Angola (Oct. 13, 1596), Teresa Angola (Oct. 13, 1596), Pedro Angola (Oct. 9, 1596), Ynes Angola (Oct. 27, 1596), Ana Angola (Oct. 28, 1596), Francisco Angola (Nov. 17, 1596), Susana Angola (Nov. 17, 1596), Xpobal Angola (Nov. 25, 1596), Juan Angola (Dec. 25, 1596), Juliana Angola (Dec. 26, 1596), Catalina Angola (Jan. 12, 1597), Francisco Angola (Jan. 19, 1597), Lucrecia Angola (Jan. 19, 1597), Anton Angola (Feb. 2, 1597), Luis Angola (Feb. 2, 1597), Antonio Angola (Feb. 2, 1597), Miguel negro Anguola (Feb. 24, 1597), Ysabel Enguola (Mar. 16, 1597), Lucreçia Angola (Mar. 13, 1597), Ophelia Enguola (Mar. 13, 1597), Jeronimo negro Anguola (Mar. 13, 1597), Andrea negra Anguola (Mar. 31, 1597), Luisa Angola (Apr. 13, 1597), María Angola (May 8, 1597), Bitoria Angola (May 8, 1597), Sebastian Angola (May 11, 1597), Francisco Angola (May 11, 1597), Francisco Angola (May 11, 1597), Juan Angola (May 11, 1597), María Angola (May 15, 1597), Lucia Angola (May 18, 1597), Juliana Angola (May 18, 1597), Guiomar Angola (June 1, 1597), Graçia Angola (June 1, 1597), Leonor Angola (June 1, 1597), Ana Angola (June 15, 1597), Juan Angola (June 15, 1597), María Angola (June 22, 1597), Juan Angola (July 6, 1597), María Angola (July 6, 1597), Antona Angola (July 6, 1597), Juan Angola (July 13, 1597), Pedro Angola (July 13, 1597), Francisco Angola (July 13, 1597), Francisco Anguola (July 20, 1597), Diego Enguola (July 27, 1597), María Angola (July 27, 1597), Juana Angola (July 27, 1597), Lucrecia Angola (July 27, 1597), Ysabel Angola (Aug. 3, 1597), Pedro Angola (Aug. 17, 1597), María Angola (Aug. 17, 1597), Madalena Angola (Aug. 17, 1597), Cristina Angola (Aug. 24, 1597), Catalina Angola (Aug. 24, 1597), Juan Angola (Sept. 7, 1597), Anton Angola (Sept. 28, 1597), Felipa Angola (Oct. 5, 1597), Pedro Angola (Oct. 19, 1597), María Angola (Oct. 26, 1597), Juana Angola (Oct. 26, 1597), Sebastian Angola (Oct. 26, 1597), Anton Angola (Oct. 26, 1597), María Angola (Nov. 2, 1597), Juan Engola (Nov. 2, 1597), María Angola (Nov. 9, 1597), Francisco Angola (Nov. 16, 1597), Lucrecia Angola (Nov. 16, 1597), María Angola (Nov. 23, 1597), Ynes Angola (Dec. 21, 1597), Melchor Angola (Dec. 26, 1597), Francisco Engola (Dec. 27, 1597), Pedro Angola (Mar. 28, 1598), Anton Angola (Mar. 28, 1598), Anton Angola (Mar. 28, 1598), Esperança Angola (Mar. 28, 1598), Francisco Engola (Mar. 29, 1598), Marco Angola (Mar. 29, 1598), Felipa Angola (Apr. 12, 1598), María Angola (Apr. 19, 1598), Pablo Engola (Apr. 19, 1598), Ysabel Angola (Apr. 26, 1598), Catalina Angola (Apr. 26, 1598), Costantino moreno Angola (May 3, 1598), Anton Angola (May 3, 1598), Manuel Angola (May 3, 1598), María Engola (May 3, 1598), María Angola (May 10, 1598), María Angola (May 10, 1598), Simon Engola (May 10, 1598), Lucas Angola (May 12, 1598), Migel Engola (May 12, 1598), Ysabel Engola (May 12, 1598), María Engola (May 17, 1598), María Angola (May 17, 1598), Anton Engola (May 17, 1598), Ysabel Angola (June 7, 1598), Catalina Angola (June 7, 1598), Antonio Angola (June 8, 1598), Pedro Angola (June 21, 1598), María Angola (June 28, 1598), Juana Angola (June 28, 1598), Felipa Engola (July 25, 1598), Juan Engola (July 26, 1598), Pedro Engola (July 26, 1598), Catalina Angola (Aug. 16, 1598), Pedro Angola (Aug. 30, 1598), Domingo Angola (Sept. 6, 1598), Pedro Angola (Sept. 20, 1598), Lucia Angola (Sept. 20, 1598), Mateo Angola (Oct. 4, 1598), Andres Angola (Jan. 10, 1599), Pedro Engola (Jan. 10, 1599), Pedro Angola (Jan. 17, 1599), Alexandre Angola (Jan. 17, 1599), Lucresia Angola (Jan. 24, 1599), Juan Engola (Jan. 24, 1599), Pedro Angola

(Jan. 24, 1599), Juan Angola (Feb. 7, 1599), Francisco Angola (Feb. 12, 1599), María Angola (Feb. 14, 1599), Juan Engola (Feb. 28, 1599), Diego negro Angola (Apr. 18, 1599), Francisco Angola (Oct. 10, 1599), Rufina Angola (Oct. 17, 1599), Ysabel Angola (Oct. 24, 1599), Anton Angola (Oct. 24, 1599), Juan Angola (Nov. 14, 1599), Pedro Angola (Nov. 12, 1599), Cecilia Angola (Dec. 5, 1599), Mateo Angola (Dec. 26, 1599), María Angola (Dec. 26, 1599), Gracia Angola (Dec. 27, 1599), María Angola (Dec. 27, 1599), Francisco Angola (Jan. 2, 1600), Francisco Angola (Jan. 6, 1600), Hernando Angola (Jan. 6, 1600), Esperança Angola (Jan. 9, 1600), Xpobal Angola (Jan. 9, 1600), and Baltasar Angola (Jan. 9, 1600), fols. 1r, 2r–3r, 5r–6v, 9r, 14r–14v, 20v, 23r–23v, 24v, 25v, 27r, 29r, 37r, 39r, 40r, 41v–42r, 45r–45v, 47r–47v, 48v, 51v, 52v–53r, 56v, 59r, 60v, 62r–62v, 63v–66r, 70v–71v, 72v–73r, 74v, 75v, 77v, 78v, 80r–80v, 82v, 83v, 84v–86r, 87r, 88r, 89r–92r, 93v, 94v, 95v–96r, 97v–101r, 102r–102v, 103v, 104v–105v, 106v, 107v–108r, 109r–109v, 111r–111v, 112v–113v, 114v–115v, 117r–117v, 120r–121r, 122r, 123r–124v, 125v–127r, 128v–130r, 131r–131v, 137v, 138v–139v, 140r–141r, 144r, 149v, 150v, 152v–153r, 154r, 155r–157r.

For individuals listed as "Congo" and, in one case, "Manicongo," see the baptisms of Mateo Manicongo (June 10–12, 1590), Ysabella Conga (Jan. 10, 1593), Miguel Congo (Aug. 27, 1595), Diego Congo (Sept. 8, 1596), Geronimo Congo (Oct. 6, 1596), María Conga (Oct. 13, 1596), Ysabel Congua (Jan. 25, 1597), Melchora Conga (Feb. 16, 1597), Luçia Conga (Mar. 9, 1597), Anton Congo (Mar. 23, 1597), Ana Conga (June 22, 1597), Manuel Congo (July 6, 1597), Miguel Congo (July 13, 1597), Domingo Congo (Aug. 17, 1597), Mateo Congo (Nov. 16, 1597), Anton Congo (Mar. 28, 1598), Ysabel Conga (Mar. 30, 1598), Gaspar Congo (Mar. 29, 1598), Catalina Congo (Apr. 5, 1598), Pedro Congo (Apr. 12, 1598), Pedro Congo (Dec. 28, 1598), Agustin Congo (Oct. 24, 1599), Francisco Congo (Dec. 26, 1599), Manuel Congo (Jan. 9, 1600), fols. 6v, 23v, 60v, 84r, 85r–85v, 92v, 95r, 96r, 97r, 102v, 103v, 104v, 108r, 115r, 120v–122r, 136v, 150v, 155v, 157r.

For one remaining West Central African described as "Moçongo," see the baptism of Anton Moçongo (Aug. 24, 1597), fol. 108v.

The category "Unspecified" includes newly baptized enslaved people identified only as *negros* or *morenos* (and in one case, *mulato*)—with no African ethnonym, and no parents listed—and who were not described as children or newborns; see the baptisms of María (Mar. 4, 1590), Catalina (May 13, 1590), Juan (June 10–12, 1590), Ale[jandro?] (Sept. 22, 1591), Sebastian (Feb. 28, 1593), Catalina (Sept. 19, 1593), María (Sept. 21, 1593), Catalina (Sept. 26, 1593), Pedro (Oct. 24, 1593), Ysabel (Dec. 18, 1594), Juan (Dec. 18, 1594), Leonor (Dec. 26, 1594), Ana (Dec. 27, 1594), Anton (Jan. 1, 1595), Francisco (Mar. 28, 1595), Anton (July 25, 1595), Mateo (July 25, 1595), María (Aug. 13, 1595), Lucia (Aug. 13, 1595), Ysabel (Aug. 15, 1595), Ana (Aug. 20, 1595), Dominga (Sept. 10, 1595), Leonor (Sept. 17, 1595), Ysabel (Sept. 17, 1595), Bentura (Nov. 5, 1595), Esperança (Nov. 25, 1595), Lucrecia (Dec. 25, 1595), Catalina (Dec. 26, 1595), Lucreçia (Dec. 26, 1595), Simon (Dec. 26, 1595), Francisco (Dec. 26, 1595), Francisco (Dec. 26, 1595), Anton (Dec. 28, 1595), Francisco (Dec. 28, 1595), Mariana (Dec. 28, 1595), Catalina (Jan. 1, 1596), Andres (Jan. 1, 1596), Pedro (Jan. 14, 1596), Guiomar (Jan. 14, 1596), Pedro (Jan. 14, 1596), Mañuel (Jan. 14, 1596), Ysabel (Jan. 14, 1596), María (Jan. 14, 1596), Melchor (Jan. 21, 1596), Francisco (Jan. 21, 1596), Matheo (Jan. 21, 1596), Catalina (Jan. 21, 1596), Simon (Jan. 28, 1596), Lucia (Feb. 4, 1596), Mateo (Feb. 18, 1596), Tomas (Apr. 7, 1596), Manuel (May 1, 1596), Domingo (July 21, 1596), María (July 21, 1596), Ysabel (Sept. 1, 1596), Sebastian (Sept. 22, 1596), Juana (Oct. 20, 1596), Anton (Nov. 25, 1596), Graçia (Jan. 25, 1597), Luis (Feb. 24, 1597), María (Mar. 16, 1597), Marta (Mar. 16, 1597), Mateo (Mar. 25, 1597), Anton (early Apr. 1597), María (June 8, 1597), Pedro (Aug. 10, 1597), Lucia (July 22, 1598), fols. 3v, 5r, 6v, 15v, 28r, 31r, 34v, 50v–51r, 52r, 56r, 58v, 59v–61v, 65r, 67r, 69r–70r, 71r–72r, 73r, 74v, 78r–79v, 83r, 84v, 86v, 89r, 92v, 94v, 95v, 97v–98r, 101v, 107r, 128v.

APPENDIX 5

Table 19 Free People of Color in Havana's Baptismal Records, 1590–1600

	Name	Sex	CH-LB/B fols.	Notes
1	Agustina de Carreño morena horra	F	37r, 41v, 78r	
2	Agustina Xoara [horra?]	F	109r	
3	Ana de Rojas morena horra / libre	F	39r, 71v, 99v	
4	Ana de Salazar mulata horra	F	20r	
5	Ana Maldonado morena horra	F	43r	
6	Ana mulata horra	F	138v, 141v	
7	Anbrosia de Luna mulata horra	F	22v	Recently manumitted; see fol. 12r
8	Beatriz de Cavallos mulata horra	F	140r	
9	Beatriz Rezio morena horra	F	15r, 96v	"esclaba que fue de Ju[an] Recio"
10	Bitoria negra horra	F	27v	
11	Catalina Bañon morena horra	F	115r	
12	Catalina Biafara morena horra	F	102r	
13	Catalina de Bañales morena horra	F	96r	
14	Catalina de Çebadilla morena horra	F	88r	
15	Catalina de Horta morena horra	F	68r	
16	Catalina de los Reyes morena horra	F	78r	
17	Catalina de Morales morena horra	F	31r	
18	Catalina negra libre	F	71r	
19	Catalina Perez morena libre	F	72r, 101v	
20	Dominga Criolla morena horra	F	8v, 18v	
21	Dominga Rodrigues mulata horra	F	9v	Owner of María Çape
22	Fabiana de Balberde morena horra	F	24v	

Table 19 (*continued*)

	Name	Sex	CH-LB/B fols.	Notes
23	Fabiana de Miranda morena horra	F	83r, 85v	
24	Felipa Lopes morena horra	F	119v	
25	Felipa Perez morena horra	F	153v	
26	Felipa Zape morena horra	F	66r	
27	Francisca Criolla morena horra	F	51v	
28	Francisca de Luna morena horra	F	149r	
29	Francisca de Miranda morena horra	F	24r, 66r, 78v, 82v	Owner of Catalina Bioho
30	Francisca de Sepulbeda morena horra	F	26v	
31	Francisca del padre morena horra	F	86r	
32	Francisca Delgada morena horra	F	34v, 48v, 114r, 141v	
33	Francisca Lorenço morena horra	F	32v, 137v	
34	Francisca Rezia morena horra	F	45v, 113r	
35	Gostança Çape morena horra	F	24v	Owner of Ysabel Bañon
36	Jeronima Conga morena horra	F	6v	
37	Juana Alfonso morena libre	F	69r	
38	Juana Angola horra	F	71v	
39	Juana Ba morena horra	F	33v	
40	Juana Bañon morena horra	F	156v	
41	Juana Batista morena horra	F	81v	
42	Juana Costilla morena horra	F	135r	
43	Juana Criolla libre	F	141r	
44	Juana Criolla morena horra	F	157v	
45	Juana de Cepe[des?] negra libre	F	60v	
46	Juana de Soto morena horra	F	66r, 86v	
47	Juana Hernandez morena horra	F	34v	
48	Juana Lopez morena horra	F	84v	
49	Juana Martin morena horra	F	131r	

	Name	Sex	CH-LB/B fols.	Notes
50	Juana morena horra	F	152v	
51	Juana Peñalosa morena horra	F	22r, 42r	
52	[Leo?]nor morena horra	F	74v	
53	Leonor Çape morena horra	F	150v	
54	Leonor de Abalos morena horra	F	145r	
55	Leonor de Raia morena horra	F	136v	
56	Leonor Rodrigues morena horra	F	77v	
57	Luisa Belazquez horra	F	73r, 142v	
58	Luisa Garcia mulata horra	F	116r	
59	Luisa mulata cri[olla?] horra	F	47v	
60	Madalena Criolla morena horra	F	124r	
61	Madalena morena horra	F	32v	
62	Madalena Nalu morena horra	F	84r	
63	Madalena Rodriguez morena libre / horra	F	73r, 94v	
64	Marçela Biafara morena horra	F	43v, 45r, 111r	
65	Mari Fernandes mulata	F	115v	(No owner mentioned)
66	María Batista morena horra	F	121r	Owner of María Bran
67	María Biafara morena horra	F	123v	
68	María Bran morena horra	F	66r	
69	María Çape morena horra	F	6v, 88r	
70	María Corderos morena horra	F	31r	
71	María Criolla morena horra	F	42v	
72	María Cuba morena horra	F	46r	
73	María Gutierres mulata libre	F	63v	
74	María Linba morena horra	F	35v	
75	María Maldonado morena horra	F	114r	

Table 19 (*continued*)

	Name	Sex	CH-LB/B fols.	Notes
76	María Sanchez mulata	F	56v, 66r	Owner of María Angola
77	Marina Hernandez morena horra	F	25r	
78	Rufina Monteo morena libre	F	94v	
79	Vitoria Bran morena horra	F	62r, 121r	
80	Ynes Criolla morena horra	F	3v	
81	Ynes de Figueroa morena horra	F	105r	
82	Ynes de Ganboa morena horra	F	88v	
83	Ynes de Luna morena horra	F	8r	
84	Ynes del Comendador morena horra	F	14v, 66r	Owner of Leonor Bran
85	Ynes Juares morena horra	F	17r, 60r, 68r, 142r	
86	Ynes morena horra	F	127r	
87	Ysabel Belasques morena horra	F	54r	
88	Ysabel Biafara morena horra	F	83r, 87v, 111r	
89	Ysabel Criolla morena horra	F	19r	
90	Ysabel Ganboa morena horra	F	19v	
91	Ysabel Hernandez mulata horra	F	48r, 84r, 141v	
92	Ysabel morena horra	F	27r	
93	[. . . ?] moreno horro	M	19r	Page torn
94	Agustin Çuares moreno horro	M	90v	
95	Alonso Rodriguez moreno horro	M	119v	
96	Anton Bran moreno horro	M	34v, 66r	Owner of Pedro Nalu
97	Antonio Peres moreno horro	M	109v	Owner of Juan Angola
98	Damian moreno libre	M	22r	
99	Diego de Rojas moreno	M	50v	Owner of María de Rojas morena
100	Francisco Çape moreno horro	M	94r	

	Name	Sex	CH-LB/B fols.	Notes
101	Francisco Mandinga moreno horro	M	20v, 103v, 153v	Owner of Juan Angola
102	Gaspar Criollo moreno horro	M	158r	
103	Grabiel Rodriguez moreno horro	M	145r	
104	Hernando Biafara moreno horro	M	1v, 28v, 57v, 58v, 83r, 120v	
105	Hernando Nabara mulato	M	56r	(No owner mentioned)
106	Joan de Ygola moreno horro	M	66r, 136r	
107	Jorge Criollo horro	M	120r	
108	Jorge Rodriguez moreno horro	M	98r, 125r	
109	Juan Criollo moreno horro	M	85v	
110	Juan Ma[. . . ?] moreno horro	M	70v	Owner of Juan Bran
111	Juan Portugues moreno horro	M	39r	
112	Lorenso Gomes mulato	M	51v	(No owner mentioned)
113	Luis Bran moreno horro	M	116r	
114	Marco Criollo moreno horro	M	85r, 111v	
115	Martin negro libre	M	71r	
116	Matheo moreno español	M	70r	
117	Miguel Çape	M	24v	(No owner mentioned)
118	Nicolas Rezio moreno horro	M	96v, 104r	
119	Rodrigo Hernandes mulato	M	38v	(No owner mentioned)

Source: CH-LB/B.

Note: The total number of free people of color listed here is approximate because many individuals appear in the baptismal records multiple times, often in various capacities, such as parent, godparent, spouse, and slaveowner. In some entries, individuals are identified only in vague terms, making it impossible to confirm or reject a match with individuals listed elsewhere in the baptismal register. Thus, some of the individuals listed here could be repeated.

A Note on Sources

This study of western Africa's influence on the early Spanish Caribbean would not have been possible without a rich, preexisting historiography of the region, most of which is published only in Spanish. Although a number of documents are discussed here in English for the first time, readers should be aware that many have already been analyzed—sometimes in considerably greater depth—by historians such as Irene A. Wright, Miguel Acosta Saignes, Leví Marrero, Enriqueta Vila Vilar, Kenneth R. Andrews, Roberto Cassá, Nicolás del Castillo Mathieu, Alfredo Castillero Calvo, María del Carmen Mena García, Alejandro de la Fuente, María Cristina Navarrete, Juana Gil-Bermejo García, María del Carmen Borrego Plá, Carlos Esteban Deive, Elsa Gelpí Baíz, Genaro Rodríguez Morel, Jean-Pierre Tardieu, Antonino Vidal Ortega, and Isabelo Macías Domínguez, among others. This historiography remains essential for anyone attempting to understand the early Spanish Caribbean, and, though my interpretations sometimes differ, my debt to this earlier scholarship is substantial, as I hope my footnotes demonstrate.

The majority of the archival materials cited in this study are housed in the Archivo General de Indias (AGI) in Seville, Spain. Although collections relative to the Spanish Caribbean constitute only a fraction of the AGI's holdings, this archive is by far the most important repository of sources generated in the sixteenth- and seventeenth-century Spanish Caribbean. Voluminous legal investigations regarding smuggling and slave ship emergency landings, among other topics, are found in the section Escribanía de Cámara. I also relied heavily on accounting records drawn up in diverse Spanish Caribbean seaports (Contaduría): dense lists of revenues and expenses that include shipping records, slave rosters, fines levied for crimes and misdemeanors, and information on exports and imports. No less significant were the various types of correspondence that form the vast trove known as Gobierno, especially those pertaining to the Audiencias of Santa Fe and Santo Domingo: letters from governors, bishops, royal officials, ecclesiastical and city council members, and individual clergymen and laypeople—even slaves—addressed to the Spanish crown or to the Council of the Indies.

The Fondo Negros y Esclavos, a collection housed in the Archivo General de la Nación (AGN) in Bogotá, Colombia, was also of fundamental importance for this study. It contains a wealth of legal suits, criminal records, and other types of colonial-era documentation relating to slavery and people of African descent in regions corresponding to the present-day nations of Colombia, Panama, and Venezuela. I was delighted to be able to view some of these files at the AGN on familiar ArchiDOC software. They are also available online, accompanied by very useful indices and abstracts, at http://negrosyesclavos.archivogeneral.gov.co.

Among other parish records housed in the Sagrada Catedral de San Cristóbal de La Habana in Havana, Cuba, the Libro de Barajas (miscellaneous book) of marriages (1584–1622) and baptisms (1590–1600) represents an unparalleled source for early Spanish Caribbean social history. It portrays people of African origin in relation to one another—and in relation to other Havana residents—as godparents, spouses, children, parents, slaves, and even, occasionally, as slaveowners. Digital images of the original documents, and my partial transcriptions of the baptismal register, can be viewed online at http://www.vanderbilt.edu/esss/.

I was also very fortunate to have access to several excellent documentary collections and primary sources in print. For Panama, I drew heavily on Carol F. Jopling's superb collection *Indios y negros en Panamá en los siglos XVI y XVII: Selecciones de los documentos del Archivo General de Indias* (Antigua, Guatemala, 1994). I also frequently relied on abstracts and transcriptions of sixteenth-century Havana town council and notarial records, published in Emilio Roig de Leuchsenring, dir., *Actas capitulares del ayuntamiento de la Habana* (Havana, Cuba, 1937–1946), and María Teresa de Rojas, comp., *Índice y extractos del archivo de protocolos de la Habana, 1578–1588,* 3 vols. (Havana, Cuba, 1947–1957). António Duarte Brásio's *Monumenta missionária africana: África ocidental,* 1st Ser. (Lisbon, 1952–1988), and 2d ser. (Lisbon, 1958–1991)—a twenty-two-volume corpus of documents concerning European missionary activities in Africa—was of great value in helping me view the Spanish Caribbean in light of precolonial African history. A two-volume collection compiled by Beatrix Heintze, with Maria Adélia de Carvalho Mendes, entitled *Fontes para a história de Angola do século XVII* (Stuttgart, Germany, 1985–1988), was also exceptionally useful.

Two additional published sources related to Jesuit missionary activities in Cartagena de Indias deserve special mention. In his treatise *De instauranda Aethiopum salute,* originally published in Seville in 1627, Alonso de Sandoval (1577–1652) discussed the sub-Saharan Africans he encountered in Cartagena, along with evangelization methods and theological arguments that justified his labor. Fascinatingly, Sandoval paid close attention to their ethnolinguistic and historical backgrounds, drawing on information supplied by Jesuits based in Africa, slave traders, and African migrants themselves. I used the most widely available, unabridged, Spanish-language edition, *Un tratado sobre la esclavitud,* with introduction and transcription by Enriqueta Vila Vilar (Madrid, 1987). The beatification proceedings of Saint Peter Claver (1581–1654), published in Spanish as *Proceso de beatificación y canonización de San Pedro Claver, edición de 1696* (Bogotá, Colombia, 2002), edited and translated by Anna María Splendiani and Tulio Aristizábal, are another invaluable source. The proceedings consist of testimonies recorded in Cartagena shortly after Claver's death describing his work among the city's enslaved Africans. These accounts—including several provided by Africans who worked closely with Claver as interpreters—provide tremendous insight into aspects of daily life in Cartagena during the first half of the seventeenth century.

Glossary

Afrocreole People of African origin born within the Spanish Americas. See *criollo*

Afro-Iberian People of African origin born in Spain or Portugal

Agregación (Sp.) The incorporation of additional towns or populations into a nearby *doctrina,* or missionary post

Alcalde (Sp.) Mayor or magistrate

Alcalde mayor (Sp.) Deputy governor or chief local magistrate of a district within a large province.

Alcalde ordinario (Sp.) Municipal magistrate or mayor of a municipality within a larger district

Alférez (Sp.) Ensign or lieutenant

Algarabio (Sp.) Someone from the Algarve (southern Portugal)

Alguacil (Sp.) Constable or sheriff

Amancebamiento (Sp.) Informal sexual union; concubinage

Armador (Sp.) Financial backer or organizer; here, of a slave trade voyage

Arribada (Sp.) Reference to a ship making an unforeseen, emergency landing; commonly used as an excuse to justify contraband trade, including unauthorized slave trafficking

Asentista (Sp.) Holder of an "asiento"

Asiento (Sp.) Agreement or contract; often refers specifically to slave trade contracts

Audiencia (Sp.) High court with the power to govern over a specific region; region under the high court's jurisdiction (for example, the Audiencia of Santo Domingo)

Bambo Small child or infant, especially child captives of very young age arriving on a slave ship (see also *cañengue, cría, cría de pecho*)

Bodega (Sp.) Storehouse or warehouse

Boga (Sp.) Literally, the act of paddling or rowing; specifically refers to labor on an organized system of canoe transportation in which first Amerindians and, later, enslaved Africans hauled merchandise and passengers up and down the Magdalena River

Bozal (Sp.) Non-Iberians who were unable to speak Spanish or Portuguese, and unfamiliar with Catholic practices and other Iberian customs. In the Spanish Caribbean, this term was nearly always reserved for un-Hispanicized, sub-Saharan Africans. In Portuguese, the equivalent term was "*boçal.*"

Cabildo (Sp.) Town council or city council

Cañengue (Kimbundu?); small boy or young child; also spelled *canengue*

Capitán (Sp.) Captain; term signifying military rank or shipboard authority but also, at times, an honorary title; leaders of free black militias and commanders of enslaved African work crews

Capitão-mor (Port.) Captain-major

Cargador (Sp.) Person responsible for loading merchandise—or African captives—onto a ship

Chalona Term used on the Upper Guinea coast (tchalona) to refer to an African interpreter. See also "negro chalán"

Chapetón, Chapetona (Sp.) Newly arrived migrant from Spain; "greenhorn"

Conuco (Sp.) Originally a Taíno term for small, raised mounds of soil used for growing vegetables; later, a small garden or cultivated plot of land

Corral (Sp.) Enclosure for raising livestock, often pigs

Cría (Sp.) Infant

Cría de pecho (Sp.) Nursing infant

Criado, Criada (Sp.) Servant

Criatura (Sp.) Small child

Criollo, Criolla (Sp.) "Creole"; typically, a person of African or Iberian origin born in the Spanish Americas. Among adults, creoles of African descent were usually outnumbered by sub-Saharan Africans, who were ascribed ethnonyms instead. During the late sixteenth and early seventeenth centuries, the term was used regularly to describe people of African origin but far less frequently for locally born people of Iberian ancestry.

Criollo de Cabo Verde (Sp.) "Creole of Cape Verde"; person, usually of African descent, born in the Cape Verde Islands. According to Sandoval, this could also refer to a sub-Saharan African born on the Upper Guinean mainland but brought to the Cape Verde Islands as a child and subsequently raised there.

Criollo del monte (Sp.) People of African origin born in the Americas but beyond the fringes of Spanish colonial society; children born in maroon communities

Criollo de San Tomé (Sp.) "Creole of São Tomé"; person, usually of African ancestry, born on the islands of São Tomé or Príncipe

De ley (Sp.) High quality or authentic, especially with reference to gold or silver; in the Spanish Caribbean, enslaved Upper Guineans were considered *negros de ley,* or "top quality blacks"

Doctrina (Sp.) Non-Iberian population center designated as a site for periodical evangelization; a missionary post, usually an Amerindian town that did not yet belong to a Catholic parish or curate but was visited regularly by a priest

Donzella (Sp.) Maiden

Ducado (Sp.) Ducat; gold coin worth 375 *maravedís*

Esclavo, Esclava (Sp.) Slave (in Portuguese, *escravo*)

Español, Española (Sp.) "Spanish"; also the island Española, or Hispaniola

Estancia (Sp.) Farm

Fanega (Sp.) Measurement for (1) land, ranging anywhere from half of 1 square hectare (a little more than 1 square acre) to 3.5 hectares (nearly 9 acres), depending on location; and (2) the volume of grains or cereals, typically around 55 liters, or 1.5 bushels

Farim (Mande) Mande title indicating regional political authority; roughly equivalent to "governor"

Feitoria (Port.) Overseas "factory" or commercial outpost

Fidalgo (Port.) Noble or individual of high social and political standing (in Spanish, *hidalgo*)

Forzado (Sp.) Convict laborer (in Portuguese, *degredado*)

Gampisa (Biafada) Renegade or bandit who kidnapped people and sold them into slavery

Grumete (Sp., Port.) "Grometto"; in Spanish, an apprentice seaman whose rank was higher than that of a page or cabin boy *(paje)*; in Portuguese, particularly in coastal western African contexts, the individuals who performed a wide range of tasks for Iberian merchants and ship captains, such as pilots, interpreters, mariners, stevedores, and slave ship guards

Hato (Sp.) Ranch for raising livestock, often cattle

Hembra (Sp.) Female

Herrero (Sp.) Blacksmith

Hombre del campo (Sp.) "Man of the countryside," a person of middling or higher status who typically lived in an urban settlement but whose wealth was based on the ownership of rural properties operated by hired workers or slaves

Horro, Horra (Sp.) Freed; often used interchangeably with *libre* (free)

Hortaliza (Sp.) Vegetables; produce

Indio, India (Sp.) "Indian"; Amerindian

Ingenio (Sp.) Sugar mill or sugar estate (in Portuguese, *engenho*)

Jornalero (Sp.) Day laborer or agricultural worker who possessed neither land, nor farming implements, nor work animals. Synonymous with *trabajador*

Kikumba (Kimbundu?) West Central African term designating an army's baggage train, including porters, family members, and other noncombatants; these could be very large and often constituted the most valuable spoils of war for victorious opposing armies

Labrador (Sp.) Rural worker or peasant farmer who possessed draft animals, farming tools, or their own plot of land

Lançado (Port.) See *tangomão*

Libre (Sp.) Free; often used interchangeably with *horra* or *horro* (freed)

Ladino, Ladina (Sp., Port.) "Latinized," referring to a person of non-Iberian origin who had acquired substantial familiarity with Iberian culture and values, particularly as manifested by fluency in Spanish or Portuguese and participation in the Catholic church; the opposite of *bozal*

Licenciado (Sp.) Person who holds a "license" or degree; a graduate of an institution of higher education

Loro, Lora (Sp.) Light brown or tawny skin tone. Used less frequently than *mulato,* this term might have referred to slightly lighter skin or might have simply carried a more positive connotation, like *moreno,* as opposed to *negro.*

Lower Guinea Vast coastal region of West Africa stretching from Cape Palmas in present-day Liberia to the Cross River estuary in southeastern Nigeria, encompassing the Bights of Benin and Biafra. The major slave trading areas in Lower Guinea during the sixteenth and early seventeenth centuries were Arda, or Ardra (Allada), and Carabalí (Calabar).

Lower Guinean People who originated in Lower Guinea, typically described in Spanish Caribbean sources as "Arda," "Carabalí," and "Terranova" or "Lucumí"

Luso-African Individuals of African, Iberian, or mixed African and Iberian origin born in Portuguese colonies in Africa, such as Angola, or in islands along the African coast, including the Cape Verde Islands and São Tomé; also Portuguese persons who resided in sub-Saharan Africa for many years

Maestre (Sp.) Shipmaster (not always the same as "captain"); also owner, teacher, or "master" in the broadest sense

Maravedi (Sp.) Common, base unit of Castilian currency

Marinero (Sp.) Seaman; professional sailor

Mayordomo (Sp.) Chief steward; manager of household staff

Monte (Sp.) Wilderness or unsettled area; "the hills" or "the woods"

Montear (Sp.) To hunt; here, could also refer to locating and catching free-range livestock, especially cattle

Morada (Sp.) Rental house or other place of residence (usually temporary)

Morador (Port.) Dweller; resident; inhabitant

Moreno, Morena (Sp.) "Brown"; adjective used to describe the skin tone of Iberians (for example sailors) but also commonly used as a noun to refer to Africans and people of African descent (*moreno* generally had more positive connotations than *negro,* or "black")

Mozo, Moza (Sp.) Lad or lass; youth (in Portuguese, *moço, moça*)

Muchacho, Muchacha (Sp.) Children or adolescents approximately twelve to fourteen years old

Mulato, Mulata (Sp.) Person of mixed African and Iberian ancestry

Muleca, Muleque (Port.) Youth or child

Natural (Sp.) Native to or originating from a certain place

Negrito, Negrita (Sp.) "Little black boy" or "little black girl"; a diminutive form of negro / negra

Negro, Negra (Sp.) "Black"; commonly used as a noun to refer to sub-Saharan Africans and to people of African descent

Negro chalán (Sp.) African interpreter. *Chalanear* could also mean to bargain or haggle. (On the Upper Guinea coast, *tchalonas*)

Negro del trato (Sp.) Trade captive; slave trade terminology referring to an enslaved African intended for export and resale

Nhara (Port.) Title of respect and honor accorded to female merchants in coastal western Africa, ostensibly derived from *senhora;* also *dona* and, later, in French, *signare*

Oidor (Sp.) Judge or magistrate of an *audiencia* (in Portuguese, *ouvidor*)

Paje (Sp.) Page or cabin boy

Paño (Sp.) Unit of measurement for cloth, equivalent to about 24 *varas* in length; in Portuguese, *pano,* a length of cloth used as currency in slave trafficking and other forms of commerce along the Upper Guinea coast and elsewhere in western Africa

Pieza (Sp.) One unit; a "head" or a "piece." Among slave merchants and royal officials in the Spanish Caribbean, the term was often used to refer to enslaved Africans (*pieza de negro*) but could also be used for Amerindians (in Portuguese, *peça*).

Pipa (Sp.) Unit of volume used for both wine and water

Plata corriente (Sp.) Unassayed silver

Procurador (Sp., Port.) Legal representative or lawyer

Pulpería (Sp.) Neighborhood shop or grocery store

Pulpero (Sp.) A grocer or neighborhood shopkeeper

Quintal (Sp.) Hundredweight or one hundred Castilian pounds

Real (Sp.) Castilian unit of money worth thirty-four *maravedís*

Regidor (Sp.) Member of a "cabildo" or city council

Rescate (Sp.) Rescue; ransom; barter; the redemption of captives or the purchase of slaves. In the Spanish Caribbean, *rescate* typically referred to unauthorized trade with non-Hispanic interlopers.

Soba (Kimbundu) Mbundu title for political authority; leaders of various ministates in West Central Africa. Under Portuguese colonial rule, *sobas* were responsible for paying tribute on behalf of their communities.

Sobado (Port.) Region over which a *soba,* or Mbundu political leader, had authority; grant authorizing the holder to exact tribute from a soba and his followers (similar to the Spanish *encomienda* system)

Solar (Sp.) Plot of land

Tangomão, Tangomã Widely used in Portuguese to refer to a person of Iberian of Capeverdean origin who went to Upper Guinea to conduct trade, remaining beyond the limits of Portuguese authority for longer than a year and a day; also used interchangeably with *lançado,* meaning "those who threw themselves among the blacks" (rarely appears in Spanish as *tangomango* or *tangomanga*)

Tierra adentro (Sp.) Hinterlands or interior of a province or island, away from the coast

Tierra firme (Sp.) The mainland; a loose designation for the entire Caribbean coastline stretching from Panama to Venezuela (in English, "the Spanish Main"). The Audiencia or Kingdom of Tierra Firme, also known as Castillo de Oro and later the Audiencia of Panama, referred more specifically to an administrative area of jurisdiction that encompassed the provinces of Panama and Veragua.

Trabajador (Sp.) Day laborer or agricultural worker who possessed neither land, nor farming implements, nor work animals. Synonymous with *jornalero*

Tratante (Sp.) Merchant or trader

Upper Guinea Broad geographical designation with various definitions, roughly analogous to competing terms such as "Greater Senegambia," encompassing areas that early modern Iberians described as "the Rivers of Guinea" and "Sierra Leone": an extensive West African coastal region stretching from the Senegal River in the north to Cape Palmas (in modern Liberia) to the south. The peoples and ports most relevant for this study were primarily located along the coasts and rivers of what are today the Gambia, southern Senegal, Guinea-Bissau, and Guinea-Conakry.

Upper Guineans Individuals who originated in Upper Guinea; for major ports, polities, and ethnolinguistic groups commonly depicted in Spanish Caribbean sources, see Chapter 1

Varón (Sp.) Male

Vecino, Vecina (Sp.) Inhabitant or permanent resident; heads of household; free, propertyowning residents

West Central Africa Geographical term referring primarily to the Kongo-Angola region on Africa's Atlantic coast; includes Luanda and the Mbundu territories that became the Portuguese colony of Angola as well as the Kingdom of Kongo, Benguela, and the Tyo or Anziku kingdom farther inland

West Central Africans People who originated in West Central African communities other than the Portuguese colony of Angola, including people typically described in Spanish Caribbean sources as "Angolas," "Congos," and "Anchicos"

Zambahigo (Sp.) Individuals of mixed African and Amerindian ancestry

Index

Bruco, 41, 63
Bruto family, 83n
Buena Ventura (Española), 212
Buenos Aires, 12, 71–72n, 79–80, 90, 92, 93n
Buguendo (São Domingos), 28, 30, 32–33,
    37–39, 41, 44, 47, 62, 94–95, 104–105,
    118–119, 122, 140, 154
Bulloms, 48, 65. *See also* Zape (ethnonym)
Burga (ethnonym), 48–49
Butter, 193

Cabo San Antón, 68, 196n, 275n
Cabo Verde. *See* Cape Verde Islands
Cabo Verde, Francisca de, 125, 288n
Cabo Verde, Manuel de, 125–126
Cabo Verde, Margarita de, 126n
Cabo Verde, Mariana de, 125–126
Cacanda, 46
Caçanga (ethnonym). *See* Cassangas
Caçanga, Isabel, 163
Caçanga, Juan, 56n
Caçanga, Madalena, 241
Cacao, 11–12, 110
Caceres, Pedro Gonçales de, 137–139
Cacheu, 21, 28, 38, 45–47, 50, 125, 127, 224,
    226–227, 231
Cacheu River, 28, 38, 45–47, 64, 104
Caculo Quehacango, 87
Cádiz (Spain), 98–99
Camacho, Diego, 173, 175
Camacho, Juan, 285
Camacho, Lucía, 169
Camargo, Francisco, 133–135
Camelo, Roque, 91–92
Camino de la Barranca, 283–284
Campeche, 13, 59
Campos, Pedro de, 169
Cana, Aña, 169
Canary Islands, 30, 71, 81–82, 124, 167, 169,
    237
Cano, Catalina, 148
Canoeros, 117–118
Canoes, 12, 42–43, 117, 133, 135, 141, 201–202,
    253
Canpisa, Antón, 61–62, 65
Cañengues, 99–101
Capelino, 232
Cape Verde Islands, 16–17, 20, 23–26, 29–33,
    37, 39, 43–44, 46–47, 49–51, 54, 57, 67, 69,
    72, 77, 94, 104–105, 107, 119–123, 125–126,
    132, 137, 140, 144, 184, 222–228, 230,
    236–237, 244, 256–258, 279, 288, 289n
Capuchins, 139
Carabalí, Damián, 253

Carabalí, Miguel, 204
Carabalí, Salbador, 204
Caracas, 13, 77, 114–116, 151n, 269.
    See also La Guaira
Caravajal, Cristóbal de, 173
Caravali (ethnonym), 230, 235–257
Cardoso, Bento Banho, 81, 82n
Cardosso, Atanácio, 123
Careño, Rodrigo de, 174
Caricuri, Dom Pedro de, 227
Carlos, Francisco, 176
Carmelites, 125, 186, 191, 270
Carmona, Leonor de, 251
Carmonesa, Inés, 169
Caro, Diego, 283
Carora, 114
Carpenters, 12, 117, 175, 213
Carreño, Agustina de, 299
Carreño, Ana de, 172, 174, 179
Carrera de Indias. *See* Indies fleets
Cartagena de Indias, 5, 9n, 11, 13–15, 18, 20,
    22, 23n, 25–27, 34, 38, 57, 74–75, 77–80,
    82–83, 86, 88–93, 98–101, 102n, 106–108,
    113, 123–138, 140, 142–144, 146–148,
    154–155, 162–164, 167, 169n, 170, 180–182,
    192n, 194n, 197–198, 200–211, 217–218,
    220–221, 223–230, 232–235, 238, 249–253,
    255–259, 261, 263, 267, 272–273, 277–281,
    288, 306; as slave trade hub, 7, 29, 75,
    78–80, 128–129, 198, 200, 225, 257; province
    of, 14–15, 18, 27, 133, 182, 197, 200–207,
    209–211, 217, 223–224, 227–228, 250, 254,
    258–260, 262–263, 272–273, 278–281,
    283–285. *See also* Mompox; Tolú
Carvalho, João Mendes de, 89
Carvalho, Pasqual, 136, 225n, 250–251
Carvalho, Sebastião de, 92
Casa, 37–39, 41, 62–63, 240. *See also* Cassangas
Casal, Sebastiana de, 169n
Casamance River, 21, 28, 37–38
Casa mansa, 37, 62–63. *See also* Masatamba
Cassangas, 21, 26, 28, 32–33, 37–40, 42, 47,
    52, 56n, 58–60, 62–65, 137, 163, 218, 226,
    239–242, 295–296
Cassanze, 85–86, 95
Cassava (or yuca), 11, 182, 184–194, 196, 202,
    209–212, 275
Castañeda, Juan de, 211–212
Castaño, Manuel, 90, 92
Castelo Branco, Garcia Mendes de, 87–88, 90
Castile, xvii, 17, 82n, 107, 109, 172, 208
Castilho, Nicolau de, 228
Castillo, Antonio del, 162
Castro, Catalina de, 285